FREEDOM OF EXPRESSION

**Recent Titles in
Major Issues in American History**

America and the World
Jolyon P. Girard

Immigration Issues
Henry Bischoff

Issues of War and Peace
Nancy Gentile Ford

Church-State Relations
Francis Graham Lee

Federalism
Robert P. Sutton

Issues of Westward Expansion
Mitchel Roth

FREEDOM OF EXPRESSION

James Magee

Major Issues in American History
Randall M. Miller, Series Editor

GREENWOOD PRESS
Westport, Connecticut • London

Library of Congress Cataloging-in-Publication Data

Magee, James J.
  Freedom of expression / James Magee.
      p. cm.—(Major issues in American history, ISSN 1535–3192)
  Includes bibliographical references and index.
  ISBN 0–313–31384–9 (alk. paper)
  1. Freedom of speech—United States—History. I. Title. II. Series.
KF4770.M34 2002
323.44'3'0973—dc21   2002021625

British Library Cataloguing in Publication Data is available.

Library of Congress Catalog Card Number: 2002021625
ISBN: 0–313–31384–9
ISSN: 1535–3192

First published in 2002

Greenwood Press, 88 Post Road West, Westport, CT 06881
An imprint of Greenwood Publishing Group, Inc.
www.greenwood.com

Printed in the United States of America

∞™

The paper used in this book complies with the
Permanent Paper Standard issued by the National
Information Standards Organization (Z39.48–1984).

10 9 8 7 6 5 4 3 2 1

ADVISORY BOARD

*To the memory of my mother, Frances A. Magee,
and to her great granddaughter,
Lauren Elizabeth Magee*

Contents

Series Foreword by Randall M. Miller   ix

Preface   xiii

Chronology of Events   xvii

1. Historical Narrative   1

2. The Alien and Sedition Acts of 1798   19

3. The Abolitionist Movement   43

4. The Civil War   69

5. The Comstock Law   95

6. World War I and Its Aftermath   121

7. The Cold War and the "Red Menace"   147

8. The Civil Rights Movement   175

9. The Vietnam War   199

10. The Nazi March on Skokie   223

11. Political Correctness and Free Speech on Campus   245

12. The Internet   275

Selected Bibliography   311

Index   317

Series Foreword

This series of books presents major issues in American history as they have developed since the Republic's inception to their present incarnation. The issues range across the spectrum of American experience and encompass political, economic, social, and cultural concerns. By focusing on the "major issues" in American history, the series emphasizes the importance of an issues-centered approach to teaching and thinking about America's past. *Major Issues in American History* thus reframes historical inquiry in terms of themes and problems rather than as mere chronology. In so doing, the series addresses the current, pressing need among educators and policymakers for case studies charting the development of major issues over time, so as to make it possible to approach such issues intelligently in our time.

The series is premised on the belief that understanding America demands grasping the contentious nature of its past and applying that understanding to current issues in politics, law, government, society, and culture. If "America" was born, and remains, as an idea and an experiment, as so many thinkers and observers have argued, issues inevitably have shaped whatever that America was and is. In 1801, in his presidential inaugural, Thomas Jefferson reminded Americans that the great strength of the new nation resided in the broad consensus citizens shared as to the rightness and necessity of republican government and the Constitution. That consensus, Jefferson continued, made dissent possible and tolerable and, we might add, encouraged dissent and debate about critical issues thereafter. Every generation of Americans has wrestled with such issues as defining and defending freedom(s), determining America's place in the world, waging war and making peace, receiving and assimilating new peoples, balancing church and state, forming a "more perfect union," and pursuing "happiness." American identity(ies) and interest(s) are not fixed. A nation of many peoples on the move across space and up and down the socioeconomic ladder cannot have it so. A nation charged with ensuring that, in Lincoln's words, "government of the people, by the people, and for the people shall not perish from the earth" cannot have it so. A nation whose heroes are not only soldiers and statesmen but also ex-slaves, women reformers, inventors, thinkers, and cowboys and Indians cannot have it so. Americans have never rested content locked into set molds in thinking and doing—not as long as dissent and difference are built into the character of a people that dates its birth to an American Revolution and annually celebrates that lineage. As such, Americans have been, and are, by heritage and habit an issues-oriented people.

We are also a political people. Issues as varied as race relations, labor organizing, women's place in the work force, the practice of religious beliefs, immigration, westward movement, and environmental protection have been, and remain, matters of public concern and debate and readily intrude into politics. A people committed to "rights" invariably argues for them, low voter turnout in recent elections notwithstanding. All the major issues in American history have involved political controversies as to their meaning and application. But the extent to which issues assume a political cast varies.

As the public interest spread to virtually every aspect of life during the twentieth century—into boardrooms, ballparks, and even bedrooms—the political compass enlarged with it. In time, every economic, social, and cultural issue of consequence in the United States has entered the public realm of debate and political engagement. Questions of rights—for example, to free speech, to freedom of religion, to equality before the law—and authority are political by nature. So, too, are questions about war and society, foreign policy, law and order, the delivery of public services, the control of the nation's borders, and access to and the uses of public land and resources. The books in *Major Issues in American History* take up just those issues. Thus, all the books in this series build political and public policy concerns into their basic framework.

The format for the series speaks directly to the issues-oriented character of the American people and the democratic polity and to the teaching of issues-centered history. The issues-centered approach to history views the past thematically. Such a history respects chronology but does not attempt to recite a single narrative or simple historical chronology of "facts." Rather, issues-centered history is problem-solving history. It organizes historical inquiry around a series of questions central to understanding the character and functions of American life, culture, ideas, politics, and institutions. Such questions invariably derive from current concerns that demand historical perspective. Whether determining the role of women and minorities and shaping public policy, or considering the "proper" relationship between church and state, or thinking about U.S. military obligations in the global context, to name several persistent issues, the teacher and student—indeed, responsible citizens everywhere—must ask such questions as "How and why did the present circumstance and interests come to be as they are?" and "What other choices as to policy and practice have there been?" so as to measure the dimensions and point the direction of the issue. History matters in that regard.

Each book in the series focuses on a particular issue, with an eye to encouraging readers and users to consider how Americans at different times engaged the issue based on the particular values, interests, and political and social structures of the day. As such, each book is also necessarily events-based in that the key event that triggered public concern and debate about a major issue at a particular moment serves as the case study for the issue as it was understood and presented during that historical period. Each book offers a historical narrative overview of a major issue as it evolved; the narrative provides both the context for understanding the issue's place in the larger American experience and the touchstone for considering the ways Americans encountered and engaged the issue at different times. A timeline further establishes the chronology and place of the issue in American history. The core of each book is the series of ten to fifteen case studies of watershed events that defined the issue, arranged chronologically to make it possible to track the development of the issue closely over time. Each case study stands as a separate chapter. Each case study opens with a historical overview of the event and a discussion of the significant contemporary opposing views of the issue as occasioned by the event. A selection of four to nine critical primary documents (printed whole or in excerpts and introduced with brief headnotes) from the period under review presents differing points of view on the issue. In some volumes, each chapter also includes an annotated research guide of print and nonprint sources to guide further research and reflection on the event and the issue. Each volume in the series concludes with a general bibliography that provides ready reference to the key works on the subject at issue.

Such an arrangement ensures that readers and users—students and teachers alike—will approach the major issues within a problem-solving framework. Indeed, the design of the series and each book in it demands that students and teachers understand that the crucial issues of American history have histories and that the significance of those issues might best be discovered and recovered by understanding how Americans at different times addressed them, shaped them, and bequeathed them to the next generation. Such a dialectic for each issue encourages a comparative perspective not only in seeing America's past but also, and perhaps even more so, in thinking about its present. Individually and collectively, the books in the *Major Issues in American History* series thereby demonstrate anew William Faulkner's dictum that the past is never past.

Randall M. Miller
Series Editor

Preface

Freedom of expression is a "sacred right" of the American people, enshrined in the Constitution, the highest law of the Republic. Justice Hugo L. Black of the U.S. Supreme Court insisted that the First Amendment was best served if only lawmakers and judges would follow its terms, written, he insisted, "in plain words, easily understood." The appeal of the language seems clear enough: "Congress shall make no law . . . abridging the freedom of speech, or of the press." Yet American history is filled with freedom of expression issues that plain words could never explain nor resolve. Very early in the life of the Republic, political leaders, many of whom, in fact, had helped to ratify the First Amendment, divided over the meaning of freedom of speech and press when the United States almost went to war against France in 1798. Its meaning was not entirely clear then, and it is not completely clear today. The realization of free expression in a free society often depends on a balance of competing social needs and interests.

When tension and fear arise, free speech is endangered. During the 1830s, abolitionist literature was often suppressed as "incendiary" expression designed to incite insurrection, and abolitionist presses were destroyed by angry mobs while local law enforcement looked the other way. The murder of antislavery advocate Elijah Lovejoy in 1837 defending his press and the assassination of civil rights leaders more than a century later demonstrated the extent of violent opposition to what Justice Oliver Wendell Holmes, Jr., later called "the thought we hate."

Freedom of expression also has facilitated triumphs for protesters seek-

ing political and social change. The unrelenting determination of zealous
abolitionists eventually altered public opinion, at least outside the South,
on the evil of slavery, although a bloody civil war was necessary to
eliminate it from American life. In the 1950s and 1960s, symbolic protest
by civil rights activists against unjust laws helped produce major legislation that finally gave meaning to constitutional rights neglected for
nearly a century. Sometimes good intentions abridge free speech. Beginning in the late 1980s, American colleges and universities adopted codes
of conduct to curb speech vilifying individuals or groups because of their
race, religion, gender, sexual orientation, or other attribute. Liberals who
supported both free speech and respect for diversity divided over this
issue.

America's experience has shown that the strongest challenges to free
speech rights have come in wartime—during the Civil War, during
World War I, and even during the "Cold War." After the shocking and
horrifying events of September 11, 2001, in New York City and Washington, D.C., the United States government declared "war on terrorism."
This challenging war, directed against both domestic and international
but unfocused targets, will again test the allegiance of the nation, its
leaders, and its courts to the constitutional principle of freedom of expression. When a nation goes to war, mounting tensions and passions
often make it difficult to distinguish legitimate dissent from disloyalty
and even treason. In announcing America's resolve, President George W.
Bush cautioned world audiences: "Either you are with us or you are
against us." That message no doubt reverberated to draw domestic fault
lines, too, pitting patriotism against legitimate dissent and, possibly, disloyalty. This process has already begun. The principal of Sissonville High
School in Kanawha County, West Virginia, suspended a fifteen-year-old
student for wearing T-shirts bearing anarchy symbols and messages opposing the bombing of Afghanistan. Many students, parents, and other
residents of the local community sided with the principal, but after the
Associated Press distributed the story worldwide, the student, Katie Sierra, became a *cause célèbre* for proponents of free expression.

Recounted in this book are eleven episodes in American history as seen
through the lenses of freedom of expression. By looking closely at particular instances when freedom of speech or press was challenged, it is
possible to observe how First Amendment principles, sometimes battered
but always resilient, grew in strength and breadth after each new storm.

The book has been the work of many people. Professor Randall M.
Miller of Saint Joseph's University was an indefatigable guide and source
of new information every step of the way. His careful combing of several
drafts and his helpful additions, suggestions, and general comments
have made this a better book. Kevin Ohe, and his staff at Greenwood
Press, particularly Betty C. Pessagno and Susan E. Badger, moved the

book along with a combination of professionalism and flexibility. Many at the University of Delaware were supportive. Joseph A. Pika encouraged this enterprise from the beginning and, as chairperson of my department, helped in many ways to facilitate its timely completion. The Morris Library provided an invaluable research study where I could hide and work uninterruptedly. Mary McGlynn expertly typed some nearly illegible documents. Karen M. Kral of Information Technologies-User Services was indispensable and exceptionally patient in helping me format the manuscript. Undergraduate students in my First Amendment courses helped to sharpen understanding of established free speech issues and to shed light on more obscure dimensions. Special thanks go to Katherine Lewis and Emily Russell. David J. M. Frederick mastered the art of locating documents and useful library and Internet sources, and he provided an incisive and bright mind to help me test ideas. My wife, Patricia, answered occasional questions of style and citation despite her busy schedule with her own book, teaching, and indispensable volunteer work for the Delaware Humane Association.

I am grateful to all of them. However, I take full responsibility for any errors made in this book.

Chronology of Events

1791	First Amendment is ratified.
1797	John Adams is inaugurated president of the United States.
1798	Congress enacts the Alien and Sedition Acts; James Madison writes the Virginia Resolution.
1799	Thomas Jefferson pens the Kentucky Resolution.
1801	Sedition Act expires; Thomas Jefferson is inaugurated president of the United States.
1820	Missouri Compromise is enacted.
1821	Benjamin Lundy publishes the *Genius of Universal Emancipation*.
1831	William Lloyd Garrison publishes *The Liberator*; the Nat Turner slave rebellion in Virginia erupts.
1833	American Anti-Slavery Society is established.
1835	President Andrew Jackson delivers Message to Congress on the Post Office.
1836	Senator John C. Calhoun defends the Postal Bill; first Gag Rule of antislavery petitions appears in Congress.

1837   Elijah Lovejoy is murdered in Alton, Illinois.

1844   Gag Rules are abolished in Congress.

1857   Supreme Court rules in *Dred Scott v. Sandford.*

1861   Abraham Lincoln is inaugurated president of the United States.

1861–1865   American Civil War is fought.

1862   Congress enacts the Treason Act.

1863   President Lincoln issues the Emancipation Proclamation; Congress authorizes military draft and suspension of habeas corpus; Clement Vallandigham is arrested and tried by a military court.

1864   Lincoln administration shuts down the New York *World* and *Journal of Commerce.*

1865   President Lincoln is assassinated.

1866   Supreme Court rules in *Ex parte Milligan.*

1868   Fourteenth Amendment is ratified; *Regina v. Hicklin* establishes legal definition of obscenity.

1870   Fifteenth Amendment is ratified.

1873   Comstock Act is enacted.

1878   There is a petition to Congress to repeal the Comstock Act.

1902   Free Speech League is founded.

1907   Supreme Court rules in *Patterson v. Colorado.*

1913   Woodrow Wilson is inaugurated president of the United States.

1915   Anthony Comstock dies; Supreme Court rules in *Mutual Film Corporation v. Ohio Industrial Commission.*

1917   Woodrow Wilson is inaugurated president of the United States for a second term; Committee on Public Information is created; Espionage Act passed; Senator Robert LaFollette delivers a speech in the Senate.

1917–1918   United States participates in World War I.

1918   Sedition Act is passed.

1919   Supreme Court rules in three cases—*Debs v. United States,*
            Schenck v. United States, and *Abrams v. United States;* first
            round of Palmer Raids takes place.

1920   Second round of Palmer Raids occurs; American Civil
            Liberties Union (ACLU) is founded.

1921   Sedition Act is repealed.

1925   Supreme Court rules in *Gitlow v. New York.*

1931   Supreme Court rules in *Near v. Minnesota.*

1934   Hollywood "Production Code" is established.

1938   Supreme Court rules in *Lovell v. City of Griffin.*

1939   Supreme Court rules in *Schneider v. State (Town of Irving-
            ton).*

1940   Supreme Court rules in *Cantwell v. Connecticut.*

1941–1945   United States fights World War II.

1942   Supreme Court rules in *Chaplinsky v. New Hampshire.*

1943   Supreme Court rules in *West Virginia State Board of Edu-
            cation v. Barnette.*

1945   President Franklin D. Roosevelt dies; Harry S. Truman
            becomes president of the United States; House Un-
            American Activities Committee (HUAC) is permanently
            established.

1946   Congress passes the Atomic Energy Act.

1947   Loyalty Review Board is created by executive order;
            HUAC investigates Hollywood.

1950   Internal Security Act is passed.

1951   Supreme Court rules in *Dennis v. United States.*

1952   Supreme Court rules in *Beauharnais v. Illinois.*

1953   Dwight D. Eisenhower is inaugurated president of the
            United States.

1954   Communist Control Act is passed; Senator Joseph Mc-
            Carthy is censured by the Senate; Supreme Court rules
            in *Brown v. Board of Education.*

1955–1956   Bus boycott takes place in Montgomery, Alabama.

1956   Supreme Court rules in *Gayle v. Browder.*

1957   Southern Christian Leadership Conference is formed;
            Dwight D. Eisenhower is inaugurated president of the
            United States for second term; Supreme Court rules in
            Yates v. United States, Watkins v. United States, and *Roth
            v. United States.*

1958   Supreme Court rules in *NAACP v. Alabama.*

1959   Supreme Court rules in *Barenblatt v. United States.*

1960   "Sit-ins" and "freedom rides" begin; Student Non-
            Violent Coordinating Committee (SNCC) is formed.

1961   John F. Kennedy is inaugurated president of the United
            States.

1962   *Port Huron Statement of the Students for a Democratic Society*
            is issued.

1963   Supreme Court rules in *Edwards v. South Carolina;* Martin
            Luther King, Jr., gives his "I Have a Dream" speech at
            Lincoln Memorial; President John F. Kennedy is assassi-
            nated; Lyndon Baines Johnson is sworn in as president
            of the United States.

1963–1964   Free Speech Movement begins on the University of Cal-
            ifornia at Berkeley.

1964   "Freedom Summer" takes place in Mississippi; Supreme
            Court rules in *New York Times v. Sullivan;* Civil Rights
            Act is passed; Tonkin Gulf Resolution is enacted; Lyndon
            Baines Johnson is elected president of the United States.

1965   First U.S. combat troops arrive in Vietnam; Voting Rights
            Act is passed; "Malcom X" is murdered.

1966   Supreme Court rules in *Adderley v. Florida.*

1967   Congress passes the Freedom of Information Act.

1968   Martin Luther King, Jr., and Robert F. Kennedy are as-
            sassinated; Supreme Court rules in *United States v.
            O'Brien;* President Johnson announces that he will not
            run for a second term.

1969   Richard M. Nixon is inaugurated president of the United
            States; Supreme Court rules in *Tinker v. Des Moines School
            District;* Supreme Court rules in *Brandenburg v. Ohio;* Na-
            tional Vietnam Moratorium takes place.

1970   *Report of the Presidential Commission on Campus Unrest* is released.

1971   Supreme Court rules in *Cohen v. California and Pentagon Papers Case.*

1973   *Miller v. California* establishes modern legal definition of obscenity/pornography; Paris Peace Accords is signed.

1974   Congress amends and expands the Freedom of Information Act; President Richard Nixon resigns.

1976   Supreme Court rules in *Greer v. Spock.*

1977   American Nazis plan march on Skokie, Illinois; Supreme Court rules in *National Socialist Party v. Skokie.*

1978   Supreme Court declines to rule in *Smith v. Collin* and thus refuses to ban Skokie march.

1981   Ronald Reagan is inaugurated president of the United States.

1987   Ronald Reagan is inaugurated president of the United States for a second term.

1989   George H.W. Bush is inaugurated president of the United States; Supreme Court rules in *Texas v. Johnson*; University of Michigan hate speech code is invalidated.

1990   Stanford University hate speech code is implemented; Supreme Court rules in *United States v. Eichman.*

1992   Supreme Court rules in *R.A.V. v. St. Paul.*

1993   William J. Clinton is inaugurated president of the United States.

1995   Stanford University hate speech code is invalidated.

1996   Communications Decency Act (CDA) is passed; Child Pornography Prevention Act (CPPA) is passed.

1997   William J. Clinton is inaugurated president of the United States for a second term; Supreme Court rules in *Reno v. ACLU* and invalidates CDA.

1998   Child Online Protection Act (COPA) is passed.

1999   Federal Court of Appeals invalidates CPPA.

2000   Federal Court of Appeals invalidates COPA; Children's Internet Protection Act (CIPA) is passed.

2001   George W. Bush is inaugurated president of the United States; Supreme Court agrees to review constitutionality of COPA and CPPA; World Trade Center and Pentagon are attacked by international terrorists on September 11; Uniting and Strengthening America by Providing Appropriate Tools Required to Intercept and Obstruct Terrorism (USA Patriot) Act is passed. United States launches war on international terrorism.

2002   Federal district court in Philadelphia rules on the constitutionality of CIPA; Supreme Court decides *Ashcroft v. Free Speech Coalition*.

1

Historical Narrative

Few nations have enjoyed the freedom of speech to which Americans are today accustomed, but speech in the United States has not always been as free or robust as it seems in the beginning of this new millennium. Ratified as part of the U.S. Constitution in 1791, the First Amendment proclaims that "Congress shall make no law . . . abridging the freedom of speech, or of the press." The United States was the first modern experiment with a free and open political regime where monarchs and emperors were forbidden to rule and in which freedom of speech was inscribed as fundamental law. The Founding Fathers who launched this system in the late eighteenth century understood the connection between free speech and representative government and the dangers attached to both. The First Amendment was written to restrict only the national government, not the states. Its framers recognized that free speech must have limits but also that mere inscription in the Constitution would not assure its protection, especially when political crises generate tension and fear. As a legal principle and as a fundamental feature of the American republic, freedom of speech has faced challenges but has adapted in accord with events in American history. It has weathered storms but has emerged after each more robust than before.

Discovering and defining the boundaries of free speech began early. The rise of party politics, unanticipated and unwanted by the framers of the Constitution, in the 1790s tested stated First Amendment principles of freedom of speech and assembly. The new American government closed off free speech during a major public policy dispute by jailing and fining critics not too long after the ink had dried on the words of the First Amendment. The notorious Alien and Sedition Acts of 1798 were passed during the administration of President John Adams when the United States engaged in an undeclared naval war against revolutionary France. The idea of a legitimate and loyal opposition had not yet developed in America's new experiment in self-government, and therefore many in power equated criticism of government as disloyalty, especially in time of crisis or uncertainty. Proponents of the Alien and Sedition Acts harbored fears of subversion by revolutionaries from France and Ireland who were resident aliens in the United States. Emerging from the throes of one of the most bloody and convulsive revolutions in modern history, France and the burgeoning Napoleonic wars threatened all of Europe. Adams and the Federalist Party sympathized with the British, enemies of France, and distrusted any opposition to their policies.

Three of these four federal laws dealt with citizenship and deportation of aliens suspected of treason, though not much enforced. The fourth—the Sedition Act—took aim at domestic political opponents who made "false" criticisms of government or its leaders by threatening them with arrest and, if convicted, with fines reaching $2,000 and as much as two years in prison. The Federalist government prosecuted more than two dozen people, newspaper editors, private citizens, and at least one member of Congress—all of whom were supporters of Thomas Jefferson and his budding political party in opposition.

In response to the Alien and Sedition Acts, James Madison, a disciple of Jefferson and "father of the Constitution," wrote the Virginia Resolution attacking the law's constitutionality, and fellow Virginian Jefferson furtively wrote a similar resolution under the auspices of the state of Kentucky. The Virginia and Kentucky Resolutions asserted the power of individual states to "interpose" their view of the Constitution against questionable acts of the national government, thereby unilaterally "nullifying" an act of Congress. Today we resort to the judiciary, through judicial review, to interpret and enforce the Constitution, but in 1798–1799, that practice was not yet established as one of the "checks and balances" on governmental power. Madison and Jefferson also knew that federal judges at the time were staunch Federalists appointed by President George Washington or by President John Adams, and virtually all of them supported and enforced the sedition law. The Sedition Act curiously expired by its own terms on March 3, 1801, the last day of the presidential term of John Adams, but the episode generated important questions, not just about freedom of speech. Neither Virginia nor Kentucky attempted to "interpose" state authority to protect its citizens, but the doctrine of "interposition" claimed by Madison and Jefferson threatened the viability of the federal government by suggesting that state authority might disregard as unconstitutional any national law. The idea lay fallow until the late 1820s when South Carolina, concerned about rising antislavery influence and high tariffs, invoked it to protect states' rights.

In the 1790s it was unclear what freedom of speech actually meant in practice. The prevailing British view was expressed through England's towering voice on the law, Sir William Blackstone—namely, that freedom of speech and press prohibited governmental "prior restraints" but that speakers or the press could subsequently be punished for what they had "freely" said or published. British law on "seditious libel" gave birth to American law with the important American addition that truth was a defense against libel. Many Americans naturally assumed that Blackstone's definition was infused in the First Amendment. If so, there was nothing unconstitutional about the Sedition Act, as it did not muzzle—though it certainly did punish—critics who made "false, scandalous" statements against the government with the intent of defaming it or bringing it into disrepute. After the political commotion had subsided and the Federalist Party had been soundly defeated in the elections of 1800, the right of the citizens of the Republic to criticize their government was no longer in doubt and became an irreducible component of freedom of speech and press. This, at least, was a right of citizens vis-à-vis the federal government. State governments, not yet constrained by the First Amendment, were free to establish their own standards of free speech, and many well into the nineteenth century prohibited libelous speech, even speech critical of government. While no court ever formally declared the Sedition Act unconstitutional, history has judged the law invalid. When Jefferson assumed the office of president in 1801, he pardoned those convicted and repaid their fines.

Freedom of speech issues continued in particular states where the protection of the First Amendment did not reach but did not resurface in the national arena until the 1830s. Slavery was the cause of the new concern over First Amendment protections. It blighted the image of the Republic from its inception, but during the first three decades of the nineteenth century, slavery was not the heated and divisive political and moral issue that it soon became in the 1830s. Until 1831, opponents of slavery as an institution were generally unobtrusive and largely ineffectual, though they did achieve the gradual abolition of slavery in all the states above the Mason-Dixon Line by the early nineteenth century and with the exception of the state of Missouri had closed slavery off the vast territory above the 36° 30' line from the Mississippi River to the Pacific. Quakers and others morally or religiously troubled by slavery deployed what little power and persuasion they could summon to challenge the South's "peculiar institution." In the 1830s, however, firebrand abolitionists demanding the immediate emancipation of the slaves burst onto the political stage and boldly pushed this divisive dispute to the front pages of the press and to the nation's capital. They assembled into abolition societies (modern-day interest groups)—locally, regionally, and nationally. They also published newspapers and pamphlets to attack slavery as immoral and sinful and blanketed the country with such works appealing to slaveholders to give up the sin of slavery. Although fragmented and disparate in organization, financing, and influence, the abolition movement grew into an irrepressible political contender and a formidable threat to the slave states, or so southerners came to believe. The antislavery mission was reinforced by the reigning intellectual climate of the day—a blend of romanticism, idealism, and transcendentalism promoting the view that human institutions should and could be reformed and even perfected. The immediate emancipation of slaves followed as a logical imperative.

To the worried planter class of the South, termination of slavery meant an end to their way of life; indeed, slaveholders viewed any interference with slavery as tantamount to a spur to slave rebellion. The Denmark Vesey conspiracy in Charleston in 1822 and the bloody Nat Turner revolt in Virginia in 1831, among several incidents, confirmed such fears. Southern states tolerated no opposition to slavery, at least within their own borders. By the mid-1830s slave states made publication of "inflammatory" or "incendiary" literature a capital crime if committed as a second offense (first convictions brought public whippings). The slaveholders fought abolition with state laws severely punishing speech critical of slavery, especially if it incited slaves to rebel (most slaves, of course, could not read). Political leaders and common citizens from the North—who found the abolitionists' preaching obnoxious and disruptive of both union and commerce with the South to the extent that such agitation might cause the emigration of freed slaves to the North—initially joined the proslavery forces to repress the abolitionist crusade.

The southern and most northern delegations in Congress thwarted every effort to entreat the national government to debate a practice that abolitionists were certain was indefensible in a country committed to freedom and equality. The "second party system" that had stabilized politics was premised on keeping the divisive slavery issue out of politics. Abolitionists cared little about party priorities and flooded the House of Representatives, and to a lesser extent the Senate, with "petitions" to restrict slavery. Between 1836 and 1844, both chambers either formally or informally adopted "Gag" rules to bar the subject of slavery from the political agenda, refusing even to having the petitions read and entered into the public record. At the behest of southern postmasters who complained of antislavery tracts flooding the mails, President Andrew Jackson urged Congress to cleanse the mails of "incendiary" literature. Mailbags were the primary means of spreading the word, and this bill was designed to keep antislavery literature out of circulation. Its principal manager in the Senate was John C. Calhoun of South Carolina, among the most forceful and uncompromising public officials representing the South in the nation's capital. The bill failed, but southern postmasters interdicted antislavery literature on their own account with the blessing of the postmaster general. The formally imposed Gag Rules lasted and were abandoned only after bitter debates in the Congress.

At the state and local level, the federal principle of free speech did not protect abolitionists from mob violence. Their literature, when sent in bulk to southern destinations, was usually burned or thrown away by angry locals. In northern towns and cities, for most of the 1830s, whites opposed, for various reasons, to freeing slaves unleashed in lawless ways their hostility on abolitionists. The most famous incident occurred in Alton, Illinois, when Elijah Lovejoy—a minister and newspaper editor—was murdered defending his press in November 1837. Local mobs inflamed by his editorials denouncing slavery had several times destroyed his printing press when he was in St. Louis and finally drove him from Missouri. After he settled in the free state of Illinois, opponents harassed him and his family, wrecked his press, and on the night of November 7 killed him as Lovejoy stood with his supporters guarding from vandals his recently arrived and final printing press. This tragic event made news across the free states and generated sympathy for the abolition movement, which capitalized on the demonstrated danger to civil liberties "the slave power" posed to northerners. After Lovejoy's death, abolition and freedom of speech and press became practically synonymous.

As the nation approached the Civil War, the abolition movement hardened, and so did the South's resistance. The "slave power" issue had serious repercussions for civil liberties. States in which it existed, or territories where it might have spread, severely restricted free speech. Visitors to slave states from free states lost the right to criticize slavery and could be severely punished for doing so. In the 1850s, especially after John Brown's raid and the panic that ensued, slave states clamped down even more. The newly emerging Republican Party capitalized on this, particularly in the 1856 presidential election with its slogan on behalf of their candidate, John C. Frémont: "Free soil, free labor, free speech, free men, and Frémont." The boundaries of free speech and the ability of the political system to mend deep fissures were both dearly tested, but the slavery issue was nonnegotiable in the minds of both sides, and the political process, more suited to compromise and reconciliation, was ultimately unable to resolve the problem. Abolition triumphed and so did free speech, but only after the American nation nearly drowned itself in blood.

The Civil War suspended the normal operations of the political system, including provisions of the Constitution. In the early months of his presidency, Abraham Lincoln governed by executive fiat, though once in session, Congress endorsed an array of executive decisions made to force the seceded southern states back to what Lincoln had always maintained was an indestructible Union. Freedom of speech and press was constrained by the necessities of war. Given the circumstances of a nation divided in civil war, and compared to the hysteria induced by World War I, speech and press during the Civil War were not so severely repressed. Edicts against aiding and abetting the enemy by publications or otherwise were decreed, and they cautioned many to keep still and sent more courageous critics to military prisons.

In the North, Democratic newspapers critical of Lincoln's war policies competed with the pro-Union press of the abolitionist and radical Republicans. New York newspapers were of special concern to Lincoln's administration because stories and editorials printed in New York were frequently reprinted in newspapers elsewhere. Northern Democrats and newspapers against the war were denounced as "Copperheads" and often targets of mob violence. After the Union's first major defeat at Bull Run in July 1861, Democratic newspapers of the North hurling invectives at the Union army or the Lincoln administration suffered the frustration of angry, pro-Union local mobs or disgruntled soldiers stationed nearby. The Lincoln administration reacted to publications that appeared to aid or comfort the enemy by denying postal privileges, which could cripple or even destroy a newspaper's business. Other measures included military orders to shut down the press by force or arrest and court-martial of incendiary critics who disrupted or discouraged recruitment of soldiers and the "normal" mobilization of resources for war. Still, no general muzzling of the opposition press or speech occurred. The Lincoln administration approached the issue of "unfree speech" in wartime on a case-by-case basis. More important, political opposition to the Republican administration went on unabated. Elections were held regularly, and Republicans defeated at the polls accepted the legitimacy of Democratic victory.

Lincoln only occasionally directed the military to take action against a supposedly "treasonous" publication. This happened in 1864 when two New York newspapers—the *World* and the *Journal of Commerce*—on May 18 unwittingly published a forged document dressed as a presidential plea for 400,000 more troops. Incensed, Lincoln issued direct orders to his general overseeing New York to arrest the perpetrators and close down the two offending papers. After it was clear that the editors had been duped, they were freed and the newspapers returned to publishing. More pervasive was the administration's practice of tolerating military generals in the field issuing orders substantially restricting the range of permissible expression. With very few exceptions, Lincoln countenanced them all. The most controversial episode was the 1863 arrest and court-martial of the outspoken "Copperhead" critic Clement L. Vallandigham, who sought the Democratic Party's nomination for governor of Ohio. At a rally Vallandigham expressed disloyal opinions, in violation of General Ambrose E. Burnside's orders, and was arrested and tried in a military court for disloyalty. The Ohioan appealed all the way to the Supreme Court, which rejected his case for lack of jurisdiction. In a related case, *Ex parte Milligan* (1866), the Court later ruled that the executive and its military had violated the Bill of Rights by prosecuting a civilian in an area where the civil courts had been functioning, but the ruling came after the Civil War had ended.

The *Milligan* case held that the Constitution speaks with "one voice" in times of both war and peace and served to reprimand the military under Lincoln's administration for its disregard of constitutional rights. The ruling also cast constitutional doubt on the Reconstruction Acts that deployed the Union army to oversee the rebuilding of the defeated Confederate states. Constitutional confrontations were studiously avoided, however, as a cautious Court found ways to deny itself jurisdiction in cases bringing such issues to its attention. The Civil War amendments, especially the Fourteenth, planted the seeds of new, national rights against the states, though the Court was initially reluctant to use them to protect civil liberties. Later, in the twentieth century, the Court breathed new life into these provisions and effectively "nationalized" the most important provisions of the Bill of Rights, such as freedom of speech, to restrict the states.

Like their abolitionist predecessors, other social reformers looked for new ways to perfect and purify postbellum America, and they found suitable causes. Many would soon discover, however, that a powerful crusade was in the making, authorized by law and directed at them and their followers. These "libertarian radicals" opposed the oppressive social conformity enforced by both government and organized religion. Many were intellectual women who saw their place in the social hierarchy as little better than that of recently freed slaves. They had fought to abolish slavery and promote equality only to be bitterly disappointed when the "freedom amendments"—the Thirteenth, Fourteenth, and Fifteenth—closing the Civil War and expanding definitions of civil rights, voting rights, and the equal protection of the laws, had nothing to say about the rights of women.

Fueling the free speech debate up to and through the Civil War were issues of national political significance—such as the Sedition Act of 1798, slavery, and the war itself. From 1873 until World War I, another issue became an obsession of a single, unrestrained man, Anthony Comstock, who loathed obscene and immoral books and magazines, which he believed polluted the urban centers of America and threatened the welfare of the nation's youth. Hundreds of thousands of abolitionists had been unable for almost a decade between 1836 and 1844 to persuade Congress even to discuss the slavery issue, yet Comstock managed almost by himself and virtually overnight to energize Congress to enact legislation in 1873 assigning carte blanche authority to purge the mails of "lewd," "indecent," "immoral," or "obscene" materials, which the law left undefined. The majority of post–Civil War Americans reacted to obscenity in ways similar to their counterparts in Victorian England. Natural human sexual urges and temptations competed with the proper Victorian attitude and demeanor that obscenity was to be rooted out wherever found. The new federal legislation charged the Post Office with this responsibility, but at the urging of his contacts in the Senate, Comstock was commissioned as a special agent entrusted with the task of enforcing the law that contemporaries equated with his name.

At age twenty-nine Comstock was chairman of New York's Society for the Suppression of Vice, and from 1873 until his death in 1915, he wielded censorial power unmatched in American history, through this society and his command of the postal service. The Comstock Law affected "obscene" and "immoral" publications and also the advertisement or sale through the mail of any materials, devices, or instructions pertaining to contraception and abortion. His absolute enforcement of the contraception ban stifled the birth control movement in America. Medical professionals were convicted, fined, and jailed for counseling women on ways to prevent pregnancy, and those who wrote manuals for inexperienced newlyweds were convicted of federal crimes (one committed suicide rather than serve the jail sentence she received).

Literature with a sexual content was subject to the uncertainties of the law and Comstock's uncertain willingness to tolerate erotic publications. Obscenity was unprotected expression, and its legal definition, which stood until 1957, perfectly accommodated Comstock's mission. Known as the *Hicklin* test and imported in the 1860s from Victorian England, it judged a publication, pictorial, or painting as obscene if the work, even in part, had a depraving influence on the most susceptible members of society. Material fit for adults but not for immature children was thus legally obscene and unprotected.

For more than four decades postal agents followed Comstock's instructions to suppress birth control literature and to protect the nation's artistic and literary culture from the harmful influences of indecent and obscene materials. In an interview near the end of his life, Comstock bragged that he had convicted enough people to load a train equipped with sixty passenger cars, each holding sixty seats, and had destroyed 170 tons of what he called the "monstrous evil." In fairness to his reign of censorship, he did not aim his law very often at genuine works of literature with sexual content, though his zeal sometimes overwhelmed his judgment, as when he tried to shut down a play by the Irish playwright George Bernard Shaw, who coined the term "Comstockery" to ridicule American prudishness. Opposition to Comstock brought about a well-orchestrated but ultimately unsuccessful petition, in 1878, in Congress to repeal the law. In 1902 the Free Speech League, one of whose prominent leaders was the prolific free speech attorney Theodore Schroeder, was established to confront Comstock and to protect the rights of political dissenters as well. Comstock died in 1915, but challenges to the law continued. Margaret Sanger was the most important pioneer in the American birth control movement, and she repeatedly challenged the Comstock Law, particularly as it pertained to abortion and birth control. Her persistence ultimately triumphed, as courts began in the 1930s liberally to interpret the law to protect patients and to save women's lives. In 1971, following the Supreme Court's discovery of a right of "marital privacy" in the Bill of Rights, Congress removed the proscriptions on contraception from the Comstock Law.

The entry of the United States into World War I led to the greatest repression of speech and dissent that the country had yet witnessed. America entered the war almost three years after it had begun in Europe in August 1914. Although aware that American participation in the war was almost inevitable, President Woodrow Wilson nonetheless successfully campaigned in 1916 for a second term on the slogan "He kept us out of war." But Wilson could not do so, and shortly after his second inauguration, Congress declared war on Germany and, with a barrage of legislation, entrusted to Wilson virtually complete authority to prosecute the war, galvanize public support, and severely punish dissent. The Committee on Public Information (CPI), headed up by George Creel, was established to encourage the mass media, including the embryonic film industry, to comply with governmental guidelines. Artists, journalists, and professional propagandists directed media campaigns to mold and maintain public support. But by casting America's involvement in the war as a "holy crusade," the Wilson administration invited repression of counterviews. Also, the United States as an immigrant nation was not of one mind regarding the war. Fearing divisions at home, the Creel Commission, as the CPI was known, painted the enemy as evil incarnate in its "Hate the Hun" campaigns. The clear message was that "you are with us or against us"—no middle ground. The Espionage Act of 1917 targeted genuine issues of espionage and deliberate disclosure of military secrets, both crimes of treason. That law was amended by Congress with the Sedition Act of 1918, which punished expression critical of the government or its political symbols with fines up to $10,000 and as many as twenty years in federal prison. The Army, Navy, and Post Office and Justice Departments were all deployed to intercept or suppress dangerous messages or expressions.

More than 2,000 people were convicted in federal courts under these two laws. One case involved the prominent Socialist Party leader Eugene

V. Debs, who on June 18, 1918, in Canton, Ohio, delivered a stirring public address to an audience of more than 1,200 in which he criticized and denounced America's participation in the war as a capitalist contrivance to enrich the arms industry. Convicted of obstructing the war effort under the Espionage Act, Debs was sentenced to ten years in prison. His conviction made him a martyr in the cause of socialism. In four presidential elections he had been the Socialist Party's presidential candidate (in 1900, 1904, 1908, and 1912—in the latter, he received more than 900,000 votes—almost 6 percent of all votes cast). The party ran his name for a fifth time in 1920, and from his prison cell he received more than 900,000 votes.

Several defendants appealed to the Supreme Court of the United States, which, in landmark cases raising First Amendment issues, upheld every criminal conviction it reviewed by ruling that the First Amendment did not protect "dangerous" expression. Prior to 1919, the Supreme Court had never specifically addressed the limits or dimensions of the First Amendment's speech and press clauses. Now it addressed the issue in the hothouse of national emergency that no doubt impelled organized efforts to protect free speech, most prominently in 1920 with the formation of the American Civil Liberties Union (ACLU). The principal instruments used by the ACLU were "test cases" to challenge governmental action or to defend in court the constitutional rights of victims of governmental abuse.

The judiciary's foray into the uncharted field of First Amendment law yielded very little that survived in calmer times. Judges and courts a generation later cited the *dissenting* opinions of the World War I cases as if they were the rules of law. Justices Oliver Wendell Holmes, Jr., and Louis D. Brandeis, though initially willing to uphold convictions of political dissenters, wrote some of the greatest defenses of free speech and its relationship to democratic government. Both Holmes and Brandeis insisted that the First Amendment protected dissenting political speech up to the point where such speech presented a "clear and present danger" that the government had the authority to prevent. The Court officially made at least one rule that triumphed as precedent for the future when it held in *Gitlow v. New York* (1925) that freedom of speech was fundamental enough to be applied against states through the mysterious avenue of the Fourteenth Amendment's "due process clause." This monumental rule paradoxically arose from a case in which the Court meekly sustained state power to punish a socialist publication.

The ugly consequences of a concerned nation deliberately whipped up by propaganda produced an assault on dissidents well after the war had ended. During the war anti-German sentiments were expressed in editorials across the country, and German immigrants and German-language newspapers were victims of a growing distrust of foreigners that, by the time war had ended, boiled over into xenophobia bordering on hysteria. The Communist Party had engineered the Russian Revolution, and A. Mitchell Palmer, President Wilson's attorney general in 1919–1920, was so certain that Communists in America were plotting a similar and imminent insurrection in the United States that he ordered a series of raids to round up dangerous immigrants and to ship them off to Russia. Hundreds were deported during the "Red Scare" that gripped the nation. Palmer and the government had reasons to be suspicious and alert; he was, in fact, a target of bombings in Washington, and there were dangerous radicals prone to violence. But in retrospect, it is clear that the government overreacted and severely damaged constitutional rights. When no great Communist uprising occurred in May 1921, as Palmer and the witchhunters had portended, the Red Scare abated. Good times were returning to America as the "Roaring Twenties" began. Still, at the state and local level nativism and suppression of free speech continued, sometimes violently through extralegal organizations such as the Ku Klux Klan. Meanwhile, the Congress dealt with the supposed problem of unassimilated foreigners and "radicals" from abroad by passing the National Origins Act of the 1920s that severely limited immigration from southern, central, and eastern Europe.

Despite the catastrophic Great Depression and World War II, freedom of speech in the 1930s and especially in the 1940s enjoyed a renaissance supervised by the Supreme Court whose members by 1943 were all appointees of Democratic President Franklin D. Roosevelt. This was the era of the "preferred position" doctrine, which held that in the inevitable collision between speech rights and other important societal interests, courts must balance interests, but in the scales of justice, speech rights occupied a preferred place. But, in 1949, two of the Court's reliable free speech liberals suddenly died and were replaced by more cautious conservatives. This unexpected shift came in the early stages of the protracted "Cold War." American leaders after World War II were convinced that the Soviet Union, with a far less robust economy and much more limited technology, rapidly acquired atomic weapons only because of Communist spies and traitors. Another "Red Scare" was under way, but very different from the post–World War I experience. The first aimed mostly at immigrants; the Cold War Red Scare targeted suspects in all walks of American life. The enemy without supposedly advanced in the struggle for world domination because of enemies within the United States. Several sensational "spy trials," such as that of the Rosenbergs in the early 1950s, lent credence to the idea that Communists had infiltrated American society.

Membership in the Communist Party was circumscribed by law and then flatly outlawed, and current, former, and suspected members suffered criminal and social reprisals that they and many others thought had vanished along with the first Red Scare. Communist Party leaders in the late 1940s and 1950s were imprisoned for advocating the violent overthrow of the government. Congressional committees investigated witnesses about their political associations and beliefs and those of their friends and fellow workers, actors, producers, artists, union organizers, teachers, and nearly anyone else. Republican Senator Joseph McCarthy of Wisconsin claimed that the State Department and the military knowingly harbored Communists in strategic positions in government. His colleagues in the Senate eventually censured him, but not before "McCarthyism" raged for several years. Freedom of speech and association suffered heavy losses in the late 1940s through the end of the 1950s. The Supreme Court tended to side with governmental efforts to suppress Communist Party propaganda, as when in *Dennis v. United States* (1951) a majority of justices found little in the First Amendment to prevent the punishment of advocacy of the violent overthrow of government—a staple of Communist dogma. Liberal justices, such as William O. Douglas and Hugo L. Black, registered strong dissenting opinions urging greater respect for the principles of the First Amendment. With very few exceptions, such as *Yates v. United States* (1957) and *Watkins v. United States* (1957), political dissidents suspected of ties with the Communist Party throughout the 1950s received little judicial support, as the Court catered to the government's crusade against communism; and given the anti-Communist hysteria that gripped the nation during the Cold War, it is unlikely that even a judiciary fully stocked with champions of free speech could have prevented the assault on the free speech right of real or suspected dissidents that developed during this period. In the 1960s a more liberal Supreme Court replenished First Amendment law with doctrines and rules designed to protect, not weaken, the rights of political dissidents. Protecting suspected Communists was possible, however, because by the early 1960s the fervor of the anti-Communist crusade in American politics had largely dissipated.

While the 1950s was a decade of judicial timidity and neglect on the free speech front, the Court was willing to confront and invalidate much official racial segregation in postwar America, a reality traceable in part to unfulfilled constitutional promises made after the Civil War. In 1954 in the landmark *Brown v. Board of Education* case, the Court unanimously struck down the "separate but equal" doctrine that had undergirded state-mandated racial segregation in the South. But blacks did not wait on the Court to assert their constitutional rights.

Seamstress Rosa Parks refused in December 1955 to surrender her seat reserved for whites on a Montgomery, Alabama, public bus. To some observers, this symbolic act of defiance began the civil rights movement that would fundamentally alter the status of blacks in American society. Courageous activists began a ten-year period of civil disobedience and peaceful protest that challenged official segregation policies and private discrimination all over the South and that spread to attacks on discrimination in employment, education, and housing outside the South. Students conducted "sit-ins" at racially segregated lunch counters, libraries, and other "public" facilities. With little political power to effect the changes they sought, civil rights activists exercised the only power available outside the courtroom: their right to petition and assemble to call attention to the wholesale failure of the Civil War amendments and the subsequent segregation and discrimination that signaled the vast racial inequality in the United States. National press attention was eventually ignited when white southerners retaliated with murders, beatings, the burning of busses, and other mob violence. State and local governments in the South also reacted with arrests and criminal convictions for various violations of law and clamped down on free speech and freedom of assembly.

Civil rights protests raised new questions as to whether the First Amendment protected marching in the streets or near a state capital building, sit-ins, and even civil disobedience. Did the First Amendment protect libel—false publications defaming someone? A police commissioner in Alabama sued the *New York Times* for defamation of character after the newspaper had run an advertisement in 1960 bearing some factual errors but critical of the city's handling of racial demonstrations in Montgomery. A local jury awarded the commissioner $500,000 in damages even though the ad made no mention of him. The Supreme Court had consistently held that the First Amendment did not protect libel at all, but when the *New York Times* appealed to the Court, all nine justices reversed the libel judgment in the watershed decision of *New York Times v. Sullivan* (1964).

As activists on behalf of black Americans became more militant in the mid- to late 1960s, and after the passage of the Civil Rights Act of 1964 and the Voting Rights Act of 1965, which killed Jim Crow laws and promised to protect blacks, and others, in their civil and political rights, the movement began to lose the support of the American people who thought that the nation had done enough to secure liberty for all citizens. In 1968 disturbing domestic turmoil rocked America as the civil rights movement unraveled and mingled with growing protests over the escalated war in Vietnam. National leaders Martin Luther King, Jr., and Senator Robert F. Kennedy were both assassinated in the spring of 1968. Race riots erupted in urban centers all over the country. The Democratic Party's divisive convention in Chicago in 1968 coincided with demonstrators and police clashing in bloody confrontations in the city's streets—broadcast on TV to the entire nation. The "breakdown in law and order," not the Vietnam War itself, became the major issue of the 1968 presidential election.

The antiwar movement picked up where the civil rights movement had left off, raising a host of free speech issues arising from more protests, demonstrations, and symbolic conduct such as wearing black armbands, burning draft cards, invoking images of the American flag, and publicly using the "F-word" to denounce the draft, and from efforts by the Nixon administration to enjoin the *New York Times* and *Washington Post* from publishing what became known as the *Pentagon Papers*. On balance, the Supreme Court supported freedom of speech during this era, though the justices grew increasingly less likely to do so midway through the presidency of Republican Richard M. Nixon. He had campaigned in 1968 on a pledge to restore "law and order" and to stop the war, and in his first term alone he filled nearly half the Court's membership with four new conservative justices, substantially affecting the ideological balance on the Court. He also brought the war to an end before he himself was forced to resign from office under a welter of evidence of illegal spying, sabotage, break-ins, conspiracy, lying, destruction of justice, and other abuses of office.

The deception and deceit in prosecuting the Vietnam War, during the presidencies of both Lyndon Baines Johnson and Nixon, combined with the Nixon administration's secrecy and illegalities that culminated in the Watergate scandal, substantially weakened public confidence in American government. To many Americans, the affairs of state had been reduced to deceit and deception, as David Wise recounted in his aptly titled book *The Politics of Lying* (1973). The free speech legacy of the Vietnam War was mixed. In 1967, in accord with complaints about the public's "right to know," Congress had passed the Freedom of Information Act requiring governmental agencies to disclose unclassified public documents. In 1974 Congress, by amendment, expanded the reach of this law. The Nixon administration's paranoia, manifest, for example, in the famous "enemies list," about opponents and an unfriendly press, ironically helped launch a new genre of investigative reporting, as seen in Bob Woodward and Carl Bernstein's bestseller *All the President's Men*, reporting that helped bring down the Nixon presidency. However, the more conservative Court that emerged after Nixon's four appointments was less willing to support press claims such as a reporter's privilege to withhold, even from a grand jury, confidential notes gathered to produce news stories.

The *Gitlow* case (1925), in which the Court upheld Benjamin Gitlow's conviction for publishing the *Left Wing Manifesto*, left one lasting doctrinal legacy: that states are bound by federal free speech standards. Many cases that came to the Court involved state restrictions of speech rights, and several years after the Vietnam War had ended, the limits of free speech were tested again by expression so offensive that even liberals divided on whether it was worthy of constitutional protection.

In 1977, the National Socialist Party of America, a neo-Nazi hate group, planned to march on Adolf Hitler's birthday (April 20), in full Nazi uniform and regalia, in the village of Skokie, Illinois, a place targeted specifically because it was home to thousands of Jews who had survived the Holocaust. The purpose of the march was to incite a hostile reaction and garner media attention. After city officials had unsuccessfully sought a court order to stop the march, they enacted three regulations to prevent the Nazis from hurling hateful messages at the residents of Skokie. Frank Collin, the organizer of the march, recruited the country's premier defender of individual rights, the ACLU, whose lawyers convinced federal courts that the Skokie ordinances violated the First Amendment. The ACLU suffered tens of thousands of protest resignations nationwide, as debate over free speech raged in newspapers, magazines, and journals, at cocktail parties, and in classrooms across the country.

Some proponents of free speech insist that government cannot be trusted to define permissible expression, a view reinforced by judicial doctrine requiring governmental regulations affecting free expression to be "content neutral." Thus, if civil rights and antiwar demonstrators deserve constitutional protection, so do Nazis despite what many regard as their obnoxious, offensive, or hateful beliefs. This principle produced two judicial First Amendment decisions, *Texas v. Johnson* (1989) and *United States v. Eichman* (1990), denying state and federal governments the authority to punish flag burning as offensive behavior. Yet courts have always held that pornography, however difficult to define, is "unprotected speech" because it is patently offensive and unworthy of constitutional protection. Could one say the same about the Nazis' message to Skokie's residents? Other exceptions are "fighting words," words or epithets that might provoke a fight or words that insult and degrade. The Nazis selected Skokie to insult and abuse Jewish residents by using what many call "hate speech."

Some theorists assert that free speech is indispensable to individual self-fulfillment and autonomy, that a person has a right of self-expression, whether through feminist, racist, artistic, or even incomprehensible ideas—however distasteful or inappropriate to someone else, and even in a place like Skokie. Someone may possess an "autonomous" right to express homophobic ideas, but on the same theory gays have the right autonomously to develop their personalities and to expect government to protect them from homophobic assaults. The collision of "autonomy" interests is almost endless. Is verbal flirtation in the workplace freedom of speech or sexual harassment? When states set up "buffer zones" to protect women seeking abortions and doctors who provide them from antiabortion picketers, are the latter's rights of free speech abridged?

Academics and others have heatedly debated the limits of speech reduced to hate directed at victims of discrimination. In the 1980s and 1990s that debate intensified at colleges and universities, hundreds of which implemented "hate speech" codes forbidding particular kinds of speech, even the use of particular words, that might be harmful to specially identified groups. Liberals remain divided in their support for these measures because two fundamental principles of contemporary liberalism have collided. Freedom to believe and say what one thinks conflicts with the expectation that people should be treated equally and fairly and that none should be demeaned, even by words, because of one's race, ethnic background, religion, sex, sexual orientation, weight, height, and so forth. This tension has turned liberals against each other. Those who emphasize freedom to speak oppose these codes; others who emphasize the dignity of all groups endorse them. Conservatives criticized speech codes as "political correctness," a form of brainwashing or regimentation by liberals who, during the Republican era of Ronald Reagan and George Bush, had lost their influence in Washington. When challenged in court, these codes were almost everywhere invalidated, but the debate continues today.

Technology continually refashions the meaning of free speech because it affects the quantity, quality, and speed of communication, as well as the nature and size of the audience. The appearance of the printing press in the fifteenth century was a momentous event in history, prior to which ideas spread via the limited means of human voices or painstakingly produced handwritten documents. As print media expanded, so did literacy rates. When motion pictures came along, courts at first refused to treat them as free expression. Radio and television revolutionized the capacity to reach a wider general public. Instantaneous digital, satellite, and laser transmission of information today assures that virtually nothing escapes the attention of the media. And the audience has become global. On September 11, 2001, a world community of eyewitnesses watched in disbelief as the twin skyscrapers of New York's World Trade Center collapsed into millions of tons of smoldering steel and molten debris that entombed thousands of American and international victims of horrifying terrorist attacks.

The information revolution spawned the Internet and its most familiar component, the World Wide Web, that accelerated globalization and built the framework of a new "e-commerce." All technological advances in history that have magnified expression have brought both good and evil. The Internet augmented and empowered the voice of the average citizen, but it also created venues for peddlers of sexually explicit images and hate speech, and it provides a means of instantaneous and anonymous exchange of information among international terrorists. Established law was not suited to manage the contents or structures of "cyberspace," and novel and awkward challenges confronted existing regulations that raced to keep pace with the faster changes of a new medium. In the final years of the twentieth century, government fought the same goblins and dragons of obscenity that Comstock, a century before, had suppressed but failed to conquer. Congress enacted laws almost annually, mostly on behalf of children and conservatives groups, to remove offensive sexual images and messages from the Internet. Just as quickly, however, these laws were challenged in court, and judges undid much of Congress's work, invoking the same but more seasoned principle that had inspired free speech advocates in the earliest days of the Republic to chastise government for passing the Sedition Act.

On October 25, 2001, President George W. Bush signed into law the "USA Patriot Act," one provision of which permits federal and state government to "wiretap" the Internet through a software program called Carnivore, including tracking down anonymous users with fake identities. This raises issues covered by the Fourth Amendment's protection against "unreasonable" searches and seizures, as no judicial warrant is needed by government to undertake this kind of surveillance. The law also implicates free speech because a loss of privacy might prompt Internet users to curb their online speech and because freedom of association can be invaded.

This brief historical narrative has shown at least that the simple words of the First Amendment cannot explain the uneven progress of freedom of expression in the political development of the United States. Events and political movements have influenced the contours of free speech far more than the language of the Constitution or any doctrines announced by the Supreme Court. Technology, fear (for example, during World War I and the Cold War), public tolerance and acceptance, education, leadership, and the underlying political culture of the American nation: These have had more to do with how free speech fares in periods of disturbance, tension, or crisis than the sweeping terms of the First Amendment. As the United States wages what will be a long, if not indefinite, war against international terrorism, the nation's commitment to freedom of expression, especially the right to dissent, Thomas Jefferson's monument to the strength of the Republic, will be continually tested.

2

The Alien and Sedition Acts of 1798

Less than a decade as a new constitutional republic, the United States faced off against France, ostensibly an American ally, in a diplomatic crisis that included the real possibility of war. The French Revolution of 1789 and its tumultuous repercussions destroyed the "old regime" of monarchy and privileged aristocracy (King Louis XVI and his queen, Marie Antoinette, were beheaded) and displayed to the world one of the most violent revolutions in modern history. For most of the 1790s, France was in a state of revolutionary turmoil and instability and embarked upon a crusade to destroy monarchies in, and thus conquer, other parts of Europe. Soon war raged across Europe and on the oceans and threatened to spread to America. Desperate to avoid entanglements, the United States negotiated the Jay Treaty with Great Britain in 1794, which settled most outstanding differences between them but also made the French believe that the United States had betrayed its own revolution and aligned with the British in the "world war." Tension increased when in the summer of 1797 some 300 American ships were captured in the West Indies by privateers supported by the French revolutionary regime. Though no formal declaration of war took place, a "quasi war" was under way during which the U.S. Navy captured more than eighty French ships. At the close of the eighteenth century, President John Adams and the Federalist Party controlled the government of the United States. Vice-President Thomas Jefferson, who together with his growing number of followers formed an alternative Jeffersonian party, led the political opposition.

Unlike the modern presidency in which the president and vice-president work as a team (or at least are elected together on the same political ticket), in the early years of the Republic the president and vice-president could be—and were, in the case of Adams and Jefferson—political rivals. Under the constitutionally established electoral process at that time, the president was the candidate receiving a majority of electoral votes in the Electoral College; the vice-president was the runner-up. In the presidential election of 1796, Adams obtained a majority of electoral votes, and Jefferson came in second. The Twelfth Amendment to the Constitution, the development of a mature, competitive political party system, and custom have changed all this into the system we have today. The original process, which the Founding Fathers had designed without anticipating the rise of political parties, created strange political rivalries such as that between Jefferson and Adams and their respective burgeoning political parties: the Jeffersonian Republicans and the Federalists.

The diplomatic crisis with France moved Federalists to pass a series of repressive laws in the early summer of 1798, known collectively as the "Alien and Sedition Acts." Three of these laws (the Alien Acts) dealt with issues pertaining to citizenship and the status and fate of aliens. The first (the Naturalization Act, passed on June 18, 1798) made aliens seeking citizenship reside for fourteen, instead of five, years before becoming eligible. The Federalists clearly feared the growing immigrant population, including as many as 25,000 French resident aliens, who tended to side with Jefferson and his Republican critics of the Federalists. (In 1802, this law was repealed and the shorter residency requirement was reinstated.) The two controversial Alien Acts followed within the next two weeks. One authorized the president to deport aliens whom he (or his administrative assistants) deemed to be "dangerous to the peace and safety of the United States" during peacetime or who were suspected of "treasonable or secret machinations against the government." This law had a limited period of operation (by its own terms, it expired in June of 1800). The other, the Alien Enemies Act, which still exists as part of the modern president's emergency war powers, authorized during wartime the arrest, imprisonment, and deportation of any alien subject to an enemy power. If war with France had, in fact, occurred, French aliens residing in the United States would have been subject to arrest, imprisonment, or expulsion from the country. War, however, never officially was declared, and President Adams never invoked the Alien Act of June 25 to apprehend and deport any resident aliens. Nonetheless, laws like the Alien Acts, even though not applied directly to any individuals, threatened resident aliens; many fled in fear from the United States or simply hid from authorities.

The fourth piece of legislation caused the most uproar and outrage, because it appeared, in the minds of many, to be politically motivated and a direct violation of the First Amendment. Federalists suspected Republicans of being irresponsible radicals bent on bringing to America the excesses of the French Revolution. Jeffersonian Republicans were enthusiastic opponents of monarchy and aristocracy, which the French revolutionaries were determined to eradicate in Europe. Republicans, too, were suspicious of their Federalist opponents, whom they regarded as reactionaries eager to cultivate an aristocracy of privilege in the United States. Jefferson and James Madison were convinced that the Federalist majority in Congress was exploiting tensions with France to justify suppressing domestic opposition. They were not wholly wrong. Several Federalists suspected that many of Jefferson's followers, and even Jefferson himself, were agents of the French government, and they sought ways to silence what they considered enemies of good government and the new Constitution. The Sedition Act ironically passed the Senate on the Fourth of July and was signed into national law on July 14 (Bastille Day—a major holiday when the French celebrate their Revolution). The law made it a crime to publish "any false, scandalous and malicious" writing against the government of the United States or any speech or writing intended to defame the government, to bring it into disrepute, or to arouse suspicions in the people that the government was acting unconstitutionally. Violations carried penalties of fines and/or imprisonment.

More than two dozen men were charged and convicted under this law, and almost all of them were editors of newspapers supporting Jefferson and his Republican followers. They were arrested and prosecuted, and their newspapers were forced to close. One victim was a member of Congress (Matthew Lyon of Vermont), and another was Benjamin Franklin Bache, grandson of Benjamin Franklin, who edited the pro-Jefferson newspaper *Aurora*, published in Philadelphia (at that time the capital of the United States). Bache was actually arrested for seditious criticism even *before* the Sedition Act was passed (among several canards tossed at the Federalists, Bache described Adams as "blind, bald, toothless, and querulous," which was libelous in that Adams was not blind). Federal authorities apprehending Bache invoked the common law. The "common law" consisted of traditional case law, inherited largely from Britain, made by judges, and practiced exclusively in the states.

Fuming at what they regarded as a brazen invasion of individual freedom to criticize government, Jefferson and his followers publicly questioned the constitutionality of the Alien and Sedition laws. The dividing line between Jeffersonian Republicans and the Federalists sharpened and hardened, and tempers flared. Jefferson and Madison privately drafted the Kentucky and Virginia Resolutions protesting the Alien and Sedition Acts on the grounds that they violated First Amendment rights and suggested, but did not press for, that states might interdict such unconstitutional acts to protect their citizens.

These "Resolves" generated a genuine national debate, not only in the Congress but among the citizenry. Public anger over the repressive Sedition Act eventually grew to the extent that the fateful laws enacted to silence political opposition paradoxically contributed to the defeat of Adams and his Federalists in the election of 1800. Adams hardly helped the Federalist cause when he found a way to settle the quasi war with France and showed that Federalist fears of imminent French invasion had been trumped up to justify a large increase in military and naval spending and vigorous prosecution of the Sedition Act. Once in office, President Jefferson pardoned those convicted under the Sedition Act who were still in prison, and the new Congress repaid all fines *with interest*. Congressman Lyon won reelection to the House of Representatives from his prison cell. By its own terms, the Sedition law expired on March 3, 1801—the last day of Adams's term of office. The expiration date reinforced suspicions that the Federalists had created the Sedition law just to silence their Republican opponents; if the Federalists lost the election in 1800, there would be no Sedition law to silence their criticism of their triumphant Republican opponents.

The First Amendment to the U.S. Constitution proclaims in sweeping terms that "Congress shall make no law ... abridging the freedom of speech, or of the press." Thomas Jefferson was certain that the Sedition Act was "palpably in the teeth of the constitution," proving that the Federalists "mean to pay no respect to it."[1] The amendment seems to guarantee in absolute terms that the people's right to speak would be unrestricted in the new constitutional regime launched in 1787. Yet the absolutist language of the "no law" portion of the amendment offers no clue as to the meaning of "the freedom of speech, or of the press" (as well as the other freedoms contained in the First Amendment, such as freedom of religion). These terms are not defined anywhere in the amendment, and for practical reasons the judiciary has never interpreted the amendment as supporting absolute rights—for example, no one would contend that perjury (lying under oath) is freedom of speech. Some critics of absolutism suggest that the absolutist language was employed not for any libertarian purposes but only to establish rigorous boundaries around national authority. Since the amendment's terms are directed at Congress, the argument claims that this constitutional principle was structured solely to establish jurisdictional limits to the new national government—that the First Amendment had actually little to do with "liberty," as such, but principally with curtailing the reach of federal power. In other words, in circumscribing the national lawmaking power, the First Amendment left the field of speech and press entirely to the various states to regulate. There is substantial evidence that Jefferson subscribed to this view.

In hindsight, it might seem strange that the generation of political leaders who inscribed freedom of speech and press in the Constitution would very soon create a national law to jail political opponents who criticized government and its public officials. Neither the concept nor the reality of a loyal political opposition had yet taken root in the young republic. Political parties were only just beginning to develop, and there was little practical experience with the notion that there could be a political opposition both loyal and yet expected to criticize those in power. The Federalists were the first leaders of the new republic, and as the first and only "party" in power since 1789, they did not accept the novel concept of a legitimate opposition. The opposing Jeffersonians hardly made it easy for the Federalists to see them as a loyal opposition. Aside from their sympathies and intrigues with a foreign power, the Jeffersonians formed Democratic-Republican Societies, supported the Whiskey Rebellion, and resorted to a strident press to attack the Adams administration. Perhaps political passions in 1798 were so inflamed by reports from France of the excesses of revolutionaries as to overtake the sound constitutional judgment of Federalist leaders.

In defense of the Federalists, one can argue that the Sedition Act did *not* contravene the First Amendment if the original meaning of "freedom of speech" was identical to its legal meaning in Britain before the American Revolution. The American legal system was a direct descendant of the "common-law" legal system of Britain, the mother country. The great eighteenth-century English legal writer Sir William Blackstone had concluded in his massive *Commentaries on the Laws of England* (1771) that freedom of speech and press meant only a right to speak or publish something at least once without being censored but that the speakers or publishers must suffer the consequences of their actions. If they abuse their right to speak, they can be punished. This meaning of freedom of speech and press was simply understood as a prohibition against "prior restraint." Blackstone's *Commentaries* were considered standard reading for aspiring lawyers, and therefore if Blackstone's view of free speech had been transferred to the First Amendment, it would have meant that the amendment prohibited only "prior restraints" on publication. If what speakers or publishers had to say were punishable by law, freedom of speech was not violated as long as they had a chance to air their views. The Sedition Act, therefore, did not violate this narrow version of freedom of speech.

One of America's most prominent constitutional historians, Leonard Levy concluded in a major study, *The Legacy of Suppression* (1960), that while it is difficult to pinpoint the exact "original meaning" of freedom of speech or press, there is abundant evidence to support the very narrow Blackstone conception of free speech. Moreover, seditious libel (malicious or false criticism of government or governmental officials—the kind of speech prohibited by the Sedition Act) was a common-law crime, a legacy also of the British legal system into which the American legal system was born. In fact, the common law inherited by the American states from British rule did not allow truth as a defense in a prosecution for seditious libel (that is, criticism of government or its officials). And no explicit effort was ever made (either in the Constitutional Convention of 1787 or in the Bill of Rights) to modify or delete the common law of seditious libel. At least the Sedition Act of 1798 allowed defendants to demonstrate that their criticism was truthful. Therefore, a case can be made that the Sedition Act of 1798 was at least consistent with the British tradition of freedom of expression, and presumably the First Amendment, even if that law had been politically motivated by Federalists to silence Jefferson and the opposition.

Moreover, the Sedition Act punished only false statements leaving "truth" as a defense, unlike the British common-law crime of seditious libel. Truth was established as a legal defense in the American colonies in 1735, when a jury in New York acquitted John Peter Zenger who published a local newspaper in which he "scandalized" the governor and his administration. Zenger's lawyer, Andrew G. Hamilton of Philadelphia, insisted, over initial objections by the judge, that seditious libel did not exist if the published statements were true. The judge ultimately allowed the jury to decide if Zenger's published statements produced an "ill opinion" of the government. The jury acquitted Zenger, and the case set a general precedent that truth was a defense in a common-law prosecution for seditious libel.

The era of the Alien and Sedition Acts produced some positive results for the development of freedom of speech and "government by the people." The machinations of the Federalists (and the vigorous efforts of the Federalist-appointed judiciary) to fine and jail political opponents were short-lived; their party suffered a humiliating electoral defeat in both houses of Congress in the election of 1800. Jefferson won the presidency but only after some thirty-five ballots in the House of Representatives (dominated by outgoing Federalists who tried to block his election). Adams had received sixty-five electoral votes, Jefferson received seventy-three, and Aaron Burr (whom Republican electors in the Electoral College expected would become vice-president) also received seventy-three. Since no candidate had a clear majority of electoral votes, the Constitution requires the House of Representatives to determine the winner—with each state having one vote. After attempting to block Jefferson for thirty-five ballots, Alexander Hamilton (who knew Adams had no chance) persuaded some Federalists that Burr would be worse than Jefferson, and thus the latter won the presidency with a substantial margin (ten to four) in the House of Representatives (with each state delegation casting one vote).

Free speech was strengthened and so was democracy. Indeed, these two traditions were now permanently sewn together and the lesson learned was that free speech is essential to self-government. While seditious libel continued in the states, the "reign of witches," as Jefferson described this era of national suppression, faded away eventually, and so too did the Federalist Party. Before leaving office the Federalists managed to create scores of new judicial posts that Adams filled with good Federalists. The emerging judiciary of unelected and life-appointed Federalists would become one of Jefferson's nemeses. In fact, the new Congress controlled by Jeffersonians impeached (though did not convict) a sitting Supreme Court justice (Samuel Chase) who had vigorously enforced the Sedition Act against Jefferson's followers. The regime of the new Republic survived and was strengthened by the painful lesson in self-government.

In his first inaugural address, President Thomas Jefferson alluded several times to the centrality of free speech in an aspiring democracy. He said: "We are all republicans—we are all federalists. If there be any among us who would wish to dissolve this Union or to change its republican form, let them stand undisturbed as monuments of the safety with which error of opinion may be tolerated where reason is left free to combat it."[2] The idea of a loyal opposition was realized.

The peaceful transfer of political authority from one political party to its opponent, from the Adams administration to the Jefferson administration, in 1801 was a sign that democratic government was in the making.

NOTES

1. Letter to James Madison, June 7, 1798, in James Morton Smith, ed., *The Republic of Letters: The Correspondence between Jefferson and Madison* (New York: W.W. Norton, 1995), 2: 1056–1057.

2. Paul Leicester Ford, ed., *The Writings of Thomas Jefferson* (New York: G.P. Putnam's Sons, 1897), 8:3.

DOCUMENTS

2.1.   The Sedition Act of 1798

This was the first and only time in the eighteenth or nineteenth century that Congress made it a crime to criticize government. "Truth" was a defense, but the accuracy of "opinions" is very difficult to document. This fear often leads to self-censorship, which in turn weakens democratic self-government, though their strident publications attacking the Adams administrations portray the Jeffersonians as unusually bold and courageous critics. Significantly, too, in revealing its partisan purpose, Thomas Jefferson, the vice-president, was the only governmental officer not protected from seditious libel in the act. The 1798 law was written deliberately to expire on the last day of the presidency of John Adams, and ironically, it was signed into law on what is today Independence Day in France. What follows is the section making seditious libel a federal crime.

An Act in addition to the act, entitled "An act for the punishment of certain crimes against the United States." . . .

SEC. 2. And be it further enacted, That if any person shall write, print, utter or publish, or shall cause or procure to be written, printed, uttered or published, or shall knowingly and willingly assist or aid in writing, printing, uttering or publishing any false, scandalous and malicious writing or writings against the government of the United States, or either house of the Congress of the United States, or the President of the United States, with intent to defame the said government, or either house of the said Congress, or the said President, or to bring them, or either of them, into contempt or disrepute; or to excite against them, or either or any of them, the hatred of the good people of the United States, or to excite any unlawful combinations therein, for opposing or resisting any law of the United States, or any act of the President of the United States, done in pursuance of any such law, or of the powers in him vested by the constitution of the United States, or to resist, oppose, or defeat any such law or act, or to aid, encourage or abet any hostile designs of any foreign nation against the United States, their people or government, then such person, being thereof convicted before any court of the United States having jurisdiction thereof, shall be punished by a fine not exceeding two thousand dollars, and by imprisonment not exceeding two years.

SEC. 3. And be it further enacted, and declared, That if any person shall be prosecuted under this act, for the writing or publishing any libel aforesaid, it shall be lawful for the defendant, upon the trial of the cause, to give in evidence in his defence, the truth of the matter contained in the publication charged as a libel. And the jury who shall try the cause, shall have a right to determine the law and the fact, under the direction of the court, as in other cases.

SEC. 4. And be it further enacted, That this act shall continue and be in force until the third day of March, one thousand eight hundred and one, and no longer: Provided. That the expiration of the act shall not prevent or defeat a prosecution and punishment of any offence against the law, during the time it shall be in force.

Source: Statutes at Large 1 (1798): 596–597.

2.2.   The "Virginia Resolution"

Both Jefferson and Madison agreed that Congress had no power to enact either the Sedition Act or the Alien Acts, because such power was, in their view, not delegated to the national government and contrary to the First Amendment. Madison wrote the Virginia Resolution in December 1798 expressing the sentiments of the Virginia state legislature in a document to be submitted to Congress. The resolution held that sovereign states could "interpose" their legal judgment on the constitutionality of federal laws.

RESOLVED, . . .

That this Assembly doth explicitly and peremptorily declare, that it views the powers of the federal government, as resulting from the compact, to which the states are parties; as limited by the plain sense and intention of the instrument constituting the compact; as no further valid that they are authorized by the grants enumerated in that compact; and that in case of a deliberate, palpable, and dangerous exercise of other powers, not granted by the said compact, the states who are parties thereto, have the right, and are in duty bound, to interpose for arresting the progress of the evil, and for maintaining within their respective limits, the authorities, rights and liberties appertaining to them.

That the General Assembly doth also express its deep regret, that a spirit has in sundry instances, been manifested by the federal government, to enlarge its powers by forced constructions of the constitutional charter which defines them; and that implications have appeared of a design to expound certain general phrases (which having been copied from the very limited grant of power, in the former articles of confederation were the less liable to be misconstrued) so as to destroy the meaning and effect, of the particular enumeration which necessarily explains and limits the general phrases; and so as to consolidate the states by degrees, into one sovereignty, the obvious tendency and inevitable consequence of which would be, to transform the present republican system of the United States, into an absolute, or at best a mixed monarchy.

That the General Assembly doth particularly PROTEST against the palpable and alarming infractions of the Constitution, in the two late cases of the "Alien and Sedition Acts," passed at the last session of Congress; the first of which exercises a power nowhere delegated to the federal government, and which, by uniting legislative and judicial powers to those of executive, subverts the general principles of free government, as well as the particular organization and positive provisions of the Federal Constitution; and the other of which acts exercises, in like manner, a power not delegated by the Constitution, but on the contrary, expressly and positively forbidden by one of the amendments thererto,—a power which, more than any other, ought to produce universal alarm, because it is levelled against that right of freely examining public characters and measures, and of free communication among the people thereon, which has ever been justly deemed the only effectual guardian of every other right.

That this state having by its Convention, which ratified the Federal Constitution, expressly declared, that among other essential rights, "the Liberty of Conscience and of the Press cannot be cancelled, abridged, restrained, or modified by any authority of the United States," and from its extreme anxiety to guard these rights from every possible attack of sophistry or ambition, having with other states, recommended an amendment for that purpose, which amendment was, in due time, annexed to the Constitution; it would mark a reproachable inconsistency, and criminal degeneracy, if an indifference were now shown, to the most palpable violation of one of the Rights, thus declared and secured; and to the establishment of a precedent which may be fatal to the other.

... [T]he General Assembly doth solemnly appeal to the like dispositions of the other states, in confidence that they will concur with this commonwealth in declaring, as it does hereby declare, that the acts aforesaid, are unconstitutional; and that the necessary and proper measures will be taken by each, for co-operating with this state, in maintaining the Authorities, Rights, and Liberties, referred to the states respectively, or to the people.

That the Governor be desired, to transmit a copy of the foregoing Resolutions to the executive authority of each of the other states, with a request that the same may be communicated to the Legislature thereof;

and that a copy be furnished to each of the Senators and Representatives representing this state in the Congress of the United States.

Source: *Elliot's Debates on the Federal Constitution,* 2nd ed. (Philadelphia: J.B. Lippincott, 1896), 4:528–529.

2.3.   Massachusetts Responds to Virginia

More than a half-dozen states responded to the Virginia Resolution and presented their own resolutions to Congress supporting the validity of the Alien and Sedition Acts and criticizing Virginia. Delaware's General Assembly, for example, responded with a curt, one-sentence accusation that the Virginia Resolution was an unjustifiable and dangerous interference in the affairs of the federal government and unworthy of any more of Delaware's time. Massachusetts—home of President John Adams—responded more fully in February 1799 and defended the laws in question.

The *Sedition Act,* so called, is, in the opinion of this legislature, equally defensible. The General Assembly of Virginia, in their resolve under consideration, observe, that when that state, by its Convention, ratified the Federal Constitution, it expressly declared, "that, among other essential rights, the liberty of conscience and of the press cannot be cancelled, abridged, restrained, or modified, by any authority of the United States," and, from its extreme anxiety to guard these rights from every possible attack of sophistry or ambition, with other states, recommended an amendment for that purpose; which amendment was, in due time, annexed to the Constitution; but they did not surely expect that the proceedings of their state Convention were to explain the amendment adopted by the Union. The words of that amendment, on this subject, are, "Congress shall make no law abridging the freedom of speech or of the press."

The act complained of is no abridgment of the freedom of either. The genuine liberty of speech and the press is the liberty to utter and publish the truth; but the constitutional right of the citizen to utter and publish the truth is not to be confounded with the licentiousness, in speaking and writing, that is only employed in propagating falsehood and slander. This freedom of the press has been explicitly secured by most, if not all the state constitutions; and of this provision there has been generally but one construction among enlightened men—that it is a security for the rational use, and not the abuse of the press; of which the courts of law, the juries and people will judge: this right is not infringed, but confirmed and established, by the late act of Congress.

. . . the President of the United States is bound by his oath "to preserve, protect, and defend, the Constitution"; and it is expressly made his duty "to take care that the laws be faithfully executed." But this would be impracticable by any created being, if there could be no legal restraint of those scandalous misrepresentations of his measures and motives which directly tend to rob him of the public confidence; and equally impotent would be every other public officer, if thus left to the mercy of the seditious.

It is holden to be a truth most clear, that the important trusts before enumerated cannot be discharged by the government to which they are committed, without the power to restrain seditious practices and unlawful combinations against itself, and to protect the officers thereof from abusive misrepresentations. Had the Constitution withheld this power, it would have made the government responsible for the effects, without any control over the causes which naturally produce them, and would have essentially failed of answering the great ends for which the people of the United States declare, in the first clause of that instrument, that they establish the same—viz, "to form a more perfect union, establish justice, insure domestic tranquillity, provide for the common defence, promote the general welfare, and secure the blessings of liberty to ourselves and posterity."

Seditious practices and unlawful combinations against the federal government, or any officer thereof, in the performance of his duty, as well as licentiousness of speech and of the press, were punishable, on the principles of common law, in the courts of the United States, before the act in question was passed. This act, then, is an amelioration of that law in favor of the party accused, as it mitigates the punishment which that authorizes, and admits of any investigation of public men and measures which is regulated by truth. It is not intended to protect men in office, only as they are agents of the people. Its object is to afford legal security to public offices and trusts created for the safety and happiness of the people, and therefore the security derived from it is for the benefit of the people, and is their right.

This construction of the Constitution, and of the existing law of the land, as well as the act complained of; the legislature of Massachusetts most deliberately and firmly believe, results from a just and full view of the several parts of the Constitution; and they consider that act to be wise and necessary, as an audacious arid unprincipled spirit of falsehood and abuse had been too long unremittingly exerted for the purpose of perverting public opinion, and threatened to undermine and destroy the whole fabric of government.

The legislature further declare, that in the foregoing sentiments they have expressed the general opinion of their constituents, who have not only acquiesced without complaint in those particular measures of the federal government, but have given their explicit approbation by ree-lecting those men who voted for the adoption of them. Nor is it appre-hended that the citizens of this state will be accused of supineness, or of an indifference to their constitutional rights; for while, on the one hand, they regard with due vigilance the conduct of the government, on the other, their freedom, safety, and happiness require that they should de-fend that government and its constitutional measures against the open or insidious attacks of any foe, whether foreign or domestic.

Source: *Elliot's Debates on the Federal Constitution*, 2nd ed. (Philadelphia: J.B. Lip-pincott, 1896), 4: 535–537.

2.4.   Congressional Committee Report Defends the Laws

As a result of the quarrels stirred among Virginia, Massachusetts, and other states, the Federalist-controlled Congress established a special committee to draft a report on whether to repeal the Alien and Sedition Acts. The committee reported on February 21, 1799, and concluded that the laws were within the consti-tutional authority of Congress and that they not be repealed.

The "Act in addition to an act entitled an act for the punishment of certain crimes against the United States," commonly called the "sedition act," contains provisions of a two-fold nature: first, against seditious acts; and, second, against libellous and seditious writings. The first have never been complained of; nor has any objection been made to its validity. The objection applies solely to the second; and on the ground, in the first place, that Congress have no power by the constitution to pass any act for punishing libels, no such power being expressly given; and all pow-ers not given to Congress being reserved to the States, respectively, or the people thereof.

To this objection it is answered, that a law to punish false, scandalous, and malicious writings against the Government, with intent to stir up sedition, is a law necessary for carrying into effect the power vested by the constitution in the Government of the United States and in the De-partments and officers thereof; and, consequently, such a law as Con-gress may pass; because the direct tendency of such writings is to obstruct the acts of the Government by exciting opposition to them, to endanger its existence, by rendering it odious and contemptible in the eyes of the people, and to produce seditious combinations against the laws, the power to punish which has never been questioned; because it would be manifestly absurd to suppose that a Government might punish sedition, and yet be void of power to prevent it by punishing those acts which plainly and necessarily lead to it; and because, under the general power to make all laws proper and necessary for carrying into effect the powers vested by the constitution in the Government of the United States, Congress has passed many laws for which no express provision can be found in the constitution, and the constitutionality of which has never been questioned; such as the first section of the act now under consideration, for punishing seditious combinations. . . .

It is objected to this act, in the second place, that it is expressly contrary to that part of the constitution which declares that "Congress shall make no law respecting an establishment of religion, or prohibiting the free exercise thereof; or abridging the liberty of the press." The act in question is said to be an abridgment of the liberty of the press, and therefore unconstitutional.

To this it is answered, in the first place, that the liberty of the press consists, not in a license for every man to publish what he pleases, without being liable to punishment if he should abuse this license to the injury of others, but in a permission to publish, without previous restraint, whatever he may think proper, being answerable to the public and individuals for any abuse of this permission to their prejudice; in like manner as the liberty of speech does not authorize a man to speak malicious slanders against his neighbor, nor the liberty of action justify him in going by violence into another man's house, or in assaulting any person whom he may meet in the streets. In the several States the liberty of the press has always been understood in this manner, and no other; and the constitution of every State, which has been framed and adopted since the declaration of independence, asserts "the liberty of the press"; while in several, if not all, their laws provide for the punishment of libellous publications, which would be a manifest absurdity and contradiction, if the liberty of the press meant to publish any and every thing, without being amenable to the laws for the abuse of this license. According to this just, legal, and universally admitted definition of "the liberty of the press," a law to restrain its licentiousness, in publishing false, scandalous, and malicious libels against the Government, cannot be considered as an "abridgment" of its "liberty."

It is answered, in the second place, that the liberty of the press did never extend, according to the laws of any State, or of the United States, or of England, from whence our laws are derived, to the publication of false, scandalous, and malicious writings against the Government, written or published with intent to do mischief; such publications being unlawful and punishable in every State; from whence it follows, undeniably, that a law to punish seditious and malicious publications is not an abridgment of the "liberty of the press"; for it would be a manifest absurdity to say that a man's liberty was abridged by punishing him for doing that which he never had a liberty to do.

It is answered, thirdly, that the act in question cannot be unconstitutional, because it makes nothing penal that was not penal before, and gives no new powers to the court, but is merely declaratory of the common law, and useful for rendering that law more generally known and more easily understood. . . . the act . . . has enlarged instead of abridging the "liberty of the press": for, at common law, libels against the Government might be punished with fine and imprisonment at the discretion of the court, whereas the act limits the fine to two thousand dollars, and the imprisonment to two years; and it also allows the party accused to give the *truth* in evidence for his justification, which, by the common law, was expressly forbidden.

And lastly, it is answered, that had the constitution intended to prohibit Congress from legislating at all on the subject of the press, which is the construction whereon the objections to this law are founded, it would have used the same expressions as in that part of the clause which relates to religion and religious tests; whereas the words are wholly different: "Congress," says the [First Amendment], "shall make no law *respecting* an establishment of religion, or *prohibiting* the free exercise thereof or *abridging* the freedom of speech, or the press." Here it is manifest that the constitution intended to prohibit Congress from legislating at all on the subject *of religious establishments,* and the prohibition is made in the most express terms. Had the same intention prevailed respecting the press, the same expressions would have been used, and Congress would have been "prohibited from passing any law *respecting* the press." They are not, however, "prohibited" from legislating at all on the subject, but merely from *abridging* the liberty of the press. It is evident they may legislate respecting the press, may pass laws for its regulation, and to punish those who pervert it into an engine of mischief; provided those laws do not "abridge" its "liberty." Its *liberty,* according to the well-known and universally admitted definition, consists in permission to publish, without previous restraint upon the press, but subject to punishment afterwards for improper publications. A law, therefore, to impose previous restraint upon the press, and not one to inflict punishment on wicked and malicious publications, would be a law to abridge the liberty of the press, and, as such, unconstitutional.

The foregoing reasoning is submitted as vindicating the validity of the laws in question.

Source: *Annals of Congress*, 5th Congress 1797–1799 (Washington, DC: Gales and Seaton, 1851), 3: 2987–2993.

2.5.   Representative John Nicholas Challenges the Report

> *Soon after the Committee Report was released, the House of
> Representatives began a debate with many lengthy orations. The
> excerpt below was made on February 25, 1799. Nicholas, a
> member of the House of Representatives from Virginia, rejected
> the claim that the First Amendment embodied Blackstone's very
> limited view that freedom of speech and press meant nothing
> more than a prohibition against prior restraint. This speech is
> one of the earliest to link the function of free speech with dem-
> ocratic self-government.*

It must be agreed that the nature of our Government makes a diffusion
of knowledge of public affairs necessary and proper, and that the people
have no mode of obtaining it but through the press. The necessity for
their having this information, results from its being their duty to elect
all the parts of the Government, and, in this way, to sit in judgment over
the conduct of those who have been heretofore employed. The most important and necessary information for the people to receive is, of the
misconduct of the Government; because their good deeds, although they
will produce affection and gratitude to public officers, will only confirm
the existing confidence, and will therefore, make no change in the conduct of the people. The question, then, whether the Government ought
to have control over the persons who alone can give information
throughout a country, is nothing more than this, whether men interested
in suppressing information necessary for the people to have, ought to be
intrusted with the power, or whether they ought to have a power which
their personal interest leads to the abuse of? I am sure no candid man
will hesitate about the answer; and it may also safely be left with ingen-
uous men to say whether the misconduct which we sometimes see in the
press, had not better be borne with, than to run the risk of confiding the
power of correction to men who will be constantly urged by their own
feelings to destroy its usefulness.

The mode of thinking which countenances this law, and the doctrines
on which it is built, are derived from a country whose government is so
different from ours, that the situation of public officers ought to be very
different. In Great Britain, the King is hereditary, and, according to the
theory or their government, can do no wrong. Public officers are his
representatives, and derive some portion of his inviolability from theory,
but more from the practice of the government, which has, for the most
part, been very arbitrary. It was, therefore, of course, that they should

receive a different sort of respect from that which is proper in our Government, where the officers of government are the servants of the people, are amenable to them, and liable to be turned out of office at periodical elections. In Great Britain, writings are seditious, though they are true, if they tend to bring a public officer into contempt.

. . . It is asserted by the select committee, and by every body who has gone before them in this discussion, that the "freedom of the press," according to the universally received acceptation of the expression, means only an exemption from all previous restraints on publication, but not to an exemption from any punishment Government pleases to inflict for what is published. This definition does not at all distinguish between publications of different sorts, but leaves all to the regulation of the law, only forbidding Government to interfere until the publication is really made. This definition, if true, so reduces the effect of the amendment, that the power of Congress is left unlimited over the productions of the press, and they are merely deprived of one mode of restraint.

The amendment was certainly intended to produce some limitation to legislative discretion, and it must be construed so as to produce such an effect, if it is possible. This is required in the construction of all solemn acts, but must be more particularly due to this on account of the various examinations it underwent, previous to its adoption. . . . To give it such a construction as will bring it to a mere nullity, would violate the strongest injunctions of common sense and decorum; and yet that appears to me to be the effect of the construction adopted by the committee. If subsequent punishments are sufficient to deter printers from publishing anything which is prohibited, there is no stint to the power of Congress; and yet, it appears to me that a limitation was clearly intended. . . . The result is, that the Government may forbid any species of writing, true as well as false, to be published; may inflict the heaviest punishments they can devise for disobedience; and yet we are very gravely assured that this is "the freedom of the press." . . .

But it is said, that the States have all adopted the same construction which is given to freedom of the press by the committee, for that all the State constitutions provide for it, and yet the law of [seditious] libels remains part of their codes. If this is fact, about which however I am uninformed, it is easily to be accounted for. At the Revolution, the State laws were either the law of England, or were built on it, and, of course, they would contain the monarchical doctrine respecting [seditious] libels. When the State constitutions were formed, the old law was continued in force indiscriminately, and only a general exception made of what should be found inconsistent with the State constitutions. Now, to prove that the States have considered the *law* of libels consistent with the freedom of the press, gentlemen should show that this law has been practised on since the Revolution, and that the attention of the States had been called to it by its execution, and that it still remains in force. I believe this cannot be done. So far as I know, it has been a dead letter.

... [T]he Convention who formed the constitution of Virginia ... passed a law similar to the [Sedition Act] of Congress, after having provided for the liberty of the press in their bill of rights. Let us examine that law. The first section is to punish these who shall "by any word, open deed, or act, advisedly and willingly maintain or defend the authority, jurisdiction, or power of the King, or Parliament of Great Britain, heretofore claimed over this Colony, or shall attribute any such authority," &c. This section, passed at the beginning of the most awful contest in which ever man was engaged, a contest for the right of self-government against one of the most powerful nations in the world, was to establish what? Not the inviolability of the Governor of the State, nor of the majority of either House of the Legislature, but to punish men who should promote resistance to the right of the people to govern themselves, to the principle of the constitution, to the republican principle. So different is this from the object of the law of Congress, that it would have been impossible to believe that they should have been compared, if we had not seen it done [in the committee report] ... [The Virginia law was aimed at seditious behavior designed to restore the rule of England, acts that] belong to the class enumerated in the first section of the sedition law, which nobody wishes to repeal, as the committee declare....

A distinction is very frequently relied on, between the freedom and the licentiousness of the press, which it is proper to examine. This seems to me to refute every other argument which is used on this subject; it amounts to an admission that there are some acts of the press which Congress ought not to have power to restrain, and that by the amendment they are prohibited to restrain these acts. Now, to justify any act of Congress, they ought to show the boundary between what is prohibited and what is permitted, and that the act is not within the prohibited class. The constitution has fixed no such boundary, therefore they can pretend to no power over the press, without claiming the right of defining what is freedom, and what is licentiousness, and that would claim a right which would defeat the constitution; for every Congress would have the same right, and the freedom of the press would fluctuate according to the will of the Legislature. This is, therefore, only a new mode of claiming absolute power over the press....

Upon the whole, therefore, I am fully satisfied, that no power is given by the constitution to control the press, and that such laws are expressly prohibited by the amendment. I think it inconsistent with the nature of our Government, that its administration should have power to restrain animadversions on public measures; and for protection from private injury from defamation, the States are, fully competent. It is to them that our officers most look for protection of persons, estates, and every other personal right; and, therefore, I see no reason why it is not proper to rely upon it, for defence against private libels.

Source: Congressional Debates (New York: D. Appleton, 1857), 2: 380–384.

2.6.   The "Kentucky Resolution"

A native and resident of Virginia, friend and confidant of Madison, and the sitting vice-president at the time, Thomas Jefferson surreptitiously wrote the Kentucky Resolutions, which also attacked the Alien and Sedition Acts. He was disturbed by some states' reactions—such as Delaware's—to the Virginia Resolution. The original draft was much longer, but the document below, submitted almost a year later in November 1799, is what the Kentucky legislature finally approved two weeks later.

THE representatives of the good people of this commonwealth in general assembly convened, having maturely considered the answers of sundry states in the Union, to their resolutions passed at the last session, respecting certain unconstitutional laws of Congress, commonly called the alien and sedition laws, would be faithless indeed to themselves, and to those they represent, were they silently to acquiesce in principles and doctrines attempted to be maintained in all those answers, that of Virginia only excepted. To again enter the field of argument, and attempt more fully or forcibly to expose the unconstitutionality of those obnoxious laws, would, it is apprehended be as unnecessary as unavailing.

We cannot however but lament, that in the discussion of those interesting subjects, by sundry of the legislatures of our sister states, unfounded suggestions, and uncandid insinuations, derogatory of the true character and principles of the good people of this commonwealth, have been substituted in place of fair reasoning and sound argument. Our opinions of those alarming measures of the general government, together with our reasons for those opinions, were detailed with decency and with temper, and submitted to the discussion and judgment of our fellow citizens throughout the Union. Whether the decency and temper have been observed in the answers of most of those states who have denied or attempted to obviate the great truths contained in those resolutions, we have now only to submit to a candid world. Faithful to the true principles of the federal union, unconscious of any designs to disturb the harmony of that Union, and anxious only to escape the fangs of

despotism, the good people of this commonwealth are regardless of censure or calumniation.

Lest, however the silence of this commonwealth should be construed
into an acquiescence in the doctrines and principles advanced and attempted to be maintained by the said answers, or least those of our
fellow citizens throughout the Union, who so widely differ from us on
those important subjects, should be deluded by the expectation, that we
shall be deterred from what we conceive our duty; or shrink from the
principles contained in those resolutions,—therefore.

Resolved, That this commonwealth considers the federal union, upon
the terms and for the purposes specified in the late compact, as condu-
cive to the liberty and happiness of the several states: That it does now
unequivocally declare its attachment to the Union, and to that compact,
agreeable to its obvious and real intention, and will be among the last
to seek its dissolution: That if those who administer the general government be permitted to transgress the limits fixed by that compact, by a
total disregard to the special delegations of power therein contained,
annihilation of the state governments, and the erection upon their ruins,
of a general consolidated government, will be the inevitable consequence: That the principle and construction contended for by sundry of
the state legislatures, that the general government is the exclusive judge
of the extent of the powers delegated to it, stop not short of *despotism*—
since the discretion of those who administer the government, and not
the *Constitution*, would be the measure of their powers: That the several
states who formed that instrument, being sovereign and independent,
have the unquestionable right to judge of its infraction; and *That a nul-
lification, by those sovereignties, of all unauthorized acts done under colour of
that instrument, is the rightful remedy:* That this commonwealth does upon
the most deliberate reconsideration declare, that the said Alien and Sedition Laws, are in their opinion, palpable violations of the said Constitution; and however cheerfully it may be disposed to surrender its
opinion to a majority of its sister states, in matters of ordinary or doubtful policy, yet, in momentous regulations like the present, which so vitally wound the best rights of the citizen, it would consider a silent
acquiescence as highly criminal: That although this commonwealth, as a
party to the federal compact, will bow to the laws of the Union, yet it
does, at the same time declare, that it will not now, or ever hereafter,
cease to oppose in a constitutional manner, every attempt, at what quarter soever offered, to violate that compact: And finally, in order that no
pretext or arguments may be drawn from a supposed acquiescence, on
the part of this commonwealth, in the constitutionality of those laws,
and be thereby used as precedents for similar future violations of the
federal compact, this commonwealth does now enter against them its
solemn PROTEST.

Source: *Elliot's Debates on the Federal Constitution*, 2nd ed. (Philadelphia: J.B. Lippincott, 1896), 4: 544–545.

2.7.   Letter from Mathew Lyon to President John Adams

Mathew Lyon was a member of the House of Representatives from the state of Vermont and a rabid critic of John Adams. His earlier criticism got him prosecuted and imprisoned by the Adams administration for breaching the "common law" against seditious libel before the Sedition Act became law. There was even a movement to expel him from Congress. Lyon wrote this abrasive farewell letter to the defeated and outgoing John Adams, dated March 4, 1801, the day the Sedition Act expired and Jefferson became president.

Fellow Citizen,

Four years ago, this day, you became President of the United States, and I a Representative of the people in Congress; this day has brought us once more on a level; the acquaintance we have had together entitles me to the liberty I take, when you are going to depart for Quincy, [Massachusetts] by and with the consent and advice of the good people of the United States, to bid you a hearty farewell. This appears to me more proper, as I am going to retire, of my own accord, to the extreme western parts of the United States, where I had fixed myself an asylum from the persecutions of a party, the most base, cruel, assuming and faithless, that ever disgraced the councils of any nation. That party are not happily humbled in "dust and ashes, before the indignant frowns of an injured country," but their deeds never can be forgotten.

In this valedictory, I propose, without further ceremony, to bring to your view, a retrospect of some part, at least, of your public conduct during the last four years. . . .

Perhaps in no one instant has our constitution—our sacred bill of rights been more shamefully, more bare-facedly trampled on, than in the case of the passage of the bill called the sedition law. This, Sir, was your darling hobby horse. By this law, you expected to have all your follies, your absurdities, and your atrocities buried in oblivion. You thought by its terror, to shut the mouths of all but sycophants and flatterers, and to secure yourself in the presidency at least; but, how happily have you been disappointed—the truth has issued from many a patriot pen and press—and you have fallen, never—never to rise again.

It has availed you little, Sir, to have me fined 1000 dollars and imprisoned four months for declaring truth long before the sedition law was past, to have Holt and Haswell fined 200 dollars and imprisoned two months each, the one for calling the late disbanded army a standing army and the other for publishing the sentiments of your secretary of war, in his letter to General Darke, to have Cooper fined 400 dollars and imprisoned six months because he resented your publishing his confidential application to you for an office he was truly worthy of.

I must finish my letter, Sir, where you finish your administration, that is with your late nominations. . . . [T]he Judiciary was the only permanent fund to be applied to, and so long as there was a brother or sister to make claim, they it seems have been ordered to draw upon it until all were satisfied, the same fund has served you an excellent purpose for legacies to your poor and distant relatives, as well as for rewarding the [T]ories, who have been the firmest friends to your administration, through the whole of your late nominations you have proceeded, Sir, as if you took counsel from the infernal regions, (some men who are not thought very highly of) have spurned your nominations avowedly to avoid the disgrace they confer.

. . . You seem now more than ever bent on mischief, your vindictive spirit prompts you to do every thing in your power to give the succeeding administration trouble, but you are as unfortunate in this, as in most of your calculations, your creatures are generally pliant reeds, they will bend to and fawn upon any body that is in power; it was power they worshipped in you, not John Adams.

Come pray, Sir, cool yourself a little, do not coil round like the rattlesnake, and bite yourself, no, betake yourself to fasting and prayer awhile, it may be good for both body and soul, that is a safer remedy for an old man in your situation, than the letting of blood.

Suffer me to recommend to you that patience and resignation which is characteristic of the holy religion you profess, I hope and pray that your fate may be a warning to all usurpers and tyrants, and that you may before you leave this world become a true and sincere penitent, and be forgiven all your manifold sins in the next. I repeat it, this is the sincere wish and prayer of your fellow citizen.   M. Lyon

Source: "Letter from Mathew Lyon" (Baltimore, MD: Printed for George Keatinge's Bookstore, 1801).

ANNOTATED RESEARCH GUIDE

Chapin, Bradley. *Early America*. Rev. ed. Englewood, NJ: J.S. Ozer, 1984. A standard reference to legal antecedents of England and the Revolutionary era.
Levy, Leonard. *The Legacy of Suppression: Freedom of Speech and Press in Early American History Students*. Cambridge, MA: Harvard University Press, 1960. Casts more than a shadow of doubt on the idea that the First Amend-

ment was intended to deny the federal government power to punish seditious libel. It competes with Zechariah Chafee, Jr.'s very influential treatise *Free Speech in the United States* (Cambridge, MA: Harvard University Press, 1948). Chafee claimed that the First Amendment was written for the very purpose of making seditious libel no longer a criminal offense, at least against the U.S. government. For a more contemporary criticism of Levy's thesis, see David M. Rabban, "An Ahistorical Historian," *Stanford Law Review* 37 (February 1986): 795–856.

Martin, James P. "When Repression Is Democratic and Constitutional: The Federalist Theory of Representation and the Sedition Act of 1798." In *First Amendment Law Handbook*, ed. James L. Swanson. St. Paul, MN: West Group, 1999, pp. 567–637. This interesting essay supports the minority claim that the Sedition Act was not unconstitutional.

McCullough, David. *John Adams*. New York: Simon & Schuster, 2001. A complex biography that sheds more favorable light on the nation's second president, especially in comparison to his rival Thomas Jefferson, than have most other works.

Miller, John Chester. *Crisis in Freedom: The Alien and Sedition Acts*. Boston: Little, Brown, 1951. Although somewhat eclipsed by Morton's *Freedom's Fetters*, this remains a useful resource.

Smith, James Morton. *Freedom's Fetters: The Alien and Sedition Laws and American Civil Liberties*. Ithaca, NY: Cornell University Press, 1956. This work is generally regarded as the definitive study of the Alien and Sedition Laws and the political events of this period of American history. The book is a chronological analysis of the events that triggered the passage of the laws, detailed accounts of the enforcement of the laws and prosecutions of suspected subversives, and finally the election of 1800.

Smith, James Morton. *The Republic of Letters: The Correspondence between Jefferson and Madison*. Vol. 2. New York: W.W. Norton, 1995. A collection of the letters (chronologically arranged) between Madison and Jefferson with introductory chapters providing background of the era and the issues prompting the exchange of letters. Chapters 23–27 focus on the events surrounding the Alien and Sedition Acts.

Smith, Jeffrey A. *War and Press Freedom*. New York: Oxford University Press, 1999. Examines the stress that free speech and press endure during wartime. Chapter 4 of this book, "The Federalists and the French Revolution," is a succinct illustration of his thesis regarding the Alien and Sedition Acts.

Web Site

http://www.yale.edu/lawweb/avalon/alsedact.htm. This contains the *Avalon Project*, created and maintained by Yale University. One page on this site is devoted to the Alien and Sedition Acts.

3

The Abolitionist Movement

Various Americans had objected to slavery before the Constitution was written and thereafter until the Civil War and the Thirteenth Amendment ended slavery in the United States. Religious groups, such as the Quakers, saw slavery as a sin; others saw it as immoral, especially in a country built on the notion of equality. Followers of the Enlightenment thought that slavery retarded progress because it debased labor. Criticism was continuous but relatively mild. By the mid-1830s, however, opponents had become a formidable political voice that refused to be silenced. A new brand of abolitionists burst onto the political scene and equated slavery with sin but now demanded its "immediate" eradication. Their political pressure threatened the slaveholding economy of the South, and the planter class resisted. Abolitionists also irritated northerners who feared southern boycotts of their manufactured goods and others who dreaded the prospect of millions of freed slaves in search of a better life in the North. Politics was another important factor; the South had electoral votes, and neither Democratic nor Whig Party leaders in the North were inclined to write off the South by siding with the enemies of slavery.

Abolitionists were inspired by the intellectual and social theories of their time: idealism, transcendentalism, and other reform movements whose objectives were to perfect human institutions of all sorts. Women's rights, penal reform, temperance, society's obligations to the poor, and other worthy causes initiated campaigns to redress wrongs and to better society. Abolitionists became convinced that only immediate emancipation was an acceptable end to slavery, and they embarked on a crusade that implicated a number of free speech issues. Prominent antislavery newspapers appeared even as early as 1821, when Benjamin Lundy, a Quaker, launched the *Genius of Universal Emancipation*. William Lloyd Garrison of Massachusetts became one of the most famous and determined abolitionists of all when, on January 1, 1831, he inaugurated the first edition of his *Liberator*, a fiery newspaper emanating from Boston and devoted to condemning the evils of slavery and hastening its demise. By the end of the next two decades, more than twenty-five abolitionist journals and newspapers appeared. Among the most famous of these earlier papers—besides *The Liberator*—was the *Philanthropist* from Cincinnati (edited by James Birney, a former slave owner in Alabama who turned fiercely abolitionist). Frederick Douglass escaped from slavery and founded the black journal *North Star*. Distinguished literary writers in the North also edited antislavery journals: for example, James Russell Lowell's *National Anti-Slavery Standard* and William Cullen Bryant's New York *Evening Post*.

Antislavery societies emerged throughout the free states and in such major cities as Boston, New York, and Philadelphia. Women were very instrumental in this movement. Mary Weston Chapman, who helped Garrison edit *The Liberator*, established with twelve other women in 1832 the Boston Anti-Slavery Society. Regional societies emerged from smaller ones, such as the New England Anti-Slavery Society, and eventually in 1833 a national convention calling itself the American Anti-Slavery Society was instituted, first in Philadelphia and eventually situated in New York, the leadership of which Garrison began to command in 1840. These organizations also published their own newspapers or journals or collaborated with others advocating the end of slavery, so that by the mid-1830s and 1840s journals, newspapers, pamphlets, and leaflets burgeoned all across the country outside the South denouncing the institution of slavery. Other newspapers, most of them in the South, supported slavery, joined by many more in the North that strongly opposed abolitionists as fanatics bent on stirring up domestic trouble.

Eight months after Garrison's first edition of *The Liberator*, Nat Turner led a small group of fellow slaves in August 1831 on a rampage through farms and plantations in rural Southampton, Virginia, slaughtering whites and freeing and enlisting dozens of other slaves along the way to the destination town of Jerusalem, Virginia. Some slaves actually resisted Turner and fought side-by-side with their white masters. At least fifty-five whites were killed in the revolt. Authorities quickly crushed the bloody uprising, and Turner was hanged six weeks after the revolt. Stunned Virginians for a while openly wondered aloud and in the press about the merits of slavery, but this impulse of free thought disappeared almost as quickly as it arose. Little more was needed to convince abolition's enemies in the South that black slaves were a class of brutes that if set loose would kill again. It was certain that abolitionist literature itself did not provoke this rebellion, but slaveholders readily linked "the black terror" to incendiary publications. Since the 1820s, when South Carolinians had charged that the Denmark Vesey slave conspiracy resulted from Vesey having read antislavery debates in Congress from the Missouri crisis of 1819–1820, southerners feared antislavery sentiments might enter the South and bestir the slaves to violence. Virginians and others juxtaposed the publication of *The Liberator* with Turner's revolt and assumed the one begat the other. Across the South, states clamped down on criticism of slavery and tightened the slave codes. Georgia even offered a bounty of $5,000 for the arrest and conviction of Garrison.

Especially galling to southerners was the antislavery societies' massive mail campaigns of "moral suasion" in the 1830s, which entailed flooding the South with antislavery literature and images encouraging slaveholders to throw off the sin of slavery. In one year between 1835 and 1836, the American Anti-Slavery Society alone printed and distributed more than a million leaflets pregnant with abolitionist criticisms of slavery. Angry citizens frequently intercepted this "detestable" literature when destined in bulk for the South, where it was either publicly burned or thrown into the river.

By the mid-1830s apprehensive and worried slaveholders recognized that the abolitionist movement was no longer confined to a small band of peaceful Quakers equipped with little capacity to make any real political impact. To the southern "men of property and standing," the end of slavery was a genuine and dreaded possibility that threatened complete upheaval in their economy and social arrangements. The horrors of the slave revolt in Haiti early in the century and the British moves to abolish slavery in the British West Indies pointed to the dangers to slavery that might come from within or without a slave society. Strong measures were undertaken in an effort to crush the abolitionists and still their potentially incendiary appeal.

The political battle over the Alien and Sedition Acts of 1798 had forced the nation's political and intellectual elite to accept free speech and a free press in matters of public affairs, and by the early 1830s, even though the First Amendment did not yet apply against the states, the tradition of freedom of speech was firmly established in the political culture. Even in slave states such as Virginia public criticism of slavery was tolerated until the fatal Turner uprising, after which repression ruled. The vital significance of slavery to the propertied class of the South transcended any commitment to free speech once abolitionism threatened social disruption and slavers' interest.

Measures to contain the abolitionist movement included "Gag Rules" in Congress against abolitionist petitions; efforts to throttle abolitionist literature by eliminating it from the mails; state laws punishing speech advocating, or even discussing, abolition; and mob violence, particularly outside the South, coordinated by self-appointed local vigilante groups or committees. Between 1836 and 1844 Congress divided on the propriety of Gag Rules to bar the national legislature from raising or debating subjects pertaining to slavery—such as the slave trade, whether a territory should be admitted as a slave state, or whether abolition of slavery should continue in the nation's capital. Such rules clashed with the spirit, if not the letter, of the First Amendment's "right of the people to petition the government for a redress of grievances," and opponents attacked the rules as unconstitutional. Abolitionists brought endless petitions to both the Senate and House in a coordinated political strategy to force the confrontation onto the front pages of newspapers across the United States.

Senator John C. Calhoun of South Carolina was the South's most outspoken champion of its vested interests. In March 1836 he argued on the Senate floor that Congress was not obligated by the Constitution to take up any or every petition presented by a handful—or even thousands—of citizens. Proper legislative discretion did not violate the First Amendment, and as a pragmatic argument it was not unreasonable. A busy collegial body with urgent public business cannot be required to take up every issue presented to it. But Calhoun went further and dismissed the right to petition as among the least important constitutional rights, even an anachronism in a modern representative republic, because it implied that the "people" (the master) must beg the "government" (their servant). This logic, of course, refuted him: The servant, Congress, was obliged to accept the requests of the master, the people petitioning—including abolitionists. His most uncompromising reply was that Congress simply had no power at all over slavery, that it was a subject for the states alone, and therefore proposals or petitions to have Congress regulate that subject were simply out of order. The Senate's version of a Gag Rule emerged in a compromise attributed in part to Senator Henry Clay of Kentucky but was principally the work of Senator James Buchanan of Pennsylvania: The Senate would *receive* the abolitionist petitions but leave them unattended and thus effectively tabled.

The House of Representatives accumulated more than twice as many petitions because it contained a more visible and enthusiastic but small bloc of antislavery sympathizers. Gag Rules were adopted in successive legislative sessions, beginning in 1836, and they lasted until 1844 when they no longer were able to command majority support or because the antislavery bloc outfoxed its opponents in a parliamentary game of wits. Fashioned by Congressman William Pinckney of South Carolina, and adopted on May 26, 1836, the first House Gag Rule required "all petitions, memorials, resolutions, propositions, or papers relating in any way or to any extent whatever to the subject of slavery or the abolition of slavery shall, without being printed or referred, be laid upon the table and that no further action whatever be taken thereon."[1] Seventy percent of the House votes to impose this Gag Rule were cast by members from free states, an indication of a strong desire to keep the troublesome antislavery issue out of the chamber. John Quincy Adams of Massachusetts was neither an advocate for slavery nor an abolitionist, but he staunchly opposed all Gag Rules from his prominent seat in the House of Representatives (he was the only former president of the United States subsequently elected to Congress). To Adams and others, these measures were blatantly unconstitutional.

Zealous abolitionists aggressively collected more than half a million signatures to create hundreds of thousands of petitions inundating Congress. One abolitionist newspaper later reflected on this organized petition drive as a tactic "to take possession of Congress and turn it into a vast Anti Slavery Debating Society, with the whole country as an audience."[2] Sympathy for abolitionists increased following critical news coverage of proslavery efforts to silence the aging and articulate former President Adams, who adamantly fought for what he deemed the citizens' right to petition their government.

When abolitionists sent their antislavery tracts through the mails, no federal law existed to restrain them, and when such literature arrived in the South, angry crowds frequently destroyed it. Birney's *Philanthropist* recorded some one hundred episodes of mob destruction of abolitionist propaganda sent by mail in just three slave states. The Post Office Department was unsure of what to do, and Postmaster General Amos Kendall eventually, in the summer of 1835, granted local postal officials discretion to remove from the mails "incendiary" publications that could cause disturbances. Most northern newspapers applauded Kendall's position, but eventually the northern press, for the most part, learned to support the abolitionist right to use the mails. Inducing this change was partly revulsion to extreme hostility displayed by southern mobs and, in part, the indignity of the South's criticism of the North for not passing laws themselves to muzzle abolitionist speech. It was also increasingly clear that abolition societies did not advocate violence in their calls to end slavery; their appeal was to morality and conscience, equating slavery with sin, and they did not address their publications to illiterate slaves.

Opponents of abolition pushed for national legislation requiring the Post Office to purge provocative abolitionist literature from circulation via the postal system. Their goal was to create an intellectual blockade by choking off the most important vehicle for transmitting information. President Andrew Jackson in December 1835 urged Congress to pass the law. Calhoun led an ad hoc special committee in the Senate to develop a Postal Bill, and he fought vigorously against any law assigning authority to the federal Post Office to control the content of the mail. Calhoun insisted that the "inflammatory" literature in question dealt with slavery, the regulation of which was exclusively reserved to the states. He also argued that the First Amendment barred federal censorship, but it did not restrict the states. Calhoun worried that if the national government could intrude to prohibit abolitionist literature from the mails, it could step in to protect it. He eventually reported a bill that instructed postal officials not to deliver or receive any literature or pictorials in any state where they were forbidden. Sufficient opposition erupted in the North to kill Calhoun's bill. It appeared to go too far in the direction of censorship just to cater to the South and its "peculiar institution." Many editorials questioned both its reach and the vague meaning of words like "incendiary" and "inflammatory" found in southern states' antiabolition suppression laws. The House was more sympathetic to the free speech rights involved and passed a "hands-off" position, to which the Senate, accepting defeat, subscribed in July 1836, and a measure that year became law ordering the Post Office not to interfere.

Slave states had already begun to deal directly with the issue at home. "Slave" and "Black" Codes governing legal arrangements and responsibilities between slave and master were read to make dissemination of abolitionist literature a crime, but many states wrote new laws specifically targeting speech or publications in any way critical of slavery, and violators were severely punished—usually with a whipping for the first offense and death for the next. Expression tending to incite a slave insurrection was a capital crime in many states. Some states floated the curious legal argument that their laws against abolitionist publications operated beyond their own borders, so that even states like Massachusetts, Ohio, or New York were obliged to make similar laws to punish abolitionists or at least hand them over for trial in slave states where their dangerous publications were prohibited. This backfired, as the northern press, even erstwhile antiabolitionists, valued their freedom to publish and criticize.

Suppression had the perverse and disastrous consequence of encasing southern society in a culture frozen in time. Universities and colleges steered clear of hiring controversial faculty, however brilliant and promising, or teaching or discussing subjects that might cast a pall of doubt or shame on a slave society. Teachers and curricula in the lower schools were similarly affected. An institution to liberate minds, education became a tool to socialize southern children into believing that slavery was natural and just and even encouraged by God. As historian Russell Nye concluded, "By 1850 the control of Southern education by slaveholding interests was virtually complete."[3] A disproportionate number of southerners sought higher education in northern institutions. In the early

1840s nearly half the student body of the University of Pennsylvania, mostly in the medical school, were from the South. "Such an alarming patronage of Northern institutions by the gifted youth of the South," wrote historian Clement Eaton, "seemed to be a confession of weakness in the idyllic slave regime, as though the repression of free thought in the South had dwarfed her institutions of learning."[4] To counteract this, a strong movement began to create a great "Central Southern University" to keep talented youth in the South.

Southern censors scoured northern books for "pernicious" doctrines. Efforts were undertaken to assure that southern texts and teachers were deployed in the schools. What few northern texts made their way into the South were usually alternative editions, excised of any offensive discussion. A separate nation had been socialized to resist any criticism; even constructive criticism, in public, was generally silenced. Repercussions were also felt to some extent in northern universities and colleges, for example, Amherst College, with influential southern alumni and student bodies, where the taboo subject was often avoided to avert disturbance, offense, or retaliation.

Educating blacks was a crime in many parts of the South. A Virginia state legislator explained the utility of enforced ignorance a year after Turner's aborted rebellion: "If we could extinguish the capacity to see the light, our work would be completed; they would then be on a level with the beasts of the field, and we should be safe."[5] Only free blacks might find any schooling, but in some states such as Missouri operating a school even for freed slaves was a crime. The rhythms of plantation life combined with slave codes, forbidding even the assembly of slaves without a white presence, to keep most slaves isolated.

The strongest force trying to suppress antislavery free speech in the short term proved ultimately counterproductive in the long run: the angry hostility and brutality of the multitude. Mob violence was not much needed in the South as hostile state laws drove out or silenced what few identifiable abolitionists there were. But incidents of this form of social control occurred across the North and in the border states. The perpetrators were usually, but not always, lower-class whites driven by the racism they learned and economic competition with small enclaves of free blacks who settled in urban areas outside the South. In Boston on October 21, 1835, for example, angry protesters thronged the hearty apostle Garrison himself. In July 1836, a squad of hooligans in what was called the Cincinnati riots vandalized and destroyed James Birney's influential *Philanthropist*, which had become an organ of the Ohio Anti-Slavery Society. Birney rebuilt and operated his press with even greater determination. Perpetrators of mob violence were sometimes sympathetically excused, even in courtrooms, and portrayed before judges and

juries as innocent victims whose belligerence had been provoked by inflammatory and obnoxious abolitionists.

The murder on November 7, 1837, of Elijah Lovejoy in Alton, Illinois,
was the most notorious moment of mob rule during the entire abolition
movement, and it generated sympathy for abolitionists everywhere outside the South. Lovejoy was a Princeton-educated minister from Maine
who started a newspaper, the *Observer*, in St. Louis. After learning that
a free black Pennsylvanian, brought by work to St. Louis, had been
dragged from a local jail awaiting trial for killing a policeman and then
burned alive by an angry mob, Lovejoy wrote in his newspaper: "Our
hands tremble as we record the story."[6] The editorial condemned the
incident, the judicial inquiry (conducted by the peculiarly named Judge
Luke Edward Lawless, who had instructed the grand jury to dismiss the
charges), and slavery itself. In July 1836 irate whites wrecked Lovejoy's
press. Antislavery societies sent him another printing press, which mobs
destroyed again and then dumped in the Mississippi River. Later that
summer he abandoned St. Louis for Alton—in Illinois, a free state—
thirty miles further north along the Mississippi River, where he began
publishing the Alton *Observer*.

Angry mobs there, too, would not leave Lovejoy alone and repeatedly
demolished his press. Committees of concerned citizens denounced his
critical editorials as incendiary and warned him that if he continued, mob
unrest could unleash again on him and his family. He tried to reason
with them, but their response foretold threats of further destruction of
his press—or worse. On the night of November 7 he and about twenty
supporters stood guard over his fourth, recently arrived new printing
press that sat still unassembled in the warehouse on the banks of the
Mississippi River. An intoxicated horde of white vigilantes approached
the building throwing rocks and stones, and one man tried to set fire to
the roof of the warehouse. As Lovejoy and others tried to extinguish the
blaze, an exchange of gunfire was heard. Lovejoy came out to see what
might have happened, when five bullets hit him. He staggered to the
second floor and fell dead. His death in defense of a free press now fused
abolition with freedom of expression and galvanized support for abolition all over the North.

The "slave power," and the slaveholders' determination to keep it,
suppressed free speech in many ways. In slave states criticism of slavery
was a criminal offense. Travelers to such states risked prosecution for
wondering aloud, or having in their possession literature, about the evils
of slavery. As the American republic spread across the continent into
new territories, the range of free speech was sharply curtailed wherever
slavery was permitted. Even in the free North, at least during the early
years of the abolition movement, criticism of slavery was curbed to avoid
offending southern interests wielding political and economic power. In

1856 the emerging Republican Party capitalized on slave power's suppression of speech with a slogan in support of its presidential candidate, John C. Frémont: "Free soil, free labor, free speech, free work, and Frémont."

The Civil War and its immediate aftermath imposed a resolution on the wrenching national problem that the Constitution in 1787 had initially accommodated in tenuous compromise. The free speech determination of abolitionists catapulted slavery to the national agenda in the 1830s, and the problem of slavery steadily grew into the most divisive issue in American history until it could be settled only by a bloody civil war.

NOTES

1. *Niles Register of Debates* (Baltimore, MD: Franklin Press, 1836), 5: 241.

2. The Salem, Ohio, *Anti Slavery Bugle*, June 15, 1850, as quoted in Russel B. Nye, *Fettered Freedom: Civil Liberties and the Slavery Controversy 1830–1860* (Lansing: Michigan State University Press, 1963), p. 46.

3. Ibid., p. 91.

4. Clement Eaton, *Freedom of Thought in the Old South* (Durham, NC: Duke University Press, 1940), p. 210.

5. As quoted in William Goodell, *The American Slave Code in Theory and Practice* (London: Clarke, Beeton & Co., 1853), p. 323.

6. As quoted in Paul Simon, *Freedom's Champion: Elijah Lovejoy* (Carbondale: Southern Illinois University Press, 1994), p. 48.

DOCUMENTS

3.1.   William Lloyd Garrison Calls for Immediate Emancipation

---

*Garrison had supported gradual emancipation and "coloniza-
tion," whereby slaves were freed but shipped away to a colony
perhaps in Liberia. By 1830 he recanted and denounced that
position as indefensible. In Boston—which he said needed lessons on the injustice of slavery—he inaugurated on January 1,
1831, his own newspaper,* The Liberator. *In the first edition,
excerpted below, he astonished readers with blunt language announcing his new views.*

In the month of August, I issued proposals for publishing "The Liberator" in Washington City; but the enterprise, though hailed in different
sections of the country, was palsied by public indifference. Since that
time, the removal of the *Genius of Universal Emancipation* [from Baltimore]
to the Seat of Government has rendered less imperious the establishment
of a similar periodical in that quarter.

During my recent tour for the purpose of exciting the minds of the
people by a series of discussions of the subject of slavery, every place
that I visited gave fresh evidence of the fact that a great revolution in
public sentiment was to be effected in the free states—*and particularly in
New-England*—than at the South. I find contempt more bitter, opposition
more active, detraction more relentless, prejudice more stubborn, and
apathy more frozen, than among slave-owners themselves. Of course,
there were individual exceptions to the contrary.

This state of things afflicted but did not dishearten me. I determined,
at every hazard, to lift up the standard of emancipation in the eyes of
the nation, *within sight of Bunker Hill and in the birthplace of liberty*. That
standard is now unfurled; and long may it float, unhurt by the spolia-
tions of time or the missiles of a desperate foe—yea, till every chain be
broken, and every bondman set free! Let Southern oppressors tremble—
let their secret abettors tremble—let their Northern apologists tremble—
let all enemies of the persecuted blacks tremble. . . .

Assenting to the "self-evident truth" maintained in the American Declaration of Independence "that all men are created equal, and endowed
by their Creator with certain inalienable rights—among which are life,
liberty, and the pursuit of happiness," I shall strenuously contend for

the immediate enfranchisement of our slave population. . . . In Park-Street Church [in Boston], on the Fourth of July, 1829, in an address on slavery, I unreflectingly assented to the popular but pernicious doctrine of *gradual* abolition. I seize this opportunity to make a full and unequivocal recantation, and thus publicly to ask pardon of my God, of my country, and of my brethren the poor slaves, for having uttered a sentiment so full of timidity, injustice, and absurdity. . . .

I am aware that many object to the severity of my language; but is there not cause for severity? I *will be* as harsh as truth, and as uncompromising as justice. On this subject I do not wish to think, or speak, or write, with moderation. No! No! Tell a man whose house is on fire to give a moderate alarm; tell him to moderately rescue his wife from the hands of the ravisher; tell the mother to gradually extricate her babe from the fire into which it has fallen—but urge me not to use moderation in a cause like the present. I am in earnest—I will not equivocate—I will not excuse—I will not retreat in a single inch—and I will be heard. The apathy of the people is enough to make every statue leap from its pedestal, and to hasten the resurrection of the dead.

It is pretended that I am retarding the cause of emancipation by the coarseness of my invective and the precipitancy of my measures. *The charge is not true.* On this question my influence,—humble as it is—is felt at this moment to a considerable extent, and shall be felt in coming years—not perniciously, but beneficially—not as a curse, but as a blessing. And posterity will bear testimony that I was right. I desire to thank God, that he enables me to disregard "the fear of man which bringeth a snare," and to speak his truth in its simplicity and power.

Source: *The Liberator* (January 1, 1831), 1: 1–4.

3.2. President Andrew Jackson Proposes Post Office Censorship

---

Aware of slaveholders' bitter opposition to abolitionist publications after Nat Turner's insurrection, in his second term and in his seventh Annual Message to Congress (submitted to the House of Representatives on December 7, 1835), President Jackson called on Congress to pass legislation requiring the Post Office Department to expurgate the mails of "incendiary" publications.

In connection with these provisions in relation to the Post-Office Department, I must also invite your attention to the painful excitement produced in the South by attempts to circulate through the mails inflammatory appeals addressed to the passions of the slaves, in prints and in various sorts of publications, calculated to stimulate them to insurrection and to produce all the horrors of a servile war. There is doubtless no respectable portion of our countrymen who can be so far misled as to feel any other sentiment than that of indignant regret at conduct so destructive of the harmony and peace of the country, and so repugnant to the principles of our national compact and to the dictates of humanity and religion. Our happiness and prosperity essentially depend upon peace within our borders, and peace depends upon the maintenance in good faith of those compromises of the Constitution upon which the Union is founded. It is fortunate for the country that the good sense, the generous feeling, and the deep-rooted attachment of the people of the nonslaveholding States to the Union and to their fellow-citizens of the same blood in the South have given so strong and impressive a tone to the sentiments entertained against the proceedings of the misguided persons who have engaged in these unconstitutional and wicked attempts, and especially against the emissaries from foreign parts who have dared to interfere in this matter, as to authorize the hope that those attempts will no longer be persisted in. But if these expressions of the public will shall not be sufficient to effect so desirable a result, not a doubt can be entertained that the nonslaveholding States, so far from countenancing the slightest interference with the constitutional rights of the South, will be prompt to exercise their authority in suppressing so far as in them lies whatever is calculated to produce this evil.

In leaving the care of other branches of this interesting subject to the State authorities, to whom they properly belong, it is nevertheless proper for Congress to take such measures as will prevent the Post-Office Department, which was designed to foster an amicable intercourse and correspondence between all the members of the Confederacy, from being used as an instrument of an opposite character. The General Government, to which the great trust is confided of preserving inviolate the relations created among the States by the Constitution, is especially bound to avoid in its own action anything that may disturb them. I would therefore call the special attention of Congress to the subject, and respectfully suggest the propriety of passing such a law as will prohibit, under severe penalties, the circulation in the Southern States, through the mail, of incendiary publications intended to instigate the slaves to insurrection.

Source: *A Compilation of the Messages and Papers of the Presidents of the United States: 1789–1897*, (Washington, DC: Government Printing Office, 1896), 3:175–176.

3.3.   John C. Calhoun on the Postal Bill

Like Jefferson and Madison during the crisis over the Alien and Sedition Acts, Senator Calhoun of South Carolina advocated "interposition," the right of a sovereign state like South Carolina to nullify a federal law that the state found unconstitutional. In a speech he delivered in the Senate on April 12, 1836, he defended the states' exclusive authority over slavery and attacked President Jackson's Postal Bill, which was designed to protect slave interests from abolitionist literature. Interestingly, Calhoun argued that Jackson's approach violated the First Amendment. The Postal Bill failed in the Senate.

As soon as the subject of abolition began to agitate the South, last summer, in consequence of the transmission of incendiary publications through the mail, I saw at once that it would force itself on the notice of Congress at the present session; and that it involved questions of great delicacy and difficulty. I immediately turned my attention in consequence to the subject, and after due reflection arrived at the conclusion, that Congress could exercise no direct power over it; and that, if acted at all, the only mode in which it could act, consistent with the constitution and the rights of the slaveholding States, would be in the manner proposed by this bill. I also saw that there was no inconsiderable danger in the excited states of the feelings of the South; that the power, however dangerous and unconstitutional, might be thoroughly yielded to Congress—knowing full well how apt the weak and timid are, in a state of excitement and alarm, to seek temporary protection in any quarter, regardless of after consequences; and how ready the artful and designing are to seize on such occasions to extend and perpetuate their power.

. . . The President's Message . . . assumed for Congress direct power over the subject, and that on the broadest, most unqualified, and dangerous principles. . . . [It] implies that Congress has jurisdiction over the subject; that is, of discriminating as to what papers ought or ought not to be transmitted by the mail . . . [and] assumes for Congress jurisdiction over the liberty of the press. The framers of the constitution (or rather those jealous patriots who refused to consent to its adoption without amendments to guard against the abuse of power) have, by the first amended article, provided that Congress shall pass no law abridging the liberty of the press—with the view of placing the press beyond the control of Congressional legislation . . . [I]f we should concede to Congress the power which the President assumes of discriminating, in reference to character, what publications shall not be transmitted by the mail . . . [i]t would place in the hands of the General Government an instrument more potent to control the freedom of the press than the Sedition Law [of 1798] itself. . . . I could not but apprehend that the authority of the President . . . would go far to rivet in the public mind the dangerous principles which it was my design to defeat. . . .

The first and leading principle is, that the subject of slavery is under the sole and exclusive control of the States where the institution exists. It belongs to them to determine what may endanger its existence, and when and how it may be defended. In the exercise of this right, they may prohibit the introduction or circulation of any paper or publication, which may, in their opinion, disturb or endanger the institution. Thus far all are agreed. To this extent no one has questioned the right of the States. . . .

The health of the State, like that of the subject of slavery, belongs exclusively to the States. It is reserved and not delegated; and, of course, each State has a right to judge for itself, what may endanger the health of its citizens, what measures are necessary to prevent it, and when and how such measures are to be carried into effect. . . .

States [can] adopt such measures as they may think proper, to prevent their domestic institutions from being endangered. They may be endangered, not only by introducing and circulating inflammatory publications, calculated to incite insurrection, but also by the introduction of free people of color from abroad, who may come as emissaries, or with opinions and sentiments hostile to the peace and security of those States. . . .

We have arrived at a new and important point in reference to the abolition question. It is no longer in the hands of quiet and peaceful, but I cannot add, harmless Quakers. It is now the control of ferocious zealots, blinded by fanaticism, and in pursuit of their object, regardless of the obligations of religion or morality. They are organized throughout every section of the non-slaveholding States; they have the disposition of almost unlimited funds, and are in possession of a powerful press, which, for the first time, is enlisted in the cause of abolition, and turned against the domestic institutions, and the peace and security of the South. To guard against the danger in this new and more menacing form, the slaveholding States will be compelled to revise their laws against the introduction and circulation of publications calculated to disturb their peace and endanger their security, and to render them far more full and efficient than they have heretofore been. In this new state of things, the probable conflict between the laws which those States may think proper to adopt, and those of the General Government regulating the mail, becomes far more important than at any former stage of the controversy; and Congress is now called upon to say what part it will take in reference in this deeply interesting subject. We of the slaveholding States ask nothing of the Government, but that it should abstain from violating laws passed within our acknowledged constitutional competency, and conceded to be essential to our peace and security. . . . I am desirous that my constituents should know what they have to expect, either from this Government or from the non-slaveholding States. Much that I have said and done during this session, has been with the view of affording them correct information on this point, in order that they might know to what extent they might rely upon others, and how far they must depend on themselves.

Thus far (I say it with regret) our just hopes have not been realized. The legislatures of the South, backed by the voice of their constituents, expressed through innumerable meetings, have called upon the non-slaveholding States to repress the movements made within the jurisdiction of those States, against their peace and security. Not a step has been taken; not a law has been passed or even proposed; and I venture to assert that none will be. . . .

Nor have we been less disappointed as to the proceedings of Congress. Believing that the General Government has no right or authority over the subject of slavery, we had just grounds to hope that Congress would refuse all jurisdiction in reference to it, in whatever form it might be presented. The very opposite course has been pursued. Abolition petitions have not only been received in both Houses, and received on the most obnoxious and dangerous grounds—*that we are bound to receive them*; that is, to take jurisdiction of the question of slavery whenever the abolitionists may think proper to petition for its abolition, either here [in Washington, D.C.] or in the States.

Thus far, then, we of the slaveholding States have been grievously disappointed. [Calhoun had helped draft a substitute bill for that of Jackson's supporters that gave the slave states the right to decide for themselves what publications could enter the states.] . . . To refuse to pass this bill would be virtually to co-operate with the abolitionists—would be to make the officer and agents of the post-office department, in effect, their agents and abettors in the circulation of their incendiary publications in violation of the laws of the States. It is your unquestionable duty, as I have demonstrably proved, to abstain from their violation; and by refusing or neglecting to discharge this duty, you would clearly enlist, in the existing controversy, on the side of the abolitionists, against the Southern States. Should such be your decision, by refusing to pass this bill, I shall say to the people of the South, look to yourselves—you have nothing to hope from others. But I must tell the Senate, be your decision what it may, the South will never abandon the principles of this bill. If you refuse co-operation with our laws, and conflict should ensue between yours and ours, the Southern States will never yield to the superiority of yours. We have a remedy in our hands, which, in such event, we shall not fail to apply. We have the high authority for asserting, that, in such cases, "State interposition is the rightful remedy"—a doctrine first announced by Jefferson—adopted by the patriotic and republican State of Kentucky, by a solemn resolution in [1799], and finally carried out into successful practice on a recent occasion, ever to be remembered, by the gallant State, which I, in part, have the honor to represent. In this well tested and efficient remedy . . . the slaveholding States have ample protection. Let it be fixed—let it be riveted into every Southern mind, that the laws of the slaveholding States for the protection of their domestic institutions are paramount to the laws of the General Government in regulation of commerce and the mail;—that the latter must yield to the former in the event of conflict; and that if the Government should refuse to yield, the States have the right to interpose, and we are safe. With these principles, nothing but concert would be wanting to bid defiance to the movements of the abolitionists, whether at home or abroad; and to place our domestic institutions, and with them our security and peace, under our own protection, and beyond the reach of danger.

Source: Richard Crallé, ed., *Speeches of John C. Calhoun* (New York: D. Appleton & Company, 1853), 2: 509–533.

3.4.   The Bible and Jesus Sanction Slavery

On October 24, 1835, a group of sixty white citizens on their own initiative voted 40–20 to convict two white men of trying to decoy slaves out of St. Louis. Rather than hang the two men, the self-anointed citizen-judges took turns whipping them. The episode inspired a public meeting of citizens of St. Louis, which issued the following resolutions expressing a prominent sentiment of their time—the fusion of religious fervor with slavery.

2. *Resolved*, That the right of free discussion and freedom of speech exist under the Constitution; but that, being a conventional reservation made by the people in their sovereign capacity, does not imply a moral right, on the part of the Abolitionists, to freely discuss the subject of Slavery, either orally or through the medium of the press. It is the agitation of a question too nearly allied to the vital interests of the slaveholding States to admit of public disputation; and so far from the fact, that the movements of the Abolitionists . . . are in the greatest degree seditious, and

calculated to excite insurrection and anarchy, and, ultimately, a disseverment of our prosperous Union.

3. *Resolved*, That we consider the course pursued by the Abolitionists,
as one calculated to paralyze every social tie by which we are now united
to our fellow-man, and that, if persisted in, it must eventually be the
cause of the disseverment of these United States; and that the doctrine
of *amalgamation* is peculiarly baneful to the interests and happiness of
society. The union of black and white, in a moral point of view, we
consider as the most preposterous and impudent doctrine advanced by
the infatuated Abolitionists—as repugnant to judgment and science as it
is degrading to the feelings of all sensitive minds—destructive to intellect
of after generations, as the advance of science and literature has contributed to the improvement of our own. In short, its practice would reduce
the high intellectual standard of the American mind to a level with the
Hottentot; and the United States, now second to no nation on earth,
would, in a few years, be what Europe was in the darkest ages.

4. *Resolved*, That the Sacred Writings furnish abundant evidence of the
existence of slavery from the earliest periods. The patriarchs and prophets possessed slaves—our Saviour recognized the relation between master and slave, and deprecated it not: hence, we know that He did not
condemn that relation; on the contrary, His disciples, in all countries,
designated their respective duties to each other.

Therefore, *Resolved*, That we consider Slavery, as it now exists in the
United States, as sanctioned by the sacred Scriptures.

Source: Horace Greeley, *The American Conflict: A History of the Great Rebellion in
the United States of America*, vol. I, 1860–1864 (Hartford, CT: Case, 1864), pp. 132–
133.

3.5.   Elijah Lovejoy Responds

---

*On November 2 and 3, 1837, concerned citizens of Alton, Illi-
nois, held public meetings at the City Courthouse in response
to the vigilante violence triggered by Lovejoy's abolitionist editorials. They discussed and agreed to a set of resolutions supporting freedom of the press and criticizing mob rule but calling
on Lovejoy to abandon his newspaper. In the afternoon of November 3, Lovejoy met with them and offered an emotional reply. Four days later he was shot dead defending freedom of the
press. The parenthetical insertions below are those of Lovejoy's
brothers, the editors of this Memoir.*

Mr. Chairman—it is not true, as has been charged upon me, that I hold in contempt the feelings and sentiments of this community, in reference to the question which is now agitating it. I respect and appreciate the feelings of my fellow-citizens, and it is one of the most painful and unpleasant duties of my life, that I am called upon to act in opposition to them. If you suppose, sir, that I have published sentiments contrary to those generally held in this community, because I delighted in differing from them, or in occasioning a disturbance, you have entirely misapprehended me. But, sir, while I value the good opinion of my fellow-citizens, as highly as any one, I may be permitted to say, that I am governed by higher considerations than either the favour or the fear of man. I am impelled to the course I have taken, because I fear God. As I shall answer it to my God in the great day, I dare not abandon my sentiments, or cease in all proper ways to propagate them.

I, Mr. Chairman, have not desired nor asked any *compromise*. I have asked for nothing but to be protected in my rights as a citizen—rights which God has given me, and which are guaranteed to me by the constitution of my country. Have I, sir, been guilty of any infraction of the laws? Whose good name have I injured? When and where have I published any thing injurious to the reputation of Alton? Have I not, on the other hand, laboured, in common with the rest of my fellow-citizens, to promote the reputation and interests of this city? What, sir, I ask, has been my offence? Put your finger upon it—define it—and I stand ready to answer for it. If I have committed any crime, you can easily convict me. You have public sentiment in your favour. You have your juries, and you have your attorney, (looking at the Attorney-General,) and I have *no doubt* you can *convict* me. But if I have been guilty of no violation of law, why am I hunted up and down continually like a partridge upon the mountains? Why am I threatened with the *tar-barrel*? Why am I waylaid every day, and from night to night, and my life in jeopardy every hour?

You have, sir, made up, as the lawyers say, a false issue; there are not two parties between whom there can be a *compromise*. I plant myself, sir, down on my unquestionable *rights*, and the question to be decided is, whether I shall be protected in the exercise, and enjoyment of those rights—*that is the question, sir;*—whether my property shall be protected, whether I shall be suffered to go home to my family at night without being assailed, and threatened with tar and feathers, and assassination; whether my afflicted wife, whose life has been in jeopardy from continued alarm and excitement, shall night after night be driven from a sick bed into the garret to save her life from the brickbats and violence of the mobs; *that, sir, is the question.* (Here, much affected and overcome by his feelings, he burst into tears. Many, not excepting even his enemies, wept—several sobbed aloud, and the sympathies of the whole meeting were deeply excited. He continued.) Forgive me, sir, that I have thus betrayed my weakness. It was the allusion to my family that overcame my feelings. Not, sir, I assure you, from any fears on my part. I have no personal fears. Not that I feel able to contest the matter with the whole community, I know perfectly well that I am not. I know, sir, that you can tar and feather me, hang me up, or put me into the Mississippi, without the least difficulty. But what then? Where shall I go? I have been made to feel that if I am not safe at Alton, I shall not be safe any where. I recently visited St. Charles to bring home my family, and was torn from their frantic embrace by a mob. I have been beset night and day at Alton. And now if I leave here and go elsewhere, violence may overtake me in my retreat, and I have no more claim upon the protection of another community than I have upon this; and I have concluded, after consultation with my friends, and earnestly seeking counsel of God, *to remain at Alton*, and here to insist on protection in the exercise of my rights. If the civil authorities refuse to protect me, I must look to God; and, if I die, I have determined to make my grave in Alton.

Source: Joseph C. Lovejoy and Owen Lovejoy, eds., *Memoir of the Rev. Elijah Lovejoy* (New York: John S. Taylor, 1838), pp. 278–280.

3.6.   A Central Southern University to Preserve the South

As the North increasingly embraced abolition, proslavery southerners sought ways to maintain their culture and way of life, even if it meant withdrawal from the Union. Educated at the University of Virginia, John Richardson predicted that secession was inevitable but without southern unity would be disastrous. Like many other southern intellectuals, he called for the creation of a general or central southern university to educate and "socialize" young southerners with proslavery ideas to perpetuate the slave-based way of life in the South.

The opinion that it is vitally important to the interests and general welfare of the South, for the slaveholding States to endow and organize as speedily as possible a great Central Southern University seems to be rapidly gaining ground. . . .

That there does exist a political necessity for the establishment of an institution of learning of the character alluded to—an institution around which shall cluster the hopes and the pride of the South; the teachings of which shall be thoroughly Southern, one pledged to the defense and perpetuation of that form of civilization peculiar to the slaveholding

States, will not, perhaps, be questioned, although some may entertain doubts as to the pressure of that necessity. . . . It is sufficient for the South to know that the necessity, *actually* exists. . . .

It is absurd to suppose that the people of the North will ever unsay what they have said, undo what they have done, or retrace their steps in any particular whatever. They have gone too far. They have persisted in saying what they know to be false, and in doing what they know to be ungenerous and unjust, until they have come at last either to believe what they say and do to be true and just, or have become wedded to falsehood and injustice. The difficulty between the South and the North can never arrive at a peaceable settlement. The supreme and ultimate arbiter in the dispute now pending between them must be the sword. To that complexion it must come at last. The first step then which the South should take in preparing for the great contest ahead of her, is to secure harmony at home. "The union of the South for the sake of the South" should be the sentiment of every patriotic son and daughter of the South, and each should endeavor to contribute his or her mite towards gaining so desirable an end. The safety of the South, the integrity of the South, not the permanence of the Union, should be regarded as the "paramount political good." No true Southerner, no loyal son of the South can possibly desire the continuance of the Union *as it is*. To secure her rights, and to guard her interests the South must be a *unit*. . . .

The educational facilities of the South offer no center of attraction tending to draw together the young men from the various slaveholding States; and of all the various colleges and institutions of learning in our midst, many of which, are of the most deserving character, there is but *one* which appears to look beyond the educational wants of the State in which it is located, and which has made provision on a scale at all commensurate with its importance, for the thorough education of the youth of other States as well as of those at home. Allusion of course is made to the University of Virginia; and I speak of it with pride, for it is not only the first institution of learning in point of excellence in the South, but it is probably superior to any other in the Union. But the University of Virginia is not sufficiently Southern, sufficiently central, sufficiently cottonized to become the great educational center of the South. . . .

But a University of the character of the one for whose establishment we are laboring, one destined to be fountain of light and honor to the South, the source of her prosperity, the center and support of her peculiar form of civilization, the great central intellectual light of the South, whose rays shall radiate over the entire land, and illuminate every nook and corner, and around which the other institutions of learning shall circle as planets round their central sun, should be located in the *very heart* of the South. Should be removed as far as possible from every malign influence which may be brought to bear upon it, threatening its corruption. As the great fortress and stronghold of the South it should not be located near the confines of her empire, on the outskirts of her civilization, but should occupy the most impregnable position within her borders. The *political center* of the South is the proper location for such an institution. . . .

Southerners must be educated as Southerners, as slaveholders, and be taught to support and defend the institution of slavery, and all the rights of the South, at all times and in all places. This education can be had no where else than in the South, and no where else so thoroughly imparted as an institution organized expressly for that purpose. . . . [N]o people can expect to retain their domestic peculiarities and institutions, when in diametrical opposition to those of most other nations, unless they will keep their sons at home, and educate them in those peculiarities, teaching them to defend and perpetuate their institutions at all hazards and costs.

. . . The remedy, as I conceive, is simply this—establish a Central University in the South, in which all the States shall have a direct and immediate interest, organize it upon the most extensive scale, the most thorough and comprehensive basis; let merit and scholarship, not money and time, be the means by which the degrees may be obtained; and let the course of study be so complete and thorough, that the various colleges may hold to it the same relation which the preparatory schools all over the country hold to them. . . .

If the South be divided she will be conquered in detail, and one by one of the slaveholding States will sink into the embraces of Free-soilism, and be abandoned to all the horrors, and evils, and abominations which characterize free society in the North and in Europe, and which disgraces humanity. The establishment of the university has been proposed as a measure certain to produce, by its working, unity and concord of action on the part of the slaveholding States. The young men of the South will then assemble and drink pure and invigorating draughts from unpolluted fountains. They will meet together as brethren, and be educated in one common political faith, at one common *alma mater*. And when they return home to their native States they will not be a whit less Kentuckians, or Georgians, or Texans, but more thorough Southerners. Can any one who has the interests of the South *at heart* object to the enterprise? . . .

Could the Union be restored to what it was in the days of Washington, and the Government administered as under him, then would no one think of disunion. The fraternal feeling would be restored between the Northern and Southern States. But is that possible? Is there a single individual in the South who really, honestly, conscientiously thinks in his "heart of hearts" that it is possible? Is there one? If there is, let him go [to] the North, and there study Northern feeling and sentiment on the subject of slavery.

Source: John M. Richardson, "Central Southern University," *Debow's Review* 23 (November 1857): 490–503.

3.7.   Slavery Suppresses Free Speech

The Supreme Court in 1857 had ruled in the Dred Scott *Case that Congress had no authority to halt the spread of slavery in the United States, and, as in southern slave states, free speech was jeopardized in territories or new states opting for slavery. William Cullen Bryant was a poet and journalist who served for years as the chief editorialist for the New York* Evening Post, *an influential literary outlet and an opponent of slavery. Aware of the reign of censorship that had prevailed and solidified in slave states, Bryant urged "free speech" reasons why slavery should not be allowed to spread its suffocating censorship any further.*

Probably there are few of our readers who would like to be smeared with tar and then equipped with a covering of feathers. Nor would many of them, we fancy, be much delighted with receiving thirty-nine lashes with a cow-skin, well laid on. A ride on a rail might be less unpleasant, but we doubt whether many of them would think it an agreeable diversion. To come down to matters of less moment, we do not suppose that they would take pleasure in being summarily expelled from the country for the offence of speaking their minds respecting a political institution which they desired to reform, or that they would be even satisfied to have the newspapers for which they subscribed, withheld from them by the creatures of the government. A reasonable man, let him live in what part of the country he might, would, we are sure, pardon any of our readers for not taking a fancy to be treated in either of the ways we have enumerated.

In saying this we but state some of the objections to the extension of slavery which have not hitherto received the attention they deserve. We of the free states object to legalizing the relation of master and slave in the territories, because, if slavery goes thither, we are not allowed to go. It is true that those who favor the enlargement of the area of slavery tell us that, although they claim the right of carrying it into the territories, yet the moment the inhabitants of any territory in which it is established frame their constitution, they have the liberty to abolish it.

That is not true; every mail that we receive from the slave states brings evidence that it is false. Wherever slavery goes, whether into a territory or a state, there is no longer any liberty of speech or even of thought in regard to that question. If any man denies its benefits, the practice of the day is to mob him, to shave his head on one side, to push him off a railway train to the danger of his life, to tar and feather him, to give him a public flogging. If he simply comes from the North, and endeavors to escape this rough treatment by observing a prudent silence in regard to slavery, his trunks are opened, his baggage searched for incendiary publications; if a northern newspaper is found, he is a subject for Lynch law; if the search be fruitless, he is warned to leave the state immediately. A bare suspicion of abolitionism is enough to cause the unfortunate traveler to be ejected from the community without further ceremony. A man selling maps, who never troubled himself to know whether he was an abolitionist or not, is admonished that he is regarded as a dangerous personage, and obliged to decamp with the next train. Commercial travelers who attend Union meetings at home, and do their best to keep on good terms with the slaveholders, are met by committees, who tell them that they will save their friends at the North a good deal of anxiety by making the best of their way back again.

Is not the theatre in which these enormities are acted large enough already, but must we open to them all that mighty area of territory which lies between the states on the Atlantic and those on the Pacific coast? Are we, as citizens of the free states, comprising two-thirds of the whole population of the Union, ready to introduce into the territories a system which will bar the whole of that vast region against us and against our children? Are we willing that the territories should become a part of the country into which we cannot enter without the certainty of being mobbed and the danger of losing our lives; in which we cannot express our opinions on public questions with that freedom which has hitherto been the boast of our institutions; in which we cannot read what books we please, and into which the newspapers of the free states, for the very reason they discuss public questions freely, are not allowed to circulate? Are we ready to establish over those extensive regions a censorship of opinions and a censorship of the press which shall make a residence in them impossible to a northern man deserving of the name of freeman?

Yet this is precisely what we are asked to do. The institution of slavery, when it reaches its full and consummate growth, which it now seems to have done in the southern states, demands all these sacrifices, all these abnegations of personal liberty. Wherever it goes it establishes a cruel, relentless, remorseless despotism, which exacts a conformity as rigid as is required in the absolute governments of the Old World, and punishes men on mere suspicion with the same ferocious severity.

No, we must keep the territories open for freedom—open for freedom of speech, open for freedom of the press; hospitably open for emigrants who carry with them only their own strong arms and their love of liberty; freely open to the commerce of the free states, and to all the civilizing influences of the older settlements. If we allow, upon any pretext, the institution of slavery to be established in them, we sign away our own birthright and the birthright of millions of freemen besides; we give them up to be the patrimony of an oligarchy which will remorselessly exclude us the moment they have it in their possession.

Source: "Who Is for a Coat of Tar and Feathers?" New York *Evening Post*, (January 9, 1860).

ANNOTATED RESEARCH GUIDE

Dickerson, Donna Lee. *The Course of Tolerance: Freedom of the Press in Nineteenth-Century America*. Westport, CT: Greenwood Press, 1990. Chapters 4–5 deal comprehensively yet succinctly with both the Post Office debate and mob violence vented against abolitionists.

Dillon, Lynn Merton. *Slavery Attacked: Southern Slaves and Their Allies, 1619–1865*. Baton Rouge: Louisiana State University Press, 1990. An examination of slavery and its opponents from the arrival of the Pilgrims through the end of the Civil War.

Eaton, Clement. *Freedom of Thought in the Old South*. Durham, NC: Duke University Press, 1940. Though published more than six decades ago, this book still presents a thorough and beautifully written overview of restricted flow of information and ideas in antebellum southern life.

Miller, William Lee. *Arguing About Slavery: The Great Battle in the United States Congress*. New York: Alfred A. Knopf, 1996. Comprehensively recounts the political drama in both the House and Senate that produced the Gag Rules against petitions. The hero of this story is former president John Quincy Adams, who, as a member of the House, fought the southern delegation (and northern allies) determined to cut off all discussion of matters relating to slavery in the national legislature.

Nye, Russell B. *Fettered Freedom: Civil Liberties and the Slavery Controversy 1830–1860*. East Lansing: Michigan State University Press, 1963. A classic, standard reference on abolition, slavery, and civil liberties. The author covers the Gag Rule controversy, debates about the postal authority, academic and press freedom, and also the hostile and violent mob reactions to abolitionists, including the death of Lovejoy.

Simon, Paul. *Freedom's Champion: Elijah Lovejoy*. Carbondale: Southern Illinois University Press, 1994. The most recent and detailed account of the travails of Elijah Lovejoy.

Stewart, James Brewer, *Holy Warriors: The Abolitionists and American Slavery*, Rev. ed. New York: Hill & Wang, 1997. A comprehensive examination of the zeal and determination of the abolitionists.

Web Site

http://memory.loc.gov/ammem/aapchtml/aapchome.html. The Rare Book and Special Collections Division of the Library of Congress has compiled this

Web site that is replete with hundreds of readily accessible documents related to slavery and abolition: *From Slavery to Freedom: The African-American Pamphlet Collection 1824–1909*. It is an outstanding and easy-to-use collection.

4

The Civil War

With slavery unabated—indeed, reinforced by judicial decree—the United States in 1860 elected its sixteenth president and soon broke into a devastating civil war that left, beyond indescribable carnage, a legacy profoundly influencing nearly everything in the country. This tumultuous era has been widely recorded, yet it is difficult to recreate the picture of freedom of speech and press from a war-torn America where military edicts frequently substituted for the rule of law and partisanship more often than not passed for news reporting of events. Preserving civil rights is always tested in time of war. President Abraham Lincoln's administration, the Confederacy, the armies of both sides, and the American people faced uncommon challenges trying to comply with the rule of law amidst countervailing pressures of both wartime necessity and a divided and passionate public whipped up by partisanship, hostility, and fear. Lincoln's prosecution of the war was—and still is—the subject of mixed reviews. Supporters exalt him as a "benevolent dictator" who had little choice but temporarily to curtail certain rights, such as due process of law and freedom of speech, in order to preserve the Union. Lincoln frankly acknowledged this gloomy reality, explaining that amputation of a diseased limb is sometimes necessary to save the life of the body. His critics, instead, detect in his actions not just military orders to root out dangerous disloyalty and betrayal but also arbitrary suppression of public speakers and newspapers lawfully opposed to the war policies of the administration.

When Lincoln was inaugurated on March 4, 1861, seven states of the

"Lower South" had already seceded from the Union. Little more than a month into the new administration, after the "first shots" of the Civil War at Fort Sumter, South Carolina, in April, Virginia seceded and joined the Confederacy, leaving the federal capital of Washington, D.C., literally on the frontier of burgeoning enemy territory. The president summoned the able-bodied to defend the city from possible Confederate attack. Just forty miles northeast of Washington, Baltimore was the hub of several intersecting rail lines that would transport the thousands of volunteers from the North heeding their president's call to arms in defense of the Union. Known by some as "Mob City," Baltimore also was home to many Confederate sympathizers. As troops from the Northeast began arriving in Baltimore, riots erupted in which crowds of onlookers threw stones and soldiers fired shots. Several lay dead. The violence in Baltimore led Lincoln to worry that the capital might fall even before the Union mobilized to put down "the rebellion" of the seceding states of the South.

The magnitude and urgency of the dangers ahead induced Lincoln to act almost by fiat, at least during the first critical stages of the rebellion. Congress was not even in session until the president reconvened the legislature on July 4, 1861, four months into his administration. Many historians have characterized this period as a "temporary dictatorship" when the president prosecuted his own war against the South. Lincoln's response to the Fort Sumter crisis went forward without waiting for Congress to declare war. Even the Supreme Court, though very closely divided (5–4) in the *Prize Cases* (1863), retroactively discovered among the many folds of the Constitution authority for presidential use of military force without a declaration of war from Congress. The Court itself was still suffering from hostile criticism after its debacle in *Dred Scott v. Sandford* (1857), ruling that slaves were private property protected from national governmental prohibition and that Congress had no authority to keep slavery out of the territories, a decision that did not settle the slavery issue but doubtless pushed a nation divided on the matter closer to civil war. However, Lincoln's unilateral actions went further than defensive reactions to rebellious attack. With Congress adjourned, he began an aggressive and comprehensive military strategy, requesting and receiving $2 million from the federal treasury and substantially expanding the size of the army and navy.

The Lincoln administration's reaction to sabotage in Baltimore drew much criticism regarding violations of First Amendment principles, a response that for Lincoln established precedent for later actions. What emerged were measures that effectively nullified constitutional rights. Baltimore's chief of police and its mayor, both Confederate sympathizers, conspired to dynamite railway bridges that fed into the city from the North. Interrupted rail access deprived the Union of a vital link through which to transport Northern volunteer troops. Without congressional support, Lincoln authorized his generals to suspend the writ of habeas corpus anywhere along the rail lines from Philadelphia to Washington; he also authorized Secretary of State William H. Seward to initiate further detentions wherever needed. The Constitution permits suspension of the writ only in situations of war, rebellion, or when public safety requires, but neither the judiciary nor anyone else has ever authoritatively determined whether congressional assent is needed to suspend the writ of habeas corpus. Chief Justice of the United States Roger B. Taney, who had written the proslavery *Dred Scott* decision in 1857 and was sitting as a circuit court judge in 1861, wrote an opinion condemning unilateral presidential suspension of the writ, but Lincoln and the Union military ignored the aging Taney's legal argument. Union forces apprehended and imprisoned the Baltimore culprits, and many others were arrested or detained as suspects in several acts of disloyalty. Thus began a widespread abeyance of constitutional rights during the war, for without the writ of habeas corpus anyone remotely suspected of disloyalty or treason or hampering the war effort could be confined in military prisons without bail, without charges or trial, and with no fixed date of release. It was, indeed, a form of martial law—brought about by urgencies facing and met by a "temporary dictatorship." Almost two years later, on March 3, 1863, Congress by law authorized presidential suspension of habeas corpus.

Newspapers in the North also became targets of the war machine being assembled to break the Confederacy and preserve the Union. The census of 1860 counted almost 400 daily newspapers, most of which were very political and partisan in character. Balanced reporting and professional objectivity were not yet developed attributes of American journalism. The political orientation of Northern journals tended to reflect the political alignment of the Northern population. Radical Republicans found their voice in the New York and Chicago *Tribunes* and the Philadelphia *Inquirer*; and their primary objective was the abolition of slavery. Moderate Republicans justified the war as necessary to save the Union itself, and the New York *Times*, the Boston *Journal*, and the Cincinnati *Commercial* defended that political view. The New York *Herald* steered toward an independent center, but this only depicted the newspaper as unsupportive of the Union's position. Outspoken Democratic newspapers competed with pro-Union journals within nearly every Northern city, for example, the strident Chicago *Times*, the Cincinnati *Enquirer*, and the New York *World* and *Journal of Commerce*. Southern newspapers were almost all Democratic and either opposed the Union war effort or ceased to exist. The Democratic press in the South (and in many places in the North) viewed Lincoln as a "demented despot" determined to destroy civil liberties; they saw the African American slaves as unfit for anything but bondage and inferior to whites and saw black freedom as dangerous to the labor markets and racial order.

Northern Democrats and their newspapers calling for peace were frequently denounced as "Copperheads," named after a venomous snake akin to the Southern rattlesnake—a comparison that branded them as traitors. The Copperhead movement centered primarily in the Midwest—in Ohio, Indiana, Michigan, Illinois, and Wisconsin—but it also had support further east. Followers were ordinary Americans, including Irish immigrants, steeped in the tradition of Jacksonian democracy, of states rights and the "common man," remnants of an era gradually disappearing into history. They used local papers as well as larger dailies such as the Chicago *Times*, Dubuque *Herald*, and Cincinnati *Enquirer* to articulate and galvanize opposition to Union war policies as well as to what they interpreted as threats from the abolition movement, from large papers like the New York *Tribune*, or from popular literature such as *Uncle Tom's Cabin*. They knew very well that the only mode of mobilizing the public to counteract these threats was through journalism, which, however disjointed and partisan, was the only means of mass communications capable of reaching the masses.

Party allegiance sharpened in the 1860s, as interest in politics and the war intensified and divided the nation. People identified themselves as either Democrats or Republicans with very few independents or moderates. Such political polarization, combined with fervent nationalism, provided ample fodder for the growing newspaper business sweeping the country. Each major city in the North had at least two rival papers appealing to either Democrats or Republicans. "Editorial wars" and unabashedly biased "advocacy journalism" were rampant during the war, evincing a style of journalism more closely resembling the art of the passionate revolutionary pamphleteer than an impartial reporting of events. Newspapers provided the most powerful forum for expressing political opinions during a period of history that abounded with heated ideas. They supplied the most effective form of mass media available during the 1860s, as they were the most popular form of literature available; some Americans read nothing else. Democrats used newspapers to espouse their anti-Lincoln views and Republicans to support the war effort. Democrats expressed discontent with Lincoln for not supporting popular sovereignty over the issue of slavery and for limiting the authority of individual states. Their criticisms aroused the attention of the federal government once the war was under way and were of special concern to the maintenance of a ready and disciplined army. Many antiwar newspapers discouraged enlistment when the government sought volunteers, or called for honorable Americans to resist compulsory conscription once in place. Some few even urged desertion.

The Lincoln administration focused especially on the New York press because of its disproportionate impact on what was printed elsewhere in the country. The telegraph was in its early stages of development and very expensive to use; the military, rather than the press, more profitably exploited and expanded this technology (as it would a century later create the rudimentary structure upon which the modern Internet has been built). Moreover, the telegraph lines were censored by the military. Wire services were also rare or in their incipient stages, and editors of newspapers in small towns and cities often reprinted stories published earlier by larger papers in the metropolitan areas, such as New York. The *Herald* on occasion, and the *Journal of Commerce* almost from the onset, opposed the administration's war policies. In one of its published stories, New York's *Journal of Commerce* reported that more than 150 Northern newspapers opposed "the present unholy war" (the list had already been published earlier by the New York *Daily News*). An annoyed and angry federal grand jury, on the eve of its own expiration, found this article sufficiently unpatriotic and disloyal to warrant some form of official rebuke. Without any other evidence or instructions from a judge or governmental attorney, the furious jurors prepared a "presentment"—a written notice of an indictable offense. This document prompted the U.S. Post Office to exclude from the mail not just the *Journal of Commerce* but also four other New York newspapers.

Postal suppression of these five papers seriously curtailed the news industry of the 1860s for two important reasons. In the first place, newspaper circulation at the time was almost completely dependent on mail delivery; moreover, as stated earlier, stories and articles appearing in big city papers, such as those in New York, were reprinted across the country in smaller local papers. The threat of lost mailing privileges succeeded in discouraging less profitable papers from printing critical stories. Denied use of the postal system, Gerald Hallock—the paper's principal editor opposing the war and part owner of the *Journal of Commerce*—agreed to retire and sell off his holdings in the company as preconditions for the restoration of postal privileges. The New York *News*, on the other hand, was emboldened to defy the government's ban by utilizing newsboys hired to deliver the newspaper in local markets. U.S. marshals quickly responded by seizing all copies of the *News*, and even one newsboy was arrested.

The first major Union defeat, at Bull Run/Manassas in July 1861, was a momentous turning point in newspaper coverage of the war and the Union government's response to criticism. Democrats responded with editorials harshly critical of both the Lincoln administration as well as Union generalships and some individual regiments. Disgruntled Union soldiers and sympathetic local civilians took turns attacking critical local papers and subjecting them to various displays of mob law. Paraphernalia of the newspaper industry, such as copy, paper, ink, printers, and other items were either burned, thrown from windows, or smashed to pieces. On August 8, 1861, Union volunteers destroyed the *Democratic Standard* of Concord, New Hampshire, because it refused to retract criticism of the regiment. The editor referred to Confederates as "the honest men of the south," and his offices were destroyed by mob violence. Two weeks later in Missouri a federal marshal exhorted the press to abstain from publishing anything of a "political character" that could "inflame the passions of men" during these times of heated discussion and civil war. Ambrose Kimball, the editor of the Massachusetts, Essex County *Democrat*, was tarred and feathered and dragged through the town streets for uttering derogatory comments about the Union army. Other newspaper offices were similarly demolished by unrestrained citizens after their editors had denounced the war effort: For example, the Easton, Pennsylvania, *Sentinel*; the West Chester, Pennsylvania, *Jeffersonian*; the Ohio, Stark County *Democrat*; and the Connecticut, Bridgeport *Farmer*. The charred ruins that remained of these Democratic presses following their criticism of Union conduct at the Battle of Bull Run and opposition to Lincoln's war policies bore grim witness to the cost of speaking out against current war policies and practices.

In 1862 Secretary of War Edwin M. Stanton, who now was the engine driving wartime censorship, issued a general order prohibiting newspapers from publishing anything regarding "intelligence," with violations subject to criminal penalties. This provoked the House Judiciary Committee publicly to proclaim that a reign of censorship was not, in fact, under way, though there was little the legislature could do to circumscribe military censorship as the war raged on.

Fighting a war whose intensity and destruction he could hardly have anticipated or even imagined, Lincoln was sensitive to the importance of First Amendment freedoms and other constitutional limits. However, historians have shown that although Lincoln rarely and reluctantly ordered official suppression of free speech and press, he did countenance or permit all of the instances that had been authorized or tolerated by his subordinates. The president fashioned a cabinet of secretaries on whom he could depend and who could operate independently. One of the most dominant figures was Secretary of State Seward, who strangely enough became a leading figure in newspaper suppression at a time when his primary attention pertained to foreign, not domestic, affairs (however, in a war like this, such distinctions are often blurred). In fact, the responsibility for censorship actually rotated within the Lincoln administration (as did some cabinet secretaries), placed first in the Treasury Department, then in the War Department, from there to the State Department, and then back to the War Department. Eager to silence disagreeable opposition, Seward relied on reports from local officials informing his office as to "seditious" speech and from what newspaper;

he then authorized their closing and/or the arrest of publishers, editors, and reporters. On July 17, 1862, Congress created the Treason Act targeting individuals who through their actions "aided and comforted the enemy." While the statute itself did not single out words or opinion, its terms could be—and were—construed to reach the kind of offensive and potentially damaging tirades unleashed by antiwar newspapers. More than 40 percent of the arrests made while Seward was in charge were initiated outside of the State Department by local and state authorities or by private citizens. In fairness to Seward, his reputation as a ruthless enforcer of war policy is exaggerated. Of the more than 13,000 arrests made during the entire war, only 864 could be traced directly to Seward.

Still, his actions had a substantial impact on the course of events during the Civil War. He was accused by many of strategically arranging arrests of Democrats during or near important elections. For instance, the secretary authorized the arrests of members of the Maryland state legislature during a period when that border state was contemplating secession. The Maryland incident resulted in the arrests of a congressman, a mayor, a state senator, and several others, including editors and publishers. Lincoln permitted the arrests and also allowed Union troops to monitor the election following the arrests. "Loyal" citizens stood with soldiers to identify possible Southern sympathizers attempting to vote.

The Union military machine was perhaps, and not surprisingly, responsible for most suppressions of expression during the war. Starting in April 1861, the Departments of War, Treasury, and State took control of the limited telegraph lines running from Washington in order to interdict all messages. Censors were instructed to intercept communications disclosing military information or actions of the government. The military also negotiated terms of news coverage with war correspondents. General George B. McClellan wrought a "treaty of Peace and Amity" that limited press coverage to avoid divulging information that would aid the enemy. Under its terms the military not surprisingly dispensed the information permissible to print. This "treaty" soon collapsed in the whirlwind of journalistic forces of various papers competing for the latest war updates and no doubt because of fundamental disagreements over what news constituted "aiding the enemy." As a new genre of reporters, war correspondents continued to cover the war despite the failed treaty and to the dismay of many generals, including General William T. Sherman who is said to have proclaimed that all reporters were spies and should be shot. Reporters who upset the military brass could be excluded from the front lines when officers withheld clearance passes. However, many papers secretly employed reporters as nurses, government clerks, and signal officers, and ambitious officers gave information to reporters who favored them in accounts of battle.

The military's fear of "aiding the enemy" through published press reports was certainly genuine and legitimate. Commanding the Confederate forces, General Robert E. Lee admitted to reading Northern papers to learn the locations, strength, and maneuvers of Union armies. Posing as a presidential appeal to an anguished nation for 400,000 more troops, a forged document appeared in the May 18, 1864, morning editions of the New York *World* and *Journal of Commerce*. That evening on direct orders from the president wired to Major General John A. Dix, who commanded the military in the New York area, both newspapers were shut down and their editors and publishers arrested. Apparently, both papers had been hoodwinked into publishing the phony document, sending a message that Union forces were urgently in need of reinforcements. The military occupied the offices of the newspapers for two days until it was clear that the editors had been deceived into publishing what they had assumed was a genuine presidential proclamation.

There was, in fact, some truth to the forgery after all, for later that summer, E.N. Fuller, the irrepressible editor of the Newark, New Jersey, *Evening Journal*, was arrested—on orders again from General Dix—for publishing an editorial castigating Lincoln's eventually real call, approved by Congress on July 4, for 500,000 additional men who, wrote Fuller, "wish to be butchered." He paid a fine for words that convicted him of inciting insurrection and discouraging enlistment, in violation of Section 25 of the March 3, 1863, federal conscription act.

Using articles of military law, underwritten by congressional legislation, military leaders dealt with rogue reporters convicted of conveying intelligence to the enemy, either directly or indirectly. The severest penalty was death, though apparently never actually invoked against reporters for their publications. Generals dealt with disloyal reporters or papers by banning their distribution in areas under their command for the entire time the army was present or by suppressing specific editions of the papers. Generals also issued military orders that limited free speech both within and outside of the military. For instance, a Union general terminated the circulation of the Chicago *Times*, the Milwaukee *News*, and the La Crosse *Democrat* in the Military Division of the Southwest.

Among the more controversial orders were those issuing from General Ambrose E. Burnside, emanating mainly from his headquarters in Cincinnati, Ohio. General Order No. 38, promulgated on April 13, 1863, vaguely proclaimed that any declaration of sympathy for the enemy would no longer be tolerated. On June 1, Burnside announced General Order No. 84 that temporarily closed the Chicago *Times* for disloyal and incendiary publications and ended circulation of the New York *World* in Ohio. The Chicago *Times* obtained an injunction from a circuit court judge in Illinois, but soldiers following commands of General Burnside seized the newspaper and warned the publisher not to repeat such disloyal behavior. The Illinois state legislature convened in special session on June 2 to denounce the general's order as a violation of the U.S. Constitution. President Lincoln specifically directed Burnside to revoke the order shutting down the Chicago *Times*, and on June 4 from Lexington, Kentucky, the general followed presidential orders and even magnanimously extended the revocation to the New York *World*, thus allowing it to circulate once again within the general's territory of command.

Critics were given firmer ground on which to base a charge of despotism when Burnside had his soldiers arrest Ohio's outspoken "Copperhead," Clement L. Vallandigham. Arrested late at night in his Dayton home, Vallandigham was taken to headquarters in Cincinnati. At the time he was a prominent candidate for the Democratic nomination for governor of Ohio. What prompted the arrest was his May 1 repudiation of Burnside's general order suppressing and punishing speech deemed intolerably disloyal by the general. Soldiers in citizens' clothing who had heard Vallandigham's remarks alerted their superiors, who then informed a fuming general. The specific charge read: "Publicly expressing, in violation of General Order No. 38, from headquarters department of the Ohio, his sympathy for those in arms against the Government of the United States, declaring disloyal sentiments and opinions, with the object and purpose of weakening the power of the Government in its efforts to suppress an unlawful rebellion."[1] Vallandigham challenged his military arrest all the way to the Supreme Court, but the justices in the midst of a war were fortunate enough to discover that they were without jurisdiction to hear the appeal. Later, however, in *Ex parte Milligan*, the Court—contrary to Lincoln's repeated position—unanimously concluded that the Constitution speaks with one voice in time of war and peace and thus the Union army acted unconstitutionally in subjecting one Lambdin P. Milligan to court-martial when the civilian courts were open and available to try Milligan for treason. The *Milligan* case, a landmark in constitutional law, was decided in 1866, after the war had ended and Lincoln had been assassinated. On June 26, 1863, about twenty prominent political leaders wrote the president protesting and challenging the military's apprehension and treatment of Vallandigham. Embarrassed perhaps once again by his zealous General Burnside, Lincoln commuted Vallandigham's sentence but, in a gesture that raised even more heated condemnation of the administration, ordered him banished behind enemy lines, in territory held by the Confederate army.

Episodes of destruction or suppression of Southern newspapers by the Confederate army or anti-Yankee mobs were far less rampant simply because there were fewer presses and fewer dissidents. In a region of America braced for secession, pro-Union newspapers did not last very long. There were some holdouts—but they quickly fell into line soon

into the war. One historian has written: "[N]o newspaper was ever suppressed by state or Confederate authority throughout the war."[2] However, other research shows that at least one in Knoxville, Tennessee, was
shut down. Nevertheless, the number of dailies in the Confederacy simply dwindled, in large measure because healthy men—including workers in the news industry—were urgently needed in the Confederate
army. Many presses also went out of business in the face of the advanc-
ing Union army, or the victorious Union army simply abolished them if
they were still operating.

Unlike the Sedition Act of 1798 or the legislation passed to deal with
sedition and espionage during World War I, the authoritative restrictions
of the federal government in fighting the Civil War never made citizens
or the press aware as to what speech was prohibited. Edicts were written
in broad sweeping language that could easily characterize as seditious
almost any and all speech or behavior that expressed an opinion on the
war. Even clergy seemed to pose threats sufficient to warrant detention,
as when an Episcopal minister failed during his service to pray for the
president on two consecutive Sundays. A Southern sympathizer, the
minister was apprehended in midservice in his pulpit, though he was
eventually released.

The federal government did not sanction every instance of repression,
but it did little to protect speech that criticized the government. Suppression of dissident speech during the Civil War was severe and very
often arbitrary, despite Lincoln's occasional orders to reopen papers or
release prisoners. Indeed, the president was well aware of the toll taken
on freedom of expression, but he knew, too, that suppression was often
necessary. In a letter to Erastus Corning, one of New York's most prominent and wealthy political leaders, Lincoln pithily illustrated the dilemma: "Must I shoot a simple-minded soldier boy who deserts, while
I must not touch a hair of the wiley [sic] agitator who induces him to
desert? . . . I think that in such a case, to silence the agitator, and save
the boy, is not only constitutional, but, withal, a great mercy."[3]

During this period of unprecedented stress, destruction, and gunfire,
the constitutional rights of free speech and free press were very often
ignored, but it is inaccurate to conclude that freedom of expression was
crushed. The vast majority of Northern journals that opposed the war or
criticized the Lincoln administration operated in defiance of the omni-
present threat of mob violence and official suppression. It would be a
mistake to conclude, however, that free speech more or less prevailed
amidst isolated episodes of outright suppression. Self-censorship never
completely overcame courageous, zealous, or foolhardy editors and reporters, but there was always an unclear and fuzzy threshold that even
the heartiest newspapers dared not cross. In wartime the judiciary is
often not politically able to protect dissident speech and constitutional

rights generally. The Supreme Court announced in *Milligan* that the Constitution was to be honored in wartime as in peacetime, but that bold proclamation occurred after the shooting had stopped. As Justice Oliver Wendell Holmes, Jr., would later explain, when a nation is at war, freedom of speech is often one of war's casualties. Yet, paradoxically, few events in the nation's history have subsequently received as much published expression. Almost a book a day, on average, has appeared in print since the last soldier fell almost 140 years ago. And whatever appraisal one makes of Lincoln's prosecution of the war against his respect for free speech and other rights, the nation today praises his presidency as one of the greatest in its history. Testament to that is a stately and moving monument in his honor that still overlooks the nation's capital.

NOTES

1. Reported in *The American Annual Cyclopaedia* (New York: D. Appleton & Co., 1864), 3: 484.

2. E. Merton Coulter, *The Confederate States of America, 1861–1865* (Baton Rouge: Louisiana State University Press, 1950), p. 503.

3. Roy B. Basler, ed., *The Collected Works of Abraham Lincoln* (New Brunswick, NJ: Rutgers University Press, 1953), 6: 266–267.

DOCUMENTS

4.1.   "Mob Law" and Freedom of Speech and Press

This editorial summarizes the tension between freedom of the press and necessities in prosecuting war. It appeared in the New York Herald, *which tried to steer a course of nonpartisanship, a very tricky road to follow especially as the war prolonged and became more destructive than anyone might have anticipated.*

Within the last ten days some four or five newspaper establishments in our Northern States, devoted more or less to the cause of our Southern rebellion, have been suppressed under the summary visitation of mob law. Considering the present critical positions of our government and our free institutions, resulting from this Southern rebellion, and the tremendous losses and sacrifices which it has entailed upon all classes of our loyal people, it is not surprising that the excitable spirits of an indignant community, here and there, should forget the counsels of prudence and law and order, and take the law into their own hands.

But notwithstanding the peculiar provocations of this awful crisis of life or death to our beneficent government, there can be no justification in the loyal States of the Union for the suppression of the liberty of speech or of the press by the dangerous interposition of mob law. This sort of law, always too much in vogue in our rebellious Southern States, has become the supreme law among them under the loose and irresponsible despotism of Jeff. Davis and his managing confederates; but even under all the stern necessities of this war in behalf of the Union and of liberty, regulated by law, there is no necessity and no safety in any case in a popular resort to the tribunal of Judge Lynch. Our constituted legal authorities—federal, State and local—are armed with the necessary powers for meeting all cases of treason; for, with the very broad margin which in our federal constitution is given to the freedom of speech and of the press, this freedom has its constitutional limitations.

For example, the constitution declares that against the United States shall consist only in levying war against them, or in adhering to their enemies, "giving them aid and comfort." This is a comprehensive definition, and doubtless may be justly applied at this time to every citizen and every public journal cooperating in any way in support of the treason of the Southern rebellion. But the remedy of mob law is as bad as the disease. The United States Marshal at Philadelphia, however, has lately interposed his authority against some of our Northern seditious and secession journals in another form. He has caused the detention at Philadelphia of the mail packages of the Journal of Commerce, Daily News and Day Book, of this city, destined further South and West; and here the question of the legal power of the Marshal in the premises, which, under a peace establishment, could be readily answered in the negative, demands some consideration on the side of the government.

We are in a state of war, and inter arma silent leges—the laws are silent pending a state of war. We are involved in a tremendous struggle for the maintenance of our government against a rebellion aiming at its overthrow—a rebellion which has today two hundred and fifty thousand men in arms against us of the loyal States. All our available resources and full harmony among our people are called for to put down this gigantic rebellion. They who are not with us are against us, for there can be no halfway house of diplomatic rest pending this terrible struggle. The whole country is more or less reduced to the necessities of the laws of war; and if the government, under such circumstances, positively refuses to assist in the circulation of newspapers, which are "giving aid and comfort to the enemy" in the wicked enterprise to overthrow the government, it must be conceded that this course of action against the enemy is consistent at least with the supreme law of self-preservation. Pushed to the wall, a man is justified in taking the life of a murderous assailant; and a government, menaced by an armed rebellion, cannot be expected to stand upon legal technicalities in the work of putting this rebellion down. It cannot be expected to work with its hands tied, while its active enemy is released from all restraints. The rebellion must be met at every point, and specially within our own camp.

We know not which are our most mischievous organs of treason and discord, those such as the Tribune, the Anti-Slavery Standard and the Boston Liberator, which have been preaching the bloody extermination of slavery and union with slaveholders, or those such as our Journal of Commerce, Daily News and Day Book, which have devoted themselves to the treason of "giving aid and comfort to the enemy." While the government is about it, it would perhaps be as well to deal alike with pestilent abolition and hypocritical secession peace organs, and exclude them all from the benefits of the United States mails.

Source: New York *Herald*, August 24, 1861.

4.2.   "Presentment" of a Federal Grand Jury

The New York Journal of Commerce *seemed to invite more than its share of retaliation and scorn from the pro-Union, pro-Lincoln circles of power. In the early months of the war the newspaper published an article listing some 150 other journals opposing the war. Incensed by such unpatriotic reporting, a federal grand jury in New York on August 16, 1861, issued a "presentment" (a written notice of indictable actions) even though the grand jury was about to expire. Its foreman, Charles Gould, signed the following presentment on behalf of the grand jury.*

The Grand Inquest of the United States of America for the Southern District of New York, beg leave to present the following facts to the Court, and to ask its advice thereon:

There are certain newspapers within this district which are in the frequent practice of encouraging the rebels now in arms against the Federal government by expressing sympathy and agreement with them, the duty of acceding to their demands, and dissatisfaction with the employment of force to overcome them. These papers are the New York daily and weekly "Journal of Commerce," the daily and weekly "News," the daily and weekly "Day Book," the "Freeman's Journal," all published in the city of New York, and the daily and weekly "Eagle," published in the city of Brooklyn. The first-named of these has just published a list of newspapers in the Free States opposed to what it calls "the present unholy war"—a war in defense of our country and its institutions, and our most sacred rights, and carried on solely for the restoration of the authority of the Government.

The Grand Jury are aware that free governments allow liberty of speech and of the press to their utmost limit, but there is, nevertheless, a limit. If a person in a fortress or an army were to preach to the soldiers submission to the enemy, he would be treated as an offender. Would he be more culpable than the citizen who, in the midst of the most formidable conspiracy and rebellion, tells the conspirators and rebels that they are right, encourages them to persevere in resistance and condemns the effort of loyal citizens to overcome and punish them as an "unholy war"? If the utterance of such language in the streets or through the press is not a crime, then there is a great defect in our laws, or they were not made for such an emergency.

The conduct of these disloyal presses is, of course, condemned and abhorred by all loyal men; but the Grand Jury will be glad to learn from the Court that it is also subject to indictment and condign [merited] punishment.

Source: The American Annual Cyclopaedia (New York: D. Appleton & Co., 1864), 1: 329.

4.3.   President Lincoln Defends His Administration

In mid-May 1863, Erastus Corning and other influential political leaders in New York were so disturbed by many of the Lincoln administration's harsh war measures, in particular, the military arrest of Ohio Democratic politician Clement Vallandigham, that they met in Albany to fashion their complaints into "resolutions" and sent them directly to the White House. These men censured the administration for unconstitutional measures employed in pursuit of a valid objective, the Union itself, to which the New York leaders pledged their support. On June 12, Lincoln handwrote a lengthy and detailed reply, an amended version of which he dispatched for publication in the New York Tribune, *founded and edited by his friend and sometime ally Horace Greeley. Lincoln defended the administration's actions as constitutional. The excerpt that follows appeared in the June 15, 1863, edition of the newspaper.*

GENTLEMEN: . . .

The resolutions . . . assert and argue, that certain military arrests and proceedings following them for which I am ultimately responsible, are unconstitutional. I think they are not.

. . . Prior to my installation here it had been inculcated that any State had a lawful right to secede from the national Union; and that it would be expedient to exercise the right, whenever the devotees of the doctrine should fail to elect a President to their own liking. I was elected contrary to their liking; and accordingly, so far as it was legally possible, they had taken seven states out of the Union, had seized many of the United States Forts, and had fired upon the United States' Flag, all before I was inaugurated; and, of course, before I had done any official act whatever. The rebellion, thus began soon ran into the present civil war; and, in certain respects, it began on very unequal terms between the parties. The insurgents had been preparing for it more than thirty years, while the government had taken no steps to resist them. The former had carefully considered all the means which could be turned to their account. It undoubtedly was a well pondered reliance with them that in their own unrestricted effort to destroy Union, constitution, and law, all together, the government would, in great degree, be restrained by the same constitution and law, from arresting their progress. Their sympathizers pervaded all departments of the government, and nearly all communities of the people. From this material, under cover of "liberty of speech," "liberty of the press" and "habeas corpus" they hoped to keep on foot amongst us a most efficient corps of spies, informers, suppliers, and aiders and abettors of their cause in a thousand ways. . . . Yet, thoroughly imbued with a reverence for the guaranteed rights of individuals, I was slow to adopt the strong measures, which by degrees I have been forced to regard as being within the exceptions of the constitution, and as indispensable to the public Safety. . . .

Ours is a case of rebellion—so called by the resolutions before me—in fact, a clear, flagrant, and gigantic case of rebellion; and the provision of the constitution that "the privilege of the writ of habeas corpus shall not be suspended, unless when in cases of Rebellion or Invasion, the public Safety may require it," is the provision which specially applies to our present case. This provision plainly attests the understanding of those who made the constitution that ordinary courts of justice are inadequate to "cases of rebellion"—attests their purpose that in such cases, men may be held in custody whom the courts acting on ordinary rules, would discharge. Habeas corpus, . . . its suspension is allowed by the constitution on purpose that, men may be arrested and held, who can not be proved to be guilty of defined crime, "when, in cases of rebellion or invasion the public safety may require it." This is precisely our present case—a case of rebellion, wherein the public safety does require the suspension. . . . Of how little value the constitutional provision I have quoted will be rendered, if arrests shall never be made until defined crimes shall have been committed, may be illustrated by a few notable examples. [Many high-ranking military officers] now occupying the very highest places in the rebel war service were all within the power of the government since the rebellion began, and were nearly as well known to be traitors then as now. Unquestionably if we had seized and held them, the insurgent cause would be much weaker. But no one of them had then committed any crime defined in the law. Every one of them if arrested would have been discharged on habeas corpus, were the writ allowed to operate. In view of these and similar cases, I think the time not unlikely to come when I shall be blamed for having made too few arrests rather than too many.

[T]he third resolution [argues] that military arrests may be constitutional in localities where rebellion actually exists; but that such arrests are unconstitutional in localities where rebellion, or insurrection, does not actually exist. . . . Inasmuch, however, as the constitution itself makes no such distinction, I am unable to believe that there is any such constitutional distinction. I concede that the class of arrests complained of, can be constitutional only when, in cases of rebellion or invasion, the public safety may require them; and I insist that in such cases, they are constitutional wherever the public safety does require them. . . . Take the particular case mentioned by [your] meeting. It is asserted in substance that

Mr. Vallandigham was by a military commander, seized and tried "for no other reason than words addressed to a public meeting, in criticism of the course of the administration, and in condemnation of the military orders of that general." Now, if there be no mistake about this—if this assertion is the truth and the whole truth—if there was no other reason for the arrest, then I concede that the arrest was wrong. But the arrest, as I understand, was made for a very different reason. Mr. Vallandigham avows his hostility to the war on the part of the Union; and his arrest was made because he was laboring, with some effect, to prevent the raising of troops, to encourage desertions from the army, and to leave the rebellion without an adequate military force to suppress it. He was not arrested because he was damaging the political prospects of the administration, or the personal interests of the commanding general; but because he was damaging the army, upon the existence, and vigor of which, the life of the nation depends. He was warring upon the military; and this gave the military constitutional jurisdiction to lay hands upon him. If Mr. Vallandigham was not damaging the military power of the country, then his arrest was made on mistake of fact, which I would be glad to correct, on reasonably satisfactory evidence.

I understand [that you favor] suppressing the rebellion by military force—by armies. Long experience has shown that armies cannot be maintained unless desertion shall be punished by the severe penalty of death. The case requires, and the law and the constitution, sanction this punishment. Must I shoot a simple-minded soldier boy who deserts, while I must not touch a hair of a wiley [sic] agitator who induces him to desert? This is none the less injurious when effected by getting a father, or brother, or friend, into a public meeting, and there working upon his feelings, till he is persuaded to write the soldier boy, that he is fighting in a bad cause, for a wicked administration of a contemptible government, too weak to arrest and punish him if he shall desert. I think that in such a case, to silence the agitator, and save the boy, is not only constitutional, but, withal a great mercy.

If I be wrong on this question of constitutional power, my error lies in believing that certain proceedings are constitutional when, in cases of rebellion or invasion, the public safety requires them, which would not be constitutional when, in absence of rebellion or invasion, the public safety does not require them—in other words, that the constitution is not in its application in all respects the same, in cases of rebellion or invasion, involving the public safety, as it is in times of profound peace and public security. The constitution itself makes the distinction; and I can no more be persuaded that the government can constitutionally take no strong measure in time of rebellion, because it can be shown that the same could not be lawfully taken in time of peace, than I can be persuaded that a particular drug is not good medicine for a sick man, be-

cause it can be shown to not be good food for a well one. Nor am I able
to appreciate the danger, apprehended by [your] meeting that the American people will, by means of military arrests during the rebellion, lose
the right of public discussion, the liberty of speech and the press, the
law of evidence, trial by jury, and habeas corpus, throughout the indefinite peaceful future which I trust lies before them, any more than I am
able to believe that a man could contract so strong an appetite for emetics
during temporary illness, as to persist in feeding upon them through the
remainder of his healthful life.

In giving the resolutions that earnest consideration which you request
of me, I cannot overlook the fact that [you] speak as "Democrats." Nor
can I . . . be permitted to suppose that this occurred by accident, or in
any way other than that they preferred to designate themselves "democrats" rather than "American citizens." In this time of national peril I
would have preferred to meet you upon a level one step higher than any
party platform; because I am sure that from such [a] more elevated position, we could do better battle for the country we all love, than we
possibly can from those lower ones, where from the force of habit, the
prejudices of the past, and selfish hopes of the future, we are sure to
expend much of our ingenuity and strength, in finding fault with, and
aiming blows at each other. But since you have denied me this, I will
yet be thankful, for the country's sake, that not all democrats have done
so. He on whose discretionary judgment Mr. Vallandigham was arrested
and tried, is a Democrat, having no old party affinity with me; and the
judge who rejected the constitutional view expressed in these resolutions,
by refusing to discharge Mr. Vallandigham on habeas corpus, is a Democrat of better days than these, having received his judicial mantle at the
hands of President Jackson [a Democrat]. And still more, of all those
democrats who are nobly exposing their lives and shedding their blood
on the battle field, I have learned that many approve the course taken
with Mr. Vallandigham, while I have not heard of a single one condemning it. I can assert that there are none such. . . .

[While a general in the War of 1812, Andrew Jackson also summarily
arrested those deemed disloyal and dangerous, and he suspended habeas
corpus.] . . . It may be remarked: First, that we had the same constitution
then, as now; secondly, that we then had a case of invasion, and that
now we have a case of rebellion; and, thirdly, that the permanent right
of the people to public discussion, the liberty of speech and the press,
the trial by jury, the law of evidence, and the habeas corpus, suffered no
detriment whatever by that conduct of Gen. Jackson, or its subsequent
approval by the American Congress.

And yet, let me say that in my own discretion, I do not know whether
I would have ordered the arrest of Mr. Vallandigham. While I cannot

shift the responsibility from myself, I hold that, as a general rule, the commander in the field is the better judge of the necessity in any particular case.

[In one] of the resolutions . . . I am specifically called on to discharge Mr. Vallandigham. I regard this act as at least a fair appeal to me, on the expediency of exercising a constitutional power which I think exists. In response to such appeal I have to say . . . I was pained that there should have seemed to be a necessity for arresting him—and that it will afford me great pleasure to discharge him so soon as I can, by any means, believe the public safety will not suffer by it. I further say that, as the war progresses, it appears to me that opinion and action, which were in great confusion at first, take shape and fall into more regular channels, so that the necessity for strong dealing with them gradually decreases. I have every reason to desire that it would cease altogether, and far from the least is my regard for the opinions and wishes of those who, like the meeting at Albany, declare their purpose to sustain the Government in every constitutional and lawful measure to suppress the rebellion. Still, I must continue to do so much as may seem to be required by the public safety.

Source: *The American Annual Cyclopaedia* (New York: D. Appleton & Co., 1864), 3:800–802.

4.4.   The Albany Committee Is Unpersuaded

Two weeks later, on June 30, the Committee replied to President Lincoln. They had met, discussed, and rejected the president's explanations and justifications for the actions of his administration. Corning spoke for a unanimous committee of citizens.

To His Excellency the President of the United States:

SIR: . . . The fact has already passed into history that the sacred rights and immunities which were designed to be protected by these constitutional guarantees, have not been preserved to the people during your Administration. In violation of the first of them, the freedom of the press has been denied. In repeated instances newspapers have been suppressed in the loyal States, because they criticized, as constitutionally they might, those fatal errors of policy which have characterized the conduct of public affairs since your advent to power. In violation of the second of the, hundreds, and we believe, thousands of men, have been seized and immured in prisons and bastiles, not only without warrant upon probable cause, but without any warrant, and for no other reason than a constitutional exercise of freedom of speech. In violation of all these guarantees, a distinguished citizen of a peaceful and loyal State has been torn from his home at midnight by a band of soldiers, acting under orders of one of your generals, tried before a military commission, without judge or jury, convicted, and sentenced without even the suggestion of any offence known to the Constitution or laws of this country. For all these acts you avow yourself ultimately responsible. In the special case of Mr. Vallandigham, the injustice commenced by your subordinate was consummated by a sentence of exile from his home, pronounced by you. That great wrong, more than any other which preceded it, asserts the principles of a supreme despotism.

These repeated and continued invasions of constitutional liberty and private right, have occasioned profound anxiety in the public mind. The apprehension and alarm which they have calculated to produce, have been greatly enhanced by your attempt to justify them, because in that attempt you assume to yourself a rightful authority possessed by no constitutional monarch on earth. We accept the declaration that you prefer to exercise this authority with a moderation not hitherto exhibited. But, believing, as we do, that your forbearance is not the tenure by which liberty is enjoyed in this country, we propose to challenge the grounds on which your claim of supreme power is based. While yielding to you as a constitutional magistrate the deference to which you are entitled, we cannot accord to you the despotic power you claim, however indulgent and gracious you may promise to be in wielding it.

We have carefully considered the grounds on which your pretensions to more than regal authority are claimed to rest; and if we do not misinterpret the misty and cloudy forms of expression in which those pretensions are set forth, your meaning is, that while the rights of the citizen are protected by the Constitution in time of peace, they are suspended or lost in time of war, when invasion or rebellion exists. You do not, like many others in whose minds reason and the love of regulated liberty seem to be overthrown by the excitements of the hour, attempt to base this conclusion upon a supposed military necessity existing outside of, and transcending the Constitution, a military necessity behind which the Constitution itself disappears in a total eclipse. We do not find this gigantic and monstrous heresy put forth in your plea for absolute power, but we do find another equally subversive of liberty and law, and quite as certainly tending to the establishment of despotism. Your claim to have found, not outside, but within the Constitution, a principle or germ of arbitrary power, which in time of war expands once into an absolute sovereignty, wielded by one man; so that liberty perishes, or is dependent on his will, his discretion, or his caprice. This extraordinary doctrine you claim to derive wholly from that clause of the Constitution which, in case of invasion or rebellion, permits the writ of habeas corpus to be suspended. Upon this ground your whole argument is based.

Source: *The American Annual Cyclopaedia* (New York: D. Appleton & Co., 1864), 3:802–803.

4.5.   Message from Clement L. Vallandigham

The day before Clement L. Vallandigham appeared before a military commission he had sent this message on May 5, 1863, from his military prison cell in Cincinnati, addressed to the people of Ohio. He was a candidate for governor of Ohio and had been arrested in his home in Dayton for earlier criticizing General Ambrose Burnside's military order, part of which declared that in the area under the general's command any sign of sympathy for the enemy would not be tolerated and violators would be arrested at once.

To the Democracy of Ohio:—I am here in a military bastile for no other offence than my political opinions, and the defence of them, and the rights of the people, and of your constitutional liberties. Speeches made in the hearing of thousands of you in denunciation of the usurpations of power, infractions of the Constitution and laws, and of military despotism, were the sole cause of my arrest and imprisonment. I am a Democrat—for the Constitution, for law, for the Union, for liberty—that is my only "crime." For no disobedience to the Constitution; for no violation of law; for no word, sign, or gesture of sympathy with the men of the South, who are for disunion and Southern independence, but in obedience to *their* demand as well as the demand of Northern abolition disunionists and traitors, I am here in bonds to-day; but

"Time, at last, sets all things even!"

Meanwhile, Democrats of Ohio, of the Northwest, of the United States, be firm, be true to your principles, to the Constitution, to the Union, and all will yet be well. As for myself, I adhere to every principle, and will make good, through imprisonment and life itself, every pledge and declaration which I have ever made, uttered, or maintained, from the beginning. To you, to the whole people, to TIME, I again appeal. Stand firm! Falter not an instant!

Source: *The American Annual Cyclopaedia* (New York: D. Appleton & Co., 1864), 3:474.

4.6.   Deceived Newsmen Defend Their Publication

On May 18, 1864, the New York Journal of Commerce *and* World *published a bogus proclamation ostensibly signed by the president and the secretary of state and calling for a national day of fasting and a request for 400,000 more soldiers. That very day the president ordered General John A. Dix immediately to arrest the editors and proprietors and to shut down both papers. On July 4, 1864, Congress by law, in fact, approved the president's actual call for 500,000 more troops. The newsmen tried to clear the record and their reputations and to protest their humiliating arrests and military suppression of their newspapers. They wrote this letter to the editor of the New York* Herald *to vent their claims.*

To the Editor of the "Herald":

Will you oblige us by publishing in your columns the following statement of the proceedings of the Government this evening toward the "World" and the "Journal of Commerce," regarding the publication in our morning's issues of the forged proclamation, purporting to be signed by President Lincoln, appointing a day of fasting and prayer, and calling into the military service 400,000 men.

The document in question was written on their manifold paper, such as is used for all of the dispatches sent to the several newspapers of our association, and had every external appearance and mark to identify it as a genuine dispatch arriving in the regular course of business.

It was delivered at our office late at night at the time of our receipt of our latest news, too late, of course, for editorial supervision, but, as it happened, not before our printing offices were closed.

It was delivered at all, or nearly all, of the newspaper offices, and published in part of the "Journal of Commerce" and "World," and, as we are informed, in a part of the editions of one or more of our contemporaries.

Early this morning the fact that the dispatch had not been sent by the agent of the Associated Press became known to us, and its fraudulent character was at once announced upon our bulletin boards, and a reward of five hundred dollars offered by us for the discovery of the forger. The Executive Committee of the Associated Press also offered a similar reward of one thousand dollars, as the fraud had been attempted to be perpetrated upon all the journals composing our association.

We took pains in the afternoon to apprise Gen. Dix of the facts in this case, and gave him such information in regard to the circumstances of the forgery as might assist him in the discovery of its author. The Government was at once put in possession of the facts in this case. Nevertheless, this evening Gen. Dix, acting under peremptory orders from the Government, placed our officers under a strong military guard, and issued warrants for the arrests of the editors and proprietors of the "World" and the "Journal of Commerce," and their imprisonment at Fort Lafayette. A vessel was lying, under steam, at one of the wharves to convey us thither.

Chancing to meet one of the officers of Gen. Dix's staff, charged with the execution of this order, we proceeded in his company to the headquarters of the Department of the East, and were informed by Gen. Dix that the order for our arrest had been suspended, but that the order for the suppression of the publication of the "World" and "Journal of Commerce" had not been rescinded, and that we could not be permitted to enter into our offices, which continue under the charge of the military guards.

We protest against this proceeding. We protest against the assumption of our complicity with this shameless forgery, implied in the order for our arrest. We protest against the suppression of our journal for the misfortune of being deceived by a forgery not less ingenious nor plausible than the forged report of the Confederate Secretary of War, which Secretary Seward made the basis of diplomatic action.

Source: The American Annual Cyclopaedia (New York: D. Appleton & Co., 1866), 4:389.

4.7.   Opposition to the Draft

On July 4, 1864, Congress approved by law Lincoln's request for 500,000 additional men. E.N. Fuller was the editor of the Newark, New Jersey, Evening Journal, *and he printed an editorial critical of this new draft. General Dix ordered a U.S. attorney to arrest and indict Fuller, who was convicted in a federal court of violating an act of Congress. What he wrote below was the basis of his arrest and conviction.*

It will be seen that Mr. Lincoln has called for another half million of men. Those who wish to be butchered will please step forward. All others will please stay home and defy old Abe and his minions to drag them from their families. We hope that the people of New Jersey will at once put their feet down and insist that not a man shall be forced out of the state to engage in the Abolition butchery, and swear to die at their own doors rather than march one step to fulfill the dictates of the mad, revolutionary fanaticism which has destroyed the best government the world ever saw, and now would butcher its remaining inhabitants to carry out a more fanatical sentiment. This has gone far enough and must be stopped. Let the people rise as one man and demand that this wholesale murder shall cease.

Source: Springfield, Illinois, *Daily State Journal*, July 30, 1864.

ANNOTATED RESEARCH GUIDE

Belz, Herman. *Lincoln and the Constitution: The Dictatorship Question Reconsidered.* Fort Wayne, IN: Louis A. Warren Lincoln Library and Museum, 1984. A reassessment of the Lincoln presidency from the perspective of constitutional limitations.

Curtis, Michael Kent. "Lincoln, Vallandigham, and Anti-War Speech in the Civil War." In *First Amendment Law Handbook*, ed. James L. Swanson (St. Paul, MN: West Group, 1999, pp. 461–566. An excellent analysis of antiwar speech during the Civil War.

Harris, Brayton. *Blue & Gray in Black & White: Newspapers in the Civil War.* Washington, DC: Batsford Brassey, 1999. A well-written and richly documented work detailing the Civil War through the observations of editors and the newly emerging "war correspondents." Contains a useful, current bibliography.

Hyman, Harold M. *A More Perfect Union: The Impact of the Civil War and Reconstruction on the Constitution.* New York: Alfred A. Knopf, 1973. Examines the Constitution's survival through the difficulties of the Civil War and the Reconstruction era.

Hyman, Harold M. and William M. Wiecek. *Equal Justice under Law: Constitutional Development, 1835–1875.* New York: Harper & Row, 1982. A standard work on the events that paved the way for equality as a constitutional principle, from the abolition period through the Civil War.

Kutler, Stanley I. *Judicial Power and Reconstruction Politics.* Chicago: University of Chicago Press, 1968. Examines the Supreme Court's role in the heated politics of the Reconstruction era.

Neely, Mark E., Jr. *The Fate of Liberty: Abraham Lincoln and Civil Liberties.* New York: Oxford University Press, 1991. Pulitzer Prize–winning book that examines the treatment of constitutional freedoms during Lincoln's prosecution of the Civil War.

Neely, Mark E., Jr. *Southern Rights: Political Prisoners and the Myth of Confederate Constitutionalism.* Charlottesville: University Press of Virginia, 1999. Makes the case that while Lincoln was no "dictator," the Confederacy was no monument to constitutional rectitude.

Paludan, Phillip Shaw. *A Covenant with Death: The Constitution, Law, and Equality in the Civil War Era.* Urbana: University of Illinois Press, 1975. A comprehensive and sensitive evaluation of the price paid for the victory in the Civil War.

Paludan, Philip Shaw. *The Presidency of Abraham Lincoln*. Lawrence: University Press of Kansas, 1994. A sympathetic but still critical modern appraisal of Lincoln, civil liberties, and wartime policy.

Reynolds, Donald E. *Editors Make War: Southern Newspapers in the Secession Crisis*. Nashville, TN: Vanderbilt University Press, 1970. Focuses on the newspaper industry in the Confederacy and is engagingly written. Includes an appendix listing virtually every newspaper that appeared at one time or another in the Confederate states.

Sachsman, David B., S. Kittrell Rushing, and Debra Reddin van Tuyll, eds. *The Civil War and the Press*. New Brunswick, NJ: Transaction Press, 2000. A collection of more than thirty-three essays exploring various dimensions of the press and press freedom before, during, and after the Civil War.

Web Site

http://www.ukans.edu/carrie/docs/amdocs_index.html. This general Web site on "American Documents," maintained by the University of Kansas, has many links to documentary materials pertaining to the Civil War.

5

The Comstock Law

Under the Constitution of 1787 the U.S. government did not possess any general "police" power to regulate morality. That power was reserved to the states. But the federal government could use the powers delegated directly to it to regulate obscenity. Under its power to regulate interstate commerce, for example, it could prohibit the sending of such materials across state borders. It also could prohibit the importation of obscenity by wielding its powers to control customs. And it could bar the use of the postal system to transport obscene materials.

The states had direct power to prohibit obscenity. The First Amendment did not restrict the states, and more important, it was widely recognized that obscenity and blasphemy were not protected forms of "free speech." Obscenity was not a significant free speech issue in colonial America, and the first known American prosecution for obscenity did not occur until 1815, in Philadelphia. Every state, however, had laws prohibiting various forms of blasphemy, and the subject of obscenity, understood as indecent sexual expression, evolved from those laws. The problem was always in defining obscenity. Not every discussion of sex, even medical manuals, could be regarded as obscene. Definitions inevitably reflected the mores of society, and post–Civil War American society was not much different from its counterpart in Victorian England, where sexual expression often confronted the strict standards of the censor. In urban centers of the United States, however, this prudishness competed with the rise of "painted ladies" and a growing supply of publications that dealt ever more explicitly with sex, especially mass circulation metropolitan dailies that regularly reported on mayhem, murder, and sexual assaults and affairs as the titillating "news" that attracted readers.

Anthony Comstock was born in Connecticut on March 7, 1844, and following his military service in the Union army during the Civil War, he moved to New York City, where he worked in Brooklyn as a dry goods salesman. A deeply religious man raised in a devoutly Christian family, Comstock believed that immoral stimuli induced immoral behavior. In one of his books he wrote: "*Lewd pictures breed hurtful thoughts. That axiom stands out above all argument.*"[1] As a salesman in New York he invoked existing state and federal antiobscenity laws to make citizens' arrests, sometimes having local newspapers cover the events to provide the publicity he sought.

He helped initiate the arrests in 1872 of Victoria Woodhull—a Wall Street speculator, journalist, and the first woman candidate for the presidency—and her sister, Tennessee Claflin. In their periodical, *Woodhull and Claflin's Weekly*, the two sisters reported an alleged sexual affair between a married woman and her minister, the famed Reverend Henry Ward Beecher. The minister's hypocrisy, not his adultery, disturbed these women because Beecher was an outspoken moralist who preached against the sin of extramarital sex. The sisters were charged with breaking federal law forbidding the sending of obscene materials through the mails. After much litigation and four weeks in jail, the two women were acquitted. The presiding federal judge dismissed the case because the prosecution had failed to demonstrate what exactly in the primly worded report was obscene.

Comstock's growing reputation as a vigilante against vice reached important circles of respectable society, including wealthy banker-attorney Morris K. Jessup, the president of the Young Men's Christian Association (YMCA). Jessup created a special Committee for the Suppression of Vice and recruited the young Comstock to lead it. Comstock accepted and pushed quickly to rename the committee the New York Society for the Suppression of Vice. He served as its secretary and supervised for four decades its enormous censorial power. The charter agreement with the state reinforced his determination to exterminate vice; it stipulated that the organization would receive half the fines imposed on those convicted under New York's antivice laws. Urban America in the 1870s witnessed the proliferation of obscene materials, and social reformers sought ways to rid society of such materials, especially to protect children. Under Comstock's leadership, the Society began purging the New York area of publications and materials about sex and other immoralities with an astounding record of confiscations, arrests, and convictions. By his own admission, Comstock arrested more than fifty dealers and destroyed 142 obscene books, 182,000 photographs, some 21,000 sheets of impure songs, about 5,000 watch and knife charms and rings, over 500 wood-cut engravings, almost 6,000 playing cards, some 30,000 "rubber articles for immoral use," and nearly 15,000 letters ordering these goods—all in a period of ten months.

When the case against Woodhull and Claflin collapsed, Comstock recognized that stronger *federal* legislation was needed to combat a persistent and nationwide threat. His prominence and connections gave him access and the leverage to persuade a Congress already inclined to divert attention from deepening recession and its own mounting scandals. In the winter of 1873 Comstock journeyed to Washington with a satchel filled with illustrations collected to document the nature of the problem that he argued before the legislators was responsible for nearly all of America's criminals. His major ally in the House, Congressman C. L. Merriam of New York, gloomily doubted if even "war, pestilence, or famine could leave deeper or more deadly scars upon a nation than the general diffusion of this pestilential literature. The history of nations admonishes us that even our fair Republic will be of but short duration unless the vigor and purity of our youth be preserved."[2]

With hardly any debate or opposition, on March 3, 1873, Congress passed an "An act for the suppression of trade in, and circulation of, obscene literature and articles of immoral use," known soon in common parlance as the Comstock Act—in honor of the man who passionately lobbied for its passage and was thereafter most eager to enforce it. Comprehensive in its reach, and reinforced with amendments in 1876, the new legislation covered not only "obscene," "immoral," and "indecent" publications but also writings or instruments pertaining to contraception and abortion, and postal officials were authorized to confiscate the prohibited matter. A few days after passage of the law, the postmaster general, at the behest of a few prominent senators, appointed Comstock special agent of the Post Office, commissioned to investigate and destroy the vice business and punish its participants anywhere in America. Until his death in 1915, he zealously discharged his newly assumed federal duties and without any pay (until after the turn of the century when he became a postal inspector and drew a federal salary for his work).

A year before his death he wrote about the importance of children as the primary assets of any nation and how easily and early children's minds are shaped by both good and evil influences. Without laws like that of 1873, filthy materials could creep through the mails and then into the hands and minds of impressionable children, all the while unbeknownst to parents and teachers. His principal concern was literature dealing with sex, but he fought against other forms of "vice" such as materials and pictures that he labeled "vampire literature." In 1891 he wrote that "many a boy or youth has been led to commit crimes which have brought him to the penitentiary or the State's prison, from the infection or seduction of this class of crime-breeding publications."[3] The power of lewd stimuli to stir up lust and its consequences, he said a year before his death, should never be underestimated: "[A] single boy having unclean books or pictures in his possession can corrupt the whole community before being detected."[4] Religious leaders were quick to defend his thesis. Nurturing children in Christian culture was one way to teach them to avoid the harmful influences of obscene literature. "Good literature," for example, provided through Sunday Schools would help inculcate wholesome, traditional values. The key was to put good books in the hands of children and keep bad books away. Comstock's friend and ally the Reverend and Dr. James M. Buckley worried that "from the corrupting influence of but one single book or picture it is doubtful if many ever wholly recover."[5] Comstock believed that the only way to protect children—and society from ruined youths—was to keep the evil influences completely away from their reach. And the only guarantee to accomplish this objective was to extirpate all such materials and influences from society at large.

The Comstock Law was remarkably thorough in its reach. Anything that could be considered obscene or immoral, or objects or writings designed to facilitate abortion or birth control or used for any "indecent or immoral" purposes, were prohibited and subject to punishment of fines and imprisonment. The law gave officials authority to search and seize materials covered by the statute, and once seized, such items could be destroyed. The only notable omission of this sweeping statute was a definition for terms like "obscene," "indecent," or "immoral." Enforcement officers were left to judge for themselves. Comstock saw the job as remarkably straightforward: "To enforce these laws according to law, and in a legal manner—simply this and nothing more."[6]

The judiciary had always assumed that the First Amendment could never be so demeaned as to protect obscene and immoral publications. The prevailing legal definition of "obscenity" was imported from English common law where it had first appeared just five years before the passage of the Comstock Act. In the case of *Regina v. Hicklin* (1868), the rule had been announced by the memorable Lord Cockburn: "I think the test is this, whether the tendency of the matter charged as obscenity is to deprave and corrupt those whose minds are open to immoral influences, and into whose hands a publication of this sort may fall."[7] This test coincided perfectly with Comstock's logic about the dangers to children and the incumbent need to expurgate society of any material that might fall into their hands. It balanced the interests entirely on the possibility that one so weak or immature might be injured by a publication yet ignored completely the benefit that thousands, or more, mature adults might derive.

Acting under cover with a fictitious name, Comstock managed to get the freewheeling libertarian radical De Robigne M. Bennett to mail him a copy of an allegedly obscene book, and upon receiving it, he had Bennett arrested for distributing the work. During Bennett's trial, in a federal court, the judge denied the defense's motion to show the jury the whole work, insisting instead that only the isolated passages charged as obscene were pertinent. The judge applied the *Hicklin* test and set a precedent that federal courts followed for at least half a century thereafter in deciding obscenity cases under the Comstock Act. Some judges were more open-minded and flexible, looking at works through mature and more modern lenses, but most judges were dogmatically committed to the *Hicklin* rule, something Comstock repeatedly stressed as proof that his convictions were lawful. It was even reported that on some occasions appalled judges refused to let jurors see the obscene matter in question, telling them that the offensive materials were too gross to view and thus assuring convictions.

Comstock made full use of the powerful weapons available. However, to his credit, he infrequently exploited the wide net of the law to dredge the literary world for classic works or masterpieces containing references to sex. Only occasionally did he or his crusaders bother with important works by prominent authors—such as Henry Fielding's *Tom Jones*, Walt Whitman's *Leaves of Grass*, or Leo Tolstoy's *Kreutzer Sonata*. He recognized that mature and serious readers should have access to some great works, though the law gave him and his agents the power to decide which works were that great. And if such classics were at all commercially exploited in the marketplace for their sexual appeal, the peddlers were answerable to the law.

Comstock and his subordinates focused principally on materials that concerned sex or reproduction, even if handled maturely and written by medical professionals, and especially if produced by social reformers or writers and advocates of radical libertarianism. These authors and reformers challenged the established norms in pursuit of progressive social goals, such as guarding against overpopulation, promoting women's liberation, and providing birth control education for ill-informed or poor people whose families were often larger than their incomes. Comstock regarded these reforms as contrary to nature and the will of God, and he had little mercy for their proponents. He also ensured that the open-ended law covered "blasphemy," thus enabling him to prosecute many reformers who irreverently rebelled against the rigidity of religion.

Enforcement of the Comstock Act directly interfered in the lives of literally thousands of people, and many thousands more no doubt curbed or gagged themselves to steer clear of the law. In an interview in *Harper's Weekly* in 1915, shortly before his death, Comstock claimed to have had 3,873 individuals arraigned in state or federal courts, and of them, 2,881, almost 75 percent, had been convicted or had pleaded guilty. The year before, he crowed that his arrestees could fill a passenger train loaded with sixty coaches, each coach filled with sixty passengers. Fines collected reached almost $250,000, and nearly 600 years in jail sentences had been meted out to those found guilty. More than 170 tons of the monstrous evil had been destroyed. His friend the Reverend Buckley, who was the editor of *The Christian Advocate*, praised Comstock as the single most successful federal official specializing in convicting criminals in the United States.

Free love advocates such as Ezra Heywood, formerly an avid abolitionist, was one of Comstock's principal targets. In 1872 Heywood had established the libertarian radical journal *The Word*, and a year later, he founded, with his wife, the New England Free Love League. In 1876 he published a pamphlet called *Cupid's Yokes*, which attacked many social restrictions as tantamount to slavery. He criticized marriage as "legalized slavery of women" and a "great social fraud." Nothing in the publication could be regarded as lascivious or obscene in any erotic way, but the tract advocated contraception as promoting greater freedom and contained some explicit instructions about birth control methods and devices. He, too, criticized the Reverend Beecher as a hypocrite and treated capitalism and marriage like slavery—forces of social oppression. The pamphlet called the Comstock Act the "National Gag-Law," a federal statute wrenched by a fanatic from an intimidated and unwitting Congress. Heywood actually opposed licentious behavior and the proliferation of obscene prints and pictures, but this did not redeem the publication in the fixed eyes of Comstock who began multiple prosecutions against Heywood.

Comstock described the events the night he personally arrested Heywood. Obtaining the warrant himself in federal court in Boston, he tracked Heywood one night while he was "holding a free-love convention." Comstock bought a ticket and took a seat unnoticed by the rest of the crowd. "I looked over the audience of about 250 men and boys. I could see lust in every face." Heywood's wife took the podium and "delivered the foulest address I ever heard. She seemed lost to all shame. The audience cheered and applauded. It was too vile; I had to go out." He wanted to arrest Heywood right then and there, but disgust drove him out of the hall. "I looked for a policeman. As usual, none was to be found when wanted. Then I sought light and help from above. I prayed for strength to do my duty, and that I might have success. I knew God was able to help me. Every manly instinct cried out against my cowardly turning my back on this horde of lusters. . . . I resolved that at least one man in America should enter a protest."[8]

Heywood's conviction resulted in a fine and two years in prison. Comstock prosecuted others who had mailed *Cupid's Yokes*. Enraged freethinkers, such as Robert G. Ingersoll, launched a petition, signed by more than 50,000 people and submitted in February 1878 to Congress as a formal request to repeal the Comstock Act. The National Liberal League, an organization that defended libertarian radical freethinkers in court, helped to organize the petition. Comstock came in person to defend not only the law but also his reputation as its principal enforcer. Congress refused to repeal what it deemed a perfectly constitutional law aimed at a vicious evil. Four years later Heywood was arrested again for publishing poems from Walt Whitman's *Leaves of Grass*, but the indictment was dismissed. Eight years later, he was arrested again. This time Comstock and the court that convicted Heywood must have been stunned to read that one of the published pieces in question used the word "fuck." Heywood was sentenced again to two years in prison.

In 1880 Moses Harmon founded a radical journal focusing on sexual liberation and reform, a publication that naturally conflicted with the Comstock Act. The journal was eventually named *Lucifer: The Light-Bearer*, an unmasked attack on established religion. Harmon used *Lucifer* as an outlet for controversial speech and letters dealing frankly with sexual reforms and women's liberation, bringing almost endless confrontations with Comstock and the vice patrol. The National Defense Association, a more radical spin-off from the National Liberal League, had a busy decade defending charges against *Lucifer*. In 1905, at age seventy-five, Harmon was finally sentenced to a year in prison at hard labor, in part for publishing a statement urging women to abstain from sex while pregnant.

Comstock's pursuits also affected the world of art and theater. The *American Student of Art* was a highly respected magazine for art students, but because it contained nude drawings and prints its June 1906 issue triggered a raid of the Art Students' League, which published the magazine, followed by prosecutions under federal law of those in charge. Years earlier, in 1887, Comstock's censors had raided the highly respected art gallery of Knoedler & Co. because some of the paintings offended moral decency. And two years before he died, while sauntering along West Forty-Sixth Street in New York City in May, the aging Comstock passed the storefront window of the art dealers Braun & Co. and suddenly caught a glimpse of Paul Chabas's masterpiece *September Morning*. He entered the shop showing his badge of office and ordered a perplexed salesman to remove the picture of the girl with no clothes. In 1912 that famous painting had received the Medal of Honor from the Art Committee of the French Academy.

Editorials in newspapers and magazines wondered whether in the hands of Comstock intellectual and artistic culture in the United States was being preserved or retarded. An angry George Bernard Shaw condescendingly coined the term "Comstockery" to describe widespread and repressive literary censorship, "the world's standing joke at the expense of the United States,"[9] a country he ridiculed as "a provincial

place, a second-rate country-town civilization after all."[10] Shaw's book
Man and Superman had been placed on the "reserved list" by the super-
visor of New York City's public libraries. Comstock apparently had little
to do with this incident—in fact, he had until then never heard of the
Irish playwright. However, once he had learned of the book's restricted
place in the city's public libraries, he discovered that Shaw's play *Mrs.
Warren's Profession* was being performed in New York. Without reading
or seeing it, he discovered that Mrs. Warren's profession was prostitution
and deduced that if Shaw had written the play, it probably contained
obscene and immoral expressions. Comstock informed the police, and
legal action was taken against the producer, who was tried but acquitted.

Comstock always vigorously enforced the sections of the law dealing
with contraception. On the illicit subject of birth control, the Comstock
Act was clear enough to permit no discretion. Targets included legitimate
physicians and pharmacists whose pamphlets, advertisements, and other
writings about sex and contraception collided with the federal statute—
even though doctors across the country regularly orally advised women
who asked during office visits. One of Comstock's earliest cases involved
prosecution of the distinguished Dr. Edward Bliss Foote, who published
a highly successful book entitled *Medical Common Sense*, a manual for the
general public explaining in lay terms a variety of medical issues, including the forbidden subject of how to prevent pregnancy and how to
obtain recommended contraceptive devices. Published in 1858, the popular book had already sold some 300,000 copies, but in January 1876
Foote was convicted and fined $3,500 for violating the Comstock Act.
Comstock later explained that the doctor had been arrested and convicted not because he had sent through the mail a purely medical publication but because the manual contained "advertisements of an
infamous article—an incentive to crime to young girls and women . . .
and other infamous things sold in connection with obscene publications,
leading the youth to speedy and positive ruin."[11] Other doctors were
similarly arrested and convicted for supplying materials explaining pregnancy and how to prevent it. One of them, for example, was sentenced
to eighteen months in jail; another fled the country after being convicted.

In part because of the stifling reign of censorship prevailing in Victorian America, many young men and women were ignorant about sex
and were often unsure what to expect. Some social reformers wanted to
supply information to better inform inexperienced newlyweds about the
wedding night. Dr. Alice Stockman published such a book and was
found guilty and heavily fined. Ida Craddock in 1902 published a similar
text, entitled *The Wedding Night*, giving advice to newlyweds about sex,
something Comstock found to be "indescribably obscene." Rather than
accept her prison term, Craddock committed suicide the day before her
sentencing (she was one of some fifteen who killed themselves rather

than pay the penalty for violating the Comstock Law). Spies and decoys in the Post Office often wrote to doctors requesting birth control information, claiming various hardships such as mentally retarded children already born and the need to avoid others. On one occasion, a federal undercover agent using two different names and stories contacted the same doctor twice, and the sympathetic physician was subsequently arrested and sentenced to ten years in prison—five years for each count of sending the requested information.

The restrictive atmosphere of Comstockery was in part responsible for the founding in 1902 of the Free Speech League, formed to defend freedom of speech itself—for anyone, not just libertarians or sex radicals. Walker, Harmon, and Edward Bond Foote, the son of the convicted Dr. Foote, helped to establish this soon very busy organization. One of its leading attorneys and eventually its principal administrator was the distinguished and prolific Theodore Schroeder, who published many scholarly attacks on censorship and Comstockery. Closely associated with the organization were two of Comstock's most wanted obscenity and birth control writers: the celebrated radical feminists Emma Goldman, founder of the anarchist magazine *Mother Earth*, and Margaret H. Sanger, a nurse and forerunner of the birth control movement in the United States. Several years before Comstock died at age seventy-one, these two determined women had defiantly flouted the Comstock Act because they were convinced that such information was badly needed.

As a nurse, Sanger treated many poor women distraught because of the number of children they could ill afford to raise and support. Some women died in childbirth because they were medically unfit for another pregnancy and often leaving working fathers with almost no time to care for the children left behind. Sanger realized that most of these women were totally uninformed about contraception, and the Comstock Law was one reason for such ignorance. With her own money she created in 1914 a monthly magazine, *The Woman Rebel*, focusing on women but especially matters of birth control. The premier edition in March was only eight pages long and barely coherent, but it was immediately suppressed by the Post Office. She continued with further additions, but the Post Office repeatedly blocked her from sending the magazine, and she was indicted in August, as World War I erupted in Europe. The night before her trial was to commence, she fled the country—as she felt that in prison there was little she could do to promote birth control awareness. While abroad, she prepared a pamphlet, *Family Limitations*, which medically and explicitly explained and demonstrated some fundamentals about contraception. One of Comstock's undercover agents visited Sanger's husband William, still in the United States, pleading for a copy for his "wife," and Sanger supplied one. On January 19, 1915, Comstock showed up to arrest William Sanger for distributing materials forbidden by the Comstock Act. William Sanger was convicted and agreed to thirty days in jail rather than pay a fine. When Margaret learned of her husband's ordeal, she returned to the United States. Her own trial was postponed several times, and eventually the charges were dropped, but the determined woman was arrested again and finally sentenced to thirty days in jail. Anthony Comstock attended her trial, where he developed pneumonia and died soon thereafter.

Courts in the 1930s began interpreting the Comstock Law to allow doctors to prescribe contraceptives to save lives and promote the well-being of patients. Margaret Sanger's resolve sustained the American birth control movement, and she lived long enough to see the Supreme Court in 1965 declare marital contraception part of a general constitutional right of privacy. This ruling induced Congress in 1971 finally to delete the birth control prohibitions from the Comstock Act.

NOTES

1. Anthony Comstock, *Traps for the Young* (New York: Funk & Wagnalls, 1883), p. 169 (emphasis in original).

2. Speeches to the House of Representatives, as reported in the New York *Times*, March 15, 1873, p. 3.

3. Anthony Comstock, "Vampire Literature," *North American Review* 153 (August 1891): 165.

4. Anthony Comstock, "The Children of Our Nation and Their Foes," *The Light* 99 (September–October 1914): 19.

5. James M. Buckley, "The Suppression of Vice," *North American Review* 135 (November 1882): 496.

6. Anthony Comstock, *Frauds Exposed* (New York: J. Howard Brown, 1880), p. 431.

7. As quoted in James C.N. Paul and Murray L. Schwartz, *Federal Censorship: Obscenity in the Mail* (New York: Free Press of Glencoe, 1961), p. 16.

8. Comstock, *Traps for the Young*, pp. 163–164.

9. As quoted in *Current Opinion* 56 (April 1914): 288.

10. As quoted in *The Literary Digest*, April 2, 1927, p. 32.

11. Comstock, *Frauds Exposed*, p. 427.

DOCUMENTS

5.1.   Comstock Defends His Law Against Repeal

In early 1878 freethinkers and others concerned with the potential dangers of such a law formally petitioned Congress to repeal the Comstock Law. More than 50,000 people signed the petition. Comstock personally went to the House of Representatives to defend both the law and his own reputation. Here he recounts what transpired.

As I entered the Committee room, I found it crowded with the long-haired men and short-haired women, there to defend, obscene publications, abortion implements, and other incentives to crime, by repealing the laws. I heard their hiss and curse as I passed through them. I saw their sneers and their looks of derision and contempt.

It was not the blackening of my reputation that weighed me down, so much as the possibility that one of the most righteous *laws* ever enacted should be repealed or changed. This law is a barrier between the youth and moral death, between the home circle and shame, between the best institutions of learning in the land and disgrace, between the souls of our children and the most subtle enemy we have to deal with. I knew of the horrors that had been scattered broadcast over the land, through the mails, and that would again flood the country, if this law was repealed. . . .

At last the suspense is over, the time came for me to speak. I had but one simple duty. Every interest paled before that, *i.e., To show the Committee reasons why the law should not be changed.* . . .

I . . . presented facts why the laws should not be changed. I showed how catalogues of schools are collected for the sake of children's names and addresses; how different devices are resorted to, to collect the names of our youth in order to send secretly by mail to them, the most demoralizing articles, giving details and sad instances coming within my own knowledge, where many youth of both sexes have been ruined. . . .

I then said to the Committee as I say to the world, "I have sought faithfully to do my duty. I have been zealous and earnest, and expect to be in the future, to keep a legal barrier between this cursed business which debauches and destroys the youth, and the children in our schools, colleges, and homes. *I challenge the closest scrutiny into all my official acts.* I am ready to meet any charge, from any person, of any act unbecoming a faithful officer; and if any member of this Committee has a suspicion that I have done any improper act, I ask them to make a most searching investigation, and do it in the most public manner." . . .

Then came the complete rout of the enemy; then came the answer to prayer; then came vindication; then came light and joy; then came a perfect victory; then came positive proof that it is better to trust God, than put confidence in men—better to walk alone with Him than go with the multitude; and as I went out of the door, the last to go out, I heard the following unanimously carried:

"I move you that we report unanimously against any repeal or change whatever."

. . . [The Committee's Report read:]

"The Committee on the Revision of the Laws, to whom was referred the petition of Robert G. Ingersoll and others, praying for the repeal or modification of sections . . . of the Revised Statutes, have had the same under consideration, and have heard the petition at length.

"In the opinion of your Committee, the post-office was not established to carry instruments of vice, or obscene writings, indecent pictures, or lewd books.

"Your Committee believe that the statutes in question do not violate the Constitution of the United States, and ought not to be changed; they recommend, therefore, that the prayer of the said petition be denied."

Source: Anthony Comstock, *Frauds Exposed* (New York: J. Howard Brown, 1880), pp. 424–434.

5.2. In Defense of Birth Control

Communal living was popular among a small sector of the American population who believed in and practiced birth control. These "socialists" were ahead of their time on the issue of birth control, and they criticized the narrow-mindedness of the Comstock Law. The following appeared in the midst of the petition to repeal the law.

An effort is now being made at Washington to procure the repeal of what are familiarly known as the "Comstock Laws," in the designing and enforcement of which Anthony Comstock, of New York, has played so conspicuous a part. A monster petition, signed by more than fifty thousand persons, praying for this repeal, has been presented to both branches of Congress, and the subject is now under consideration in one

of the Committees. Meantime those who have most interested themselves in the project are soliciting aid and influence in behalf of the movement, which induces us to say a few words about it.

It must be borne in mind that these laws represent and are sustained
by a strong public opinion which is averse to the discussion of any sexual
matters whatever. We do not consider this an enlightened opinion; certainly not if Anthony Comstock truly represents it; but it is, nevertheless,
the opinion of a large and influential class of people who have the best
intentions in the world, but who do not at all understand the tendencies
and progress of this age. These people have gone to work and procured
the passage of laws which enable them to hold in check those whom
they consider altogether too liberal and progressive. They do not believe
in any meddling with the population question, but think that if we all
go ahead in the good, old-fashioned way, trusting to "natural laws" to
limit the size of our families, all will be well with us. They do not care
to have science poking its nose into social and domestic affairs. Their
zeal and earnestness are such that they are ready to spend large sums
to enforce their opinions on others.

Now it is a question which is the wisest and most effectual way to
correct and enlarge this narrow public opinion; shall it be by fighting
and lobbying and bribing at Washington, or by taking hold to educate
the whole nation into a better understanding of the great social problems
which are pressing upon the world? We think, decidedly, that the latter
is the true way, and we are already at work upon it. The Malthusian
Doctrines must be thoroughly examined, and verified or refuted by all
procurable statistics. If Malthus was right, if it is true that we are ap-
proaching, no matter how slowly, a time when population will press on
the means of subsistence so that the whole world will be subject to periodical famines, as India and China now are, then this must be demonstrated so that all will be convinced. When that shall have been done,
the necessity of limiting population in some intelligent and scientific
manner will be conceded at once, and public opinion will demand that
the whole subject be thrown open to the freest discussion, and any laws
which interfere with this will be expunged from the statute books. There
is nothing in the "Comstock Laws" forbidding the discussion of the population question and the Malthusian theories on general principles, although they do bear hard on the matter of preventive checks. When the
people begin to see that they must sooner or later choose between famines, pestilences, and other death-producing checks, or some scientific
and unobjectionable birth-restricting check, they will no longer consider
the subject obscene and immoral, and they will see to it that the laws
are conformed to the necessities of the situation. Undoubtedly in that
time of free discussion all the checks that are now secretly known and
practiced will be brought to light and judged by science. We shall offer

a contribution to that investigation when it comes; and till it comes we shall content ourselves with urging on the preliminary investigations started by Malthus as to the importance of intelligent, voluntary control of population.

Source: American Socialist 3 (April 4, 1878): 108.

5.3.   Rev. Dr. James M. Buckley Defends Comstock

In 1882 the North American Review *held a symposium to which Comstock and several critics and supporters were invited to participate. The proceedings, entitled "The Suppression of Vice," were published in the November edition of the periodical. An acquaintance and admirer of Comstock, Buckley spoke and strongly defended his friend's efforts to suppress vice. These were some of his remarks to the gathering.*

The effect of licentious publications upon the imagination of youth is "evil and only evil, and that continually." The passions are normally and gradually developed in man as in the lower animals; but the brutes are under no restraint. Instinct, impulse, and opportunity determine their actions. Yet, as passion strengthens, it stimulates the imagination. Marriage, only, affords legitimate gratification. Lust, indulged in thought or deed apart from love, is moral impurity; sexual love with lust, apart from wedlock, is the spirit of adultery. This is the strain placed by God, human nature, and law, upon man. Divorce, polygamy, communism, illegitimacy, abortion, and the reaction and aberrations of the sexual instinct in vices that are "not so much as to be named," are but superficial indications of its power. The purity of youth is to be maintained only by repressing, under moral principle, the uprisings of passion and the play of a prurient fancy. But a filthy book or picture, by premature representations and morbid exaggerations, in which lust is a tyrant smothering love the rightful sovereign, poisons all the springs of fancy, and turns the fountains of feeling into stagnant pools, breeding disease, and agitated only by monsters of their own generation. From the corrupting influence of but one such or picture it is doubtful if many ever wholly recover; the hideous and polluting remembrance is a "damned spot that will not out."

When in the habit of conducting religions services in an asylum for the insane, [I] questioned many of the victims of their own vices who were convalescent, or who had lucid intervals, and found that most of them were led into their vile practices, or stimulated themselves therein, by lascivious publications. Pollution of the mind is self-perpetuating: "having eyes full of adultery, they cannot cease from sin."

The victims of these habits and the readers of these books are reserved. Until shame is destroyed, the last person to whom they would voluntarily reveal their thoughts, or show obscene books or engravings, are parents, teachers, or chaste friends. Even theft is not more secretive.

The Hon. Algernon S. Sullivan, of New York, when standing in Association Hall, corner Twenty-third Street and Fourth Avenue, before a large audience, said, concerning the amount of obscene matter confiscated by the society: "We found storerooms literally filled with this terrible stuff, and the piles looked like stacks of hay. I saw, when it was being prepared for the flames, that it would cover more than this platform and height of my stature." . . .

. . . A special defect of a republican form of government, pointed out by De Tocqueville and emphasized by many subsequent writers, is its weakness in the enforcement of law in advance of public interest. Private interests which are imperiled or injured by criminal acts find it necessary to stir officials to the performance of their official duty. This defect may be traced in rural districts, but it is especially disastrous in cities. The sale of obscene literature belong[s] to a class of crime in which the general public, left to itself, will take little interest. If this society were dissolved, there is every reason to believe that in a very short time, the traffic in these debauching agencies would be as open, and as large, as before it was founded.

. . . A charge often repeated is that the mails are tampered with. The Hon. Thomas L. James, ex-Postmaster-General of the United States, said in a public address in the city, on February 6th last:

. . . "I am informed that there is a widespread belief that Mr. Comstock opens letters in transit in the post-office. The idea is simply absurd. No letter is tampered with in the post-office, and it is due to Mr. Comstock to say that he never attempted to tamper with a letter. There is nothing that the American people are more sensitive than the sanctity of their correspondence, and they would hurl the postmaster from power, as they did one in England, if he allowed tampering with the mail. I say it broadly and emphatically, that Mr. Comstock never attempted to open, or opened a letter."

Other charges were that the secretary has pursued innocent and unsuspecting persons, woven a net around them, entrapped and ruined them; that the spirit of the society is vindictive, that it has interfered with legitimate medical practice. If securing the conviction of nearly sixty abortionists, and the punishment of venders of instruments and nostrums, whose sole purpose is the promotion or concealment of licentiousness, be "interfering with legitimate medical practice," no denial can be made; but if it be procuring the enforcement of just law, the accusation is the highest commendation. . . .

In fine, I write under the conviction that the most efficient modes of restricting these forms of vice have been ascertained; that the affairs of the society which adopts them have been managed with prudence; that its errors have been few and unimportant; that its work, in comparison with the means at its command, has not been surpassed in amount and value by any reformatory movement of modern times.

Its secretary, starting out from his clerkship in 1872 to save his comrades, fighting his way step by step against fearful odds, appearing single-handed in the courts, going, almost alone to Washington to meet an army of opponents,—a horde of traducers, and secret letters sent by persons high in authority, but deceived by criminals, if not in league with them,—or as he appears with his face scarred and seamed by the knife of the would-be assassin, I conceive presents one of the most impressive and noble figures which have appeared in a time prolific of strong personalities.

Source: North American Review 135 (November 1882): 495–501.

5.4.   Questioning Comstock's Judgment

On May 11,1894, the New York Times, *which had been sympathetic to Comstock's work, expressed dismay that Comstock regarded Henry Fielding's classic* Tom Jones *as the kind of "obscenity" suppressible under the federal law. In the following editorial, eighteen months later, the editors had grown more impatient with Comstock's sometimes-reckless tactics, even questioning his fitness for the job.*

The arrest and arraignment at the instance of Mr. Anthony Comstock of an established and respectable bookseller as a dealer in obscene literature, which evidently he is not, brings up once more the question whether the powers of the inquisition devolved upon or assumed by Mr. Comstock can safely be reposed in any individual, and especially whether they can safely be reposed in a person like Mr. Comstock, who is a specialist, so to speak, in pornography. It is a curious fact that a man cannot devote himself to such specialties without losing his mental balance and overdoing his business. In the case of a man who assumes the special functions which Mr. Comstock has taken upon himself the fallibility of the specialist is increased, because in order to render a fair judgment upon the question whether a work of art or literature is obscene, one needs a very wide acquaintance with literature and with art. It is of course not at all the question whether a passage or a picture might not appeal to a particularly prurient mind. Shakespeare and the Bible abound in such passages. The question is whether the intention of the author of the work, and its necessary tendency, are of an inflammatory and brutalizing character. In this "the hand of little employment hath the daintier sense." A casual citizen of equal knowledge would be a much better judge than an agent for the Society for the Suppression of Vice. And Mr. Comstock has sufficiently shown that if any man can be trusted to decide off-hand what is obscene literature or art, he is not the man. A man who thought it his duty, in the interest of morality to suppress "Tom Jones," is a man to whom no discretion can in such matters be confided. Such a suppression is a conclusive proof of the incapacity of the censor.

Certainly the fact that a bookseller is a reputable and established dealer is not a conclusive refutation of the charge that he dealt in obscene literature. Some years ago seizure and arrest were made, under the direction of Mr. Comstock, which appeared to be a persecution of such a dealer. But in that case it turned out that Comstock was in the right and that the man was guilty. In the present case it is maintained by Comstock that the question has already been adjudicated and the book pronounced indecent. But this plea requires much qualification. It is asserted that the adjudication came about as follows: Comstock called at the shop of a French bookseller and demanded that the work in question, which he thereupon proceeded to mutilate with a penknife for the purpose of extracting exhibits, thus destroying a work valued at $50 and inflicting a fine of that amount in advance of any judicial proceeding whatever. The bookseller, being arraigned, being imperfectly acquainted with English and under great apprehension, pleaded guilty of an offense which nobody really believes that he had willfully committed. It is the acceptance of this plea of guilty, it is said, that constitutes the adjudication in this case. It is true that no owner of a library would like to submit to a common jury the question whether he was not the possessor of obscene literature, but imperfect as such an adjudication would be, it seems that it is more than was had in this case. Mr. Comstock's victim has very properly demanded a trial by jury. If he is acquitted, it will clearly appear both that his arrest was an outrage and that the arrest of the French bookseller was an outrage, and the injury of his property a wrong for which he is entitled to redress.

Source: *New York Times*, November 21, 1895, p. 807.

5.5.   More "Comstockery"

Many editorials criticized Comstock and his associates for taking legal action against The American Student of Art *because one of its editions contained prints of nude figures. The* Independent *joined those who questioned the handling of the art magazine, but in general the magazine defended Comstock's overall work in keeping America pure.*

Every little while there appears in the daily press, sometimes of New York, and sometimes flowing over the country, a wave of ridicule of Anthony Comstock. He is an officer of the United States Government, whose business it is to prevent the use of the mails to carry indecent matter, tons of pictures unquestionably intended to corrupt youth. He does his work with great energy and general intelligence and usually with the approval of the courts. The most of the objects which he tries to suppress and destroy are so unquestionably and filthily bad that no decent person can complain. Indeed he is one of those scavengers who are necessary in cleansing our morals, just as other scavengers remove other offensive matter. Most of his work is never obtruded upon by the public eye, just as nightsoil is carted away when people are asleep. Equally not a little of the matter that comes before those other moral scavengers who preside over our courts, especially in divorce cases, is too disgusting to be printed. Mr. Comstock thus belongs to that needful class of public officials, including judges, prosecuting attorneys, jurymen, detectives, policemen, and street sweepers, whom we require to do much disagreeable work, all for the purification of society. It is all absolutely essential, and some of it is very unpleasant, but all honorable, and somebody must do it. It is a law in some States, written or unwritten that no buzzard shall be killed, because he does this disagreeable work.

Now, all this good work that Mr. Comstock does one never hears him praised for, any more than you hear praise for the vultures that settle on a Parsee House of Silence. But there is a class of people who would not dare to say that no restraint should be put on the circulation of indecency, but who never fail to slur his work, as if it were prurient prudery. And if this officer makes a mistake, or a doubtful arrest, they delight in the chance to attack and ridicule him, and George Bernard Shaw, as the angel of liberty, talks about "Comstockery."

Just now there is a great cry against him because he has seized the June number of *The American Student of Art*, published by the Art Students' League. This League is an excellent school of art, taught by most reputable artists, and it has done much for American art. It does not neglect studies in the nude, and it is some of these undisguisedly frank studies of naked men and women which are the chief attraction of the numbers which have been seized by Mr. Comstock. We have received a copy, and we are not pleased to have such studies selected for publication, for we should not like to see them publicly distributed. While it is doubtless necessary to make studies in the nude, a certain degree of fig-leaf decency is even here to be desired, and does not in the least interfere with study of the play of limbs and muscles. There was a time in Greece when in the gymnasium men were naked and were not ashamed, and when art followed custom: but we would arrest such people nowadays; and even children are required to be clothed, as well as older people when they walk from the bathing booths to the beach.

In this case Mr. Comstock was on the edge of his duty. He is attacked because these pictures are no worse than those in medical books. True, except that they are more life-like. But those are in books belonging to specialists, necessary for them, and not open to the public. This defense may, in a measure, apply to these pictures. They are for and by artists, in their work; and the magazine is intended mainly to attract young men and young women who wish to study art. To be sure, they are distributed freely, at a small price, to anybody who wants them, and circulars are sent out soliciting miscellaneous subscriptions, yet so much must be said in their favor. The purpose is not lubricity, as in most of Mr. Comstock's seizures; and this is a real defense, altho[ugh] the pictures are not at all such as would be decent to examine and discuss in a mixt company, nor would they be exposed even in a picture gallery. They are mere immature studies, with no idealism, just realistic pictures of nakedness and not works of art. They might not offend a student of art, scarce any more than a naked corpse offends a student of anatomy, taken from the brine in a medical school; but they would be evil if given to one who evil thinks; and no ordinary decent person would like to have them about.

We presume Mr. Comstock will fail in his attempt to prevent the distribution of this number of the magazine. The popular voice of the press is against him, and the press influences judges and jury more than we wish. It condemned Dreyfus, just as public favor has many a time acquitted those who ought to be condemned. The admirers of Whitman are numerous, who are more appreciative of his grossness than of his "My Captain." It is literary form to ridicule Puritanism; and "society plays" and "society novels" illustrate and exploit pornography; and art comes down to repulsive, coarse nakedness, level to the walls of a bar-room. If in this act of his Mr. Comstock is judged to have played the prude, it is an error that leans to virtue's side.

Source: *Independent* 61 (August 9, 1906): 343–344.

5.6.   Our Prudish Censorship

In 1902 the Free Speech League was formed to defend freedom of expression and those charged with violations of antiobscenity and laws against advocacy of anarchism and other doctrines considered dangerous. Theodore Schroeder became the League's most prominent attorney, and he published widely in defense of free speech and press. In the following essay he challenges the premises of governmental censorship of obscene and immoral literature.

"[O]bscenity," like witches, will cease to exist for you, when you cease to believe in it.... One proof lies in the fact that no man or court ever has been able to make a generally acceptable or generally applicable definition of "obscenity" in *terms of book-qualities*, and many persons, at least as decent as our moralists for revenue, are unable to see "obscenity" where the latter are quite overwhelmed by it. If it had any existence outside the mere mind and feelings of the obscenity-seeing humans, then the standard of "obscenity" would be uniform. But it is not.

   ... I believe I can make my meaning plain by a single illustration. Mr. Comstock says that in doing his work of suppression he has stood "at the mouth of a sewer" for forty years. Mr. Comstock admits that his mind is still "pure," which proves that mental sewage is harmless for some of us, at least when persistently taken for a long time, in very large doses. This suggests that the remedy against the alleged evils of "obscenity" is more "obscenity" until, by making sex as commonplace as noses, its representation will be equally void of stimulating qualities and all of us will have become as immune against "evil" results as our wild animals, and Mr. Comstock.

   It is true beyond doubt that by his most conspicuous activities, he has fixed, in the minds of millions of people, an indissoluble association between mental sewage and the name Anthony Comstock....

   Thus, the "Comstock Law" has become a synonym for the obscenity law, and "Comstockery" is an Americanism for our whole system of sex-censorship, at once suggesting to our minds all that which we think is thereby suppressed.

   So zealous and unceasing has been his work and so well advertised is its nature that one cannot think of the great suppressor without thinking also of that which he suppresses. That is to say, from the storehouse of our memory the mere words "Anthony Comstock" immediately bring to our consciousness all those impure and libidinous thoughts which we imagine he is trying to exclude from the minds of others and which we are ashamed to confess in ourselves.

The usual judicial test by which a word, book, picture or play is judged "obscene" is *"if it would have a tendency to suggest impure and libidinous thoughts in the minds of those open to the influence of such thoughts and thus deprave and corrupt their morals."* This is the test by which our courts send men to prison cells. . . . [T]he mere words "Anthony Comstock" suggest a greater variety of "impure and libidinous thoughts" than probably any other two words of the English language. It follows conclusively, *according to the judicial test*, that the mere words "Anthony Comstock" should be adjudged the most "obscene" words in the English language. I insist that this is no mere quip of levity but a literal application of the judicial test by which men are being condemned to penal servitude. If the laws were uniformly enforced the mailing of these words would entitle the publisher to five years in jail and a fine of Five Thousand Dollars ($5,000) besides. But, of course, such laws are never intended to be uniformly enforced. They are useful to our savage instinct for revenge when we are in need of a righteous pretence for inflicting pain upon those whom we dislike or fear, for other reasons.

It is obvious in this case that the "obscenity" is not in the words "Anthony Comstock," but rests wholly in the associated ideas and feelings which are attached to these words—in *our own mind*. So it is in every other case of "obscenity." It always exists exclusively in the minds of those who see it because they believe in it, and no one should be punished on the theory that it exists in a name, a picture, a book or a play.

. . . In the psychologic laboratories this law is applied under the name of association-tests. Let me illustrate. A group of people contemplating a nude figure would have many varieties of related images coming to their mind, each according to a special psychologic imperative, manifesting the dominant thought of the observer. The true artist would think first of a beauty of curves, of symmetry and of coloring; the athlete would think first of proportion and muscular development; the biologist would probably have suggested to his mind the relation of the human organs to the corresponding parts in lower forms of life, while from such a nude figure "pure" people would get mainly the idea of lewdness, *for unto the lewd all is lewd.*

The more lewd people are, the more vivid will be their imaginative lewdness and the more lewdness will they read into that which they see. . . . Lewd "pure" persons usually evince great capacity for discovering lewdness where more normal people are unable to find it, and foolishly think to conceal, rather than measure their own condition, by the vehemence of their denunciation of it—in others. Thus the psychology of hysteria has given us proof that the greatest salacity is always to be found as the source of the greatest prudery. . . .

So we come to the problem of morals and ignorance. The prevalent theory is that you cannot teach any kind of sex ethics without making contrasts with immorality, the suggestion of which, some people say, is "far worse and more seductive than is the placing of the originals in all their abhorrent, disgusting, clammy, physical details before the blood and flesh eyes and reach." ... Those who advocate such notions falsely assume that if no sexual knowledge is imparted by a relatively intelligent instructor, then sensual ideas will never come into the mind of a child. Of course, this is absurd. So, then, the only question is whether it is dangerous and immoral to supplement the information acquired from a servant or on the street, or to anticipate it with greater intelligence accompanied by better motives. ...

... [I]n the realm of sex, as everywhere else, immunity from evil must be sought in the spread of scientific truth, all the truth that is known, and by fearlessly seeking for truths yet unknown.

... Those outrageous laws which make it a crime, even for a physician by post, orally or otherwise, to inform even mature or married people how to avoid conception would soon be repealed if our eugenic babblers had any real interest in race betterment. So long as these look upon the birth of defective children as the work of God, and all voluntary sterilization of marriage as the work of the devil and criminal, so long their interest in eugenics will be the damnation of the movement. ...

In the present state of ignorance and uncertainty as to ethics and sexual psychology, our mental mechanism is too diversified, complex and obscure to enable anyone to predict with certainty the general "moral tendency" of any piece of literature or art. That which produces "good" effects upon some minds will produce "bad" effects upon other minds, according to what is already there. That which some thoughtful persons consider harmless and wholesome joy, others consider "highly immoral." In some minds the "best" books, by their distorted perspective and glaring omissions, suggest very much evil, while to other minds the "worst" books suggest very much that is humanizing and educating. Therefore no one is good enough to strike a balance for society as a whole on a book's "moral tendency" considered as a whole. The only alternative is that the destiny of our intellectual and moral progress shall be left to the whim, caprice, or superstition of an ignoramus, and this is insufferable except for other like ignoramuses. ...

Always the cure for the sorrows of misinformation and half knowledge is more information. In every field of human progress we must go through the stages of ignorance, superstition, dogma, error and half knowledge, in order to arrive at the whole truth. ... Let us then annihilate this outrageous censorship, as our American constitutions were designed to do, and thus give everybody a chance to know all that is to be known, even upon the subject of sex; let truth grapple with error in a free and open field and in so far as we have the truth we shall prevail, and where we have it not, that fact and the remedy will be the sooner discovered through freedom for the interchange of *all* ideas even those about sex morals, sex hygiene, eugenics and the physiology and psychology of sex, yes, even for the "worst" of such I demand this freedom for myself and for every other human, as a natural and constitutionally guaranteed right.

Source: *Forum* 53 (January, 1915): 87–99.

5.7.   "Unpopular But Not Undeserving"

Anthony Comstock retired from public service in 1915 shortly before he died. The New York Times, *which had been in the past a sometime supporter and a sometime critic, appraised in the following editorial Comstock's overall contributions to the well-being of the nation.*

Several of the New York papers, in recording the withdrawal from Anthony Comstock of the title and salary that have long been his as Post Office Inspector, express a kind and amount of satisfaction which to *The Times* seems to indicate inappreciation of the man's good qualities and the vast amount of good work that he has accomplished.

Mr. Comstock has more than once exercised his powers in a way to make the judicious grieve. He has a capacity, at times intensely irritating, for seeing vice where it does not exist, and occasionally he has done things which his best friends have found it difficult or impossible to defend. All these are charges on which he can fairly be convicted in the court of public opinion. After he has been condemned on every such count, however, the fact remains that to his zeal, industry, and courage New York City is very largely indebted.

He has made it in many ways a city more decent than it was when he undertook the much-needed work of purifying it, and more than one vicious trade that once flourished in open and flagrant defiance of the disgust and anger it earned has either been wholly suppressed by him or has been driven so far underground that its harmful effects are almost negligible. Like the rest of us, Mr. Comstock has his faults, but they are the faults that inevitably and invariably go with his qualities, and upon them, probably, the efficiency of those qualities has depended.

He has made an enormous number of bitter enemies. Of a great majority of them the enmity is highly creditable to him, and the hatred of not a few others is due to misunderstanding of his purposes and methods. Mr. Comstock is not unreasonable or undiscriminating. At least he is far from as unreasonable and indiscriminating as his accusers say, and anybody who talks with him will soon learn that he, too, knows that a book or a picture is to be viewed, as to its "morality," not in the abstract and the absolute, but in relation to where it is and the use that is made of it.

In the minds of fair critics, the achievements of the vice hunter far outweigh his mistakes, and his retirement from any of his activities would be something of a public calamity, not a cause for exultation.

Source: *New York Times* 64, June 14, 1915, p. 960.

ANNOTATED RESEARCH GUIDE

Bennett, D.R.M. *Anthony Comstock: His Career of Cruelty and Crimes*. New York: DaCapo Press, 1971. One of Comstock's earliest targets was the radical freethinker D.R.M. Bennett who published an account of his ordeal in 1878, again available in this republished edition.

Besiel, Nicola. *Imperiled Innocents: Anthony Comstock and Family Reproduction in Victorian America*. Princeton, NJ: Princeton University Press, 1998. Documents the devastating effects of Comstock's and the law's treatment of contraception.

Broun, Heywood, and Margaret Leech. *Anthony Comstock: Roundsman of the Lord*. New York: A.C. Boni, 1927. Though dated, still one of the best accounts of Comstock's life and his enforcement of the law.

Chesler, Ellen. *Woman of Valor: Margaret Sanger and the Birth Control Movement in America*. New York: Simon & Schuster, 1992. Recounts Sanger's tireless struggle to promote birth control, despite the Comstock Law.

Gurstein, Rochelle. *The Repeal of Reticence: A History of America's Cultural and Legal Struggles over Free Speech, Obscenity, Sexual Liberation, and Modern Art*. New York: Hill and Wang, 1996. An analysis of the evolution of the tension between free speech and antiobscenity laws and the changing social mores regarding sexual expression.

Hopkins, Mary Alden. "Birth Control and Public Morals: An Interview with Anthony Comstock." *Harper's Weekly*, May 22, 1915, pp. 489–90. Reprinted in Sheila Suess Kennedy, ed. *Free Speech in America: A Documentary History*. Westport, CT: Greenwood Press, 1999, pp. 49–55. An exceptionally frank and revealing interview with Comstock.

Horowitz, Helen Lefkowitz. "Victoria Woodhull, Anthony Comstock, and Conflict over Sex in the United States in the 1870s." *Journal of American History* 87 (September 2000): 403–434. A detailed account of the impact of the Comstock Law (with interesting pictures).

Rabban, David M. *Free Speech in Its Forgotten Years*. New York: Cambridge University Press, 1997. Chapter 1 provides the context of the post–Civil War intellectual climate in which the Comstock Law was established and enforced. Rabban also describes and analyzes some of the more prominent applications of the law that stiffened reaction from free speech advocates and led to the formation of the Free Speech League.

Reagan, Leslie J. *When Abortion Was a Crime: Women, Medicine, and Law in the United States, 1867–1973*. Berkeley: University of California Press, 1997. Focuses on the evolution of abortion from the post–Civil War era through the Comstock era, and up to the Supreme Court's historic decision in *Roe v. Wade* (1973).

Reed, James. *From Private Vice to Public Virtue: The Birth Control Movement and American Society since 1830*. Rev. ed. Princeton, NJ: Princeton University Press, 1984. A comprehensive treatment of the abortion controversy in American history.

Video Resources

Before Griswold v. Connecticut: Birth Control and the Law—1962. CBS News, 1962. Hosted by Eric Sevareid, looks at the issue of birth control and how the Comstock Law restricted access to information about contraception. An old film, and in black and white, it nonetheless has a clip of Margaret Sanger discussing public policy issues. There is a short but interesting videorecording about birth control and women's rights that examines the most prominent pioneer of the movement.

Margaret Sanger: A Public Nuisance. Produced by the Margaret Sanger Film Project. New York: Women Make Movies, 1992.

Web Sites

http://sunsite.berkeley.edu/Goldman/Curricula/WomensRights/letter.html. Devoted to the papers of Emma Goldman, this page has links to many of her important statements.

http://www.positiveatheism.org/hist/goldmanmor.htm. This page includes an essay by Emma Goldman—"Victims of Morality"—with links to some of her other essays generally discussing freedom of speech issues in pre–World War I America.

6

World War I and Its Aftermath

When war broke out in Europe in 1914, President Woodrow Wilson earnestly urged Americans to be neutral in thought and deed, but in 1917 he reluctantly led the country into World War I. Wilson feared that participation in the war would unleash intolerance at home. He told a reporter in early 1917: "Once lead this people into war and they'll forget there ever was such a thing as tolerance. To fight you must be brutal and ruthless, and the spirit of ruthless brutality will enter into the very fibre of our national life, infecting Congress, the courts, the policeman on the beat, the man in the street."[1] His fears were justified. Zealously pursuing saboteurs, spies, and traitors, governmental officials and citizens rallied behind the banner of democracy and freedom but infringed on the civil liberties of thousands of others who legitimately disagreed with the war policy. The majority of the public supported the president's goal of uniting the country and silencing opposition, especially leftist opponents who looked to the courts for protection but to no avail. Congress and many states severely abridged free speech, and even the Supreme Court found almost none of this suppression inconsistent with the First Amendment.

Initially, most Americans opposed involvement in what they considered a "European" conflict that did not threaten the interests of their own country. Irish and German ethnic groups strongly opposed pro-British American foreign or defense policies. Almost a sixth of the national population at the time could claim Irish ancestry, and the Irish were not willing to sacrifice their lives in defense of Britain. On April 6,

1917, Congress declared war against the German Empire, and the United States entered the war on Britain's side. Wilson's patriotic "Americanism" reelection campaign in 1916, with its pro-peace slogan "He kept us out of war," was triumphant, but the road to another term in the White House was strewn with campaign messages impugning the loyalty and patriotism of segments of the population, particularly "German Americans," fueling an intensifying national distrust of "hyphenated" Americans. This was not confined to campaign tactics or rhetoric. Two years earlier Wilson had questioned the patriotism of Irish Americans as immigrants who "need[ed] hyphens in their names because only part of them has ever come over [from Ireland]."[2] He recognized that America's entry into Europe's war was inevitable but that war would galvanize the prejudices of a nation accustomed to intolerance of foreign ideas and evils.

President Wilson avoided President Lincoln's measures taken during the Civil War that—perhaps of necessity—had arbitrarily and unilaterally suspended civil rights. Instead, the Wilson administration called upon Congress to draft security measures to legitimize restraint on speech and restrictions on other civil rights, laws that would otherwise be unconstitutional during peacetime. Congress passed the Selective Service Act to assure the needed number of men in arms. It also enacted laws to create a comprehensive internal security system designed to keep dissidents and opponents in place—to prevent them, at the very least, from aiding the enemy and impeding the draft. By 1915 the Justice Department had already concluded that the government was insufficiently equipped to deal with seditious conduct and needed laws such as the controversial 1798 Sedition Act. Attorney General Thomas W. Gregory proposed strong security measures to combat insurgency by propaganda and sought authority to limit free speech and press. Wilson agreed but only if Congress authorized them.

The president had little talent for masquerading behind euphemisms. On Flag Day, June 14, 1917, in a speech about freedom, justice, and self-government, he paradoxically equated advocacy of peace or pacifism, once war had already been declared, with treason. He regularly asked Congress for power to control what he regarded as disloyal anarchists. Two months prior to the official declaration of war, Congress passed the "Threats against the President Act" on February 14, 1917, which made verbal or written threats a federal crime. By June 1918, sixty cases had been brought to trial under this law, with thirty-five convictions. In April 1917, a Proclamation regarding Alien Enemies and a Confidential Executive Order regarding Federal Employees took aim at immigrants and members of unpopular political parties, seen as threats to the United States.

The entire population felt the effects of the evolving governmental security system. On April 14, 1917, the administration created the Committee on Public Information (CPI) to censor newspapers, books, and films. George Creel, a former journalist from Denver, was placed in charge of the CPI and encouraged the mass media voluntarily to exercise self-censorship and restraint. Creel used the CPI mostly as a propaganda machine to combat German influence in the United States and to rally the public in support of the war effort. The CPI hired important journalists, artists, and professionals in propaganda campaigns to distribute "information" and to correct "misinformation." In its effort to increase morale, the CPI capitalized on a fermenting nationalism to feed the growing anti-German and antiradical frenzy, which created imaginary enemies and foes among foreigners and immigrants.

The Army Index was a list of over one hundred books judged to contain "dangerous thoughts." Banned from military bases were books about war that, if read, might induce young men to question their mission and make soldiers less effective fighters. The authors were typically of German nationality, socialists, pacifists, or members of some other unpopular group. Books such as H.G. Wells's *War in the Air* were also excluded from the New York Public Library and from classrooms. Publishers doing business in this atmosphere censored their products to avoid profit losses resulting from books unfit for export or shunned in the United States. Books accused of being German propaganda or simply pro German experienced the same fate as books describing the brutality of war. The CPI utilized the Army Index in its censorship strategy.

The CPI scrutinized not only newspapers, magazines, and books but also the fledgling yet already powerful medium of motion pictures. In *Mutual Film Corporation v. Ohio Industrial Commission* (1915) the Supreme Court had ruled that films were not protected forms of speech, and thus the government could censor them without legal restraint. Filmmakers seeking to export a movie from the United States needed a letter of approval from the CPI; films that realistically portrayed the gruesome horrors of war were unlikely to be approved. Guidelines prohibited films that misrepresented American ideals or its way of life, displayed derogatory images such as domestic mob or riot scenes, or conveyed other unpleasant impressions that might be used as enemy propaganda. The guidelines encouraged films with wholesome themes of a hearty and united America. Others, such as the *Spirit of '76* that negatively portrayed Great Britain, and *Birth of a Nation* that revealed troubled domestic race relations, were suppressed because they threatened to harm the war effort.

Under presidential proclamation issued on April 28, 1917, the military took control of cable and land telegraph lines. Newspapers were the most affected by this order because 75 percent of all wire transmissions were to newspapers or news associations. Official censors read the stories filed by correspondents and gave them instructions to confine all incoming and outgoing press messages to statements of facts. Opinions, speculations, commentary, or predictions about future events or public opinion were severely censored or suppressed. Transmissions also could be altered—without any notification to the author. Journalists recognized the futility of sending stories that portrayed the war as anything other than patriotic and victorious. War correspondents needed accreditation by the military and risked losing a $10,000 surety for breaking any censorship rules, including the vague regulation against submitting stories that would cause tension between the United States and its Allies or among the Allies themselves. Approximately forty foreign newspapers had correspondents working in the United States during the war, and their coverage of internal American labor disputes, union activity, and strikes was censored to avoid any "misrepresentation."

By the end of the war, the navy had either monitored, or closed down, every radio station in the United States, especially German-speaking radio stations. Officials examined the records of these stations in search of citizens suspected of allegedly using the radio to send coded messages to the enemy. Before the war ended, some 250,000 suspects had been listed. Once the navy gained control of the stations, no messages could be sent in code. Censorship of the telegraph and radio ended on June 18, 1919, one of the few measures of censorship that ceased after the armistice was signed.

On June 15, 1917, Congress enacted the Espionage Act to prevent or punish genuine acts of espionage, sabotage, and "speech" acts such as deliberate disclosure of military secrets—all crimes of treason. However, the legislation was enforced mostly to prevent and punish many other forms of expression intended to change the mind of the nation but perceived by the Wilson administration as obstructing the prosecution of the war. Section 3 of Title I of that statute was amended by the Sedition Act of 1918 to punish virtually any expression hostile to the government's war effort, with punishment of fines of up to $10,000 and twenty years in federal prison. The Justice Department prosecuted over 2,000 people and convicted more than 1,055, including 150 leaders of the International Workers of the World (IWW) and the prominent Socialist leader Eugene Debs, who was a candidate for president five times. Debs was convicted and sentenced to ten years under the Espionage Act for delivering an antiwar speech to an audience containing men eligible for military service (while in prison his name was on the 1920 presidential ballot for the Socialist Party, and he received some 900,000 votes). The U.S. Supreme Court reviewed his and other convictions on appeal in 1919, after the war. For the first time in the history of the Republic, the country's highest tribunal formally addressed the boundaries of the First Amendment guarantee of free speech—and upheld all convictions.

The most famous constitutional doctrine that sprouted from these cases was the "clear and present danger test," developed by the distinguished Justice Oliver Wendell Holmes who wrote a unanimous opinion for the Court in *Schenck v. United States*, decided on March 3, 1919. Charles T. Schenck was the general secretary of the Socialist Party and, like Debs, an outspoken opponent of the war. He produced a leaflet entitled "Assert Your Rights" and distributed some 15,000 copies to young men subject to the military draft. The leaflet equated conscription with slavery, prohibited by the Thirteenth Amendment to the Constitution, and thus urged potential draftees to assert their constitutional right to refuse to be drafted. He was indicted and convicted of multiple violations of the Espionage Act. Holmes's opinion for the Court stated that the First Amendment protects freedom of speech but not absolutely. If a speech creates a clear and present danger, it loses its constitutional immunity.

This test implicitly accepted the idea that the First Amendment protected seditious libel, thus going beyond the narrow, eighteenth-century Blackstonian notion that government was prohibited only from restraining speech in advance of publication but could punish criticism of government once made public. If no clear and present danger could be shown, the speech critical of government would be constitutionally protected. Another feature of this case, however, is perplexing: The Court did not examine or discuss any evidence that Schenck's antiwar expression actually had any of the consequences that the legislation sought to prevent—or, indeed, any consequences at all. Holmes merely acknowledged that the country was in a state of war when otherwise protected peacetime speech loses its immunity. For all one can discern from the Court, the young men who might have read the leaflet may have been more prone to beat up Schenck than follow his exhortation to flout the draft law.

Six months later the Supreme Court upheld the convictions of Jacob Abrams and other Russian Jewish immigrants who hurled from rooftops of lower Manhattan antiwar leaflets protesting U.S. military action. During the last months of the war, in the summer of 1918, the United States and some of its Allies had invaded parts of what became the Soviet Union. Printed in both Yiddish and English, the leaflets included a call for "workers of the world" to participate in a general strike to prevent further military intervention into the Soviet Union and bitterly criticized Wilson as a coward. Abrams and three other defendants were found guilty of violating the Sedition Act of 1918, under which even general criticism of the United States (for example, its flag, institutions, Constitution) during wartime could bring severe punishments. Three of the four defendants, including Abrams, received the maximum prison sentence of twenty years in prison and fines of $4,000. When the case reached the Supreme Court, a 7–2 majority, following *Schenck*, had no trouble presuming a clear and present danger and affirmed the convictions. Justice Holmes—and Justice Louis D. Brandeis, who had endorsed the test and the earlier convictions of Schenck and others—now *dissented* and refashioned the clear and present danger test to protect, not suppress and punish, political speech. Holmes did not question the Sedition Act, but he insisted that without adducing some evidence that sufficiently dangerous results were imminent, the government could not convict and sentence Abrams and others to twenty years solely on the basis of the leaflets they had distributed.

Many cases involving the Espionage and Sedition Acts came to trial, not because the Justice Department prosecuted but because Postmaster General Albert Burleson excluded from the mail materials that he regarded as harmful and thus illegal. The Sedition Act was designed to thwart interference with enlistment, support for Germany and its allies, and disrespect of the American war effort, its leaders, or symbols. Its general language, however, covered many other activities, furnishing the postmaster general with roving authority to censor the mails. Burleson's policies targeted left-wing, radical, pacifist, socialist, anarchist, and all other groups that did not support the war effort. By denying second-class mailing privileges to twenty-two socialist newspapers, he nearly destroyed the left-wing press in the United States. In *United States ex rel. Milwaukee Social Democrat Publishing Co. v. Burleson* (1921), the Supreme Court upheld Burleson's authority to deny mailing privileges apparently without much more evidence than the critical leftist or socialist content of the papers.

The Trading with the Enemy Act added to the postmaster's arsenal, augmenting what seemed to be already unbridled discretion. The act authorized the government during wartime to make rules and regulations to censor communications by mail, cable, radio, or other means of transmission between the United States and any foreign country. Under this law, the administration required all foreign-language publications to submit an exact translation in English of articles to be mailed, which, of course, delayed publications and thereby encouraged papers to support the government or cease circulation for the duration of the war. The Yiddish *Daily Forward* acknowledged that in order to keep its mailing privileges it would no longer publish commentary on the war and would cease all criticism of American Allies.

Although the Post Office exercised severe control over the mails, its enforcement did not become reckless. This could not be said of the Justice Department. U.S. attorneys in the many different federal districts across the United States varied greatly in enforcement and prosecutions under the Espionage and Sedition Acts. The Justice Department's data disclose greater arbitrary and unnecessary enforcement than that seen in the Post

Office Department. One explanation is that federal attorneys were granted the same prosecutorial discretion in espionage cases as in all other criminal cases. Their only apparent restriction was that appropriate care should be exercised to avoid unjustified arrests and prosecutions, at least until October 28, 1918, when they now needed permission from Washington to indict espionage suspects. Another reason for arbitrary and abusive enforcement was that the Justice Department delegated some responsibility to the American Protective League (APL), a group of approximately 200,000 affluent citizens who voluntarily policed the country in search of sedition until it was disbanded after the armistice. The APL often abused its authority by making illegal arrests, using confidential records, impersonating officers, and waging dangerous propaganda campaigns against foreigners and other suspects in the United States. The Justice Department and the APL raided the offices of the National Civil Liberties Bureau (the forerunner of the American Civil Liberties Union) and harassed leaders and members of IWW without authority from the attorney general.

State and local governments also restricted civil liberties. Seven states and Alaska passed statutes limiting constitutional rights even before Congress began to act. Vermont enacted an antisabotage bill one day after Congress had declared war. Massachusetts gave its governor sweeping authority, including the right to seize private property for public use, and even instituted by law the correct way to sing the national anthem. In Pennsylvania, the Reverend William A. Prasser was arrested for praying that his parishioners, were they to be drafted, would find the solemnity to resist. States began deleting German-language programs from the public school curricula, and some cities and towns, like Menard, Texas, prohibited German from being spoken in public or private for the duration of the war. Twenty-two states banned foreign-language programs in public schools. A Nebraska law prohibited them so "that the sunshine of American ideals will permeate the life of the future citizens of this republic."[3] Colleges and universities also felt suppression of free speech and academic freedom. German programs were phased out as attendance declined and because Safety Committees investigated professors who opposed the war effort. Not unexpectedly, reactions of patriotic mobs were reported, and tar and feathering as well as horsewhipping were not uncommon retorts to individuals who denounced the war.

Following the war, Attorney General Gregory asked President Wilson to commute over 100 sentences because of undoubted injustices by jurors carried away by heated patriotism and aroused emotions. Some jurors returned guilty verdicts to display their own loyalty. Although 116 sentences were eventually commuted, more than 800 people remained in prison even after the war ended for violating wartime prohibitions. Of the 6,000 aliens who had been detained or arrested, some 2,000 were interned for potentially posing a threat to internal security, and over a hundred publications had been banned by the Post Office.

When the war ended and the armistice was signed, the repression of dissident expression did not cease. President Wilson refused to end the security legislation while he remained in office, and he retained the war powers delegated to him by Congress. After the bloody Russian Revolution, thousands of Communists, Socialists, and anarchists residing in the United States seemingly posed enough dangers that postwar Washington officials (as well as state and local governments) reacted. In 1919 Wilson appointed A. Mitchell Palmer as attorney general of the United States to replace Gregory, who had returned to private practice. Palmer was a progressive Democrat, but like many others he was profoundly affected by the turbulent events of the war era, and he suspected that Communist Party agents were plotting to reproduce in the United States what had happened in Russia.

There were frightening episodes of sabotage and other illegal conduct to deepen Palmer's fears—such as bomb explosions in Washington, D.C., one partially damaging Palmer's own residence. Authorities discovered dozens of other bombs sent to prominent public officials. With genuine reason to be alert and quick to respond, the government overreacted. Palmer instituted the Central Intelligence Division within the Justice Department, which maintained files on potentially disloyal aliens and also planned a strategy to rid the country of danger by rounding up and deporting all radicals, anarchists, and Communist Party members. The young J. Edgar Hoover headed this new division from which he built one of Washington's most feared positions of power—director of the Federal Bureau of Investigation (FBI)—and headed for half a century.

Two massive raids occurred, one in November 1919, when the government arrested thousands of suspected Communist sympathizers. In December 1919, federal agents seized 249 resident aliens and sent them to the Soviet Union by ship, an old army steamer renamed the *Buford*. In January 1920, several thousand more suspects, many of them IWW members, were apprehended and detained. Some were held for lengthy periods without trial and eventually released; many others were deported. The renowned Emma Goldman was among those deported. Later that year Palmer warned of a Communist Party revolution and predicted its occurrence on "May Day" (May 1). Panic and hysteria afflicted a nation already drained by the war. When the "revolution" never happened, the embarrassed Palmer watched his reputation collapse.

The infamous Palmer raids netted 6,000 arrests that were just part of the Red Scare that swept the country in 1919 and 1920. He and most of his subordinates too readily believed (or exploited) the wishful thinking expressed in the propaganda of domestic Communists. The Justice Department claimed that some 300,000 "Reds" were at large, armed, and ready to move. History shows that in 1920 fewer than 2,000 people were still members of the Communist Party. A governmental report prepared by Assistant Secretary of Labor Louis Post acknowledged that the arrest of some 5,000 dangerous radicals produced only three handguns discovered among their belongings. Post also reviewed 1,600 deportation warrants and canceled more than 1,100 for lack of evidence.

Some three dozen states also had laws against seditious statements and some even against displaying red flags—the symbol of the Russian Revolution. On the eve of Palmer's predicted revolution that never occurred, the New York state legislature expelled several duly elected Socialists because their ideas were thought inimical to the values of New York and the United States. Proponents of socialism were convicted and jailed in various states for speeches and pamphlets advocating the overthrow of the government, capitalism, and the constitutional system. The outstanding example was Benjamin Gitlow who had published his "Left Wing Manifesto."

Gitlow was convicted for violating New York's 1902 law (passed after President William McKinley's assassination in 1901), making it a felony to advocate the view that organized government should be overthrown by force. The First Amendment, directed at Congress, had never before been held applicable against the states. In *Gitlow v. New York* (1925) the Court grudgingly conceded that the federal Constitution established a threshold for freedom of speech that the states were required to meet. This was a watershed for free speech rights, as states were henceforth subject to some federal constitutional constraints. However, a giant step backward followed in the Court's measure of permissible speech. Justice Edward T. Sanford, who wrote the Court's opinion, did not invoke the clear and present danger test, not even the weak and ineffectual version from *Schenck*. Instead, the seven-member majority concluded that since New York had undoubted power to prevent the *act* of overthrowing of the government, it had the authority as well to punish any speech or expression that *advocates* such action—regardless of whether the advocacy had any chance of succeeding. "The State cannot reasonably be required to measure the danger from every such utterance in the nice balance of a jeweler's scale. . . . [I]t may, in the exercise of its judgment, suppress the threatened danger in its incipiency."[4] The Court was merely asking whether it was rational for a state to conclude that certain kinds of expression might have a tendency to produce undesirable consequences. This became known as the "bad tendency" test, the use of which virtually assures that expression unpleasant or offensive will be punished. Justice Holmes dissented, together with Justice Brandeis, and penned one of his briefest but most poignant opinions attacking the Court for its refusal to give freedom of speech the breadth of protection it deserves and needs in a free society.

Alexander Hamilton wrote in *The Federalist Papers* in 1787: "Whatever fine declarations may be inserted in any constitution respecting [freedom of the press] must altogether depend on public opinion, and on the general spirit of the people and of the government."[5] The real danger was what Wilson had forecast: the "spirit of ruthless brutality" and intolerance that swept across America in a very difficult period in its history. During and after World War I freedom of expression, especially the right to dissent, was severely repressed and endured its greatest challenge since the ratification of the First Amendment. In 1920 the American Civil Liberties Union was established to protect constitutional rights through education and lobbying and especially through legal representation in court. In the 1930s and 1940s, freedom of expression enjoyed far more protection in the courts than ever before, but other events would soon test the strength of free speech in America.

NOTES

1. As quoted in Arthur S. Link, *Woodrow Wilson and the Progressive Era* (New York: Harper Torchbooks, 1963), p. 277.

2. As quoted in Margaret A. Blanchard, *Revolutionary Sparks: Freedom of Expression in Modern America* (New York: Oxford University Press, 1992), p. 74.

3. Quoted in the brief filed by the state of Nebraska before the Supreme Court in *Meyer v. Nebraska*, 262 U.S. 390, 394 (1923). A 7–2 majority of justices invalidated the state's law, not on First Amendment grounds but as a violation of the "liberty . . . without due process" clause of the Fourteenth Amendment.

4. *Gitlow v. New York*, 268 U.S. 652, 669 (1925).

5. Alexander Hamilton, James Madison, and John Jay, *The Federalist Papers*, ed. Roy P. Fairfield, 2nd ed. (Garden City, NY: Anchor Books, 1966), pp. 263–264.

DOCUMENTS

6.1.   Censorship and Publicity

Soon after Congress declared war, and before harsher censorship measures were put in place, the Wilson administration established the Committee on Public Information to help manage the flow and substance of information available to the public. George Creel was appointed to chair this committee. The following editorial questioned the utility and appropriateness of the CPI—as well as the qualifications of its chairman.

While there is as yet no press censorship law, and the Espionage bill so drawn as surreptitiously to create a press censorship, has not yet reached a vote, while, indeed, the only existing authority on the subject is the mandate of the Constitution directing the Congress to pass no law abridging the freedom of the press, three members of the Cabinet have addressed to the President a communication recommending the creation of a Committee on Public Information, combining the two functions of "censorship and publicity"; and the President has appointed the committee, including the three Cabinet officers and a civilian Chairman, Mr. George Creel.

Mr. Creel may have been unjustly criticised in Denver, but we are unable to discover in his turbulent career as a municipal officer there, or in his qualities as a writer, or in his services to the Woman Suffrage Party in New York, any evidence of the ability, the experience, or the judicial temperament required "to gain the understanding and cooperation of the press," as the three Cabinet officers put it. That he is qualified for any position of authority over the press is made further doubtful by his publicly expressed hostility toward certain newspapers.

As to "rallying the authors of the country," the other function assigned to Mr. Creel, these estimable and gifted ladies and gentlemen can doubtless be made useful in various ways, but essential to the information of the public during the war will be not pleasing fictions prepared by imaginative writers but facts, even painful facts, accurately described by conscientious and competent reporters.

Source: *New York Times*, April 16, 1917, p. 12.

6.2.   Disloyalty of the German-American Press

German-language newspapers operated especially in the Mid-west, and most of them opposed America's entry into the war on the side of Germany's enemies. A month after Congress had passed the Espionage Act, the Atlantic Monthly *magazine published an essay by Frank Perry Olds accusing virtually all German-language newspapers in the United States of disloyalty, if not outright treason. Olds ended his piece asking what should be done; the editors' response to this question appears at the end, in brackets.*

Newspapers printed in this country in the German language have said that they are loyal to the United States. Other editors have read their statements and believed them. Americans in general have been led to suppose that our pro-German press, once so emphatic in defense of Germany, is now supporting the United States in the prosecution of its war against the German Empire. But nothing could be further from the truth. The pro-German press of the country has merely revised its propaganda to fit its present needs.

Carefully avoiding anything which would lay them open to the charge of treason according to the letter of the law, German-American newspapers are daily violating its spirit by spreading a fabric of anti-government lies, anti-Ally calumnies, and anti-war agitations. It is their aim to bring defeat to the cause we have espoused by discrediting our motives, by preventing assistance to the Allies, and by causing discontent and opposition in our own country. Confidently expecting a German victory, they wish to hasten that desirable event by withholding our weight from the Allied offense. . . .

Since the beginning of the world-war, the German press of the United States has consistently praised and defended every move of the Imperial German government. Every step of the American government in maintenance of its neutrality which did not redound to the credit and advantage of Germany, every step in resistance to German aggression, has been condemned. German-American newspapers went into paroxysms of joy over the sinking of the Lusitania, and their sharpest criticism of the Zimmermann note to Mexico was that it was "unwise." They deemed our neutrality "scurvy" and "one-sided." The German Emperor has been praised by them as mild, God-fearing, and faithful to the interests of his people; the President of the United States has been characterized as hypocritical, selfish, and unworthy of his high office. Count Zeppelin's services have been exaggerated; Admiral Dewey's services, in view of his defiance of Germany, have been minimized. Von Berstorff has been called a true diplomat; Ambassador Gerard has been referred to as a "thing calling itself a diplomat." Before we entered the war, the German-American press existed, apparently, for the glorification of Germany and abuse of the United States. Then our war came.

When the President's message sounded through the halls of Congress, there were some men among us sanguine enough to hope for a complete change of heart in the German-American editorial bosom. Though we knew that German-Americans had steadfastly opposed a war between Germany and America, we thought that the actuality might convert them to a semblance of Americanism. It did not, but it made them more circumspect. They began to realize that opinions would no longer be viewed as "pro-German" or "un-American," but would be labeled "patriotic" or "treasonable." For obvious reasons, their first "patriotic" effusions were of undivided loyalty to the United States. Under cloak of that loyalty, they launched their new propaganda.

Long before the sixth day of April, 1917, the German-American press had characterized our national leaders as dishonest and unfair. The foundations were all laid when war came, and it was necessary only to continue along the old lines to undermine, so far as possible, the faith of German-American readers in the justice of the American cause, to discount our declared principles, and to represent as tawdry and ignoble our real motives. But, first of all, Germany must be freed from all blame. "Germany did everything in her power to adjust herself to our one-sided neutrality," said the Cincinnati *Volksblatt*; and concluded by throwing the whole blame for the war on the President.

With never a word to show that we might be right, the hyphenated press devoted all its energies to showing that we must be wrong. "World-history is a world-court," said the Baltimore *Deutsche Correspondent*. "Its iron stylus will engrave the facts and make it difficult for America's present generation to stand with honor before coming generations." . . .

. . . The cumulative effect of such propaganda can hardly be over-estimated. If it is also remembered that the dozen largest papers are read by more than a million people, it will be seen that we have here a force worthy of notice—a force that congratulates La Follette and his like for their "courage," and denounces anti-governmental agitations in Germany as conspiracies.

Not one of these papers has expressed an iota of sympathy with the purposes announced by the President as those for which we are fighting. Before the declaration of war they supported every aim of the most extreme chauvinists in Germany, and by no word has any German-

American paper indicated a change of belief. As the Milwaukee *Germania* says,—

> Our friends know what we think and feel. This paper has coura-
> geously and consistently expressed its conviction in this matter. The
> fact that war has now been declared through the expediency of
> recognizing the existence of a state of war does not at all change
> our opinion and our convictions. But it forces us to keep silent from
> now on.

They do not dare to-day to attack directly the declared purpose of the United States, but they still can and do attack every statement of the purposes of our allies, which are now in their main outline those of the United States.

Their campaign of racial division has continued unabated. In every line is apparent the attempt to make the American citizen of German birth or descent feel that he is a man apart from the common herd of Americans: that he is of better stuff; that his ideals are different; that he is a much higher creation than the ordinary dollar-chaser of Dollarika . . .

At least one million men, women, and children living in the United States are being misinformed and misguided. Many of them are, no doubt, being converted to the propagandist's ways of thinking. The Con-stitution allows free speech. The Constitution does not allow comfort to the enemy. The case of the German-American press is between the two. What are we going to do about it? What can we do about it?

[There are several things we can about it, and it seems well to consider them.

By temper and tradition, the people of the United States are easy-going and tolerant. We believe in that temper and we respect that tradition. And, likewise, we believe in and respect the great body of American citizens of German inheritance. But, in the matter before us, we confront a situation where tolerance is defeating its own ends. Here in America we bear with the publication of newspapers in the enemy language, though in Europe such forbearance is unknown and almost inconceiva-ble. But now, these papers, unmindful of their privilege, trade upon our patience. As Mr. Olds shows, the bulk of the German-American press within this country consists frankly of enemy papers. Enemy papers, printed in the enemy language, protected by our laws and admitted to the privileges of the mails! That is coddling sedition with a vengeance.

The remedy is a sane war-time censorship upon enemy propaganda, and a substantial war-time tax on the printed use of the enemy language. Statements which would not be tolerated in American newspapers must not find immunity in the thin disguise of German type, and the publi-cation of newspapers in the German language is a privilege which should be paid for. We have singled out the German press as the subject for Mr. Olds's article and for these remarks, because here, as in Europe, it is German thinking which is the chief offender, and fortunately because it is with Germany alone that we are at war. —THE EDITORS.]

Source: Atlantic Monthly 120 (July 1917): 136–140.

6.3.   Senator LaFollete Defends Dissent

Best known in history as the independent Progressive Party candidate for president in 1924, who received almost 17 percent of the popular vote, Robert M. LaFollete was a Republican senator from Wisconsin and one of only six senators to vote against the declaration of war. An effort was made to expel him from the Senate. Reacting to the nearly hysterical and intense persecution and prosecution of persons suspected of disloyalty, he spoke on the floor of the U.S. Senate on October 6, 1917, six months after the government had formally declared war.

Six Members of the Senate and fifty Members of the House voted against the declaration of war. Immediately there was let loose upon those Senators and Representatives a flood of invective and abuse from newspapers and individuals who had been clamoring for war, unequaled, I believe, in the history of civilized society.

Prior to the declaration of war every man who had ventured to oppose our entrance into it had been condemned as a coward or worse, and even the President had by no means been immune from these attacks.

Since the declaration of war the triumphant war press has pursued those Senators and Representatives who voted against war with malicious falsehood and recklessly libelous attacks, going to the extreme limit of charging them with treason against their country.

This campaign of libel and character assassination directed against the Members of Congress who opposed our entrance into the war has been continued down to the present hour, and I have upon my desk newspaper clippings, some of them libels upon me alone, some directed as well against other Senators who voted in opposition to the declaration of war. One of these newspaper reports most widely circulated represents a Federal judge [Waller T. Burns] in the state of Texas as saying, in a charge to a grand jury . . . :

If I had a wish, I would wish that you men had jurisdiction to return bills of indictment against these men. They ought to be tried

promptly and fairly, and I believe this court could administer the
law fairly; but I have a conviction, as strong as life, that this country
should stand them up against an adobe wall tomorrow and give
them what they deserve. If any man deserves death, it is a traitor.
I wish I could pay for the ammunition. I would like to attend the
execution, and if I were in the firing squad I would not want to be
the marksman who had the blank shell.

... It is not alone Members of Congress that the war party in this
country has sought to intimidate. The mandate seems to have gone forth
to the sovereign people of this country that they must be silent while
those things are being done by their Government which most vitally
concern their well-being, their happiness, and their lives. Today and for
weeks past honest and law-abiding citizens of this country are being
terrorized and outraged in their rights by those sworn to uphold the
laws and protect the rights of the people. I have in my possession numerous affidavits establishing the fact that people are being unlawfully
arrested, thrown into jail, held incommunicado for days, only to be eventually discharged without ever having been taken into court, because
they have committed no crime. Private residences are being invaded,
loyal citizens of undoubted integrity and probity arrested, cross-
examined, and the most sacred constitutional rights guaranteed to every
American citizen are being violated.

It appears to be the purpose of those conducting this campaign to
throw the country into a state of terror, to coerce public opinion, to stifle
criticism, and suppress discussion of the great issues involved in this
war.

I think all men recognize that in time of war the citizen must surrender
some rights for the common good which he is entitled to enjoy in time
of peace. *But, sir, the right to control their own Government according to
constitutional forms is not one of the rights that the citizens of this country are
called upon to surrender in time of war....*

More than all, the citizen and his representative in Congress in time
of war must maintain his right of free speech. More than in times of
peace it is necessary that the channels for free public discussion of governmental policies shall be open and unclogged. I believe ... that I am
now touching upon the most important question in this country today—
and that is the right of the citizens of this country and their representatives in Congress to discuss in an orderly way frankly and publicly
and without fear, from the platform and through the press, every important phase of this war; its causes, and manner in which it should be
conducted, and the terms upon which peace should be made. The belief
which is becoming widespread in this land that this most fundamental
right is being denied to the citizens of this country is a fact, the tremen-

dous significance of which those in authority have not yet begun to appreciate. . . .

Suppose success attends the attempt to stifle all discussion of the issues of this war, all discussions of the terms upon which it should be concluded, all discussion of the objects and purposes to be accomplished by it, and concede the demand of the war-mad press and war extremists that they monopolize the right of public utterance upon these questions unchallenged, what think you would be the consequences to this country not only during the war but after the war?

. . . [O]ur Government, above all others, is founded on the right of the people freely to discuss all matters pertaining to their Government, in war not less than in peace. It is true, sir, that Members of the House of Representatives are elected for two years, the President for four years, and the Members of the Senate for six years, and during their temporary official terms these officers constitute what is called the Government. But back of them always is the controlling sovereign power of the people, and when the people can make their will known, the faithful officer will obey that will. Though the right of the people to express their will by ballot is suspended during the term of office of the elected official, nevertheless the duty of the official to obey the popular will continue throughout his entire term of office. How can that popular will express itself between elections except by meetings, by speeches, by publications, by petitions, and by addresses to the representatives of the people? Any man who seeks to set a limit upon those rights, whether in war or peace, aims a blow at the most vital part of our Government. And then as the time for election approaches and the official is called to account for his stewardship—not a day, not a week, not a month, before the election, but a year or more before it, if the people choose—they must have the right to the freest possible discussion of every question upon which their representative has acted, of the merits of every measure he has supported or opposed, of every vote he has cast and every speech that he has made. And before this great fundamental right every other must, if necessary, give way, for in no other manner can representative government be preserved.

Source: *Congressional Record*, 65th Cong., 1st sess., October 6, 1917, 55, pt. 8: 7878–7888.

6.4.   The Sedition Act of 1918

Not since the Sedition Act of 1798 expired in March 1801 had the U.S. government maintained a law on the books punishing speech critical of the government. In May 1918, more than a year into World War I, Congress amended the Espionage Act to punish wartime seditious expression. Unlike the statute of 1798, which at least allowed truth as a defense, the act of 1918 tolerated no dissent, at least in wartime. In March 1921, the law was repealed.

[W]hoever, when the United States is at war, shall willfully utter, print, write, or publish any disloyal, profane, scurrilous, or abusive language about the form of government of the United States, or the Constitution . . . or the military or naval forces . . . or the flag of the United States, or the uniform of the Army or Navy . . . or any language intended to bring the form of government of the United States . . . [or the Constitution, the military, the flag, or the uniform of the Army or Navy] . . . into contempt, scorn, contumely, or disrepute, or shall willfully utter, print, write, or publish any language intended to incite, provoke, or encourage resistance to the United States, or to promote the cause of its enemies, or shall willfully display the flag of any foreign enemy, or shall willfully by utterance, writing, printing, publication, or language spoken, urge, incite, or advocate any curtailment of production in this country of any thing or things, product or products, necessary or essential to the prosecution of the war . . . and whoever shall willfully advocate, teach, defend, or suggest the doing of any of the acts or things in this section enumerated, and whoever shall by word or act support or favor the cause of any country with which the United States is at war or by word or act oppose the cause of the United States therein, shall be punished by a fine of not more than $10,000 or imprisonment for not more than twenty years, or both.

Source: Statutes at Large 40 (1918): 553–554.

6.5.   Justice Holmes and the "Marketplace of Ideas"

Jacob Abrams and three other Russian Jewish immigrants circulated leaflets critical of the American military invasion of Russia in the closing months of the war. The Supreme Court upheld their convictions under the Sedition Act of 1918, but Justice Holmes, joined by Justice Brandeis, dissented in an opinion that gave far more protection to speech than his majority opinion in the Schenck *case, just six months earlier. It became a monument in the evolution of First Amendment jurisprudence.*

[T]he United States constitutionally may punish speech that produces or is intended to produce a clear and imminent danger that it will bring about forthwith certain substantive evils that the United States constitutionally may seek to prevent. The power undoubtedly is greater in time of war than in time of peace, because war opens dangers that do not exist at other times.

But . . . Congress certainly cannot forbid all effort to change the mind of the country. [N]obody can suppose that the surreptitious publishing of a silly leaflet by an unknown man, without more, would present any immediate danger that its opinions would hinder the success of the government arms or have any appreciable tendency to do so. . . .

In this case, sentences of twenty years' imprisonment have been imposed for the publishing of two leaflets that I believe the defendants had as much right to publish as the Government has to publish the Constitution of the United States now vainly invoked by them. Even if I am technically wrong, and enough can be squeezed from these poor and puny anonymities to turn the color of legal litmus paper, I will add, even if what I think the necessary intent were shown, the most nominal punishment seems to me all that possibly could be inflicted, unless the defendants are to be made to suffer not for what the indictment alleges, but for the creed that they avow—a creed that I believe to be the creed of ignorance and immaturity when honestly held, as I see no reason to doubt that it was held here, but which, although made the subject of examination at the trial, no one has a right even to consider in dealing with the charges before the Court.

Persecution for the expression of opinions seems to me perfectly logical. If you have no doubt of your premises or your power, and want a certain result with all your heart, you naturally express your wishes in law, and sweep away all opposition. To allow opposition by speech seems to indicate that you think the speech impotent, as when a man says that he has squared the circle, or that you do not care wholeheartedly for the result, or that you doubt either your power or your premises. But when men have realized that time has upset many fighting faiths, they may come to believe even more than they believe the very foundations of their own conduct that the ultimate good desired is better reached by free trade in ideas—that the best test of truth is the power of the thought to get itself accepted in the competition of the market, and that truth is the only ground upon which their wishes safely can be carried out. That, at any rate, is the theory of our Constitution. It is an experiment, as all life is an experiment. Every year, if not every day, we have to wager our salvation upon some prophecy based upon imperfect knowledge. While that experiment is part of our system, I think that we should be eternally vigilant against attempts to check the expression of opinions that we loathe and believe to be fraught with death, unless they so imminently threaten immediate interference with the lawful and pressing purposes of the law that an immediate check is required to save the country. I wholly disagree with the argument of the Government that the First Amendment left the common law as to seditious libel in force. History seems to me against the notion. I had conceived that the United States, through many years, had shown its repentance for the Sedition Act of 1798, by repaying fines that it imposed. Only the emergency that makes it immediately dangerous to leave the correction of evil counsels to time warrants making any exception to the sweeping command, "Congress shall make no law . . . abridging the freedom of speech." Of course, I am speaking only of expressions of opinion and exhortations, which were all that were uttered here, but I regret that I cannot put into more impressive words my belief that, in their conviction upon this indictment, the defendants were deprived of their rights under the Constitution of the United States.

Source: Abrams v. United States, 250 U.S. 616, 624–631 (dissenting opinion) (November 10, 1919).

6.6.   Why Is Mr. Roosevelt Unjailed?

Given the severe enforcement of the Espionage and Sedition Acts of 1917 and 1918, a fairly liberal weekly magazine asked why the enforcement of such laws was so selective. Former president Theodore Roosevelt had unsuccessfully campaigned for president when Wilson won the office in 1912. His later criticism of Wilson regarding the war was vehement enough that had the speaker been foreign or a descendant of immigrants, he or she, according to the editorial below, would have been prosecuted and jailed.

WE ask our readers what would happen if an humble citizen of the United States were to attract a crowd on the street corner and then denounce President Wilson thus: "There is not the slightest suggestion that he disapproves of disloyalty to the nation"; the resolute and straightforward soul of the American people "is being thwarted by "the obscure purposes and wavering will of Wilson," who fortunately has "stultified his own diplomacy and repudiated his own implied offer to Germany." Suppose that he should go even further and assure the crowd that in the cloak rooms of Congress it is a bitter jest to speak of the President thus: "Here's to our Czar, last in war, first toward peace, long may he waver." Suppose he should then proceed to say in connection with Mr. Wilson:

"For the very reason that I abhor Germany's trickery, treachery, and bad faith, I am most anxious that Americans shall not imitate her in these matters," and should finally assail the President thus, only slightly masking the attack: "... Men of cold heart, who do not fight themselves, whose nearest kin are not in danger, who prepared for war not at all, who helped wage the war feebly, and who are content with a craven peace." Can any one doubt that if a soapbox orator were to use these words of Mr. Roosevelt he would be given twenty years in jail for "interfering with the draft" under 'our all-embracing' Espionage Act? Yet Mr. Roosevelt is reported to have used these words in public the other day and was unmolested by any Federal agent.

Let us see how his case contrasts with some that are on record. For instance, an Indiana citizen was locked up for a month by a United States marshal for "uttering disparaging remarks about President Wilson," and then released without trial or compensation. One Oliver Smith of Faribault, Minnesota, was promptly indicted for saying that there would have been "no reason for the United States to enter the war if President Wilson had listened to the advice of La Follette and Bryan and kept Americans out of the war zone." It is surely not so reprehensible to say that "the United States might as well be under the Kaiser's government as our own" as for one of Theodore Roosevelt's influence to call the President a Czar and charge him with making a craven peace; but for the former remark Frank J. Busch was fined $500, compelled to buy a thousand dollars worth of Liberty bonds and give $100 to the Red Cross. For criticising the President's conduct of the war much more mildly than did Mr. Roosevelt, L.L. Miller of Ashland, Ohio, was promptly indicted and punished, his chief offence being that he "criticised the President for appointing his son-in-law to more offices than any one man was capable of filling."

We could fill pages of the *Nation* with similar cases; there is just one other we would cite. It is the case of Assemblyman Shiplacoff, now under indictment for "uttering disloyal, scurrilous, and abusive language about the military and naval forces," in saying that the people of Russia have much more right to feel bitterly against the American troops invading Russia than the Americans did against the Hessians in 1777. This constitutes three separate offences in the eyes of a vigilant district attorney; but it is no crime in Mr. Caffey's eyes for Theodore Roosevelt to charge the Commander-in-Chief of the Army and Navy of the United States with deliberately selling out his country's cause, with being guilty of "trickery and treachery and bad faith." What could be more monstrously unjust or more certain to bring the administration of justice into contempt than this discrimination? The truth is that Assemblyman is indicted because he is a Socialist and inconspicuous. Mr. Roosevelt goes scot free because he is a national figure.

Now our readers must not misunderstand us. We do not think that Mr. Roosevelt ought to be arrested and indicted. Far from it. We have said before this that he has rendered a public service in speaking out freely. Not that we like his manners or his language, or his reckless use of epithets; when he is excited he is hardly a gentleman. But it is largely to Mr. Roosevelt that we owe our ability to discuss peace terms and to criticise at all. The only point we make is that the administration of justice is grossly unfair when Mr. Roosevelt can escape while lesser offenders are sentenced so severely. The same unfairness has been true of the Post-Office Department censorship. It has too often laid hands upon the insignificant, the weak, and those unable to defend themselves, and permitted the New York *Tribune* to say things for which most radical papers would be barred; it does not dare touch the saucy Colonel Harvey who abuses the Government from one end of his *War Weekly* to the other. It is precisely this discrimination that is arousing deep feelings of distrust and anger in the country. Mr. Roosevelt's bad taste, his unfair abuse of a President who stands head and shoulders above him morally and mentally, will react upon himself. What we are concerned with is the effect upon the country of two kinds of justice. We ask the Attorney General, Mr. Gregory, to tell us why Mr. Roosevelt is unjailed.

Source: *The Nation* 107 (November 1918): 546.

6.7.   The Case against the Reds

> As Attorney General Palmer's 1920 dragnet raids and deportations of dangerous and all "Reds" became more widespread, criticism increased. He defended the Justice Department's actions in a statement recounting the nature and urgency of the Red menace facing the country.

In this brief review of the work which the Department of Justice has undertaken, to tear out the radical seeds that have entangled American ideas in their poisonous theories, I desire not merely to explain what the real menace of communism is, but also to tell how we have been compelled to clean up the country almost unaided by any virile legislation. . . . The time came when it was obviously hopeless to expect the hearty cooperation of Congress in the only way to stamp out these seditious societies in their open defiance of law by various forms of propaganda.

Like a prairie-fire, the blaze of revolution was sweeping over every American institution of law and order a year ago. It was eating its way into the homes of the American workmen, its sharp tongues of revolutionary heat were licking the altars of the churches, leaping into the belfry of the school bell, crawling into the sacred corners of American homes, seeking to replace marriage vows with libertine laws, burning up the foundations of society.

[Because] "Reds" were criminal aliens and secondly that the American Government must prevent crime, it was decided that there could be no nice distinctions drawn between the theoretical ideals of the radicals and their actual violations of our national laws. An assassin may have brilliant intellectuality, he may be able to excuse his murder or robbery with fine oratory, but any theory which excuses crime is not wanted in America. . . .

The Government was in jeopardy; our private information of what was being done by the organization known as the Communist Party of America, with headquarters in Chicago, of what was being done by the Communist Internationale under their manifesto planned at Moscow last March by Trotzky, Lenin and others addressed "To the Proletariats of All Countries," of what strides the Communist Labor Party was making, removed all doubt. In this conclusion we did not ignore the definite standards of personal liberty, of free speech, which is the very temperament and heart of the people. The evidence was examined with the utmost care, with a personal leaning toward freedom of thought and word on all questions. . . .

My information showed that communism in this country was an organization of thousands of aliens who were direct allies of Trotzky. Aliens of the same misshapen caste of mind and indecencies of character, and it showed that they were making the same glittering promises of lawlessness, of criminal autocracy to Americans, that they had made to the Russian peasants. How the Department of Justice discovered upwards of 60,000 of these organized agitators of the Trotzky doctrine in the United States is the confidential information upon which the Government is now sweeping the nation clean of such alien filth. . . .

Behind, and underneath, my own determination to drive from our midst the agents of Bolshevism with increasing vigor and with greater speed, until there are no more of them left among us, so long as I have the responsible duty of that task, I have discovered the hysterical methods of these revolutionary humans with increasing amazement and suspicion. . . . I have been asked . . . to what extent deportation will check radicalism in this country. Why not ask what will become of the United States Government if these alien radicals are permitted to carry out the principles of the Communist Party as embodied in its so-called laws, aims and regulations?

There wouldn't be any such thing left. In place of the United States Government we should have the horror and terrorism of bolsheviki tyranny such as is destroying Russia now. Every scrap of radical literature

demands the overthrow of our existing government. . . . The whole purpose of communism appears to be a mass formation of the criminals of
the world to overthrow the decencies of private life, to usurp property
that they have not earned, to disrupt the present order of life regardless
of health, sex or religious rights. By a literature that promises the wildest
dreams of such low aspirations, that can occur to only the criminal
minds, communism distorts our social law. . . .

It has been inferred by the "Reds" that the United States Government,
by arresting and deporting them, is returning to the autocracy of Czar-
dom, adopting the system that created the severity of Siberian banish-
ment. My reply to such charges is that in our determination to maintain
our government we are treating our alien enemies with extreme consideration. To deny them the privilege of remaining in a country which
they have openly deplored as an unenlightened community, unfit for
those who prefer the privileges of Bolshevism, should be no hardship. It
strikes me as an odd form of reasoning that these Russian Bolsheviks
who extol the Bolshevik rule should be so unwilling to return to Russia.
The nationality of most of the alien "Reds" is Russian and German. There
is almost no other nationality represented among them. . . .

The Department of Justice will pursue the attack of these "Reds" upon
the Government of the United States with vigilance, and no alien, advocating the overthrow of existing law and order in this country, shall
escape arrest and prompt deportation.

It is my belief that while they have stirred discontent in our midst,
while they have caused irritating strikes, and while they have infected
our social ideas with the disease of their own minds and their unclean
morals we can get rid of them! And not until we have done so shall we
have removed the menace of Bolshevism for good.

Source: A Mitchell Palmer, "The Case against the 'Reds,' " *Forum* 63 (February
1920): 173–185.

ANNOTATED RESEARCH GUIDE

Blanchard, Margaret A. *Revolutionary Sparks: Freedom of Expression in Modern
     America.* New York: Oxford University Press, 1992. Chapters 2–4 offer a
     rich and engaging survey of the turbulent travails of free speech during
     the first thirty years of the twentieth century.
Chafee, Zechariah, Jr. *Free Speech in the United States.* Cambridge, MA: Harvard
     University Press, 1948. Chafee's later musings on the subject.
Chafee, Zechariah, Jr. *Freedom of Speech.* 1920. Birmingham, AL: Legal Classics
     Library, 1990. Still standard reading on the subject, especially the devel-
     opments during World War I and the 1920s.
Cohen, Jeremy. *Congress Shall Make No Law: Oliver Wendell Holmes, the First
     Amendment and Judicial Decision Making.* Ames: Iowa State University

Press, 1989. An excellent study of the enigmatic Justice Holmes and the free speech guarantee of the First Amendment.

Mock, James R., and Cedric Larson. *Words That Won the War: The Story of the Committee on Public Information, 1917–1919.* Princeton, NJ: Princeton University Press, 1939. Though dated, an interesting account of the Creel Commission's role in World War I.

Murphy, Paul L. *The Meaning of Freedom of Speech: First Amendment Freedoms from Wilson to FDR.* Westport, CT: Greenwood Press, 1972. A standard reference for any exploration of this era. It provides a detailed, clearly written, and comprehensive coverage of the impact on free expression of the war and its aftermath.

Murphy, Paul L. *World War I and the Origins of Civil Liberties in the United States.* New York: W.W. Norton, 1979. Another standard reference on the development of free speech and civil liberties more generally during this period.

Polenberg, Richard. *Fighting Faiths: The Abrams Case, the Supreme Court, and Free Speech.* New York: Viking Press, 1987. An in-depth examination of the case that produced one of Justice Holmes's great dissents.

Rollins, Peter C., and John E. O'Connor, eds. *Hollywood's World War I: Motion Picture Images.* Bowling Green, OH: Bowling Green State University Popular Press, 1997. Consists of fifteen essays, including an introduction, that examine scores of films and how a new mass medium depicted and filtered both the courage and horrors of the "Great War."

Vaughn, Stephen. *Holding Fast the Inner Lines: Democracy, Nationalism, and the Committee on Public Information.* Chapel Hill: University of North Carolina Press, 1980. A more contemporary assessment of the Creel Commission's efforts to foster nationalism and patriotism during the war.

Web Sites

http://chnm.gmu.edu/courses/hist409/red.html. This page is devoted to the Palmer Raids, with links to brief descriptions of the people involved.

http://www.spartacus.schoolnet.co.uk/FWW.htm. Emanating from and maintained in the United Kingdom, this "Encyclopaedia of the First World War" is rich in links to all sorts of documents, biographies, and photos pertaining to the First World War.

http://www.spartacus.schoolnet.co.uk/USAredscare.htm. Coming from the same online teaching source as the preceding page, this Web site is devoted to the Red Scare and the "Palmer Raids" that followed shortly after the cessation of hostilities of the war.

http://www.ukans.edu/carrie/docs/amdocs_index.html. This page is maintained by the University of Kansas and is replete with documentary materials of American history. There is a whole section devoted to the events of World War I.

7

The Cold War and the "Red Menace"

During World War II the United States by military circumstance was allied with the Soviet Union (USSR)—the revolutionary regime deemed so diabolical that it frightened Americans after World War I. This alliance changed quickly and drastically after World War II when the relationship between two victorious superpowers devolved into a bitter ideological and dangerous military rivalry that lasted until the fall of the Berlin Wall in 1989 and the disintegration of the Soviet empire shortly thereafter. It was an era called the Cold War. Soon after World War II both countries possessed weapons capable of destroying each other—and the rest of the world.

American leaders were convinced that the USSR, with a far less robust economy and much more limited technology, rapidly produced these weapons only because of spies and traitors who gave the Soviets military secrets from the West. They were not wholly wrong. In 1950, for example, physicist Klaus Fuchs, who had been involved in secret research in America that produced the atomic bomb, was arrested in Britain and confessed that Americans Julius and Ethel Rosenberg, who had been members of the Communist Party, had supplied Soviet agents with crucial information needed to make its own bombs. At the height of what became another Red Scare, the Rosenbergs were convicted of violating the Espionage Act of 1917 and executed on June 19, 1953.

Ambitious politicians exploited international communism creating a national paranoia that transformed the Communist Party, which in the 1930s had been intellectually trendy but always politically insignificant, into a terrifying and dreaded plague. Given the capacity of Soviet weapons and the real political tensions, it would have been dangerously irresponsible not to investigate and to take appropriate measures to protect the nation. Records of the FBI showed that at the end of the 1940s there were about 54,000 actual members of the Communist Party in the United States. FBI director J. Edgar Hoover probably greatly exaggerated the magnitude of the danger with his announcement of "fifth column" Communists. He said that for every card-carrying member there were ten more underground awaiting the beck and call of the party for circumstances ripe for revolution. Curbs on free speech were put into law and escalated into an assault that lasted more than a decade, and it appeared in many guises and forms—some of it necessary and certainly legitimate, but much of it based on overstated claims that only increased fear.

In 1946 Congress passed the Atomic Energy Act to restrict and manage the flow of scientific data and information. The wartime Office of Strategic Services was displaced in 1947 by the new Central Intelligence Agency (CIA), whose budget was—and still is—kept secret. In 1951 President Harry S. Truman issued an executive order to implement a system to classify governmental documents to protect national security. Sensitive to charges—from conservatives among both Democrats and Republicans—that his administration was rife with Communists, Democratic President Truman temporarily instituted an employee loyalty-screening program in November 1946, and in March 1947, under another executive order, it became permanent. Federal employees in the executive branch could be discharged if the attorney general discovered that they had been members of organizations on the government's list of subversive associations. The FBI developed its own directory of untrustworthy groups and associations, and a special committee in Congress maintained still another catalog. After five years in operation, the awkward Loyalty Review Board made some 9,000 charges. After all the procedures were followed, only 378 individuals of 4 million scrutinized were either denied employment or fired—a statistical ratio of zero. The enormous investment of time and effort proved, to the relief of many and displeasure of others, that federal employees were competent and remarkably loyal. Still, the syndrome of mistrust and doubt that had paralyzed freedom of speech and association in the 1920s snowballed into effect once more, and by the time it had melted away as the Cold War thawed, profound damage had ruined thousands of lives and disabled free speech for millions.

In 1945 Congress created a permanent, standing committee with an inscrutable name: the House Committee on Un-American Activities (HUAC). Like other congressional committees, HUAC had constitutional authority to investigate and the concomitant power to cite for contempt of Congress witnesses who refused to appear or to answer "pertinent" questions—those germane to subjects on which Congress had authority to legislate. Failure to answer was a federal crime carrying punishments of fines and as much as a year in prison. One of HUAC's first postwar inquiries was its investigation of an anti-Fascist rally held in Madison Square Garden on September 24, 1945, by an organization helping refugees from the Spanish Civil War. This Joint Anti-Fascist Refugee Committee (JAFRC) had been designated on the attorney general's list as "Communist" because like the Communist Party in Europe it helped victims of one of the twentieth century's three most prominent Fascist dictators, General Francisco Franco. More than a dozen JAFRC members were cited for contempt for failure to cooperate with HUAC's requests for information, including membership lists of the organization. Journalist I.F. Stone wrote about the investigation: "A Congressional committee presumably established to expose alien propaganda against American free government has succeeded . . . in jailing for contempt Americans accused of engaging in propaganda against a totalitarian regime in Spain!"[1]

HUAC later combed Hollywood in search of Communists. Conservatives objected to films that gave respectability to Communist ideals and propaganda. The entertainment industry could propagate the wrong message and affect public opinion. Movie stars parading before a congressional committee would also provide national attention for HUAC. During the investigations the most famous and repeated question of the decade reverberated in the committee room and across the country via radio and TV: "Are you now or have you ever been a member of the Communist party?" Other invasive inquiries routinely followed about friends, associates, or coworkers. The "Hollywood Ten," mostly screenwriters, defied HUAC's questioning into their political beliefs and associations, arguing that such prying was not relevant to any legitimate congressional objective. They were not only charged with contempt of Congress but soon out of work. All were convicted, and their convictions were upheld on appeal. Employees in radio and the new medium of television were also caught in suspicions about the entertainment industry. Companies selling dozens of different products financed TV networks and most radio programs, providing revenue in return for advertisements. Shows written or directed or acted out by Communists, suspected or friends of Communists, or members of listed groups or witnesses summoned to testify before HUAC found their advertisers looking elsewhere. Management began a sweep with loyalty oaths and background checks and fired employees who failed to comply or whose backgrounds were suspect. Those with tainted memberships, even long since renounced, faced layoffs and other recriminations.

HUAC again investigated Hollywood in 1951, when some 300 more in the movie business were named, blacklisted, or socially ostracized. To save themselves from congressional contempt, many individuals invoked the Fifth Amendment right against self-incrimination—an uncomfortable midway between answering questions and outright refusal to testify followed by a jail term. "Fifth Amendment Communists" witnesses were now exposed to social and professional ostracism, an inevitable consequence, and apparent objective, of the kind of inquisition conducted by HUAC. After this thorough scouring of the movie industry for "un-American activity," not a single spy or saboteur had been discovered.

HUAC turned to labor unions, a natural link to Communist activity. Investigations were often and widespread, and many labor leaders either went to prison or were exposed as having links with the Communist Party or its "front" organizations. Many others, like their Hollywood counterparts, became Fifth Amendment Communists. HUAC also examined institutions of education, at all levels, where the minds of millions of children and young adults are shaped. State and local boards of education, as well as colleges and universities, soon followed suit. Higher education dismissed or denied tenure to Communists or even former Communists and "fellow-travelers." Loyalty oaths, blacklisting, witch hunts, and self-imposed silence soon saturated academia from the lowest to the highest levels of education. Most of those inclined to freedom of thought and inquiry were careful to conform for fear of losing their jobs and becoming unemployable as educators. State and local school boards took their cues from federal authorities that it was both lawful and dutiful to inquire into people's political beliefs and associations. The Supreme Court upheld the firing of a schoolteacher in New York accused of advocating or being a member of a group advocating the overthrow of the government. Justice William O. Douglas dissented and described American education in this way: "A deadening dogma takes the place of free inquiry. Instruction tends to become sterile; pursuit of knowledge is discouraged; discussion often leaves off where it should begin."[2]

HUAC pressured the Justice Department to shut down the Communist Party, and in 1949 the top leaders of the party were arrested for violating the Alien Registration Act, enacted by Congress in 1940 to combat something other than the menace now perceived to threaten the United States. Also called the Smith Act in honor of one of its legislative sponsors, the law made a crime of advocating the violent overthrow of the government, conspiring to organize a group so advocating, or being a member of an organization espousing that view. Eleven defendants were convicted of advocating and conspiring, though no evidence at all of attempt or incitement to overthrow the government had been assembled as proof. The prosecution's case was built on books and pamphlets, such as Karl Marx and Friedrich Engels's *The Communist Manifesto*. All defendants were found guilty, and all but one received the maximum sentence under the law of five years in prison and a $10,000 fine.

Under the name of *Dennis v. United States* (1951), the case came to the Supreme Court, but the Court limited the inquiry to the constitutionality of the challenged provisions of the Smith Act and refused to accept for evaluation any evidence against the convicted defendants. In a 6–2 decision, the Court left the convictions and the provisions of law undisturbed, though the six justices in the majority could not agree on the reasons why. A frustrated Justice Hugo L. Black complained that not one of the six justices in the majority gave the First Amendment its due respect. He understood the public paranoia but hoped that in calmer times that free speech will be restored to its rightful place in a free society. Justice Douglas applied the "clear and present danger" test the way Justices Holmes and Brandeis had finally framed it. Since there was no evidence that the defendants did anything other than advocate and join a party that advocated the abstract doctrine that organized government should be overthrown by force and replaced with a Communist society, Douglas concluded that such advocacy was what the First Amendment was designed to protect.

While the *Dennis* case was pending on appeal, and convinced that the Smith Act supplied insufficient means to beat back the danger threatening the country, Congress passed the Internal Security Act of 1950, which President Truman vetoed but which Congress overrode with stunning legislative majorities in both chambers (286–48 in the House, 57–10 in the Senate). The law required "Communist-action" and "Communist-front" organizations to register with the Subversive Activities Control Board created by the legislation. Registration meant supplying financial records as well as a list of officers; "Communist-action" groups, such as the Communist Party, were required to furnish their membership lists. Membership in such registered organizations carried numerous disabilities, such as a ban on foreign travel or working in certain sensitive industries. Punishments for failure to register under orders to do so included $10,000 in fines and a maximum five-year imprisonment. Registered organizations were also ordered to display warnings on their outgoing mail that the sender was a "Communist organization." In the event of a war or insurrection, the law also authorized wholesale detention of Communists. From within the Senate Judiciary Committee appeared the Senate Internal Security Subcommittee (SISS), a group of lawmakers who were charged with overseeing the new law, and they refused to be outperformed or upstaged by HUAC.

In 1953 the ruthless Soviet leader Josef Stalin died, and Soviet leadership shifted to the more moderate Nikita Khrushchev. Newly elected President Dwight D. Eisenhower negotiated the end of the Korean War, and later in his first term a summit meeting with Khrushchev took place, the first meeting of the top leaders of these two countries in a decade. Republicans controlled the executive and until 1955 both chambers of Congress. Republicans in Congress could no longer accuse the executive branch of being awash with Communists, as most of the executive appointees were now Republicans. This did not stop the man whose name not only defined this decade of American history but also entered the vocabulary to signify sensational, irresponsible, and unfounded allegations of disloyalty and treason about innocent people. The surfeit of legislation and investigations and the concomitant damage felt across American society in the 1950s will always be remembered by the word "McCarthyism."

Senator Joseph R. McCarthy, Republican of Wisconsin, ran a reckless and strident crusade of his own, supported by a group of intensely loyal subordinates. He exacerbated the reigning paranoia with unfounded and repeated conjectures that Communists had infiltrated virtually every level of government, including the State Department and even the U.S. Army. Fearing that he might lose a reelection bid for the Senate in 1950, McCarthy delivered a speech to a gathering of Republican women in Wheeling, West Virginia, in February 1950. He told these women that he held in his waving hand a list of more than 200 card-carrying Communists who were still working and making policy in the State Department and that the secretary of state was fully aware and doing nothing about it. There was little to his claim (at best his list was of those who eventually were screened out by Truman's earlier Loyalty Review Board), but he got the attention he sought from the press and an increasingly scared American people, both of which he manipulated.

Conducting his own inquiries from the Senate's relatively insignificant Committee on Government Operations, McCarthy accused every echelon of the American government of harboring the nation's enemies. His notorious bullying methods were prominently revealed when, in the fall of 1953, he began legislative hearings on disloyalty in the U.S. Army. Journalist Edward R. Murrow of CBS soon after publicly challenged McCarthy as a threat to freedom of speech. When newspapers or journalists criticized or questioned him or his committee, their reporters and editors were likely to receive a subpoena to appear before his committee to explain themselves. He and his supporters blamed the Truman administration for "losing" China in the 1949 revolution that brought to power Mao Zedong (Mao Tse Tung) and the Chinese Communist Party. He claimed too that the Truman administration was responsible for the prolonged Korean War that was killing American boys. McCarthy's numbing recklessness more than embarrassed his Senate colleagues, even fellow Republicans. Seven Republican senators, led by Margaret Chase Smith of Maine, signed a "Declaration of Conscience" in 1950 condemning McCarthy's behavior. A feared national figure, McCarthy was irked but unshaken. Four years later, however, after witnessing enough damage and abuse, seventy-three-year-old Republican Ralph E. Flanders of Vermont introduced a measure to expel McCarthy for conduct unbecoming a senator. Political compromise produced a 67–22 formal censure in December 1954, which was potent enough to derail him and put an end to his endless red-baiting that did little more than destroy reputations, insult and humiliate loyal governmental officials and many others, and exacerbate a fear and hysteria that swept the country. McCarthy remained in the Senate until he died in 1957.

In 1954 Congress enacted the Communist Control Act. The FBI had earlier warned Congress that outlawing the Communist Party would drive it underground and thereby make it more difficult for federal agents to monitor its actions. This warning perhaps kept Congress from banning the party in the Internal Security Act. However, the 1954 law directly outlawed the Communist Party of the United States; anyone convicted of being a member could be fined and sent to prison. Impatient and determined lawmakers were not concerned that the 1954 law contradicted the 1950 Internal Security Act's compulsory registration section. The Fifth Amendment to the Constitution prohibits compulsory self-incrimination, yet Congress in one law ordered Communists to register as members and in another law made membership a crime.

After McCarthy died the fervor of the crusade abated, and the Supreme Court in 1957 seized a propitious moment and surprised Washington and the rest of the country with unexpected, if limited, holdings protecting First Amendment rights. The government had prosecuted since 1951 some 120 lower-level Communist leaders under the Smith Act. In 1957 the Court reversed five convictions and ordered new trials for nine others, ruling that the Smith Act's ban against "advocating" the overthrow of the government had been intended to cover only advocacy coupled with action or incitement and not mere abstract advocacy. Speaking for the Court, Justice John Marshall Harlan explained: "The statute was aimed at the advocacy and teaching of concrete action for the forcible overthrow of the Government, and not of principles divorced from action. . . . The essential distinction is that those to whom advocacy is addressed must be urged to *do* something, now or in the future, rather than merely to believe in something."[3] Justice Tom Clark was the only dissenter. As attorney general, he had initiated the indictment against Eugene Dennis in 1949, and he was not persuaded by Harlan's effort in 1957 to camouflage the Court's abrupt change in direction. Dennis and his fellow Communists had been convicted not on the basis of any plans or actions but on the writings of Karl Marx and other famous Communists—abstractions, not incitements to *do* something.

On the same day the Court in a 6–2 vote reversed the contempt conviction of University of New Hampshire visiting lecturer Paul Sweezy, who had refused to answer certain questions about his political beliefs asked by the state's attorney general. In another case that momentous day the Court held in favor of John T. Watkins who, on April 29, 1954, rather than invoke the Fifth Amendment in his appearance before HUAC, instead had challenged the authority of the Congress to pry into anyone's political associations and beliefs and was charged with contempt of Congress. Chief Justice Earl Warren wrote the majority opinion to reverse the contempt conviction and subtly to rebuke Congress. Without directly condemning HUAC's motives, Warren said: "Investigations conducted solely for the personal aggrandizement of the investigators to 'punish' those investigated are indefensible. . . . We have no doubt that there is no congressional power to expose for the sake of exposure. [Legitimate investigations] cannot be inflated into a general power to expose where the predominant result can only be an invasion of the private rights of individuals."[4] The chief justice knew that exposure was about as much as HUAC in all its years in business had actually accomplished. However, the actual legal reason for reversing the conviction was a very narrow one: due process of law. Watkins had been convicted for failure to answer "pertinent" questions related to HUAC's investigations, but the Court majority concluded that, given the totally unfocused charge of the committee, the defendant could not have known whether or what questions were really pertinent to the investigation. After admonishing HUAC with First Amendment principles, the Court majority issued a very limited ruling. Still, after years of silence, the Court astonished the political establishment with its newfound interest in clarifying First Amendment protections.

An incensed Congress reacted angrily to "Red Monday" (back then Mondays were "decision days" at the Court, and Monday, June 17, 1957, has never been forgotten) and immediately introduced measures designed to strip the Court of appellate jurisdiction over cases involving "national security." Left over from the Civil War almost a century earlier was a still undisturbed judicial precedent recognizing the absolute power of Congress to make exceptions to the appellate jurisdiction of the Supreme Court, and in 1957 Congress tried to capitalize on this authority. Though the bill eventually failed, enough justices retreated. In *Barenblatt v. United States* (1959) Harlan wrote for the 5–4 majority upholding the contempt conviction of Lloyd Barenblatt for refusing to answer questions before HUAC. Barenblatt had been given the "pertinent" questions in advance, and thus he knew their relevance to the investigation into education. Addressing directly Barenblatt's First Amendment claim, Harlan balanced interests and rejected the claim, holding that one man's private right to keep still did not outweigh the self-preservation of the entire United States. An angry Justice Black dissented, joined by three of his colleagues on the Court, and attacked the Court's balancing as a masquerade to appease an angry Congress.

McCarthy, HUAC, and other legislative committees rummaged through governmental agencies, education, the labor movement, Broadway, Hollywood, left-wing groups, the army, and other institutions, places, and organizations that comprise America. The fledgling television industry got an unexpected boost as TV viewers were anxious to learn whether their neighbors, friends, coworkers, or relatives were suspected of being, knowing, or harboring Communists or Communist-"fronters," at present or ever in the past. To prove their loyalty or to avoid prison, many witnesses answered the questions of investigators who were already well informed by Hoover's FBI. Many witnesses named names. Institutions produced blacklists of undesirables, and employers often fired completely innocent people caught up in the suspicion and distrust that preoccupied the country for more than a decade.

Ironically, the real threat was not Communists plotting to overthrow the United States but, as President Truman announced in his veto of the Internal Security Act, official overreaction to a genuine concern of national security. The capacity of the Soviet Union's nuclear arsenal to destroy the United States was certainly legitimate cause for concern or even alarm, but the reaction at home was more of a threat to freedom and democracy than the minuscule American Communist Party and its faithful following. Nationwide there were probably more federal, state, and local investigators on thought patrol than the total number of Communists, including Hoover's imaginary "fifth column." The Cold War era of "McCarthyism" destroyed reputations, careers, and lives. Some victims of accusations even committed suicide. The injury, however, was not just of the government's making, though more sensible leaders or statesmen could have prevented much of the damage inflicted. Alarmed Americans believed Communism to be a genuine security threat; and elected officials (and others) lost few opportunities to exploit their fears.

By the mid-1960s the crusade against Communists had largely burned itself out, and the Supreme Court dismantled the regime of repression erected in the postwar era and restored, as Justice Black had hoped in the *Dennis* case, free speech guarantees to the high preferred place where they belong in a free society. HUAC eventually went out of business, and Americans no longer were told or believed that Communists were hiding in the American military and running foreign policy in the State Department. McCarthy and McCarthyism eventually became subjects of public resentment or ridicule, though the charges that one was "soft on communism" still carried some political weight until the end of the Cold War.

NOTES

1. I.F. Stone, "Is the Constitution Un-American?" *The Nation* 165 (September 6, 1947): 223.

2. *Adler v. Board of Education*, 342 U.S. 485, 510 (1952) (dissenting opinion).

3. *Yates v. United States*, 354 U.S. 298, 319–320, 324–325 (1957) (emphasis in original).

4. *Watkins v. United States*, 354 U.S. 178, 188, 200 (1957).

DOCUMENTS

7.1.   The Grand Inquisition

The uncertain connection between the film industry and national security was one of the first subjects investigated by HUAC once it became a permanent House committee after World War II. Liberal journalist/columnist I.F. Stone covered two weeks of ongoing investigations that took place in Washington and criticized the proceedings driven by what he derided as a Fascist mentality.

It would be easy to be cute about the pratt-fall with which the House Committee on Un-American Activities ended two weeks of hearings on the movie industry. No such inquiry is complete nowadays without the disclosure of some attempt to steal the atom bomb. By sophisticated standards the atom-bomb sensation produced by the committee was a dud; the ties between it and the film industry were of Rube Goldbergian tortuousness. Unfortunately, relatively few readers of newspapers will get beyond the flaring headlines which link Hollywood with atom-bomb spying. . . .

The committee is succeeding in its objectives: to build up an impression that Communists have penetrated everywhere; that they menace the prize national possession, the atom bomb; that something drastic will have to be done about them; that the peril warrants dismissals of appeals to constitutional rights as legal pettifogging, if not treasonable jesuitry. The state of mind being created is a kind of plot-and-persecution system akin to paranoid obsession and like paranoia impervious to correction by rational argument. The creation of this state of mind is the necessary preliminary for the emergence of a full-scale fascist movement garbed as militant Americanism. It is in this perspective, and not as some kind of unfortunate Congressional aberration, that one must view this latest in the long series of "hearings" by the Thomas committee and its predecessors. What the committee needs above all is attention, and the attention-getting potentialities of the movie star and the film industry are so much richer than anything else in American life that if there were no reds in Hollywood the committee would have to plant some.

As sheer spectacle, whether for the sophisticated or the unsophisticated, the movie hearings were the most superb performance yet put on by the committee. Outside the huge marble-walled caucus room of the old House office building on Capitol Hill a long line waited for a glimpse of the glamorous folk in attendance. "My wife," I heard a poorly dressed man plead with the policeman on duty downstairs, "wants to have a look at Humphrey Bogart." Within the guarded hearing-room the scene matched Hollywood's best in productions. On the right sat the ponderous moguls of the industry, with their handsome gray-haired counsel, Paul McNutt. A million dollars in movie names were scattered through the intent audience. In the front rows left sat perhaps the most affluent-looking group of alleged reds in modern history: earnest men, mostly young—only rich America could provide its alleged revolutionaries with such slick clothes and Sulka ties. On the aisle, out-dazzled both by their clients and by McNutt, sat Bob Kenny and Bart Crum, the determined counsel of the accused screen writers. The rows of press tables in front of them were crowded with stellar by-lines, hemmed in by Klieg lights. And on the high bench presiding was the Grand Inquisitor himself—the bald, stout, red-faced apoplectic-looking J. Parnell Thomas. One could not imagine a more perfect piece of casting for his role.

The first week's hearings were largely taken up with the lunatic fringe of the right, Hollywood's Liz Dillings, male and female. The second week was different. From the moment strong-faced John Howard Lawson hitched up his pants over a rather capitalistic paunch as he strode to the witness stand, it was clear that the committee was in for a fight. Lawson's stentorian voice, aided by a microphone, out-shouted both Thomas, no dulcet tenor, and Thomas's gavel, which broke the first day under the pounding he gave it. The committee is accustomed to quick crucifixions and docile answers to loaded questions. One screen writer after another declined to give Thomas the pleasure of watching the victim squirm, and ten were finally cited for contempt. The key question, "Are you a Communist?" brought neither denial nor affirmation nor even a flat refusal to answer, but an insistence on shouting the committee down. At one point Thomas asked a witness almost pleadingly, "Can't you answer yes, no, or maybe?" and two witnesses were even allowed to read their statements.

"The committee is determined," Thomas said at the beginning of the inquiry, "that the hearings shall be fair and impartial. We have subpoenaed witnesses representing both sides of the question." But the nearest the "accused" got to presenting their side, except for the reading of the two statements, was the chance to answer "yes" or "no" when they were asked about membership in the Screen Writers' Guild and the Communist Party. Their counsel, laying the groundwork for what will be a crucial test of the right of Congress to investigate in the sphere of ideas, were given no chance to cross-examine witnesses or rebut charges against their clients, and at one point were threatened with indictment for conspiracy if they had advised their clients not to answer. On each of the ten cited for contempt the committee released a voluminous dossier. These dossiers showed that the committee's investigators are constant readers of the Communist Party press: most of the information in them came from the *Daily Worker*, the rest from other party papers. That few of the "accused" could qualify as Republicans is hardly news. The dossiers were made up of numbered counts like an indictment; each purported to represent an "affiliation" with the Communist Party, but many of them could be brought forward against other leftists and liberals who are by no means party-liners. Aid to Spain, defense of one of a long list of leftists from Torn Mooney to Gerhard Eisler, a 1931 speech against the criminal-syndicalism laws, praise of Marx and Engels, membership in Consumers' Union or the P.C.A., showing "an active interest in the Soviet Union," and signing an ad in 1945 calling for breaking relations with Spain were among the "counts" in these indictments, which could set precedents for wider dragnet proceedings.

But the most striking feature of the hearings and the dossiers was the almost complete absence of allegations concerned with what was supposed to be the business of the inquiry—Communist propaganda in the films. The committee claims to have a list of complaints but seems hesitant to make it public. The hesitancy becomes clear when one notes the character of the only two films to which the "dossiers" object as communistic. One is "Blockade," the Lawson film about the Spanish civil war, which was covertly pro-Loyalist; the other, "The Brotherhood of Man," which Ring Lardner, Jr., helped to write for the Automobile Workers' Union. This was based on the pamphlet "The Races of Mankind," by Ruth Benedict and Gene Weltfish. It is significant that among those cited for contempt are men who have written or produced those few movies which give the Negro a break and attack anti-Semitism: for example, Edward Dmytryk and Adrian Scott, who were responsible for "Crossfire."

This inquiry must be fought by all men of good-will. The constitutional issues go to the very fundamentals of what may truly be called Americanism. If a Congressional committee can investigate ideas in the movies, it can investigate them in the press. The purpose is to terrorize all leftists, liberals, and intellectuals; to make them fearful in the film, the theater, the press, and any school of advanced ideas the Thomas committee can stigmatize as "red." In the films, as the transcript shows, the committee is out to give the moguls of the industry no rest until they not only take from the screen what little liberal and social content it has, but turn to making films which would prepare the way for fascism at home and war abroad. There were two revealing moments in the producers' testimony. Jack Warner, explaining the "subtle" methods of "red" screen writers, said, "They have the routine of the Indians and colored folks. That is always their setup." And when Louis B. Mayer said he was going to start making some "anti-Communist films promptly," Thomas leaned forward with a grin and asked, "These hearings haven't anything to do with promptness, have they?"

Source: I.F. Stone, "Grand Inquisition," *The Nation* 165 (November 8, 1947):492–494. Reprinted by permission of *The Nation*.

7.2.   Communists Should Not Teach in American Colleges

Raymond B. Allen was president of the University of Washington, at Seattle, at a time when several faculty members were dismissed or denied tenure because they had been members of the Communist Party. The decisions and termination policy of the university were subjected to a round of criticism (though the University of Washington was clearly not the only institution of higher learning to terminate Communists from the faculty). President Allen defended the university's actions and the general proposition that Communists are unfit to serve as college and university professors.

The question of whether a member of the Communist Party should be allowed to teach in an American college is by no means a simple one. Despite the fact that many persons in educational circles appear to find easy answers to this question, those of us who have examined the question most carefully perhaps find the answers more difficult.

. . . I am now convinced that a member of the Communist Party is not a free man. Freedom . . . is the most essential ingredient of American civilization and democracy. In the American scheme educational institutions are the foundation stones upon which real freedom rests . . . [and] can prosper only as they maintain free teaching and research. To maintain free teaching and research the personnel of higher education must accept grave responsibilities and duties as well as the rights and privileges of the academic profession. A teacher must, therefore, be a free seeker after the truth. If, as Jefferson taught, the real purpose of education is to seek out and teach the truth wherever it may lead, then the first obligation and duty of the teacher is to be a free man. Any restraint on the teacher's freedom is an obstacle to the accomplishment of the most important purposes of education.

. . . I have seen the free minds of scholarly men solve most of the mysteries of travel in the air. I have also seen free research evolve a whole new science of electronics that has revolutionized men's ability to communicate with one another. As a medical man I have seen free research wipe out some of the most hideous diseases that have afflicted mankind down through the centuries. Even my young children have seen free and scholarly men unlock and control the vast and frightening power of the atom. In the past decade, all of us have seen the virility of a free people win out in a death struggle with the slave-states of Germany, Italy and Japan, only now to be faced again by another and perhaps more vicious adversary. These accomplishments I submit are some of the material fruits of freedom in scholarship and teaching.

The freedom that America prizes so much . . . is not allowed the membership the Communist Party. I have come to this conclusion painfully and reluctantly through a long series of hearings and deliberations . . . by faculty and administrative agencies of the University of Washington [that] have proved beyond any shadow of a doubt that a member of the Communist Party is not a free man, that he is instead a slave to immutable dogma and to a clandestine organization masquerading as a political party. . . . [A] member of the Communist Party has abdicated control over his intellectual life.

The real issue between Communism and education is the effect of Communist Party membership upon the freedom of the teacher and upon the morale and professional standards of the profession of teaching. Many would have us believe that it is an issue of civil liberty, [but no] man has a constitutional right to membership in any profession, and those who maintain that he has are taking a narrow, legalistic point of view which sees freedom only as a privilege and entirely disregards the duties and responsibilities that are correlative with rights and privileges. The lack of freedom permitted the Communist has a great deal more than a mere passing or academic bearing upon the duties of a teacher.

. . . [T]he Communist Party [member's] lack of freedom disqualifies him from professional service as a teacher. Because he is not free . . . he is incompetent to be a teacher. Because he asserts a freedom he does not possess . . . he is intellectually dishonest to his profession. Because he has failed to be a free agent, because he is intolerant of the beliefs of others and because education cannot tolerate organized intolerance . . . he is in neglect of his most essential duty as a teacher. For these reasons I believe that Communism is an enemy of American education and that members of the Communist Party have disqualified themselves for service as teachers.

. . . Academic freedom . . . consists of something more than merely an absence of restraints placed upon the teacher by the institution that employs him. It demands as well an absence of restraints placed upon him by his political affiliations, by dogmas that stand in the way of a free search for truth, or by rigid adherence to a "party line" that sacrifices dignity, honor, and integrity to the accomplishment of political ends. Men, and especially the teacher and the scholar, must be free to think and discover and believe, else there will be no new thought, no discovery, and no progress.

. . . Thus, the University's position has been not that it wished to prescribe "the truth" but instead that it insisted that members of its faculty be free to seek the truth and be not restricted in this search by any agency other than the intellectual faculties of the individual himself. . . .

. . . Essentially the issue posed by the presence of Communists on our faculties is much larger than that merely between Communism and free education. . . . Communists are not qualified to be teachers [because] freedom has little meaning apart from the integrity of the men and women who enjoy that freedom. The larger issue is the . . . integrity of the teacher and, beyond that, the corporate integrity of education as a whole. Certainly no one will argue that an educational institution, can have greater integrity than that of the individuals who make it up. The Communist Party, with its concealed aims and objectives, with its clandestine methods and techniques, with its consistent failure to put its full face forward, is a serious reflection upon the integrity of educational institutions that employ its members and upon a whole educational system that has failed to take the Communist issue seriously.

Individual faculty members have a duty and a responsibility to defend the corporate integrity of scholarship and teaching. . . . [E]ducation's free and unfettered search for truth . . . is our most precious asset and should be defended at all costs. Without it education as a whole is without orientation. . . . Without responsible freedom, democracy and all we hold dear lacks meaning and the possibility of achievement. We as a people have chosen to live by the hopeful, positive tenets of freedom. Communism is the antithesis and the negation of these tenets. Communism would substitute a doctrine of fear, of little faith and would submerge the human spirit to the vicious ends of a crass materialism. Free education and its endless search for truth cannot gain by association with this doctrine of fear and hate and inhumanity. The American idea and the idea behind free education, and to my mind the two are inseparable, are "the last best hope on earth." In the final analysis, both rest upon the dignity, the integrity, and the goodwill of free men. As Americans and as educators, it is our responsibility to cherish and sustain this dignity, this integrity, this goodwill and this freedom.

The classroom has been called "the chapel of democracy." As the priests of the temple of education, members of the teaching profession have a sacred duty to remove from their ranks the false and robot prophets of Communism or of any other doctrine of slavery that seeks to be in, but never of, our traditions of freedom.

Never before has this country needed as it does today the leadership of thoroughly trained men and women. We must have leaders inspired from their earliest years with the ideals of true democracy. Education is our first line of defense. In the conflict of principle and policy which divides the world today, America's hope, our hope, the hope of the world, is in education. Through education alone can we combat the tenets of Communism.

Source: Raymond B. Allen, "Communists Should Not Teach in American Colleges," *Educational Forum* 13, no. 4 (May 1949): 433–440. Reprinted by permission of Kappa Delta Pi, International Honor Society in Education.

7.3.   Declaration of Conscience

Republican Senator Margaret Chase Smith of Maine gave a brief speech on June 1, 1950, from the Senate floor in the presence of Senator McCarthy. Without naming him, she castigated his reckless and irresponsible accusations, which she linked to electioneering tactics that had degraded the Senate and threatened individual dignity and rights. Seven other Republican senators publicly endorsed Smith's statement.

I would like to speak briefly and simply about a serious national condition. It is a national feeling of fear and frustration that could result in national suicide and the end of everything that we Americans hold dear. It is a condition that comes from the lack of effective leadership in either the legislative branch or the executive branch of our government. . . . I speak as a Republican. I speak as a woman. I speak as a United States senator. I speak as an American.

I think that it is high time that we remembered that we have sworn to uphold and defend the Constitution . . . that we remembered that the Constitution, as amended, speaks not only of the freedom of speech but also of trial by jury instead of trial by accusation.

Whether it be a criminal prosecution in court or a character prosecution in the Senate, there is little practical distinction when the life of a person has been ruined. Those of us who shout the loudest about Americanism in making character assassinations are all too frequently those who, by our own words and acts, ignore some of the basic principles of Americanism—The right to criticize; The right to hold unpopular beliefs; The right to protest; The right of independent thought.

The exercise of these rights should not cost one single American citizen his reputation or his right to a livelihood nor should he be in danger of losing his reputation or livelihood merely because he happens to know someone who holds unpopular beliefs. Who of us doesn't?

The American people are sick and tired of being afraid to speak their minds lest they be politically smeared as "Communists" or "Fascists" by their opponents. Freedom of speech is not what it used to be in America. It has been so abused by some that it is not exercised by others.

As a Republican, I say to my colleagues on this side of the aisle that the Republican Party faces a challenge today that is not unlike the challenge that it faced back in Lincoln's day. The Republican Party so successfully met that challenge that it emerged from the Civil War as the champion of a united nation—in addition to being a party that unrelentingly fought loose spending and loose programs.

Today our country is being psychologically divided by the confusion and the suspicions that are bred in the United States Senate to spread like cancerous tentacles of "know nothing, suspect everything" attitudes. . . .

[T]o displace [the current administration] with a Republican regime embracing a philosophy that lacks political integrity or intellectual honesty would prove equally disastrous to this nation. The nation sorely needs a Republican victory. But I don't want to see the Republican Party ride to political victory on the four horsemen of calumny—fear, ignorance, bigotry and smear. . . .

As a woman, I wonder how the mothers, wives, sisters and daughters feel about the way in which members of their families have been politically mangled in Senate debate—and I use the word "debate" advisedly.

As a United States senator, I am not proud of the way in which the Senate has been made a publicity platform for irresponsible sensationalism. . . .

I don't like the way the Senate has been made a rendezvous for vilification, for selfish political gain at the sacrifice of individual reputations and national unity. I am not proud of the way we smear outsiders from the floor of the Senate and hide behind the cloak of congressional immunity and still place ourselves beyond criticism on the floor of the Senate.

As an American, I am shocked at the way Republicans and Democrats alike are playing directly into the Communist design of "confuse, divide and conquer." As an American, I don't want a Democratic administration "whitewash" or "cover-up" any more than I want a Republican smear or witch hunt.

As an American, I condemn a Republican "Fascist" just as much as I condemn a Democrat "Communist." I condemn a Democrat "Fascist" just as much as I condemn a Republican "Communist." They are equally dangerous to you and me and to our country. As an American, I want to see our nation recapture the strength and unity it once had when we fought the enemy instead of ourselves.

Source: Congressional Record, 81st Cong., 2nd sess., June 1, 1950, p. 7898.

7.4.   President Truman Vetoes the Internal Security Bill

On September 22, 1950, six weeks before congressional elections, President Harry S. Truman vetoed the comprehensive Internal Security Act designed to augment national powers to deal with the threat of the Communist Party and Communist-front organizations. Truman found the bill needless, counterproductive, procedurally cumbersome, and dangerous to the freedom of Americans. The next day, 85 percent of the members of each house overrode the veto—a sign of the intensity of the issue and its place in electoral politics.

It has been claimed over and over again that this is an "anti-communist" bill—a "communist control" bill. But in actual operation the bill would have results exactly the opposite of those intended. . . . It would help the communist propagandists throughout the world who are trying to undermine freedom by discrediting as hypocrisy the efforts of the United States on behalf of freedom.

. . . [T]he language of the bill is so broad and vague that it might well result in penalizing the legitimate activities of people who are not communists at all, but loyal citizens. . . . [Its] provisions are not merely ineffective and unworkable. . . . [T]he application of the registration requirements to so-called communist-front organizations can be the greatest danger to freedom of speech, press and assembly, since the Alien and Sedition Laws of 1798. This danger arises out of the criteria or standards to be applied in determining whether an organization is a communist-front organization.

There would be no serious problem if the bill required proof that an organization was controlled and financed by the Communist Party before it could be classified as a communist-front organization. However, recognizing the difficulty of proving those matters, the bill would permit such a determination to be based solely upon "the extent to which the positions taken or advanced by it from time to time on matters of policy do not deviate from those" of the communist movement.

This provision could easily be used to classify as a communist-front organization any organization which is advocating a single policy or objective which is also being urged by the Communist Party or by a communist foreign government. . . . Thus, an organization which advocates low cost housing for sincere humanitarian reasons might be classified as a communist-front organization because the communists regularly exploit slum conditions as one of their fifth-column techniques.

It is not enough to say that this probably would not be done. The mere fact that it could be done shows clearly how the bill would open a Pandora's box of opportunities for official condemnation of organizations and individuals for perfectly honest opinions which happen to be stated also by communists.

The basic error of these sections is that they move in the direction of suppressing opinion and belief. This would be a very dangerous course to take, not because we have any sympathy for communist opinions, but because any governmental stifling of the free expression of opinion is a long step toward totalitarianism.

There is no more fundamental axiom of American freedom than the familiar statement: In a free country, we punish men for the crimes they commit, but never for the opinions they have. . . . To permit freedom of expression is primarily for the benefit of the majority, because it protects criticism, and criticism leads to progress.

We can and we will prevent espionage, sabotage, or other actions endangering our national security. But we would betray our finest traditions if we attempted, as this bill would attempt, to curb the simple expression of opinion. This we should never do, no matter how distasteful the opinion may be to the vast majority of our people. The course proposed by this bill would delight the communists, for it would make a mockery of the Bill of Rights and of our claims to stand for freedom in the world.

And what kind of effect would these provisions have on the normal expression of political views? Obviously, if this law were on the statute books, the part of prudence would be to avoid saying anything that might be considered by someone as not deviating sufficiently from the current communist propaganda line. And since no one could be sure in advance what views were safe to express, the inevitable tendency would be to express no views on controversial subjects.

The result could only be to reduce the vigor and strength of our political life—an outcome that the communists would happily welcome, but that free men should abhor.

We need not fear the expression of ideas; we do need to fear their suppression.

Our position in the vanguard of freedom rests largely on our demonstration that the free expression of opinion, coupled with government by popular consent, leads to national strength and human advancement. Let us not, in cowering and foolish fear, throw away the ideals which are the fundamental basis of our free society. . . .

Earlier this month, we launched a great Crusade for Freedom designed, in the words of General Eisenhower, to right the big lie with the big truth. I can think of no better way to make a mockery of that crusade and of the deep American belief in human freedom and dignity which underlie it than to put the provisions of [this bill] on our statute books.

Source: Public Papers of the Presidents of the United States: Harry S. Truman: 1950 (Washington, DC: Government Printing Office, 1965), pp. 645–653.

7.5.   "Where I Stand"

Elia Kazan—the distinguished director of films and plays, including the Broadway production of Arthur Miller's Death of a Salesman, *both the stage and film versions of Tennessee Williams's* A Streetcar Named Desire, *and the film of John Steinbeck's* East of Eden—*first appeared before HUAC on January 14, 1952, but refused to "name names." On April 10, he returned and identified eight individuals who had, with him, in the mid-1930s been members of the Communist Party when he worked in the Group Theater. His testimony injured careers and lives and reinforced the expanding Hollywood blacklist, and he was sharply rebuked by liberals for his disclosures. The day after his April appearance he wrote the following piece published as an advertisement in the* New York Times *as a response to his critics. On March 21, 1999, amidst criticism from the Left, the Academy of Motion Picture Arts and Sciences presented Kazan with a Lifetime Achievement Award.*

I want to make my stand clear:

I believe that Communist activities confront the people of this country with an unprecedented and exceptionally tough problem. That is, how to protect ourselves from a dangerous and alien conspiracy and still keep the free, open, healthy way of life that gives us self-respect.

I believe that the American people can solve this problem wisely only if they have all the facts about Communism.

I believe that any American who is in possession of such facts has the obligation to make them known, either to the public or to the appropriate Government agency.

Whatever hysteria exists—and there is some, particularly in Hollywood—is inflamed by mystery, suspicion, and secrecy. Hard and exact facts will cool it.

The facts I have are 16 years out of date, but they supply a small piece of background to the graver picture of Communism today.

I have placed these facts before the House Committee on Un-American Activities without reserve and I now place them before the public.

Seventeen and a half years ago I was a 24-year old stage manager and bit actor, making $40 a week when I worked.

At that time nearly all of us felt menaced by two things: the depression and the ever-growing power of Hitler. The streets were full of unemployed and shaken men. I was taken in by the Hard Times version of the Communists' recruiting technique. They claimed to have a cure for the depressions and a cure for Nazism and Fascism. I joined the party late in the summer of 1934. I got out a year and a half later.

I have no spy stories to tell, because I saw no spies. Nor did I understand, at the time, any opposition between American and Russian national interest. It was not even clear to me in 1936 that the American Communist Party was abjectly taking its orders from the Kremlin.

What I learned was the minimum that anyone must learn who puts his head into the noose of Party "discipline." The Communists automatically violated the daily practices of democracy to which I was accustomed. They attempted to control thought and suppress personal opinion. They tried to dictate personal conduct. They habitually distorted and disregarded and violated the truth. All this was crudely opposite to their claims of "democracy" and "the scientific approach."

To be a member of the Communist Party is to have a taste of the police state. It is a diluted taste, but it is bitter and unforgettable. It is diluted, because you can walk out.

I got out in the spring of 1936.

Why did I not tell this story sooner? I was held back, primarily, by concern for the reputations and employment of the people who may, like myself, have left the Party many years ago.

I was also held back by a piece of specious reasoning which has silenced many liberals. It goes like this: "You may hate the Communists, but you must not attack them or expose them, because if you do you are attacking the right to hold unpopular opinions and you are joining the people who attack civil liberties."

I have thought soberly about this. It is, simply, a lie.

Secrecy serves the Communists. At the other pole, it serves those who are interested in silencing liberal voices. The employment of a lot of good liberals is threatened because they have allowed themselves to become associated with or silenced by the Communists.

Liberals must speak out.

I think it is useful that certain of us had this kind of experience with the Communists, for if we had not we should not know them so well. Today, when all the world fears war and they scream peace, we know how much their professions are worth. We know tomorrow they will have a new slogan. Firsthand experience of dictatorship and thought control left me with an abiding hatred of Communist philosophy and methods, and with the conviction that these must be resisted always.

It also left me with the passionate conviction that we must never let the Communists get away with the pretense that they stand for the very things which they kill in their own countries.

I am talking about free speech, a free press, the rights of property, the rights of labor, racial equality and, above all, individual rights. I value these things. I take them seriously. I value peace, too, when it is not bought at the price of fundamental decencies.

I believe these things must be fought for whenever they are not fully honored and protected whenever they are threatened.

The motion pictures I have made and the plays I have chosen to direct represent my convictions.

I expect to continue to make the same kinds of pictures and to direct the same kinds of plays.

Source: *New York Times*, April 12, 1952, p. 412. Copyright © 1952 by the New York Times Co. Reprinted by permission.

7.6.   Justice Hugo L. Black Dissents

After the Supreme Court's Watkins v. United States *(1957) decision reprimanded HUAC and reversed a labor witness's contempt conviction, Congress threatened the Court with measures to deprive it of jurisdiction in internal security matters. The measure failed, but the Court retreated, as can be seen in this case, upholding (5–4) the conviction, of Lloyd Barenblatt, a Vassar College professor, on the grounds that national security outweighs an individual's right not to disclose his political beliefs or associations. Justice Black wrote the dissenting opinion that stated his "absolutist" view of the First Amendment but then strongly criticized the Court's "balancing" of the conflicting interests here and HUAC and McCarthyism in general.*

To apply the Court's balancing test under such circumstances is to read the First Amendment to say "Congress shall pass no law abridging freedom of speech, press, assembly and petition, unless Congress and the Supreme Court reach the joint conclusion that on balance the interest of the Government in stifling these freedoms is greater than the interest of the people in having them exercised." This is closely akin to the notion that neither the First Amendment nor any other provision of the Bill of Rights should be enforced unless the Court believes it is reasonable to do so. . . .

But even assuming what I cannot assume, that some balancing is proper in this case, I feel that the Court after stating the test ignores it completely. At most it balances the right of the Government to preserve itself, against Barenblatt's right to refrain from revealing Communist affiliations. Such a balance, however, mistakes the factors to be weighed. In the first place, it completely leaves out the real interest in Barenblatt's silence, the interest of the people as a whole in being able to join organizations, advocate causes and make political "mistakes" without later being subjected to governmental penalties for having dared to think for themselves. It is this right, the right to err politically, which keeps us strong as a Nation. For no number of laws against communism can have as much effect as the personal conviction which comes from having heard its arguments and rejected them, or from having once accepted its tenets and later recognized their worthlessness. Instead, the obloquy which results from investigations such as this not only stifles "mistakes" but prevents all but the most courageous from hazarding any views which might at some later time become disfavored. This result, whose importance cannot be overestimated, is doubly crucial when it affects the universities, on which we must largely rely for the experimentation and development of new ideas essential to our country's welfare. It is these interests of society, rather than Barenblatt's own right to silence, which I think the Court should put on the balance against the demands of the Government, if any balancing process is to be tolerated. . . .

Moreover, I cannot agree with the Court's notion that First Amendment freedoms must be abridged in order to "preserve" our country. That notion rests on the unarticulated premise that this Nation's security hangs upon its power to punish people because of what they think, speak or write about, or because of those with whom they associate for political purposes. The Government, in its brief, virtually admits this position when it speaks of the "communication of unlawful ideas." . . . The First Amendment means to me, however, that the only constitutional way our Government can preserve itself is to leave its people the fullest possible freedom to praise, criticize or discuss, as they see fit, all governmental policies and to suggest, if they desire, that even its most fundamental postulates are bad and should be changed. . . .

Today we deal with Communists or suspected Communists. In 1920, instead, the New York Assembly suspended duly elected legislators on the ground that, being Socialists, they were disloyal to the country's principles. In the 1830's the Masons were hunted as outlaws and subversives, and abolitionists were considered revolutionaries of the most dangerous kind in both North and South. Earlier still, at the time of the universally unlamented alien and sedition laws, Thomas Jefferson's party was attacked and its members were derisively called "Jacobins." . . . History should teach us then, that in times of high emotional excitement minority parties and groups which advocate extremely unpopular social or governmental innovations will always be typed as criminal gangs and attempts will always be made to drive them out. . . .

Finally, I think Barenblatt's conviction violates the Constitution because the chief aim, purpose and practice of the House Un-American Activities Committee, as disclosed by its many reports, is to try witnesses and punish them because they are or have been Communists or because they refuse to admit or deny Communist affiliations. The punishment imposed is generally punishment by humiliation and public shame. There is nothing strange or novel about this kind of punishment. It is in fact one of the oldest forms of governmental punishment known to mankind; branding, the pillory, ostracism and subjection to public hatred being but a few examples of it. . . .

To accomplish this kind of result, the Committee has called witnesses who are suspected of Communist affiliation, has subjected them to severe questioning and has insisted that each tell the name of every person he has ever known at any time to have been a Communist, and, if possible, to give the addresses and occupations of the people named. These names are then indexed, published, and reported to Congress, and often to the press. The same technique is employed to cripple the job opportunities of those who strongly criticize the Committee or take other actions it deems undesirable. Thus, in 1949, the Committee reported that it had indexed and printed some 335,000 names of people who had signed "Communist" petitions of one kind or another. All this the Committee did and does to punish by exposure the many phases of "un-American" activities that it reports cannot be reached by legislation, by administrative action, or by any other agency of Government, which, of course, includes the courts.

I do not question the Committee's patriotism and sincerity in doing all this. I merely feel that it cannot be done by Congress under our Constitution. For, even assuming that the Federal Government can compel witnesses to testify as to Communist affiliations in order to subject them to ridicule and social and economic retaliation, I cannot agree that this is a legislative function. Such publicity is clearly punishment, and the Constitution allows only one way in which people can be convicted and punished. . . .

[T]he Court today fails to see what is here for all to see—that exposure and punishment is the aim of this Committee and the reason for its existence. To deny this is to ignore the Committee's own claims and the reports it has issued ever since it was established. I cannot believe that the nature of our judicial office requires us to be so blind, and must conclude that the Un-American Activities Committee's "identification" and "exposure" of Communists and suspected Communists . . . amount to an encroachment on the judiciary which bodes ill for the liberties of the people of this land.

Ultimately all the questions in this case really boil down to one—whether we as a people will try fearfully and futilely to preserve democracy by adopting totalitarian methods, or whether in accordance with our traditions and our Constitution we will have the confidence and courage to be free. I would reverse this conviction.

Source: *Barenblatt v. United States*, 360 U.S. 108, 134–162 (June 8, 1959) (dissenting opinion).

ANNOTATED RESEARCH GUIDE

Barson, Michael. *Better Red Than Dead: A Nostalgic Look at the Golden Years of Russia Phobia, Red-baiting, and Other Commie Madness*. New York: Hyperion, 1992. A lighthearted but quite informative account of the governmental effort to round up Communists and others suspected of promoting their objectives.

Blanchard, Margaret A. *Revolutionary Sparks: Freedom of Expression in Modern America*. New York: Oxford University Press, 1992. Chapter 7 presents a brief yet comprehensive and scholarly synopsis of the era as seen from the perspective of free speech and association.

Digest of the Public Record of Communism in the United States. New York: Fund for the Republic, 1955. A compendium of federal and state laws, administrative and judicial decisions, congressional reports, and other public documents and their sources. This is a very handy reference for anyone researching this era.

Fariello, Griffin. *Red Scare: Memories of the American Inquisition—An Oral History*. New York: W.W. Norton, 1995. A marvelous collection of humorous and sometimes painful accounts told by dozens of people who were participants in the Red Scare—witnesses such as distinguished playwright Arthur Miller and folk singer Pete Seeger, ex-Communists who worked for the FBI, and Hollywood producers and screenwriters.

Foster, Stuart J. *Red Alert!: Educators Confront the "Red Scare" in American Public Schools, 1947–1954*. New York: Peter Lang, 2000. Looks at the far-reaching impact that the Red Scare and the Cold War had on America's public schools and education in general.

Kalven, Harry, Jr. *A Worthy Tradition: Freedom of Speech in America*. New York: Harper & Row, 1988. Contains many scholarly chapters dealing with free speech issues raised during the Cold War period.

Kutler, Stanley I. *The American Inquisition: Justice and Injustice in the Cold War*. New York: Hill and Wang, 1982. Examines the role of the judiciary in protecting free speech during the Cold War era.

Navasky, Victor S. *Naming Names*. New York: Viking Press, 1980. Recounts the story of suspected Communists and "blacklists" in Hollywood and the motion picture industry.

Powers, Richard Gid. *Not Without Honor: The History of American Anticommunism*.

New York: Free Press, 1995. A study of twentieth-century American anti-Communists movements that provides a context in which to evaluate the anti-Communist frenzy of the Cold War.

Rose, Lisle A. *The Cold War Comes to Main Street: America in 1950*. Lawrence: University Press of Kansas, 1999. A wonderful book that explores major concepts, such as McCarthyism, liberalism and conservatism, the Red Menace, and several other concerns, by focusing on the events of one stormy year: 1950.

Steinberg, Peter L. *The Great "Red Menace": United States Prosecution of American Communists, 1947–1952*. Westport, CT: Greenwood Press, 1984. Analyzes the U.S. government's efforts to enforce the welter of confusing and often very vague criminal laws, from the Smith Act to the Internal Security Act.

Whitfield, Stephen J. *The Culture of the Cold War*. 2nd ed. Baltimore, MD: Johns Hopkins University Press, 1996. A useful analysis providing the social and cultural background of the Cold War era.

Video Resources

Dateline—1947. Northbrook, IL: Coronet/MTI Film & Video, 1989. This is a fairly brief (twenty-three minutes) film that outlines the early stages of the Cold War and some of the personalities in the fight against communism at home, especially J. Edgar Hoover and Senator Joseph McCarthy.

A Report on Senator Joseph McCarthy. New York: CBS News Archives, 2000. A twenty-seven-minute documentary by CBS reporter Edward R. Murrow on what he coined as "McCarthyism." Followed by *McCarthy Rebuttal* (New York: CBS News Archives, 2000). A twenty-six-minute documentary in which Murrow invited McCarthy to rebut allegations that he was reckless in his investigations that the Communists had infiltrated upper echelons of American government.

Web Sites

http://webcorp.com/mccarthy. Audio playbacks of some of Senator McCarthy's speeches can be found on this Web page.

http://www.law.umkc.edu/faculty/projects/ftrials/rosenb/ROSENB.htm. This Web site is devoted to the trial and background of Julius and Ethel Rosenberg.

http://www.turnerlearning.com/cnn/coldwar/reds/reds_res.html. This site covers the period from 1947 through 1953 and focuses on the Red Scare itself. It also has links to many interesting and useful documents.

http://www.english.upenn.edu/~afilreis/50s/home.html. Professor Al Filreis of the University of Pennsylvania has created and maintained this superb and comprehensive page with scores of helpful and informative links focusing on many dimensions of the 1950s.

8

The Civil Rights Movement

The Fourteenth Amendment (1868) prohibited states from denying to anyone within their jurisdiction "the equal protection of the laws," and the Fifteenth Amendment (1870) prohibited states from racially restricting voting rights. Despite these constitutional promises, the vast majority of black Americans, even as late as the 1950s, lived as second- or third-class citizens; hardly any blacks in the South were even registered to vote. Racially segregated public transportation, schools, jails, parks, restrooms, drinking fountains, and other public facilities were the law of the land across the South, more in some states than in others, and the proscription of blacks from voting, jury duty in cases involving whites, and other means of acting in their own interest denied them "the equal protection of the laws." Racial segregation in housing and employment also characterized much of urban America across the country. The private sector was perhaps more pervasively segregated. Movie houses, for example, had their "colored balconies," and many restaurants, shops, and retail outlets refused to do business with blacks. In many states it was a crime for an individual to marry someone of another race, though peculiar exceptions were carved into law, for example, in Virginia for descendants of the Native American Pocahontas.

Before the quest for racial equality took on the dimensions of a mass political movement, African Americans had been fighting for racial equality in the courts for four decades, making important, if limited, gains in the field of civil rights. The principal engine of litigation was the National Associational for the Advancement of Colored People

(NAACP), founded in 1909. The NAACP launched various lawsuits on many fronts in America's courtrooms, and in the 1940s and 1950s a receptive Supreme Court made rulings that cut piece by piece into racial segregation. What was missing was not a sympathetic Court but political power to sweep beyond the narrow impact of judicial decrees. Activists in the emerging civil rights movement knew that much more was needed than valiant but sporadic judicial proclamations to desegregate a system so entrenched that it represented a "normal," resilient way of life in the South. Even the monumental case of *Brown v. Board of Education* (1954), in which the NAACP persuaded the Court to invalidate state-enforced segregated public schools, yielded little compliance until the president and the Congress joined the Court with political support in the "Great Society" programs of President Lyndon B. Johnson almost a decade later.

Freedom of expression and association was a fundamental component of the machinery used by the civil rights movement. This was inevitable, as free speech has been an instrument at the center of every other effort in American history to change the established order. The civil rights movement generated a host of issues and constitutional cases involving freedom of expression, many of which raised new questions, not only about the content but also the "time, place and manner" of expression. Important and respected, and thereby influential, members of the press can help change a nation's attitudes, as Walter Cronkite, the respected anchorman of the *CBS Evening News*, probably did in delivering the nightly news in the late 1960s regarding the war in Vietnam. Unlike national news anchors, however, civil rights leaders and disenfranchised blacks initially had no ready access to the national media. They sent their messages through "sit-ins," public protest and marches, demonstrations, and other forms of "symbolic" speech by which they hoped to push the degrading reality of segregation to the front of the national agenda.

The traditional means of citizen protest, voting, was largely unavailable to most blacks in the South, despite the Fifteenth Amendment. State-created tests and preconditions allowed only a very small percentage of blacks to register and vote in the South, and efforts to register and vote faced bureaucratic obstacles and violence. The strategy of leaders such as Martin Luther King, Jr., and his Southern Christian Leadership Conference (SCLC) called, instead, for nonviolent resistance and peaceful protest and civil disobedience of unjust laws. During freedom rides, sit-ins, and other protests, many blacks and their white supporters were brutally beaten; many were arrested and convicted; and some of their cases reached the U.S. Supreme Court. The Court was usually sympathetic to free speech rights in the civil rights cases and protected the speakers and protesters, finding various ways to shield this public form of protest from the criminal laws of the states.

In 1955 Rosa Parks, a forty-three-year-old black seamstress and mem-

ber of the local chapter of the NAACP, in Montgomery, Alabama, refused to surrender a "white" seat and to move, instead, to the "colored"
section of a public bus as required by local law. Many regard this symbolic act as the beginning of the civil rights movement—at least outside
the courtrooms. Her defiance led to the 381-day-long Montgomery Bus
Boycott, initiated by black leaders including King, which was designed
not just to showcase segregated public transportation but also to demonstrate that Montgomery's bus system was financially dependent on
black riders. The boycott cut deeply into the city's income, and King was
arrested and fined, but the Supreme Court, in *Gayle v. Browder* (1956),
eventually declared unconstitutional the city's policy of segregated public buses. As Henry J. Abraham has written: "[T]he successful Montgomery boycott set a precedent for similar actions in cities throughout the
South, extending to retail stores, produce markets, and a host of other
sales and service facilities."[1]

In September 1957, President Dwight D. Eisenhower sent army troops
and then some 10,000 National Guardsmen to insure that nine black
students could enroll in Central High School, a public school, with more
than 2,000 students, in Little Rock, Arkansas. Governor Orval Faubus
had defied a federal court desegregation order and had belittled the Supreme Court's *Brown* decision as a misreading of the Constitution. Angry
local citizens were thus encouraged to prevent the nine black students
from entering the school, requiring Eisenhower's actions. The following
year the school board sought postponement of the court order, claiming
the governor and the state legislature had derailed the school board's
plan. Shortly before the 1958 school year started, in a special summer
session and in an extremely rare, if not unique, Supreme Court reply, *all
nine* justices individually signed their names to an opinion denying the
request. The Court rebuked the governor for ignoring "the basic principle that the federal judiciary is supreme in the exposition of the law of
the Constitution, [a] principle [that] has ever since been respected by this
Court and the Country as a permanent and indispensable feature of our
constitutional system."[2]

The momentum of the movement increased significantly when a sustained campaign of sit-ins and "freedom rides" began in the early 1960s.
The sit-ins originated in Greensboro, North Carolina, when four young
black men, all college students, on February 1, 1960, were refused service
at Woolworth's "whites only" lunch counter. The attention spawned, in
the next few months, sit-ins in places of public accommodation in almost
sixty cities throughout every southern state, involving some 50,000 protesters. At Shaw University, a black institution in Raleigh, North Carolina, a group of students formed the Student Non-violent Coordinating
Committee (SNCC) to plan and manage a strategy of sit-ins and other
forms of public protest. Though the group initially consisted of just a

few hundred students, they were courageous enough publicly to flout the law to draw further attention to the realities of racial segregation. SNCC also worked with the Congress of Racial Equality (CORE) to staff the famous "Freedom Rides" of 1961, emulating similar protests in the late 1940s by CORE after the Supreme Court had ruled in 1946 that segregated *interstate* travel violated the Constitution's "commerce clause." After the Montgomery Boycott, the Court ruled that segregated *local* public transportation violated the "equal protection" clause of the Fourteenth Amendment, and although Montgomery public buses were desegregated in 1956, there were still many remnants and relics of segregation in bus terminals.

Civil rights activists in 1961 boarded buses on cross-country journeys beginning in Washington, D.C., and reaching one southern city after another. The first freedom ride began with seven black and six white civil rights activists. At bus terminals the black travelers peacefully entered "whites only" waiting rooms, restaurants, and restrooms. In the Deep South, angry white mobs with metal pipes along the way beat many "freedom riders," sometimes into unconsciousness. Some freedom riders were arrested. In Alabama, a mob slashed the tires of a bus as it entered the state, and another bus upon arriving in Anniston, Alabama, was burned to the ground. A second ride carried newsmen and cameramen and brought to national prominence the events of the freedom rides. When the bus reached Montgomery, a near-riot erupted. A livid crowd of whites beat a young white freedom rider as he exited the bus; some in the mob stomped his head into the ground. Members of the press were clubbed; and police eventually used tear gas to disperse the violent mob. Subsequent freedom rides were assigned a detail of federal marshals on orders from President John F. Kennedy.

A year later the Kennedy administration arranged for federal marshals to guard James Meredith as he entered the University of Mississippi as its first black student ever to enroll. The marshals were not enough to prevent violence; two students were killed and many others injured before the National Guard arrived. Increasingly, the violence in reaction to the protests was being captured on film. Protesters in 1963 in Birmingham, Alabama, staged sit-ins at lunch counters and "kneel-ins" in front of segregated churches. Reverend King and several other leaders were arrested. Police dogs and fire hoses assaulting and beating back civil rights protesters produced vivid pictures on front pages of newspapers and on network newscasts, amplifying a message for a whole nation to hear. Civil rights and racial equality were finally on the national political agenda.

SNCC and other groups conducted voter registration in Mississippi, which attracted some 600 volunteers, most of whom were white students from universities and colleges across the United States. SNCC initiated the "Freedom Summer" of 1964, and the local Ku Klux Klan (KKK) near the town of Philadelphia, Mississippi, murdered two white and one black voter registration volunteers. Undeterred, SNCC sought to challenge the white Democratic Party of Mississippi by creating the Mississippi Freedom Democratic Party and holding a "Freedom Ballot" mock election that brought out some 80,000 black "voters"—many times the number of actually registered black voters in Mississippi. Several "campaign" workers were arrested, and many white student volunteers from northern universities seen as outside agitators were attacked and beaten by local whites.

Perhaps no event more symbolizes the civil rights movement than Martin Luther King, Jr.'s "I Have a Dream" speech delivered in 1963 from the Lincoln Memorial before an assembly of over 250,000 people who had peacefully marched through the stately named streets of the nation's capital—one hundred years after Lincoln, in the midst of the Civil War, had signed the Emancipation Proclamation to free the slaves. The effect of King's march and speech was dramatic as millions watched on television. At the time, a major civil rights bill was pending but bottlenecked in Congress, and in the fall President Kennedy was assassinated, leaving Vice-President Lyndon B. Johnson his successor in the White House. The march on Washington, sympathy for the dead president, and Johnson's unmatched mastery of the lawmaking process combined in producing the following year the most comprehensive federal legislation ever enacted to promote equality—the Civil Rights Act of 1964. Inspired by that success, King and other civil rights activists on March 7, 1965, led a march of some fifty miles from Selma to Montgomery in support of voting rights. The following August, Congress passed and President Johnson signed into law the Voting Rights Act of 1965, the most powerful statute ever passed to enforce the terms of the Fifteenth Amendment. The constitutional promises of a century before were now at last coming true.

Numerous free speech issues—some based on established principles, some breaking new ground—were fused with the long and sustained events of the civil rights movement that culminated in the 1960s in these major legislative triumphs.

In 1958 the Court began a steadfast battle against Alabama's relentless efforts to pry membership lists from NAACP operations in that state. In Alabama and other states under court order to desegregate their public schools, the NAACP was more despised than the Communist Party, and if membership had become public, social ostracism and worse might have greeted those—whether black or white—working in the organization to promote civil rights. In *NAACP v. Alabama* (1958), the Court hailed the importance of freedom of association and refused Alabama's request to get the NAACP membership lists unless the state could demonstrate a compelling interest in the membership lists that was achievable in no other way except through forced disclosure. In a series of subsequent cases the Court protected the NAACP against other states' determination to disclose membership lists. Virginia tried to cramp the increasingly successful role played in the courts by the NAACP's use of "test cases" to challenge state segregation laws. For decades the NAACP had been generating such cases, but after it had effectively initiated school deseg-regation lawsuits in Virginia, the state amended its law against "im-proper solicitation" of legal business in such a way as to target organizations like the NAACP. In a 6–3 decision, the Supreme Court in *N.A.A.C.P. v. Button* (1963) ruled that the organization's litigation activ-ities were a form of free speech protected against the state's efforts to ban improper solicitation.

While the NAACP was busy in courtrooms across the South, ordinary citizens (students, ministers, and other civil rights activists, white and black, from within and beyond the South) faced criminal prosecution for their participation in various forms of symbolic protest, demonstrations, and marches in cities like Birmingham, Montgomery, and Selma, Ala-bama, Columbia, South Carolina, Baton Rouge, Louisiana, and Tallahas-see, Florida. The movement even spread to northern cities where racial discrimination was pervasive, though not always overtly required by law, in cities such as Boston, Chicago, Denver, Detroit, Philadelphia, and Seattle.

On March 2, 1961, some 187 black high school and college students demonstrated against racial inequality and official segregation and were arrested in Columbia, South Carolina. They had peacefully walked around the state capitol grounds holding placards that expressed op-position to the state's segregation policies. Police feared disturbances as a crowd of 200 to 300 curious onlookers gathered, and when the dem-onstrators refused to obey the order to disperse, they were arrested and charged with the common-law crime of disturbing the peace. The Su-preme Court, with one dissenter (Justice Tom Clark, a conservative from Texas), reversed their convictions. Clark questioned the Court's conclu-sion that the demonstration was peaceful and that there was no cause to stop it. In his view the facts "created a much greater danger of riot and disorder. It is my belief that anyone conversant with the almost spon-taneous combustion in some Southern communities in such a situation will agree that the City Manager's action may well have averted a major catastrophe."[3] But the Court thought otherwise, having concluded that the symbolic demonstration around the state capitol grounds was an exercise of freedom of speech protected by the First Amendment.

As the Court continued to protect variations of symbolic opposition to segregation, the number of justices in support of the protesters continued to dwindle as the civil rights movement intensified. One year after the South Carolina case, a divided Court reversed convictions of blacks who had refused to leave lunch counters in Baltimore, Maryland. In the earlier sit-in cases the Court either found a lack of evidence or held the ordinance too vague to enforce consistently with principles of "due process of law." In the Baltimore case most of the members of the Court's majority reversed the convictions because, while the cases were in the judicial pipeline, Maryland passed a law prohibiting racial discrimination in places of public accommodation, like restaurants. A majority of the Court, in effect, never actually ruled that sit-ins—a form of civil disobedience—were protected free speech. In 1965 another closely divided Court (5–4) reversed the convictions of protesters too near a Baton Rouge courthouse, finding the "breach of peace" city ordinance vague and insufficient evidence of disruptive conduct. In 1964 five young black men staged a protest in a Louisiana regional public library for "whites only," were arrested, and then convicted. Two years later the sharply divided 5–4 Court majority reversed all five convictions on appeal, though the majority could not agree on the reasoning. Four of the five justices, however, argued that the refusal to leave the library was, in fact, protected by the First Amendment, but that view could not command a fifth supporter.

Later that year waning judicial support produced another 5–4 majority, but this one *upheld* convictions of thirty-two students from Florida A&M University, in Tallahassee, Florida, who had assembled to protest the arrest of fellow students the day before. They had clustered close to the jail housing the arrested students, and after refusing to leave upon official request, the protesters themselves were arrested for "trespass with a malicious and mischievous intent." Justice Hugo L. Black wrote the opinion of the Court upholding the convictions. Jails were distinguished from state capitol buildings, and there was no evidence, said Black, that the trespass statute was enforced to silence the message of the protesters. No one has a constitutional right to trespass, he concluded, rejecting "the assumption that people who want to propagandize protests or views have a constitutional right to do so whenever and however and wherever they please."[4]

As important as these "symbolic speech" cases were, the civil rights movement produced one of the most important legal holdings in the development in freedom of speech and press in the United States. The *New York Times* in 1960 had published a paid advertisement ("Heed Their Rising Voices") recounting official and hostile reaction to civil rights protesters in Alabama. L.B. Sullivan, a former Montgomery police commissioner, who was unnamed in the advertisement, sued the newspaper in various Alabama courts for libel—a publication falsely defaming some-one—and was awarded damages by sympathetic juries (in one lawsuit alone the damages were $500,000). Under Alabama law, a libel existed wherever a third party read the defamatory statements; thus multiple lawsuits could result from a single publication distributed in many ju-risdictions. The Alabama defamation law also stated that libel existed if *any* factual details were untrue—and the ad here misstated some minor details. Monetary damage awards—both compensatory but especially punitive, which were virtually unlimited—could have crippled and ef-fectively muzzled any major newspaper. Yet, until this case, the Supreme Court had held that libel was *completely* outside the scope of the First Amendment. Without some protection from libel judgments made by hostile juries, the press would reduce or eliminate its coverage of con-troversial events, such as sit-ins, marches, and other symbolic protest that informed the nation and inspired sympathetic attention that changed public policy with the federal civil rights and voting laws of 1964–1965. In his concurring opinion, in fact, Justice Black noted that an angry white jury was punishing the *New York Times* for favorably covering the civil rights movement.

In the case of *New York Times v. Sullivan* (1964) a unanimous Supreme Court abolished the libel judgment awarded to Police Commissioner Sul-livan and established an unprecedented doctrine that greatly expanded the marketplace of ideas by seriously weakening state libel laws. While the case arose in the clash of civil rights protest and official conduct, the doctrine that emerged (known as the "actual malice" test) was soon ex-panded in a series of later cases so that by the mid-1970s and thereafter public—and even private—behavior of public figures became fair game for the mass media. Such "public" people must show not only that they were defamed but that the false statements about them were published by others who knew the statements were false or who acted recklessly in utter disregard of the truth. Public figures—whether they are Presi-dent George W. Bush, Michael Jackson, Britney Spears, Eminem, or Tom Cruise—face great difficulty prevailing against publications or broad-casts not driven by recklessness or based on deliberate falsehood. This was a major change in freedom of the press.

As the strategy of the civil rights movement shifted in the mid-1960s from passive resistance to "Black power," public support began to di-minish. Activists in the movement divided. Some continued peacefully to protest against a still much-segregated South; others turned to the pervasive discrimination, especially economic inequality, in the North. Another group became more militant and demanded immediate equality and even a separate state. Malcom Little changed his name to Malcom X and became a prominent member and skilled advocate of the Nation of Islam, a group that preached black racial superiority and separatism. Passive resistance and civil disobedience collided with a growing militancy and calls for violence and an end to cooperation among white and black civil rights workers. As the movement fractured, violence erupted throughout the nation's cities. Discontent spilled out into the streets of urban centers such as Los Angeles and Detroit. Urban race riots grew in number during the 1960s. In 1965 five were reported, twenty-seven erupted in 1966, and in 1967 seventy-five occurred.

On February 21, 1965, rivals from the Nation of Islam assassinated Malcolm X in Harlem while at a speaking engagement. On April 4, 1968, Martin Luther King, Jr., was murdered at a Memphis motel, setting off more than a hundred city riots nationwide. Two months later in the first hour of June 5, Senator Robert F. Kennedy of New York was shot dead in the kitchen passageway of the Ambassador Hotel in Los Angeles. Just before midnight he had proclaimed victory before a jubilant audience of supporters in the California primary for the nomination of the Democrat candidate for the presidency. At the party's national convention later in August in Chicago, a blood bath spilled onto the city's streets when antiwar protesters and police clashed, an event seen on television all over the country in millions of homes.

An astonished and blurry-eyed nation was overcome by a whirlwind of shocking public events: a new hippie drug-and-sex-filled culture, a civil rights movement that had touched the national consciousness and lost its appeal through violence and demands for immediate change, a spate of seemingly endless and violent urban riots, university and college campuses rife with protest, an increasing toll of young men dead or wounded in an unpopular and confusing war half a world away, and the assassination of prominent public leaders. The backlash elected conservative Republican Richard M. Nixon to the presidency, edging out the Democratic nominee, Vice President Hubert H. Humphrey. Nixon had developed a "southern strategy" to attract to the Republican Party disillusioned southern Democrats who had voted for a third party in 1968. Segregationist candidate of the American Independent Party, governor and former Democrat George C. Wallace of Alabama, won 13.5 percent of the popular vote and carried five southern states.

Despite two consecutive Senate rejections of his nominees, President Nixon had appointed during his first term four of the nine members of the Supreme Court, establishing a conservative Court less inclined to protect novel free speech claims of protesters and demonstrators. In 1972 Nixon was reelected to a second term with a stunning support of forty-nine of the fifty states. The liberal 1960s had come to a crashing conclusion from which liberalism as a political message has yet to recover its once prominent place in American political culture.

NOTES

1. Henry J. Abraham and Barbara Perry, *Freedom and the Court: Civil Rights and Liberties in the United States*, 7th ed. (New York: Oxford University Press, 1998), p. 386.

2. *Cooper v. Aaron*, 358 U.S. 1, 18 (1958).

3. *Edwards v. South Carolina*, 372 U.S. 229, 244 (1963) (dissenting opinion).

4. *Adderley v. Florida*, 385 U.S. 39, 48 (1966).

DOCUMENTS

8.1.   The Right to Associate

---

*A number of southern states demanded that corporations doing
business in such states divulge their membership lists. The law
targeted civil rights groups such as the NAACP. The NAACP had
prevailed in lawsuits attacking segregation, and many regarded
these orders to disclose membership lists as retaliation, designed
to expose its members to social ostracism and worse. The
NAACP challenged Alabama's order to disclose its membership
lists, claiming that the order infringed on its members' right to
associate. The Supreme Court ultimately agreed with the
NAACP.*

[Justice John Marshall Harlan delivered the opinion of the Court.]

Effective advocacy of both public and private points of view, particularly controversial ones, is undeniably enhanced by group association,
as this Court has more than once recognized by remarking upon the close
nexus between freedom of speech and assembly. . . . It is beyond debate
that the freedom to engage in association for the advancement of beliefs
and ideas is an inseparable aspect of . . . freedom of speech. Of course, it
is immaterial whether the beliefs sought to be advanced by the association pertain to political, economic, religious or cultural matters, and state
action which may have the effect of curtailing the freedom to associate
is subject to the closest scrutiny.

The fact that Alabama . . . has taken no direct action . . . to restrict the
right of [NAACP] members to associate freely, does not end the inquiry
into the effect of the production order. . . . In the domain of these indispensable liberties, whether of speech, press, or association, the decisions
of this Court recognize that abridgment of such rights, even though un-
intended, may inevitably follow from varied forms of governmental action. . . . The governmental action challenged may appear to be totally
unrelated to protected liberties. . . .

It is hardly a novel perception that compelled disclosure of affiliation
with groups engaged in advocacy may constitute as effective a restraint
on freedom of association as the forms [previously invalidated by this
Court]. This Court has recognized the vital relationship between freedom
to associate and privacy in one's associations. . . . Inviolability of privacy
in group association may in many circumstances be indispensable to

preservation of freedom of association, particularly where a group espouses dissident beliefs.

... [The NAACP] has made an uncontroverted showing that on past occasions revelation of the identity of its rank-and-file members has exposed these members to economic reprisal, loss of employment, threat of physical coercion, and other manifestations of public hostility. Under these circumstances, we think it apparent that compelled disclosure of petitioner's Alabama membership is likely to affect adversely the ability of [the NAACP] and its members to pursue their collective effort to foster beliefs which they admittedly have the right to advocate, in that it may induce members to withdraw from the Association and to dissuade others from joining it because of fear of exposure of their beliefs shown through their associations and of the consequences of this exposure.

It is not sufficient to answer, as [Alabama] does here, that whatever repressive effect compulsory disclosure of names of [the NAACP's] members may have upon participation by Alabama citizens in [the NAACP's] activities follows not from *state* action but from *private* community pressures. The crucial factor is the interplay of governmental and private action, for it is only after the initial exertion of state power represented by the production order that private action takes hold.

... It is important to bear in mind that [the NAACP] asserts no right to absolute immunity from state investigation, and no right to disregard Alabama's laws. . . . [The NAACP] has not objected to divulging the identity of its members who are employed by or hold official positions with it. It has urged the rights solely of its ordinary rank-and-file members. . . . [W]e are unable to perceive that the disclosure of the names of [NAACP's] rank-and-file members has a substantial bearing on [any state interest or justification in obtaining this information]. . . . [W]hatever interest [Alabama] may have in obtaining names of ordinary members has not been shown to be sufficient to overcome [NAACP's] constitutional objections to the production order. . . .

We hold that the immunity from state scrutiny of membership lists which the Association claims on behalf of it members is here so related to the right of its members to pursue their lawful private interests privately and to associate freely with others in doing so as to come within the protection of the [Constitution's guarantees]. And we conclude that Alabama has fallen short of showing a controlling justification for the deterrent effect on the free enjoyment of the right to associate which disclosure of membership lists is likely to have. Accordingly, the judgment of civil contempt and the $100,000 fine which resulted from [NAACP's] refusal to comply with the production order in this respect must fall.

Source: NAACP v. Alabama, 357 U.S. 449 (June 30, 1958).

8.2.   Peaceful Marching Is Protected Expression

*In March 1961, some 187 high school and college students
marched in protest in front of the state capitol in Columbia,
South Carolina, against the state's official segregation policies.
After crowds of bystanders began to gather, the police asked the
protesters to disperse, but they did not. The protesters were arrested, tried, and convicted of the common-law breach of the
peace, and the state's supreme court upheld the convictions.
The U.S. Supreme Court reversed, ruling that the conduct here
was constitutionally protected.*

[Justice Stewart delivered the opinion of the Court.]

There was no substantial conflict in the trial evidence. Late in the
morning of March 2, 1961, the petitioners, high school and college students of the Negro race, met at the Zion Baptist Church in Columbia.
From there, at about noon, they walked in separate groups of about 15
to the South Carolina State House grounds, an area of two city blocks
open to the general public. Their purpose was to submit a protest
[against racial discrimination in South Carolina]. . . . Already on the State
House grounds when the petitioners arrived were 30 or more law enforcement officers, who had advance knowledge that the petitioners were
coming. Each group of petitioners entered the grounds through a driveway and parking area known in the record as the "horseshoe." As they
entered, they were told by the law enforcement officials that "they had
a right, as a citizen, to go through the State House grounds, as any other
citizen has, as long as they were peaceful." During the next half hour or
45 minutes, the petitioners, in the same small groups, walked single file
or two abreast in an orderly way, through the grounds, each group carrying placards bearing such messages as "I am proud to be a Negro"
and "Down with segregation."

During this time, a crowd of some 200 to 300 onlookers had collected
in the horseshoe area and on the adjacent sidewalks. There was no evidence to suggest that these onlookers were anything but curious, and no
evidence at all of any threatening remarks, hostile gestures, or offensive
language on the part of any member of the crowd. The City Manager
testified that he recognized some of the onlookers, whom he did not
identify, as "possible troublemakers," but his subsequent testimony
made clear that nobody among the crowd actually caused or threatened
any trouble. There was no obstruction of pedestrian or vehicular traffic
within the State House grounds. No vehicle was prevented from entering

or leaving the horseshoe area. Although vehicular traffic at a nearby street intersection was slowed down somewhat, an officer was dispatched to keep traffic moving. There were a number of bystanders on the public sidewalks adjacent to the State House grounds, but they all moved on when asked to do so, and there was no impediment of pedestrian traffic. Police protection at the scene was at all times sufficient to meet any foreseeable possibility of disorder.

In the situation and under the circumstances thus described, the police authorities advised the petitioners that they would be arrested if they did not disperse within 15 minutes. Instead of dispersing, the petitioners engaged in what the City Manager described as "boisterous," "loud," and "flamboyant" conduct, which, as his later testimony made clear, consisted of listening to a "religious harangue" by one of their leaders, and loudly singing "The Star Spangled Banner" and other patriotic and religious songs, while stamping their feet and clapping their hands. After 15 minutes had passed, the police arrested the petitioners and marched them off to jail.

Upon this evidence, the state trial court convicted the petitioners of breach of the peace, and imposed sentences ranging from a $10 fine or five days in jail to a $100 fine or 30 days in jail. . . .

The petitioners contend that there was a complete absence of any evidence of the commission of this offense, and that they were thus denied one of the most basic elements of due process of law. Whatever the merits of this contention, we need not pass upon it in the present case. The state courts have held that the petitioners' conduct constituted breach of the peace under state law, and we may accept their decision as binding upon us to that extent. But it nevertheless remains our duty in a case such as this to make an independent examination of the whole record. And it is clear to us that, in arresting, convicting, and punishing the petitioners under the circumstances disclosed by this record, South Carolina infringed the petitioners' constitutionally protected rights of free speech, free assembly, and freedom to petition for redress of their grievances.

It has long been established that these First Amendment freedoms are protected by the Fourteenth Amendment from invasion by the States. The circumstances in this case reflect an exercise of these basic constitutional rights in their most pristine and classic form. The petitioners felt aggrieved by laws of South Carolina which allegedly "prohibited Negro privileges in this State." They peaceably assembled at the site of the State Government, and there peaceably expressed their grievances. Not until they were told by police officials that they must disperse on pain of arrest did they do more. Even then, they but sang patriotic and religious songs after one of their leaders had delivered a "religious harangue." There was no violence or threat of violence on their part, or on the part of any member of the crowd watching them. Police protection was "ample."

. . . [A] function of free speech under our system of government is to invite dispute. It may indeed best serve its high purpose when it induces a condition of unrest, creates dissatisfaction with conditions as they are, or even stirs people to anger. Speech is often provocative and challenging. It may strike at prejudices and preconceptions, and have profound unsettling effects as it presses for acceptance of an idea. That is why freedom of speech . . . is . . . protected against censorship or punishment, unless shown likely to produce a clear and present danger of a serious substantive evil that rises far above public inconvenience, annoyance, or unrest. . . . There is no room under our Constitution for a more restrictive view. For the alternative would lead to standardization of ideas either by legislatures, courts, or dominant political or community groups.

. . . [T]he courts of South Carolina have defined a criminal offense so as to permit conviction of the petitioners if their speech stirred people to anger, invited public dispute, or brought about a condition of unrest. A conviction resting on any of those grounds may not stand.

Source: Edwards v. South Carolina, 372 U.S. 229 (February 25, 1963).

8.3.   Is "Libel" Protected Expression?

The New York Times *published an advertisement supported by clergy and other civil rights activists depicting racial protests and harsh official reaction in Alabama. No public officials were mentioned by name, but some of the details of the claims in the ad were factually incorrect. Former Montgomery, Alabama, police commissioner L.B. Sullivan successfully sued the* New York Times *for libel—that is, a civil lawsuit for false defamation of character—and received a judgment of $500,000 from a jury in an Alabama court. Until this case, libel had not been protected at all by the First Amendment. Unrestricted state libel laws could thus be used, as here, to punish the news media when sympathetic to civil rights protesters. The only defense under Alabama libel law was proof of truth "in all its particulars." This* New York Times *advertisement did have some minor factual errors, which allowed Sullivan to prevail. The Supreme Court, in this watershed holding, unanimously reversed the libel judgment and announced a new test to measure when libel must be protected by the Constitution.*

[Justice Brennan delivered the opinion of the Court.]

We are required in this case to determine for the first time the extent to which the constitutional protections for speech and press limit a State's power to award damages in a libel action brought by a public official against critics of his official conduct.

[Sullivan's] complaint alleged that he had been libeled by statements in a full-page advertisement that was carried in the New York Times on March 29, 1960. Entitled "Heed Their Rising Voices," the advertisement began by stating that "As the whole world knows by now, thousands of Southern Negro students are engaged in widespread non-violent demonstrations in positive affirmation of the right to live in human dignity as guaranteed by the U.S. Constitution and the Bill of Rights." It went on to charge that "in their efforts to uphold these guarantees, they are being met by an unprecedented wave of terror by those who would deny and negate that document which the whole world looks upon as setting the pattern for modern freedom. . . ." Succeeding paragraphs purported to illustrate the "wave of terror" by describing certain alleged events. . . .

It is uncontroverted that some of the statements contained in the [advertisement] were not accurate descriptions of events which occurred in Montgomery. [For example,] Negro students . . . sang the National Anthem and not "My Country, 'Tis of Thee." . . . Dr. King had not been arrested seven times, but only four; and although he claimed to have been assaulted some years earlier in connection with his arrest for loitering outside a courtroom, one of the officers who made the arrest denied that there was such an assault. . . .

[Sullivan] relies heavily, as did the Alabama courts, on statements of this Court to the effect that the Constitution does not protect libelous publications. [However,] libel can claim no talismanic immunity from constitutional limitations. It must be measured by standards that satisfy the First Amendment. . . .

[W]e consider this case against the background of a profound national commitment to the principle that debate on public issues should be uninhibited, robust, and wide-open, and that it may well include vehement, caustic, and sometimes unpleasantly sharp attacks on government and public officials. . . . The present advertisement, as an expression of grievance and protest on one of the major public issues of our time, would seem clearly to qualify for the constitutional protection. The question is whether it forfeits that protection by the falsity of some of its factual statements and by its alleged defamation of respondent.

. . . As [James] Madison said, 'Some degree of abuse is inseparable from the proper use of every thing; and in no instance is this more true than in that of the press." . . .

[N]either factual error nor defamatory content suffices to remove the constitutional shield from criticism of official conduct, [and] the combination of the two elements is no less inadequate. This is the lesson to be drawn from the great controversy over the Sedition Act of 1798 . . . which first crystallized a national awareness of the central meaning of the First Amendment. . . . Although the Sedition Act was never tested in this Court, the attack upon its validity has carried the day in the court of history. . . . These views reflect a broad consensus that the Act, because of the restraint it imposed upon criticism of government and public officials, was inconsistent with the First Amendment.

There is no force in [Sullivan's] argument that the constitutional limitations implicit in the history of the Sedition Act apply only to Congress and not to the States. It is true that the First Amendment was originally addressed only to action by the Federal Government . . . [b]ut this distinction was eliminated with the adoption of the Fourteenth Amendment and the application to the States of the First Amendment's restrictions. . . .

The fear of damage awards under a rule such as that invoked by the Alabama courts here may be markedly more inhibiting than the fear of prosecution under a criminal statute. . . . Alabama, for example, has a criminal libel law which subjects to prosecution "any person who speaks, writes, or prints of and concerning another any accusation falsely and maliciously importing the commission by such person of a felony, or any other indictable offense involving moral turpitude," and which allows as punishment upon conviction a fine not exceeding $500 and a prison sentence of six months. . . . Presumably a person charged with violation of this statute enjoys ordinary criminal-law safeguards such as the requirements of an indictment and of proof beyond a reasonable doubt. These safeguards are not available to the defendant in a civil [libel] action. The judgment awarded in this case—without the need for any proof of actual pecuniary loss—was one thousand times greater than the maximum fine provided by the Alabama criminal statute, and one hundred times greater than that provided by the Sedition Act. And since there is no double-jeopardy limitation applicable to civil lawsuits, this is not the only judgment that may be awarded against [the *New York Times*] for the same publication. Whether or not a newspaper can survive a succession of such judgments, the pall of fear and timidity imposed upon those who would give voice to public criticism is an atmosphere in which the First Amendment freedoms cannot survive. [The *New York Times* states that four other libel suits based on the advertisement have been filed against it by others who have served as Montgomery city commissioners and by the governor of Alabama: that another $500,000 verdict has been awarded in the only one of these cases that has yet gone to trial; and that the damages sought in the other three total $2 million.] Plainly the Alabama law of civil libel is "a form of regulation that creates hazards to protected freedoms markedly greater than those that attend reliance upon the criminal law."

The state rule of law is not saved by its allowance of the defense of truth. . . . A rule compelling the critic of official conduct to guarantee the truth of all his factual assertions—and to do so on pain of libel judgments virtually unlimited in amount—leads to a comparable "self-censorship." Allowance of the defense of truth, with the burden of proving it on the defendant, does not mean that only false speech will be deterred. Even courts accepting this defense as an adequate safeguard have recognized the difficulties of adducing legal proofs that the alleged libel was true in all its factual particulars. . . . Under such a rule, would-be critics of official conduct may be deterred from voicing their criticism, even though it is believed to be true and even though it is in fact true, because of doubt whether it can be proved in court or fear of the expense of having to do so. They tend to make only statements which "steer far wider of the unlawful zone." The rule thus dampens the vigor and limits the variety of public debate. It is inconsistent with the First and Fourteenth Amendments.

The constitutional guarantees require, we think, a federal rule that prohibits a public official from recovering damages for a defamatory falsehood relating to his official conduct unless he proves that the statement was made with "actual malice"—that is, with knowledge that it was false or with reckless disregard of whether it was false or not.

It is as much [a citizen's] duty to criticize as it is the official's duty to administer. . . . As Madison said, "the censorial power is in the people over the Government, and not in the Government over the people." It would give public servants an unjustified preference over the public they serve, if critics of official conduct did not have a fair equivalent of the immunity granted to the officials themselves.

We conclude that such a privilege is required by the First and Fourteenth Amendments.

Applying these standards, we consider that the proof presented to show actual malice lacks the convincing clarity which the constitutional standard demands, and hence that it would not constitutionally sustain the judgment for respondent under the proper rule of law. . . . We think the evidence against the Times supports at most a finding of negligence in failing to discover the misstatements, and is constitutionally insufficient to show the recklessness that is required for a finding of actual malice.

We also think the evidence was constitutionally defective in another respect: it was incapable of supporting the jury's finding that the allegedly libelous statements were made "of and concerning" [Sullivan].

There was no reference to respondent in the advertisement, either by name or official position. [It cannot be assumed that criticism of government in the abstract is, in fact, criticism of specific officials.] . . . Raising as it does the possibility that a good-faith critic of government will be penalized for his criticism, the proposition relied on by the Alabama courts strikes at the very center of the constitutionally protected area of free expression. We hold that such a proposition may not constitutionally be utilized to establish that an otherwise impersonal attack on governmental operations was a libel of an official responsible for those operations. Since it was relied on exclusively here, and there was no other evidence to connect the statements with respondent, the evidence was constitutionally insufficient to support a finding that the statements referred to respondent.

Source: *New York Times v. Sullivan*, 376 U.S. 254 (March 9, 1964).

8.4.   Does the First Amendment Protect Protesting Near a City Jail?

The Supreme Court had been very protective of the expressive rights of civil rights activists—at least until 1966. About 200 Florida A&M University students had gathered in a driveway of a city jailhouse, where they danced, sang songs, and generally protested both the earlier arrests of fellow students and the segregated jail in which they were being detained. The students ignored the sheriff's warnings to leave, and 32 were subsequently arrested and convicted for "trespass with a malicious and mischievous intent." On November 14, 1966, Justice Hugo L. Black wrote the Court's (5–4) opinion upholding the convictions and rejecting the First Amendment claims, distinguishing this case from earlier decisions by ruling that a jail is not the state capitol grounds. Four justices dissented in the following opinion by Justice William O. Douglas.

[Justice Douglas, joined by Chief Justice Earl Warren, Justice Brennan, and Justice Fortas, dissenting.]

The jailhouse, like an executive mansion, a legislative chamber, a courthouse, or the statehouse itself . . . is one of the seats of government, whether it be the Tower of London, the Bastille, or a small county jail. And when it houses political prisoners or those who many think are unjustly held, it is an obvious center for protest. The [First Amendment] right to petition for the redress of grievances has an ancient history and is not limited to writing a letter or sending a telegram to a congressman; it is not confined to appearing before the local city council, or writing letters to the President or Governor or Mayor. . . . Conventional methods of petitioning may be, and often have been, shut off to large groups of our citizens. Legislators may turn deaf ears; formal complaints may be routed endlessly through a bureaucratic maze; courts may let the wheels of justice grind very slowly. Those who do not control television and radio, those who cannot afford to advertise in newspapers or circulate elaborate pamphlets may have only a more limited type of access to public officials. Their methods should not be condemned as tactics of obstruction and harassment as long as the assembly and petition are peaceable, as these were.

There is no question that petitioners had as their purpose a protest against the arrest of Florida A. & M. students for trying to integrate public theatres. The sheriff's testimony indicates that he well understood the purpose of the rally. The petitioners who testified unequivocally stated that the group was protesting the arrests, and state and local policies of segregation, including segregation of the jail. This testimony was not contradicted or even questioned. The fact that no one gave a formal speech, that no elaborate handbills were distributed, and that the group was not laden with signs would seem to be immaterial. Such methods are not the sine qua non of petitioning for the redress of grievances. The group did sing "freedom" songs. And history shows that a song can be a powerful tool of protest. . . . There was no violence; no threat of violence; no attempted jail break; no storming of a prison; no plan or plot to do anything but protest. The evidence is uncontradicted that the petitioners' conduct did not upset the jailhouse routine; things went on as they normally would. None of the group entered the jail. Indeed, they moved back from the entrance as they were instructed. There was no shoving, no pushing, no disorder or threat of riot. It is said that some of the group blocked part of the driveway leading to the jail entrance. The chief jailer, to be sure, testified that vehicles would not have been able to use the driveway. Never did the students locate themselves so as to cause interference with persons or vehicles going to or coming from the jail. Indeed, it is undisputed that the sheriff and deputy sheriff, in separate cars, were able to drive up the driveway to the parking places near the entrance and that no one obstructed their path. Further, it is undisputed that the entrance to the jail was not blocked. And whenever the students were requested to move they did so. If there was congestion, the solution was a further request to move to lawns or parking areas, not complete ejection and arrest. . . . Finally, the fact that some of the protestants may have felt their cause so just that they were willing to be arrested for making their protest outside the jail seems wholly irrelevant. A petition is nonetheless a petition, though its futility may make martyrdom attractive.

We do violence to the First Amendment when we permit this "petition for redress of grievances" to be turned into a trespass action. . . . In the first place the jailhouse grounds were not marked with "NO TRESPASS-ING!" signs, nor does respondent claim that the public was generally excluded from the grounds. Only the sheriff's fiat transformed lawful conduct into an unlawful trespass. To say that a private owner could have done the same if the rally had taken place on private property is to speak of a different case, as an assembly and a petition for redress of grievances run to government, not to private proprietors.

The Court forgets that prior to this day our decisions have drastically limited the application of state statutes inhibiting the right to go peacefully on public property to exercise First Amendment rights. . . . Such was the case of Edwards v. South Carolina, where aggrieved people "peaceably assembled at the site of the State Government" to express their grievances to the citizens of the State as well as to the legislature. Edwards was in the tradition of Cox v. New Hampshire [1941], where the public streets were said to be "immemorially associated" with "the right of assembly and the opportunities for the communication of thought and the discussion of public questions." . . . Would the case be any different if, as is common, the demonstration took place outside a building which housed both the jail and the legislative body? I think not.

. . . There may be some instances in which assemblies and petitions for redress of grievances are not consistent with other necessary purposes of public property. A noisy meeting may be out of keeping with the serenity of the statehouse or the quiet of the courthouse. No one, for example, would suggest that the Senate gallery is the proper place for a vociferous protest rally. And in other cases it may be necessary to adjust the right to petition for redress of grievances to the other interests inhering in the uses to which the public property is normally put. . . . But this is quite different from saying that all public places are off limits to people with grievances. . . . And it is farther yet from saying that the "custodian" of the public property in his discretion can decide when public places shall be used for the communication of ideas, especially the constitutional right to assemble and petition for redress of grievances. . . . For to place such discretion in any public official, be he the "custodian" of the public property or the local police commissioner . . . is to place those who assert their First Amendment rights at his mercy. It gives him the awesome power to decide whose ideas may be expressed and who shall be denied a place to air their claims and petition their government. . . .

That tragic consequence happens today when a trespass law is used to bludgeon those who peacefully exercise a First Amendment right to protest to government against one of the most grievous of all modern oppressions which some of our States are inflicting on our citizens. . . . Today a trespass law is used to penalize people for exercising a constitutional right. Tomorrow a disorderly conduct statute, a breach-of-the-peace statute, a vagrancy statute will be put to the same end. It is said that the sheriff did not make the arrests because of the views which petitioners espoused. That excuse is usually given, as we know from the many cases involving arrests of minority groups for breaches of the peace, unlawful assemblies, and parading without a permit. The charge against William Penn, who preached a nonconformist doctrine in a street in London, was that he caused "a great concourse and tumult of people" in contempt of the King and "to the great disturbance of his peace." . . . That was in 1670. In modern times, also, such arrests are usually sought to be justified by some legitimate function of government. Yet by allowing these orderly and civilized protests against injustice to be suppressed, we only increase the forces of frustration which the conditions of second-class citizenship are generating amongst us.

Source: Adderley v. Florida, 385 U.S. 39, 48–56 (1966) (dissenting opinion).

ANNOTATED RESEARCH GUIDE

Bloom, Jack M. *Class, Race, and the Civil Rights Movement*. Bloomington: Indiana University Press, 1987. Provides an economic context in which to examine the progress of the civil rights movement. Part Two of this text carries his thesis forward as the movement began to split between advocates of integration and the call for black separatism.

Branch, Taylor. *Parting the Waters: America in the King Years, 1954–1963* (New York: Simon & Schuster, 1988). An award-winning story of the civil rights movement during the ten years preceding the passage of the momentous Civil Rights Act of 1964.

Branch, Taylor. *Pillar of Fire: America in the King Years, 1963–1965*. New York: Simon & Schuster, 1998. Another fine account of the transition years of the civil rights movement, particularly in Alabama and also the "Freedom Summer" in Mississippi.

Campbell, Clarice T. *Civil Rights Chronicle*. Jackson: University Press of Mississippi, 1997. A collection of letters written and compiled by Campbell from her teaching experiences in the South during the first decade of the civil rights movement.

Carmichael, Stokely, and Charles V. Hamilton. *Black Power: The Politics of Liberation in America*. New York: Random House, 1967. A clarion call for a new, more militant approach to promote the civil rights of African Americans, coauthored by one of the most prominent leaders of that strategy.

Carson, Clayborne, et al., eds. *The Eyes on the Prize Civil Rights Reader*. New York: Penguin Books, 1991. Works in tandem with the video collection of the same title noted below. The book consists of documents, speeches, and firsthand accounts from participants in the civil rights movement.

Graham, Hugh Davis. *Civil Rights and the Presidency: Race and Gender in American Politics, 1960–1972*. New York: Oxford University Press, 1992. Focuses on the presidency in the push for racial and gender equality.

Kalven, Harry, Jr. *The Negro and the First Amendment*. Chicago: University of

Chicago Press, 1965. A brief but fairly comprehensive analysis of the free speech issues that arose during the civil rights era, written by one of the most highly regarded First Amendment scholars of the latter half of the twentieth century.

Lawson, Steven F. *Running for Freedom: Civil Rights and Black Politics in America since 1941.* 2nd ed. New York: McGraw-Hill, 1997. A study of the changing role of blacks in the American political process throughout the civil rights movement and after.

Levy, Peter B. *The Civil Rights Movement.* Westport, CT: Greenwood Press, 1998. An engaging and clearly written chronicle, which also contains some interesting and pertinent documents, photographs, and biographies of some of the principal activists.

Lewis, Anthony. *Portrait of America: The Second American Revolution.* New York: Random House, 1964. A contemporary narrative of the events of the civil rights movement by a reporter for the *New York Times*.

Tushnet, Mark V. *Making Constitutional Law: Thurgood Marshall and the Supreme Court, 1961–1991.* New York: Oxford University Press, 1997. A penetrating analysis of Thurgood Marshall, the Supreme Court's first African American justice, and his work during the civil rights movement, both on and off the Court.

Weisbrot, Robert. *Freedom Bound: A History of America's Civil Rights Movement.* New York: W.W. Norton, 1990. A comprehensive account of the civil rights movement that covers many of the free speech issues raised.

Zinn, Howard. *SNCC: The New Abolitionists.* Boston, MA: Beacon Press, 1964. Provides a close-up examination of the student group that orchestrated the freedom rides and then later questioned the tactics of nonviolent civil disobedience as a means of furthering the cause of equality.

Video Resources

Eyes on the Prize—Parts I and II. Alexandria, VA: PBS Video, 1990, 1993. A fourteen-part series of outstanding videos that focus on nearly every major aspect of the civil rights movement, with each section approximately sixty minutes in length. The collection begins in 1954–1955 with the Montgomery Bus boycott and concludes in the 1980s with various dimensions of "black pride" and affirmative action programs.

The 60s. Los Angeles: NBC Home Video, 1999. A look at the Black Panther movement in the late 1960s through the experiences of two families.

Web Sites

http://www.core-online.org/history/history%20opening.htm. This page recounts the role of the Congress of Racial Equality during the civil rights movement. It contains many interesting links to events and individuals.

http://www-dept.usm.edu/~mcrohb/. Containing numerous links to important documents pertaining to the movement, this Web site also includes interesting oral histories and a timeline of the crucial events.

9

The Vietnam War

President John F. Kennedy's inspiring inaugural address in January 1961 signaled the Cold War role history had assigned to the United States: "Let every nation know, whether it wishes us well or ill, that we shall pay any price, bear any burden, meet any hardship, support any friend, oppose any foe, in order to assure the survival and the success of liberty."[1] The youthfully vigorous president's confident words uplifted his audience and inspired the American people, especially young men and women, to participate in public affairs, but it was unclear to them at the time what this stirring message would eventually signify. The Cold War American foreign policy of containing communism everywhere put pressure on Kennedy to prevent Communist North Vietnam, supported by the insurgent Viet Cong in the South, from taking over South Vietnam. Despite his eloquent promise, Kennedy was reluctant to send troops to fight a growing war in Vietnam, though his administration did support military aid to the anti-Communist regime in South Vietnam and likely okayed the assassination of the increasingly inefficient, corrupt, and unpopular premier Ngo Diem there in an effort to provide more vigorous prosecution of the war against the local pro-Communist insurgents.

After Kennedy was assassinated in 1963, Vice-President Lyndon B. Johnson became president and promised to stay the course, making clear that "American boys should not do the fighting that Asian boys should do for themselves."[2] But in early August 1964, the Johnson administration claimed that the North Vietnamese had fired on the American destroyer *Maddox*, which was conducting reconnaissance patrols in the Gulf of Tonkin. At the president's request, Congress, by nearly unanimous votes in both houses, authorized the administration to take all necessary military measures to defend American forces against aggression and to take any appropriate steps to prevent any further assaults. This "Tonkin Gulf Resolution" was the legal authority for Johnson's subsequent massive escalation of American military involvement in Vietnam. Yet just weeks after the alleged Tonkin Gulf incident, Johnson told his secretary of defense, Robert S. McNamara: "When we got through with all the firing, we concluded maybe they [the North Vietnamese] hadn't fired at all."[3] And during the 1964 presidential election campaign, Johnson ran as the peace candidate depicting in TV advertisements his Republican rival, Senator Barry Goldwater of Arizona, as likely to blow up the world in nuclear war. By the time the Vietnam War had ended and President Richard M. Nixon had resigned under pressure from the Watergate scandal, a culture of deception in government, which had grown amid Cold War fears of espionage and disloyalty, had evolved and induced ordinary Americans to lose confidence in their leaders and their political system. Such cynicism and distrust spilled into the news business where the new art of investigative journalism presumed that political leaders were not telling the truth.

Following his landslide victory in 1964, LBJ began to escalate the U.S. presence in Vietnam at first with retaliatory measures such as the "Flaming Dart" air raids launched after a North Vietnamese attack that produced 137 American casualties, and a sustained bombing offensive, nicknamed "Rolling Thunder," soon followed. The Johnson administration apparently hoped that "gradual escalation" would preserve his domestic programs without provoking North Vietnam's backers—China and the Soviet Union—into a wider, perhaps nuclear war and without fomenting an antiwar movement at home. However, Johnson's administration underestimated the domestic reaction that mounting casualties would bring. In 1965, 61 percent of the American public approved of U.S. involvement in Vietnam. Once it became evident that the war would be both long and costly, public support, as measured in Gallup polls, began a steep and nearly uninterrupted trajectory downward. Approval slipped to 50 percent in 1966, 35 percent in 1968, and then plummeted in 1971 to an all-time low of 28 percent.[4]

As the war dragged on, disillusionment and frustration emerged from one end of the spectrum to the other. Prowar American "hawks" were impatient with history's mightiest military unable to defeat an economically backward country with comparatively primitive weaponry. Antiwar "doves" tried to stop the fighting, convinced that the United States had no good reason to wage a protracted war against a virtually unknown nation on the other side of the globe. The war effort seemed to be spinning its wheels in prolonged stalemate—except that tens of thousands on both sides were dying. In 1963–1964 Paul M. Kattenburg was the State Department's director of Vietnam Affairs, and in a book published in 1980 he reflected on this uncertain prosecution of the war:

> What the Johnson administration demanded from the American people after 1964 was not a crusade in the Kennedy spirit; but rather a long, costly, bloody, and persistent partial engagement in a constrained and limited mix of civil and military programs designed to extend secure areas and create a viable government in South Vietnam. Not at once, but in the longer run, this proved fatal to domestic support. If we could not get out in there and win, the American people would increasingly ask, then what were we doing there in the first place? This would shortly lead many Americans to ask: 'Why not get out?'[5]

President Johnson reached the lowest point of his presidency when on March 31, 1968, he stunned the country in a brief televised address announcing that he would not seek nor accept his party's nomination for another term as president.

Vietnam was also the first televised American war. Vivid and graphic footage, shown on the evening news, depicted the casualties that made Americans realize the extent of the burden borne as defender of liberty around the world. During World War I, books recounting war's ugly side were censored for fear that young men might resist the draft or that the public would become sickened by the brutality, and during World War II the film industry tempered depictions of the brutality of war, except in characterizing the "fiendish foe." From the mid-1960s onward the medium of television broadcast the awful truths of war on a daily basis into American living rooms. The mass media were relatively free in presenting the war; indeed, reporters in Vietnam could send their reports and footage back to their bureaus and networks in the United States without much censorship. With increasing and vivid press accounts of casualties a corresponding deterioration in public support occurred.

The escalation in Vietnam occurred at a time of domestic upheaval. The late 1960s were filled with protest activities rooted in the earlier civil rights movement. The "peace movement" melded with the struggle for racial equality. American culture generally came under attack. A small contingent of young Americans reacted with psychedelic music and flamboyant clothing, a drug subculture, a sexual revolution, and "flower power" as a way of tuning out of public affairs. Many others confronted the political establishment, through street demonstrations and protests on college campuses. The momentum of both the antiwar and civil rights movements unleashed frustrations of other disgruntled groups, such as women and gays who also publicly challenged their official second-class citizenship. Average American citizens still accustomed to the calm routine of life depicted on 1950s television, exemplified by the all-American families in *Ozzie and Harriet* and *Leave It to Beaver*, were in the late 1960s bombarded by culture shock.

The parallels between antiwar activism and civil rights protests were unmistakable. Both in the beginning of their campaigns did not have the national media or prominent media personalities on their sides, but their messages were eventually picked up and endorsed by the national press. Also, both protesting groups were essentially politically powerless: The Constitution gave blacks the right to vote, but it was eclipsed by the same kind of laws and practices that civil rights activists were trying to eradicate; young men of draft age could not vote until they were twenty-one. Thus demonstrations and other forms of protest provided the most readily available means of sending their political messages. The efficacy of sits-ins and other forms of earlier symbolic opposition taught antiwar activists how to convey and publicize their messages. People debated the war everywhere else—in classes, in journals and editorials, at parties and picnics, and around the dinner table. But the press always prefers to cover "disturbances," and antiwar protests disturbed the country.

College students became the driving force of the antiwar movement because young male students were directly affected. Even before the Vietnam War climbed to the top of the national agenda, a student political movement had already been underway. Reacting to "McCarthyism," racial discrimination, and the danger of nuclear weapons, many college students joined groups such as the Students for a Democratic Society (SDS), formed in the 1950s with the help of the American Socialist Party, and eventually created the "New Left," a term coined by social scientist C. Wright Mills in 1961. In 1962 students from around the country convened for a weekend to write the *Port Huron Statement of the Students for a Democratic Society*, a document officially recognizing a new ideology in American political thinking. The New Left drew support from campus-based organizations rather than from the working classes that had supported the old leftist organizations. It staged protests against racial segregation, atomic testing, and eventually the Vietnam War. One of the earliest of these protests occurred in 1963 at the "Ban the Bomb" rally in the United Nations Plaza in New York City. In 1964 the Women's International League for Peace advocated U.S. withdrawal from Vietnam. Protest activity continued to grow in 1964 when the *National Guardian* contained an advertisement "signed by almost one hundred college students saying flatly that they would refuse military service in Vietnam."[6] These earlier antiwar activities were sporadic and low key since U.S. involvement in Vietnam was still relatively limited—and unknown to most of the nation. At that time polls showed that 70 percent of Americans approved of LBJ's foreign policy.

By 1964 the New Left movement was shifting to an almost complete focus on antiwar protests. The *New York Times* featured the movement in an article entitled "The New Student Left: Movement Represents Serious Activists in Drive for Change." Then came the Free Speech Movement on the University of California at Berkeley, from September 14, 1964, to January 3, 1965. Historian Kirkpatrick Sale wrote that this was "the most direct confrontation ever seen in an American educational institution up to that time."[7] The Berkeley campus administration had restricted student fund-raisers and recruitment of members for off-campus events, sparking student protests for the freedom to operate on campus; the rough treatment of students by the administration did nothing except attract more student support. "The escalating response and counter-response evident at Berkeley established the formula for almost all future campus demonstrations."[8]

College campuses staged "teach-ins," which began at the University of Michigan and consisted of lectures, debates, and seminars on U.S. policy in Vietnam. The Michigan teach-in attracted some 3,000 students and professors and went on almost throughout the night. In May 1965, an epic teach-in at Berkeley drew 20,000 students and faculty. Some sixty colleges around the country eventually participated in similar events. Kenneth Crawford of *Newsweek* magazine wrote that teach-ins were "a splendid new way of communicating wisdom from scholars, through students, to the benighted general public."[9] Students were able to engage war supporters, antiwar activists, government officials, and other students. The Johnson administration criticized the teach-ins. Recruited by JFK to Washington from academia, Johnson adviser McGeorge Bundy accepted and then refused an invitation to participate in a teach-in, and in his withdrawal letter he wrote that these teach-ins "can give encouragement to the adversaries of our country."[10] There was something to Bundy's point of view. Teach-in participants usually did not express popular opinions. For example, Eugene D. Genovese, a professor of Marxist history at Rutgers University in New Jersey, made the following comment: "Unlike most of my distinguished colleagues here this morning, I do not fear or regret the impending Vietcong victory in Vietnam. I welcome it."[11]

The Johnson administration received several reports per week on antiwar activities in 1967 relating to comments made at the sit-ins and teach-ins. *The Nation* magazine reported that "few realize just how deeply the teach-ins are reaching into campus life. Trouble is brewing in the most unlikely places."[12] To attract attention, more extreme forms of protest replaced peaceful discussion. Todd Gitlin, an SDS activist, stated: "Where a picket line might have been news in 1965, it took tear gas and bloodied heads to make headlines in 1968."[13] Protests at Columbia University were some of the most violent and extreme domestic events during the Vietnam War era. On April 23, 1968, students led by SDS campus president Mark Rudd held Dean Henry S. Coleman hostage, and other students occupied buildings including the Low Memorial Library, the mathematics building, and a residence hall, for seven days. On April 30, the New York City police were called in. A total of 711 students were arrested in the largest campus police activity in history. After this incident at Columbia, the FBI pursued the New Left "with a vengeance almost unknown in FBI annals."[14]

College protesters, who seemed but a handful of rebellious malcontents in proportion to the total population, saw their numbers multiply each year, as antiwar protests and demonstrations became more frequent and at times almost staggering. Young men began burning their draft cards, defiling American flags, displaying Viet Cong flags, and engaging in other egregious public behavior. The antidraft movement continued to gain support, and one of the largest protests of the era occurred in New York's Central Park, where some 200,000 people gathered at the Spring Mobilization to End War in Vietnam on April 15, 1965. Opposing the draft, a Yale college student coined the phrase "We won't Go," which evolved into the more vulgar "Hell no, we won't go." Civil rights marchers had been singing "We Shall Overcome"; antiwar activists chanted: "Hey, hey, LBJ, how many kids have you killed today?" Antiwar protest reached a peak when a thirty-two-year-old Quaker with three children burned himself to death in front of the Pentagon, imitating the self-immolation protest used by Buddhist monks in South Vietnam. When another antiwar self-immolation took place in New York, protesters supporting the war carried signs saying "Burn yourself instead of your card." Anger was gathering on both sides. The nationwide Vietnam Moratorium Day planned for November 1969 culminated in one of the largest public demonstrations in American history.

Richard Nixon very narrowly lost the 1960 presidential election to JFK, then ran for governor of California and lost. A veteran of the post–World War II Red Scare, he knew domestic discord was a good political issue. Campaigning in 1965 on behalf of the Republican candidate for governor of New Jersey, Nixon was quick to criticize the teach-ins and, in particular, Professor Genovese's injudicious remarks, and he equated a Communist win in Vietnam with the end of free speech everywhere:

> Where the choice confronting us is between the lives of American men fighting to preserve the system which guarantees freedom of speech for all and the right of an individual to abuse that freedom, the lives of American fighting men must come first. . . . [W]e must never forget that if the war in Vietnam is lost and victory for the

Communists, which Professor Genovese says he "welcomes," becomes inevitable, the right of free speech will be extinguished
throughout the world.[15]

Three years later in a remarkable political comeback, Nixon won the
presidency in 1968, capitalizing on the breakdown in "law and order"
and a "secret plan" to end the war.

Once in office, he continued the negotiations secretly under way with
the North Vietnamese in Paris, and his secret plan of "Vietnamization"
was simply to increase the air war while bringing more American
ground troops home. As the fighting and bombing spread to neighboring
countries such as Laos and Cambodia, a wave of campus protests
erupted including the terrible events at Kent State and Jackson State,
where National Guardsmen killed student protesters during anti-Nixon
rallies. This set off another round of alarming demonstrations and student occupation of administrative buildings on college campuses all over
the country.

By 1970, 30 percent of American colleges and universities experienced
protests regarding U.S. involvement in the Vietnam War and federally
funded military research projects undertaken by universities. In 1970 the
President's Commission on Campus Unrest released a report noting that
violence on campus resulted from both student and law enforcement
behavior, not just the students. It urged that universities should be institutions open to every point of view where speech and conduct, protected by the First Amendment, are respected. According to the report,
the violence that occurred at Kent State, Jackson State, the University of
Wisconsin, and Columbia University were exceptional, overshadowing
the majority of protests that were peaceful.

The still functioning House Committee on Un-American Activities, the
Senate Internal Security Subcommittee, and the U.S. Justice Department
targeted students and activists for investigations. The FBI conducted
Counter Intelligence Programs (COINTELPRO), directed at the New
Left. Agents resorted to safecracking, mail interception, telephone surveillance, microphone plants, trash inspection, infiltration, and Internal
Revenue Service (IRS) investigations. FBI director J. Edgar Hoover instructed his agents to use every means available to gather the information. From 1964 to 1971, the FBI gathered noncriminal "political
intelligence" on protest groups ranging from civil rights to antiwar. College students were employed by the FBI as "plants" to gather information on college-based organizations and on university professors.
University administrators also worked directly with the FBI to monitor
both student and faculty antiwar activity. Brigham Young University
employed students to gather information that led to the dismissal of six

professors. Similar undercover activity occurred at Illinois, Indiana, Kansas, Ohio State, and Michigan State.

A small group of burglars named the Citizens' Commission to Investigate the FBI (CCIFBI) broke into bureau offices and stole classified documents that outlined the FBI's counterintelligence activities aimed at the New Left. The CCIFBI sent copies of COINTELPRO documents to journalists at the *New York Times, Washington Post,* and *Los Angeles Times.* William C. Davidson, a peace activist, was one of the first individuals to publicize the FBI burglary after he received documents from the CCIFBI. He explained that the whole purpose was to expose the extent to which the FBI was infiltrating perfectly legal groups. The pilfered FBI files contained unlisted phone numbers of political activists, files on antiwar activists including professors, and evidence that the FBI monitored checking accounts of groups by tellers and surveillance. One document entitled "The New Left Notes—Philadelphia" contained instructions that field agents were to step up contact with radical groups to increase "the paranoia endemic in these circles and to further serve to get the point across that there is an FBI agent behind every mailbox."[16] Hoover canceled COINTELPRO operations out of fear that more documents would be exposed. After the war, on November 21, 1977, the FBI released over 50,000 documents relating to various COINTELPRO activities.

In response to those who symbolically burned their draft cards, Congress in 1965 amended the selective service laws to make it a crime knowingly to destroy or mutilate a draft card, and the criminal penalties were as high as $10,000 in fines and five years in prison. Congressman L. Mendel Rivers, who chaired the House Armed Services Committee, said that the law was "a straightforward clear answer to those who would make a mockery of our efforts in South Vietnam.... If it can be proved that a person knowingly destroyed or mutilated his card, then ... he can be sent to prison, where he belongs. This is the least we can do for our men in South Vietnam fighting to preserve freedom, while a vocal minority thumb their noses at their own Government."[17]

In the 1960s the Supreme Court was inclined to protect protesters' speech rights, as it had, for the most part, during the civil rights movement. But it was not uniformly supportive; nor was it looking for ways to protect antiwar activism, as some critics have complained. Young men incarcerated for desertion or resisting the draft claimed that the draft was illegal insofar as no war had ever been formally declared by Congress. The most liberal Court in American history repeatedly refused to hear these appeals until after the Vietnam War came to an end, and then the Court simply left the matter to the political branches of government. However, the war provoked issues that directly implicated the First Amendment. One of the first dealt with burning draft cards, and the

Court ruled in *United States v. O'Brien* (1968) that Congress could punish such behavior without violating the First Amendment.

A year later, however, in *Tinker v. Des Moines School District* (1969), in a case involving high school students' free speech rights in Des Moines, Iowa, the Court held that students had a constitutional right peacefully to wear, even in school, black armbands to protest the war. Justice Abe Fortas explained: "Our problem involves direct primary First Amendment rights akin to 'pure speech.' The school officials banned and sought to punish petitioners for a silent, passive expression of opinion, unaccompanied by any disorder or disturbance on the part of petitioners."[18] The school's principal had allowed campaign buttons and even an Iron Cross, traditionally a symbol of Nazism, indicating that political statements were permitted in the schools. Unless the armbands had caused disruptions that unduly interfered with order in the school, the Court insisted that such opinions were protected, too. Red-faced and angry, the Cold War First Amendment absolutist, Justice Hugo L. Black, now in his eighties, read his caustic dissent from the bench and excoriated the Court for coddling "students [who] all over the country are already running loose conducting break-ins, sit-ins, lie-ins, and smash-ins."[19] This decision affirmed the principle that students maintain their First Amendment rights in school.

Paul Cohen had walked into a Los Angeles county courthouse wearing a jacket with the words "Fuck the Draft" emblazoned on his back. A police officer saw Cohen's defaced jacket and arrested and charged him with disturbing the peace through offensive conduct. Cohen's lawyers argued that his jacket was a form of protected symbolic speech, and on appeal the 5–4 Supreme Court majority agreed in *Cohen v. California* (1971), extending First Amendment protection to the public utterance of this particularly vulgar word. Justice John Marshall Harlan, a fairly conservative jurist, delivered the majority opinion, concluding that the state attempted to punish Cohen's words, not his actions. These words did not fall into any categories of speech that by definition are unprotected— such as "fighting words" or "pornography" (there was nothing erotic about Cohen's message). An important innovation was the Court's recognition that freedom of speech protects not just the "cognitive" message that Cohen did not support the draft but the "emotive" message conveying the intensity of his opposition. "At least so long as there is no showing of an intent to incite disobedience to or disruption of the draft, Cohen could not, consistently with the First and Fourteenth Amendments, be punished for asserting the evident position on the inutility or immorality of the draft his jacket reflected."[20] Justice Black did not see this as a matter of free speech at all; he joined three other dissenters who characterized Cohen's behavior as "mainly conduct, and little speech," even though it was this little speech that prompted his arrest. Without the expletive on his back, it is doubtful that Cohen would have been noticed, much less arrested.

The most widely covered and awaited judicial case was whether to permit two national newspapers to publish the purloined documents know as the "Pentagon Papers," a secret history of American involvement in Vietnam prepared by the Defense Department that had fallen into the hands of the *New York Times* and the *Washington Post*. The Nixon administration sought permanent injunctions to prohibit publication. In a special summer session in 1971 called to resolve what became popularly known as the *Pentagon Papers Case*, a 6–3 majority on the Court rejected the administration's request for the injunction. The common denominator upon which a majority could agree was a terse statement, in effect saying: The government had not carried the heavy burden of proving "irreparable damage," a task needed to justify the prior restraint requested. Justice Black seized the occasion—it would be his last; he died in early autumn—to proclaim once again that the First Amendment absolutely protected freedom of speech and press. Justice Harlan—who also died soon after this case—wrote in his last judicial opinion that this was not a matter for courts to decide because the issues turned upon complex national security matters that the judiciary was ill equipped to address. He would have let the executive decide the outcome here. A few other First Amendment rulings trickled down from the Court by the time the American fighting in Vietnam had stopped, but none of them fundamentally altered the Court's respect for, however grudgingly, First Amendment protections for political speech.

There were some ironic consequences to the pressures to pry open government secrecy and protect First Amendment principles. To the consternation of the press, later presidents had the military under their command more closely manage the flow and availability of information in wars fought or other military actions taken. Many attributed the failure of Vietnam to *too much* available information. Also, public trust in the political system plunged, and it diminished even further when the nation was dragged through the deceit and lies of the Watergate scandal that ultimately brought down the Nixon presidency in August 1974. A decade or more of "the politics of lying" produced unfortunate consequences for the health of the American democracy. People "turned on" to politics and public service by President Kennedy's hopeful message in 1961 were turned off by the time of Nixon's forced and premature resignation from office. An era that began with a call to public service ended in distrust and detachment from politics, especially among younger Americans who consistently have had the lowest rates of voter turnout in comparison to every other age group. Paradoxically, in the midst of the Vietnam War, in 1971 the Constitution was formally amended to extend the right to vote to eighteen-year-olds because they were old enough to die for their country.

NOTES

1. *Papers of the Presidents of the United States: John F. Kennedy, 1961* (Washington, DC: U.S. Government Printing Office, 1962), p. 1.

2. Lyndon Baines Johnson, *The Vantage Point: Perspectives on the Presidency, 1963–1969* (New York: Popular Library, 1971), p. 68.

3. As quoted in the *New York Times*, November 6, 2001, p. A16.

4. These figures are summarized in Mark Lorell and Charles Kelley, Jr., *Casualties, Public Opinion, and Presidential Policy during the Vietnam War* (Santa Monica, CA: Rand Corporation, 1985), pp. 19–20.

5. Paul M. Kattenburg, *The Vietnam Trauma in American Foreign Policy, 1945–1975* (New Brusnwick, NJ: Transaction Books, 1980), p. 211.

6. James Kirkpatrick Davis, *Assault on the Left: The FBI and the Sixties Antiwar Movement* (Westport, CT: Praeger, 1997), p. 24.

7. Kirkpatrick Sale, *SDS* (New York: Vintage, 1974), p. 163.

8. Margaret A. Blanchard, *Revolutionary Sparks: Freedom of Expression in Modern America* (New York: Oxford University Press, 1992), p. 294.

9. Kenneth Crawford, "Egghead Souffle," *Newsweek*, May 31, 1965, p. 30.

10. As quoted in Louis Menashe and Ronald Radosh, eds., *Teach-ins U.S.A.* (New York: Praeger, 1967), p. 154.

11. As quoted in ibid., p. 225.

12. Arnold S. Kaufman, "Teach-ins: New Force for the Times," *The Nation* 200 (June 25, 1965): 666–670.

13. Todd Gitlin, *The Whole World Is Watching: Mass Media in the Making & Unmaking of the New Left* (Berkeley: University of California Press, 1980), p. 182.

14. Sanford J. Unger, *FBI: An Uncensored Look behind the Walls* (Boston, MA: Little, Brown, 1975), p. 232.

15. As quoted in Menashe and Radosh, *Teach-ins U.S.A.*, pp. 234–235.

16. As quoted in Davis, *Assault on the Left*, p. 11.

17. *Congressional Record*, 89th Cong. 1st sess., August 10, 1965, p. 19871.

18. *Tinker v. Des Moines School District*, 393 U.S. 503, 508 (1969).

19. 393 U.S. at 525 (dissenting opinion).

20. *Cohen v. California*, 403 U.S. 15, 18 (1971).

DOCUMENTS

9.1.   Is Burning a Draft Card Free Speech?

> *Upon reaching the age of eighteen, young men were required
> by federal law to register with a local draft board where they
> were assigned Selective Service certificates (or draft cards). Like
> many other opponents of the Vietnam War across the country,
> David Paul O'Brien publicly burned his draft card in "symbolic"
> protest as he stood on the steps of the South Boston Courthouse.
> He was prosecuted under a 1965 congressional amendment to
> the 1948 Universal and Military Training and Service Act. The
> amendment made it a federal crime knowingly to destroy or
> mutilate a draft card. The 1948 statute already had made crim-
> inal the nonpossession of draft cards, and critics argued that the
> 1965 amendment was redundant, created purposely to punish
> a form of symbolic public protest of the war—and consequently
> a violation of the First Amendment. The issue eventually reached
> the Supreme Court, whose (8–1) decision rejected O'Brien's ap-
> peal.*

[Chief Justice Warren delivered the opinion of the Court.]

O'Brien first argues that the 1965 Amendment is unconstitutional as
applied to him because his act of burning his registration certificate was
protected "symbolic speech" within the First Amendment. His argument
is that the freedom of expression which the First Amendment guarantees
includes all modes of "communication of ideas by conduct," and that his
conduct is within this definition because he did it in "demonstration
against the war and against the draft."

We cannot accept the view that an apparently limitless variety of conduct can be labeled "speech" whenever the person engaging in the conduct intends thereby to express an idea. However, even on the
assumption that the alleged communicative element in O'Brien's conduct
is sufficient to bring into play the First Amendment, it does not necessarily follow that the destruction of a registration certificate is constitutionally protected activity. This Court has held that when "speech" and
"nonspeech" elements are combined in the same course of conduct, a
sufficiently important governmental interest in regulating the nonspeech
element can justify incidental limitations on First Amendment freedoms.

... [W]e think it clear that a government regulation is sufficiently justified if it is within the constitutional power of the Government; if it furthers an important or substantial governmental interest; if the governmental interest is unrelated to the suppression of free expression; and if the incidental restriction on alleged First Amendment freedoms is no greater than is essential to the furtherance of that interest. We find that the 1965 Amendment ... meets all of these requirements, and consequently that O'Brien can be constitutionally convicted for violating it.

The constitutional power of Congress to raise and support armies and to make all laws necessary and proper to that end is broad and sweeping. ... The power of Congress to classify and conscript manpower for military service is "beyond question." ... Pursuant to this power, Congress may establish a system of registration for individuals liable for training and service, and may require such individuals within reason to cooperate in the registration system. The issuance of certificates indicating the registration and eligibility classification of individuals is a legitimate and substantial administrative aid in the functioning of this system. And legislation to insure the continuing availability of issued certificates serves a legitimate and substantial purpose in the system's administration.

O'Brien's argument to the contrary ... essentially adopts the position that such certificates are so many pieces of paper designed to notify registrants of their registration or classification, to be retained or tossed in the wastebasket according to the convenience or taste of the registrant. Once the registrant has received notification, according to this view, there is no reason for him to retain the certificates. O'Brien notes that most of the information on a registration certificate serves no notification purpose at all; the registrant hardly needs to be told his address and physical characteristics. We agree that the registration certificate contains much information of which the registrant needs no notification. This circumstance, however, does not lead to the conclusion that the certificate serves no purpose, but that, like the classification certificate, it serves purposes in addition to initial notification. Many of these purposes would be defeated by the certificates' destruction or mutilation. Among these are:

1. The registration certificate serves as proof that the individual described thereon has registered for the draft. The classification certificate shows the eligibility classification of a named but undescribed individual. ...

2. The information supplied on the certificates facilitates communication between registrants and local boards, simplifying the system and benefiting all concerned. ...

3. Both certificates carry continual reminders that the registrant must notify his local board of any change of address, and other specified changes in his status. . . .

4. The regulatory scheme involving Selective Service certificates includes clearly valid prohibitions against the alteration, forgery, or similar deceptive misuse of certificates. The destruction or mutilation of certificates obviously increases the difficulty of detecting and tracing abuses such as these. Further, a mutilated certificate might itself be used for deceptive purposes.

The many functions performed by Selective Service certificates establish beyond doubt that Congress has a legitimate and substantial interest in preventing their wanton and unrestrained destruction and assuring their continuing availability by punishing people who knowingly and wilfully destroy or mutilate them. And we are unpersuaded that the pre-existence of the nonpossession regulations in any way negates this interest.

In the absence of a question as to multiple punishment, it has never been suggested that there is anything improper in Congress' providing alternative statutory avenues of prosecution to assure the effective protection of one and the same interest. . . .

. . . [Moreover,] the 1965 Amendment, like [the earlier law] which it amended, is concerned with abuses involving *any* issued Selective Service certificates, not only with the registrant's own certificates. The knowing destruction or mutilation of someone else's certificates would therefore violate the statute but not the nonpossession regulations.

We think it apparent that the continuing availability to each registrant of his Selective Service certificates substantially furthers the smooth and proper functioning of the system that Congress has established to raise armies. We think it also apparent that the Nation has a vital interest in having a system for raising armies that functions with maximum efficiency and is capable of easily and quickly responding to continually changing circumstances. For these reasons, the Government has a substantial interest in assuring the continuing availability of issued Selective Service certificates.

It is equally clear that the 1965 Amendment specifically protects this substantial governmental interest. We perceive no alternative means that would more precisely and narrowly assure the continuing availability of issued Selective Service certificates than a law which prohibits their wilful mutilation or destruction. . . . The 1965 Amendment prohibits such conduct and does nothing more. In other words, both the governmental interest and the operation of the 1965 Amendment are limited to the noncommunicative aspect of O'Brien's conduct. The governmental interest and the scope of the 1965 Amendment are limited to preventing harm to the smooth and efficient functioning of the Selective Service System. When O'Brien deliberately rendered unavailable his registration certificate, he wilfully frustrated this governmental interest. For this noncommunicative impact of his conduct, and for nothing else, he was convicted. . . .

O'Brien finally argues that the 1965 Amendment is unconstitutional as enacted because what he calls the "purpose" of Congress was "to suppress freedom of speech." We reject this argument because under settled principles the purpose of Congress, as O'Brien uses that term, is not a basis for declaring this legislation unconstitutional.

It is a familiar principle of constitutional law that this Court will not strike down an otherwise constitutional statute on the basis of an alleged illicit legislative motive. . . .

Inquiries into congressional motives or purposes are a hazardous matter. When the issue is simply the interpretation of legislation, the Court will look to statements by legislators for guidance as to the purpose of the legislature, because the benefit to sound decision-making in this circumstance is thought sufficient to risk the possibility of misreading Congress' purpose. It is entirely a different matter when we are asked to void a statute that is, under well-settled criteria, constitutional on its face, on the basis of what fewer than a handful of Congressmen said about it. What motivates one legislator to make a speech about a statute is not necessarily what motivates scores of others to enact it, and the stakes are sufficiently high for us to eschew guesswork.

Since the 1965 Amendment to 12(b)(3) of the Universal Military Training and Service Act is constitutional as enacted and as applied . . . we vacate the judgment of the Court of Appeals, and reinstate the judgment and sentence of the District Court. It is so ordered.

Source: *United States v. O'Brien*, 391 U.S. 367 (May 27, 1968).

9.2.   Do High School Students Have a Right to Protest the War?

On December 16, 1965, John Tinker, a fifteen-year-old high school student, and his thirteen-year-old sister, Mary Beth, a junior high school student, were sent home and suspended from school for wearing black armbands in the Des Moines, Iowa, public schools after having been warned not to do so. Wearing the armbands was part of a concerted protest among some parents and their children against the war in Vietnam. The father of the Tinker children sued the school district for violating his

children's rights. The Supreme Court agreed with his claim, stat-
ing that students have free speech rights in public school as long
as their expression is not disruptive. Justice Hugo L. Black, who
claimed to be a First Amendment "absolutist," angrily dissented.
The excerpt below is from Black's dissenting opinion.

The Court's holding in this case ushers in what I deem to be an entirely new era in which the power to control pupils by the elected "officials of state supported public schools . . ." in the United States is in ultimate effect transferred to the Supreme Court. . . .

As I read the Court's opinion it relies upon the following grounds for holding unconstitutional the judgment of the Des Moines school officials and the two courts below. First, the Court concludes that the wearing of armbands is "symbolic speech" which is "akin to 'pure speech' " and therefore protected by the First and Fourteenth Amendments. Secondly, the Court decides that the public schools are an appropriate place to exercise "symbolic speech" as long as normal school functions are not "unreasonably" disrupted. Finally, the Court arrogates to itself, rather than to the State's elected officials charged with running the schools, the decision as to which school disciplinary regulations are "reasonable."

Assuming that the Court is correct in holding that the conduct of wearing armbands for the purpose of conveying political ideas is protected by the First Amendment . . . the crucial remaining questions are whether students and teachers may use the schools at their whim as a platform for the exercise of free speech—"symbolic" or "pure"—and whether the courts will allocate to themselves the function of deciding how the pupils' school day will be spent. While I have always believed that under the First and Fourteenth Amendments neither the State nor the Federal Government has any authority to regulate or censor the content of speech, I have never believed that any person has a right to give speeches or engage in demonstrations where he pleases and when he pleases. . . .

While the record does not show that any of these armband students shouted, used profane language, or were violent in any manner, detailed testimony by some of them shows their armbands caused comments, warnings by other students, the poking of fun at them, and a warning by an older football player that other, nonprotesting students had better let them alone. There is also evidence that a teacher of mathematics had his lesson period practically "wrecked" chiefly by disputes with Mary Beth Tinker, who wore her armband for her "demonstration." Even a casual reading of the record shows that this armband did divert students' minds from their regular lessons, and that talk, comments, etc., made John Tinker "self-conscious" in attending school with his armband. While the absence of obscene remarks or boisterous and loud disorder perhaps justifies the Court's statement that the few armband students did not actually "disrupt" the classwork, I think the record over-whelmingly shows that the armbands did exactly what the elected school officials and principals foresaw they would, that is, took the students' minds off their classwork and diverted them to thoughts about the highly emotional subject of the Vietnam war. And I repeat that if the time has come when pupils of state-supported schools, kindergartens, grammar schools, or high schools, can defy and flout orders of school officials to keep their minds on their own schoolwork, it is the beginning of a new revolutionary era of permissiveness in this country fostered by the judiciary. . . .

In my view, teachers in state-controlled public schools are hired to teach there. . . . [C]ertainly a teacher is not paid to go into school and teach subjects the State does not hire him to teach as a part of its selected curriculum. Nor are public school students sent to the schools at public expense to broadcast political or any other views to educate and inform the public. The original idea of schools, which I do not believe is yet abandoned as worthless or out of date, was that children had not yet reached the point of experience and wisdom which enabled them to teach all of their elders. It may be that the Nation has outworn the old-fashioned slogan that "children are to be seen not heard," but one may, I hope, be permitted to harbor the thought that taxpayers send children to school on the premise that at their age they need to learn, not teach. . . . [E]ven if the [facts here] were silent as to protests against the Vietnam war distracting students from their assigned class work, members of this Court, like all other citizens, know, without being told, that the disputes over the wisdom of the Vietnam war have disrupted and divided this country as few other issues ever have. Of course students, like other people, cannot concentrate on lesser issues when black armbands are being ostentatiously displayed in their presence to call attention to the wounded and dead of the war, some of the wounded and the dead being their friends and neighbors. It was, of course, to distract the attention of other students that some students insisted up to the very point of their own suspension from school that they were determined to sit in school with their symbolic armbands.

Change has been said to be truly the law of life, but sometimes the old and the tried and true are worth holding. The schools of this Nation have undoubtedly contributed to giving us tranquility and to making us a more law-abiding people. Uncontrolled and uncontrollable liberty is an enemy to domestic peace. We cannot close our eyes to the fact that some of the country's greatest problems are crimes committed by the youth, too many of school age. School discipline, like parental discipline, is an integral and important part of training our children to be good citizens—to be better citizens. Here a very small number of students have crisply and summarily refused to obey a school order designed to give pupils who want to learn the opportunity to do so. One does not need to be a prophet or the son of a prophet to know that after the Court's holding today some students in Iowa schools and indeed in all schools will be ready, able, and willing to defy their teachers on practically all orders. This is the more unfortunate for the schools since groups of students all over the land are already running loose, conducting break-ins, sit-ins, lie-ins, and smash-ins. Many of these student groups, as is all too familiar to all who read the newspapers and watch the television news programs, have already engaged in rioting, property seizures, and destruction. They have picketed schools to force students not to cross their picket lines and have too often violently attacked earnest but frightened students who wanted an education that the pickets did not want them to get. Students engaged in such activities are apparently confident that they know far more about how to operate public school systems than do their parents, teachers, and elected school officials. It is no answer to say that the particular students here have not yet reached such high points in their demands to attend classes in order to exercise their political pressures. Turned loose with lawsuits for damages and injunctions against their teachers as they are here, it is nothing but wishful thinking to imagine that young, immature students will not soon believe it is their right to control the schools rather than the right of the States that collect the taxes to hire the teachers for the benefit of the pupils. This case, therefore, wholly without constitutional reasons in my judgment, subjects all the public schools in the country to the whims and caprices of their loudest-mouthed, but maybe not their brightest, students. I, for one, am not fully persuaded that school pupils are wise enough, even with this Court's expert help from Washington, to run the 23,390 public school systems in our 50 States. I wish, therefore, wholly to disclaim any purpose on my part to hold that the Federal Constitution compels the teachers, parents, and elected school officials to surrender control of the American public school system to public school students. I dissent.

Source: *Tinker v. Des Moines School District*, 393 U.S. 503, 515–526 (February 24, 1969) (dissenting opinion).

9.3.   Justice Harlan Dissents in the Pentagon Papers Case

When the New York Times *and* Washington Post *both began publishing installments of the "Pentagon Papers," a secret Pentagon chronicle of the Vietnam War, the Nixon administration went to federal court in Washington and also in New York seek-*

> *ing injunctions to block publication. On June 25, 1971, the Su-*
> *preme Court agreed to review the cases and stayed the*
> *enforcement of any injunctions against the newspapers; the next*
> *day it heard "oral arguments"; and four days later, it ruled (6–*
> *3) that the government had not met the burden to justify a "prior*
> *restraint." Justice John Marshall Harlan was one of the three dis-*
> *senters, and he thought the Court acted not only too hastily but*
> *incorrectly.*

With all respect, I consider that the Court has been almost irresponsibly feverish in dealing with these cases. . . . [The branch of government best able to decide whether publication will cause injury to national security is the Executive.] The power to evaluate the "pernicious influence" of premature disclosure is not, however, lodged in the Executive alone. I agree that, in performance of its duty to protect the values of the First Amendment against political pressures, the judiciary must review the initial Executive determination to the point of satisfying itself that the subject matter of the dispute does lie within the proper compass of the President's foreign relations power. Constitutional considerations forbid "a complete abandonment of judicial control." Moreover, the judiciary may properly insist that the determination that disclosure of the subject matter would irreparably impair the national security be made by the head of the Executive Department concerned—here, the Secretary of State or the Secretary of Defense—after actual personal consideration by that officer. This safeguard is required in the analogous area of executive claims of privilege for secrets of state.

But, in my judgment, the judiciary may not properly go beyond these two inquiries and redetermine for itself the probable impact of disclosure on the national security.

. . . [T]he very nature of executive decisions as to foreign policy is political, not judicial. Such decisions are wholly confided by our Constitution to the political departments of the government, Executive and Legislative. They are delicate, complex, and involve large elements of prophecy. They are and should be undertaken only by those directly responsible to the people whose welfare they advance or imperil. They are decisions of a kind for which the Judiciary has neither aptitude, facilities nor responsibility, and which has long been held to belong in the domain of political power not subject to judicial intrusion or inquiry.

Even if there is some room for the judiciary to override the executive determination, it is plain that the scope of review must be exceedingly narrow. I can see no indication in the opinions of either the District Court or the Court of Appeals in the *Post* litigation that the conclusions of the Executive were given even the deference owing to an administrative agency, much less that owing to a co-equal branch of the Government operating within the field of its constitutional prerogative.

Pending further hearings in each case conducted under the appropriate ground rules, I would continue the restraints on publication. I cannot believe that the doctrine prohibiting prior restraints reaches to the point of preventing courts from maintaining the *status quo* long enough to act responsibly in matters of such national importance as those involved here.

Source: New York Times v. United States, 403 U.S. 713, 752–759 (June 30, 1971) (dissenting opinion).

9.4.   Is a Military Base a "Public Forum"?

> *Famed pediatrician and antiwar activist Dr. Benjamin Spock ran an independent third-party campaign for president in 1972. He and his running mate went to Fort Dix, a basic training military reservation in central New Jersey, to campaign and distribute leaflets. The local public had full access to certain unrestricted areas of this base, but the post also prohibited political speeches and demonstrations on its grounds. Spock and his supporters were denied permission to distribute their campaign literature and were evicted from the post. They sued in federal court to enjoin enforcement of the military post's regulations. Lower federal courts agreed with Spock's First Amendment claim that he had a right to enter unrestricted areas of Fort Dix and campaign, speak, and distribute his antiwar campaign leaflets. The Supreme Court, with two dissenters, reversed and held that a military base is not a public forum for the exercise of free speech rights.*

[Justice Stewart delivered the opinion of the Court.]

One of the very purposes for which the Constitution was ordained and established was to "provide for the common defence," and this Court over the years has on countless occasions recognized the special constitutional function of the military in our national life, a function both explicit and indispensable. In short, it is "the primary business of armies and navies to fight or be ready to fight wars should the occasion arise." . . . And it is consequently the business of a military installation like Fort Dix to train soldiers, not to provide a public forum.

A necessary concomitant of the basic function of a military installation has been "the historically unquestioned power of [its] commanding officer summarily to exclude civilians from the area of his command." . . .

The notion that federal military reservations, like municipal streets and parks, have traditionally served as a place for free public assembly and communication of thoughts by private citizens is thus historically and constitutionally false.

... [Spock and others], therefore, had no generalized constitutional right to make political speeches or distribute leaflets at Fort Dix, and it follows that Fort Dix [regulations] are not constitutionally invalid on their face. These regulations, moreover, were not unconstitutionally applied in the circumstances disclosed by the record in the present case.

With respect to Reg. 210–26, there is no claim that the military authorities discriminated in any way among candidates for public office based upon the candidates' supposed political views. It is undisputed that, until the appearance of the respondent Spock at Fort Dix on November 4, 1972, as a result of a court order, no candidate of any political stripe had ever been permitted to campaign there.

What the record shows, therefore, is a considered Fort Dix policy, objectively and evenhandedly applied, of keeping official military activities there wholly free of entanglement with partisan political campaigns of any kind. Under such a policy members of the Armed Forces stationed at Fort Dix are wholly free as individuals to attend political rallies, out of uniform and off base. But the military as such is insulated from both the reality and the appearance of acting as a handmaiden for partisan political causes or candidates.

Such a policy is wholly consistent with the American constitutional tradition of a politically neutral military establishment under civilian control. It is a policy that has been reflected in numerous laws and military regulations throughout our history. And it is a policy that the military authorities at Fort Dix were constitutionally free to pursue.

With respect to Reg. 210–27, it is to be emphasized that it does not authorize the Fort Dix authorities to prohibit the distribution of conventional political campaign literature. The only publications that a military commander may disapprove are those that he finds constitute "a clear danger to [military] loyalty, discipline, or morale," and he "may not prevent distribution of a publication simply because he does not like its contents," or because it "is critical—even unfairly critical—of government policies or officials...." There is nothing in the Constitution that disables a military commander from acting to avert what he perceives to be a clear danger to the loyalty, discipline, or morale of troops on the base under his command.

It is possible, of course, that Reg. 210–27 might in the future be applied irrationally, invidiously, or arbitrarily. But none of the respondents in the present case even submitted any material for review. The noncandidate respondents were excluded from Fort Dix because they had previously distributed literature there without even attempting to obtain approval for the distribution. This case, therefore, simply does not raise any question of unconstitutional application of the regulation to any specific situation.

Source: *Greer v. Spock*, 424 U.S. 828 (March 24, 1976).

ANNOTATED RESEARCH GUIDE

De Benedetti, Charles. *An American Ordeal: The Antiwar Movement of the Vietnam Era.* Syracuse, NY: Syracuse University Press, 1990. Recounts the escalation of both the war itself and the accompanying domestic turmoil that grew up against the war.

Ferber, Michael, and Staughton Lynd. *The Resistance.* Boston: Beacon Press, 1971. Two leaders of the movement to resist the draft in the late 1960s recount its history.

Gitlin, Todd. *The Sixties: Years of Hope, Days of Rage.* New York: Bantam, 1987. A history of the New Left and the counterculture, recounted by one of the leading participants.

Heineman, Kenneth J. *Campus Wars: The Peace Movement at American State Universities in the Vietnam Era.* New York: New York University Press, 1993. A scholarly analysis focusing on how universities led the way, first on campus, and then beyond, in the spiraling antiwar movement of the 1960s and early 1970s.

Miller, James. *"Democracy in the Streets": From Port Huron to the Siege of Chicago.* New York: Simon & Schuster, 1987. Focuses on the early leaders of SDS and critically analyzes the theory of participatory democracy.

Powers, Thomas. *Vietnam: The War at Home—Vietnam and the American People, 1964–1968.* Boston, MA: G.K. Hall, 1984. Explores the American public's reaction to the war and the ensuing domestic discord that escalated into the violence of 1968.

Robbins, Mary Susannah, ed. *Against the Vietnam War: Writings by Activists.* Syracuse, NY: Syracuse University Press, 1999. A collection of essays from some of the most prominent and not-so-well-known opponents of the war, from academia, the civil rights movement, organized religion, and politics.

Rudenstine, David. *The Day the Presses Stopped: A History of the Pentagon Papers.* Berkeley: University of California Press, 1996. An in-depth case study of the litigation and politics collectively known as the *Pentagon Papers Case.*

Sale, Kirkpatrick. *SDS.* New York: Random House, 1974. A detailed history of Students for a Democratic Society, including its internal conflicts and ideological evolution.

Small, Melvin. *Covering Dissent: The Media and the Anti-Vietnam War Movement.* New Brunswick, NJ: Rutgers University Press, 1994. Presents a scholarly examination of how the media handled and thus affected some of the principal events in the evolution of the antiwar movement.

Small, Melvin, and William D. Hooper, eds. *Give Peace a Chance: Exploring the Vietnam Antiwar Movement.* Syracuse, NY: Syracuse University Press, 1992. Retrospective essays and commentaries on the character and meaning of the antiwar movement.

Zaroulis, Nancy, and Gerald Sullivan. *Who Spoke Up?: American Protest against the War in Vietnam, 1963–1975.* Garden City, NY: Doubleday, 1984. Details the antiwar movement from its earliest days when most Americans subscribed to the principle "My Country, Right or Wrong" to the late 1960s and early 1970s when public sentiment had clearly shifted against the war.

Video Resource

Vietnam: The War at Home. Oak Forest, IL: MPI Home Video, 1986. This eighty-eight-minute video recounts the developments of the war and the changing public reaction to the war within the United States.

Web Site

http://library.berkeley.edu/BANC/FSM/. This page focuses on the Free Speech Movement of 1964 at the University of California at Berkeley.

10

The Nazi March on Skokie

Recounting the events that became known as the *Skokie* case cannot reflect the deep emotional turmoil that this controversy brought to the inhabitants of the Village of Skokie, Illinois, intellectuals and commentators across the nation, and the American Civil Liberties Union, a national organization dedicated to protecting individual freedom. The immediate question in this case was whether the First Amendment protects the right of the American Nazi Party to march or demonstrate peacefully in a suburb of Chicago, Illinois, which was predominantly a Jewish community, among whom were thousands of survivors and descendants of the Holocaust. The broader free speech issue involved the extent to which government can prevent the airing of messages deemed offensive by certain groups or even by a majority of the people.

During the Cold War period the assault on freedom of speech and association that began in the late 1940s finally simmered down in the early 1960s as anti-Communist hysteria subsided and the nation turned to other matters. In the 1960s the Supreme Court in a series of major rulings gave new life to First Amendment rights. A very liberal Court majority throughout most of the decade undercut the capacity of both state and federal governments to continue the kind of anti-Communist witch hunt and crusade that characterized the 1950s, a period similar to the Red Scare immediately following World War I. In order to punish political speech, the Court insisted by the end of the 1960s that government needed to show far more than what the courts had found sufficient in the 1950s. For example, in a case called *Brandenburg v. Ohio* (1969), the

Court made it difficult to punish political speech unless the facts could show that such speech was *incitement* intended to cause a serious and *imminent* danger that the government has authority to prevent. It was a libertarian doctrine combining strands and concepts of earlier, incipient judicial efforts to determine the range of speech protected by the First Amendment.

Despite this generous speech-protective stance, courts still recognized that certain classes of speech are unprotected simply because of their very nature. That is, certain kinds of speech have no social value or do not contribute to the exchange of ideas essential to the functioning of a democratic society. This position derived from a much-cited precedent established by the Court in 1942 that emerged from the case of *Chaplinksy v. New Hampshire*. Here the Court said that "obscenity" (by which today we mean "pornography"), "commercial speech," "defamation" (such as libel and slander), and "fighting words" are classes of expression that the First Amendment does not reach. Of course, defining these categories presents the difficulty. The best illustration of this has been the nearly incomprehensible and sometimes humorous efforts of the judicial branch to determine whether certain films, pictures, books, or articles are sufficiently salacious and offensive to be deemed pornographic. As a result of ever-narrowing definitions of "obscenity," much of what was once outside the pale of the First Amendment is today protected erotica, even very explicit materials.

Also, during the civil rights movement, the Court held that some libel—false defamatory publications—must be protected in order to insure a robust public debate about important issues facing society, otherwise, critics would avoid controversial subjects for fear that they might be sued in court if they get any of their facts wrong. And beginning in the 1970s, the judiciary extended constitutional protection to commercial expression, first by protecting an advertisement appearing in a newspaper on where to obtain an abortion. Just because the issue appeared in a paid advertisement, according to the Court's new, more flexible approach, it should not be excluded from the First Amendment's coverage. In bits and pieces following this case, the Court elaborated a commercial speech doctrine that today protects even TV ads for prescription drugs, as long as the commercial promotes legal articles or objects and the advertisement is not misleading or false.

The "fighting words" exclusion, however, still stands, although the Court has whittled it down considerably since its first appearance in 1942. Nonetheless, "fighting words" remain unprotected forms of speech, and these are face-to-face utterances that are designed to provoke a fight (hence, the name of the category) or are intended to have no other purpose than to inflict injury upon the listener. For example, racial and ethnic insults and slurs, while not necessarily hate *crime*, became known as "hate speech" that many argue fit the kind of "fighting words" that the Court had in mind when it created this class of unprotected expression in the *Chaplinsky* case. This kind of expression intentionally aims at various groups and individuals in order to vilify and hurt them. It reflects intolerance still deeply ingrained in much of the American population, and it follows from the increasing fragmentation of American society into various groups, many of them frustrated with the evolution of society and their place within it. The most prominent event that catapulted this issue to national attention occurred when a small band of American Nazis scheduled a public march and demonstration not too far from Chicago, Illinois.

Frank Collin was the leader of the National Socialist Party of America, a neo-Nazi group whose objective was to exercise his and his party's right of freedom of expression in full military uniform, including the swastika. The site of the march was scheduled for the Village of Skokie, on the sidewalk in front of the Village Hall, and organizers expected that the demonstration would last only for half an hour. Collin did not intend to present a speech or distribute any literature; he wanted instead to march in full Nazi uniform amidst posters and placards proclaiming "White Free Speech." The Village of Skokie was not randomly or inadvertently chosen for this demonstration. It was a small suburban town of about 69,000 residents, 40,000 of whom were Jews. Of the Jewish refugees who had fled from Nazi Germany to the metropolitan Chicago area, a disproportionate number of them eventually settled in Skokie. In this sprawling metropolitan area a group of about 12,000 members organized the "Survivors of the Holocaust," and about 7,000 of them lived in Skokie. Collin carefully selected Skokie because from here he was sure to draw national attention completely disproportionate to the few dozen members of his Nazi political party.

Officials of the village sought a restraining order—an injunction—to prevent the march, but it was eventually overturned by the U.S. Supreme Court in *National Socialist Party v. Skokie* (1977). Village officials responded immediately in May 1977 with three local ordinances designed to thwart Collin's plans. One measure required organizers of the march to secure a permit and $350,000 of liability insurance, on the assumption that the demonstration could get out of control. The second prohibited the distribution of materials that intentionally promoted or incited hatred of persons because of their race, religion, or nationality. This claim appeared to rest on the "fighting words" exception to freedom of speech and on a 1952 Supreme Court precedent upholding a "group libel" law. The third provision forbade political party demonstrations or marches in which military-style uniforms were worn. The last of these hastily drawn measures seemed clearly unconstitutional in the light of judicial precedent. The other two could conceivably jibe with First Amendment law.

Collin enlisted the support of the ACLU to challenge these restrictions in federal court. Eventually, in the late spring of 1978, a federal judge struck down all three measures as conflicting with the First Amendment. Judge Bernard M. Decker saw the insurance requirement as prohibitively and unnecessarily expensive and thus an abridgment of First Amendment rights in the guise of a routine regulation. The prohibition against hate speech and slurs aimed at religion, race, and nationality he found to be vague and overbroad, and the ban against wearing military-style uniforms was held to be a direct collision with the First Amendment. The court maintained that the government could not intervene arbitrarily; that is, the government could not pick and choose which messages were unacceptable. The First Amendment, argued the court, requires the airing of all views and ideas, however hateful, unless clear evidence can be shown that such messages would, in fact, provoke violence—evidence the village failed to substantiate with sufficient proof. The group libel claim, though never directly overruled, had been effectively undermined by later Supreme Court cases, according to Judge Decker. In conclusion, the best guarantee that the Nazi march would be ineffectual, he concluded, was the ability of the American people to tolerate even hateful speech because of their firm commitment to democratic government.

The U.S. court of appeal that oversees federal courts in Illinois and other midwestern states affirmed the lower court ruling invalidating all three Skokie laws as violations of the free speech guarantees of the First Amendment. Having prevailed in the judicial system, Collin and his Nazis, however, curiously canceled their planned June 25, 1978, demonstration in Skokie and, instead, held an unremarkable rally with about two dozen party faithful in a public park in the city of Chicago. In the fall of 1978 (after the triumphal Nazis had completed their thinly populated demonstration in Chicago), the U.S. Supreme Court declined to review the lower federal court decisions in favor of Collin and the Nazis.

The bitter and intense controversy sparked by this episode was so great that the ACLU, which had defended most liberal causes for decades, even during some very heated periods, substantially lost membership all across the United States because it had agreed to represent the despised Nazis and their offensive messages. The issue was widely debated in weekly magazines, editorials, and just about everywhere else.

The reaction of the press to the dilemma faced by courts in the Skokie case was immediate, often vehement, and widespread. While almost all commentators conceded that the Nazi messages were repugnant, mean, uncivilized, and designed with no other purpose than to remind victims of past horror, scholars, politicians, legal professionals, and ordinary citizens disagreed over whether Nazis had a constitutional right to march in Skokie—especially in view of the population who lived there. Liberal magazines, such as *The Nation* and the *Progressive*, concluded that no matter how loathsome and vile the messages of the Nazis the First Amendment must protect their right to express them, even in a village like Skokie. The "slippery slope" argument was echoed across the nation in the liberal defense of free speech: Once an exception is made for speech as offensive as this, the exception will serve as precedent and justification for exclusion of even more offensive expression later. Embedded in this argument is the principle that government should regulate in a content-neutral way and that the First Amendment forbids government to select certain messages and suppress them and punish the messenger on the basis of the "content" of the expression.

Others who defended the right even of Nazis to demonstrate maintained that a general march, such as what Frank Collin had planned, did not present the kind of face-to-face fighting words because the march, as planned, was not directed at any particular listeners; in fact, even the survivors of the Holocaust could look away, close their windows, and avoid the painful messages being sent in their town. Some have even equated Collin's tactic of staging his demonstration where it would provoke the most attention and outrage to Martin Luther King, Jr.'s strategy of marching for civil rights and equality in predominantly white neighborhoods. Though the messages of the two demonstrators were diametrically opposed, the comparison draws attention to the sometimes controversial nature of political speech and the necessity of protecting the speaker rather than catering to the demands of the offended listeners. This was known in legal parlance as the "heckler's veto," something that if permitted would create the real potential to suppress unpopular opinions because they are too offensive to sensitive listeners. Popular opinion never really needs First Amendment protection, but offensive expression always does, and the question presented in the Skokie case was whether the message was so odious and hateful as to exceed the bounds of what the First Amendment should protect.

In 1952, in a case called *Beauharnais v. Illinois*, a narrowly divided Court upheld a "group libel" law that imposed criminal penalties on persons who publicly degraded whole classes of people because of their race, color, creed, or religion. That case has never been overruled, even though many commentators, including the federal judges who invalidated the three municipal ordinances involved in the *Skokie* case, have argued that the Court's reasoning there is obsolete, eroded by subsequent cases developing the doctrines established in the momentous 1964 *New York Times* libel case that was at the center of the civil rights movement. Still, some who wanted to prevent the Nazi march advocated the theory underlying "group libel," namely, that the Nazis here were clearly attempting to degrade one particular class of people who had suffered merciless genocide at the hands of Nazi Germany. During the national debate on this issue, Carl Cohen—then a professor of philosophy at the University of Michigan and an active supporter of the ACLU—rejected the group libel thesis because he said it was completely unworkable in practice. "First, *which* groups are to be protected against defamation? . . . Second, *what* is defamatory? . . . Certain terms . . . are used contemptuously in some contexts, affectionately in others. May they be voiced only at the risk of criminal prosecution? . . . The performance of some ethnic groups is statistically inferior to the norm in one sphere or another: some show higher rates of alcoholism and divorce, some tend to do less well in schools, and so on. . . . If our Constitution did not already prohibit legislative entry into this utterly subjective sphere, our good sense should surely do so."[1] Bigotry, even with respect to the issue of genocide, Cohen concluded, is best handled by free and open discussion.

Others disagreed, and often profoundly. One of the nation's most prominent conservative thinkers, and founder and editor of the weekly conservative magazine *The National Review*, William F. Buckley differentiated between discussion of public affairs and punishable conduct, such as a nuisance. Agreeing with and quoting historian and columnist Garry Wills, Buckley saw the situation in Skokie as one in which the Nazis were " 'not engaged in the rational airing of views, but in the provoking of irrational (but predictable) responses. They [were], in effect, broadcasting an obscene phone call to a whole neighborhood instead of a single home.' " The Nazi march, Buckley continued, would be equivalent to the KKK marching through Harlem, that is, not "the exercise of the right of assembly, but an obscene phone call acting as an impostor under the umbrella of the First Amendment."[2]

Hadley Arkes, then a political science professor at Amherst College, argued that the Nazis had forfeited their right to march and demonstrate because their "message" did not deserve constitutional protection, even for a moment, because "certain things are in themselves, in principle, despicable."[3] The residents of Skokie were entitled to be spared the horrendous and repugnant reminder of the appalling atrocities of Nazi Germany. Arkes viewed the planned Nazi march not as conveying any messages but as an assault on the dead and their descendants, an assault that any sensible interpretation of the *Chaplinsky* holding would permit government to ban as harmful, and worthless at best. Averting one's eyes by not watching from the living room or kitchen windows, from this perspective, was simply irrelevant as the assault was visible nonetheless in the minds and memories of the Holocaust survivors.

Lee C. Bollinger, at the time a law professor and later president of the University of Michigan, wrote an important book, *The Tolerant Society*, in which he defended the constitutional protection of Collin and his Nazi Party.[4] The essence of his thesis is: As difficult and as trying as this episode was, society ultimately benefits from events like the *Skokie* case, despite the suffering inflicted by the atrocious and hate-filled messages offered by organizations such as the Nazi Party. According to Bollinger, from these extreme events and the national attention they receive, a debate unfolds that reinforces democracy and teaches a lesson in tolerance. Yet in defending the Nazis, the American Civil Liberties Union suffered a wholesale drop in national membership among erstwhile, dedicated, tolerant supporters of freedom of speech; some estimates indicate that as much as one quarter of its total membership resigned in protest. Moreover, after the Skokie controversy receded from the national news, episodes of "hate speech" and hate crimes seemed to grow in number, at least in news coverage. The constitutional debate about how to handle bigotry, racial hatred, sexism, homophobia, and other manifestations of intolerance moved onto American university and college campuses, where another round of national debate and division took place and has lasted ever since.

NOTES

1. Carl Cohen, "The Case against Group Libel," *The Nation* 226 (June, 24, 1978): 759–760.

2. William F. Buckley, Jr., "Postmortem on the Nazis," *National Review*, August 18, 1978, p. 1040.

3. Hadley Arkes, "Marching Through Skokie," *National Review*, May 12, 1978, p. 589.

4. Lee C. Bollinger, *The Tolerant Society: Freedom of Speech and Extremist Speech in America* (New York: Oxford University Press, 1986).

DOCUMENTS

10.1.   Many Happy Returns

> *Frank Collin and the National Socialist Party of America sched-*
> *uled a march not only in a town with thousands of descendants*
> *and survivors of the Holocaust but also apparently to celebrate*
> *the birthday (April 20) of Adolf Hitler. In sending its birthday*
> *wishes, the editorial, which appeared in a popular conservative*
> *periodical, recognized the difficulty of the First Amendment is-*
> *sues presented by the case.*

Do Nazis have the right to march through a largely Jewish suburb to celebrate Der Führer's birthday? Morally, the issue in Skokie, Illinois could hardly be clearer. Constitutionally, it is prickly. The American Civil Liberties Union has always had a hearty appetite for test cases, but its defense of the Nazis' right in this one has resulted in massive defections of its Jewish supporters. Now the Illinois Supreme Court has ruled that the Nazis may march on schedule on April 20, swastikas and all. It is, according to the court, a First Amendment issue. "The display of these swastikas," it held, "as offensive to the principles of a free nation as the memories it recalls may be, is symbolic political speech intended to convey to the public the beliefs of those who display it [*sic*]." The court refused to allow Skokie to prohibit the display under the "fighting words" principle, and declared that "anticipation of the hostile audience [cannot] justify a prior restraint."

Of Skokie's seventy thousand people, forty thousand are Jews; of whom about five thousand are survivors of Nazi death camps. Clearly the march is "intended" to do something besides "convey beliefs" to the "public." It is intended to insult the dead, to celebrate their murderers, and to convey a threat, however impotent, against the living. And even if it were supposed that the Nazis were somehow innocent of the meaning of their actions in the context of Skokie, it would hardly be unreasonable to require them to spend the next few months figuring out what it must be.

The issue is *not* simple. Americans treasure their freedom of speech, and one does not deny rights to a group one loathes that might not, with equal reason, be denied to all. But the whole notion of "symbolic speech" needs inspection. Any act, with suitable stagesetting, might be so characterized: you might bulldoze a church to express your taste in architecture. The fact remains that vandalism is illegal, however excellent your taste.

For that matter, not all speech is protected under the Constitution. False advertising, libel, threats, crank phone calls, incitement to riot, and many other verbal acts expose one to legal penalties. Recent philosophy has given a good deal of attention to "speech acts," "performative utterances," and the like, which are not mere verbal descriptions of reality but modes of *action*. The law has always recognized that the circumstances of an utterance can determine its very nature, and British law particularly has asserted the relevance of society's *experience* of certain categories of words and utterance as provocative of violence.

We don't know the specific solution for Skokie. Maybe it is as simple as a voluntary collective avoidance of the big birthday march, with the cooperation of the press. Maybe not. In any case, no solution can ever come from a rigidly abstract and doctrinaire approach to free "speech."

Source: National Review, February 17, 1978, p. 201. © 1978 by National Review, Inc., 215 Lexington Avenue, New York, NY 10016. Reprinted by permission.

10.2.   "Springtime for Skokie"

In the film The Producers, *there is a satirical song called "Springtime for Hitler." Acknowledging the sensitivity and difficulty of the legal issues presented in the* Skokie *case, the editorial below no doubt borrowed the song title in reluctantly supporting the Nazis' right to march on Skokie.*

Under a regime of civil liberties, the true ideas rise on their own merits and the false ideas collapse under their own weight as long as the truth tellers also may speak up. False ideas have the "right" to win, but the market is rigged against them. History suggests that when these principles are abandoned it is the true ideas, rather than the false ones, that tend to be suppressed.

But of course the citizens of Skokie don't object to the proposed Nazi march through their village out of any concern that those along the parade route might find its message convincing. No one contends there is any "clear and present danger" of a Nazi triumph in this country, or even that Nazism will gain any support as a result of this march. The complaint is precisely the opposite: that those exposed to the march will find its message repugnant, and should be spared this offense to their sensibilities. Put this way, it becomes clear that the Skokie controversy is not really about "free political debate" at all. It is an obscenity case.

Seeing Skokie's campaign against the Nazi march as an attempt to suppress obscenity makes the case for the village stronger, but not strong enough. The case is stronger because it is no longer an answer to say, "Have your own march. Spread your own views." However certain it is that anti-Nazi opinions will triumph in the "free marketplace of ideas," this will not alleviate the alleged harm caused by the Nazi demonstration. If a community wishing to preserve its sexual equanimity is free to ban dirty movies inside theaters (which the Supreme Court says it is), the argument would go, surely a community with an unusually large proportion of Holocaust survivors may ban an offensive display of Nazi symbols and rhetoric in its public streets.

But the lawyers for Skokie have not made this argument, even though they have spent the past year—working in concert with the village ordinance writers—frantically searching for an acceptable route through the maze of First Amendment doctrine. The reason, of course, is that the doctrine of obscenity as an exception to the First Amendment protection of free speech—a dubious proposition in itself—cannot possibly be applied to displays that are offensive because of their political content. The current Supreme Court standard for obscenity requires the censor to prove that a banned work "lacks serious literary, artistic, political or scientific value." It would be tempting to argue that Nazism as an ideology has no political value and therefore can be banned as worthless. But then who would decide the next case? Clearly allowing the government to decide that some political ideas are too *worthless* to be protected by the First Amendment would be just as unfortunate as allowing the government to decide that some political ideas are too *dangerous* to be protected.

Since they are precluded from resting on their real objection to having Nazis march through their village—that they don't like Nazis—Skokie and its lawyers have attempted a variety of subterfuges in order to ban the demonstration. The legal wrangling has been going on now for about a year. During this time the march has been banned—a rather successful prior restraint, whatever the final outcome. The American Civil Liberties Union—which we have criticized in these columns for some apparent departures from basic civil liberties principles—has defended the First Amendment valiantly throughout this battle, at great cost in money and membership.

When the Nazis first announced their march . . . Skokie went to the Illinois state court for an injunction to prevent it. Skokie's argument was that if Nazis were allowed to march through their city, a violent response by offended residents would be inevitable. Therefore the march, however peaceable, posed a clear and present danger of civil disorder. The Supreme Court rejected this sort of argument several times in the 1960s, when it was invoked to justify police action in breaking up peaceful black protests against racial segregation. The police argued that the inevitable violent white response would pose a threat to law and order. In these less sympathetic circumstances, the fallacy of the argument is obvious: to accept it would be to provide what lawyers call a "heckler's veto" over the expression of any ideas—or over the mere presence of certain people—that a local majority might object to. The Supreme Court has struggled a bit with the problem of how much effort the police must make to quell a hostile crowd before asking a controversial speaker or demonstration to make their job easier by stopping. But the Court never would permit prior banning of a political demonstration on the *chance* that a violent response *might* result.

Despite this clear precedent, the lower Illinois court enjoined the Nazi demonstration planned for May 1, 1977. When the Nazis changed the scheduled date to April 30, Skokie asked for and got a blanket injunction against *all* Nazi demonstrations in the village "until further order of the court." The ACLU appealed this injunction and eventually, in January of this year, the Illinois Supreme Court ruled that it was unconstitutional. At the same time, the court dismissed a similar injunction request filed on behalf of Holocaust survivors in Skokie by the Anti-Defamation League of Chicago.

At this point the Nazis and the ACLU came up against Skokie's next line of defense. On May 2, 1977, the day after the march originally had been scheduled to take place, the village passed three ordinances intended to assure that it would never happen. One requires 30 days' advance notice and proof of $350,000 in liability insurance in order to get a march permit (except that the village could waive the requirement whenever it wished). Another forbids "political organizations" from demonstrating in "military style" uniforms. A third forbids display of "symbols offensive to the community" and also contains what is known as a "group libel" provision banning literature that ascribes a "lack of virtue" to any racial or ethnic group. The ACLU challenged all three ordinances in federal district court. The court ruled last month that all three—except for the 30-day waiting period requirement, which is common around the country—are unconstitutional violations of free speech.

The case is now before the Seventh Circuit Court of Appeals, which has promised a quick ruling, but inevitably there will be an appeal to the US Supreme Court. . . . The only really controvertible legal issue is the validity of the "group libel" statute. A 1952 Supreme Court case upheld such a statute, but this was long before all the later decisions bringing libel within the protection of the First Amendment. In all probability the Nazis will be able to have their horrible march—as they should—some time soon.

It is easy to be bloodless and analytical about free speech from a distance. The citizens of Skokie are the ones who must tolerate this distressing antic. We hope they will think of it as the price they pay for the privilege of living in a non-authoritarian society, where the police are used to protect minorities—no matter how offensive to the majority—rather than to harass and intimidate them. Those many citizens of Skokie who suffered under a different system are in an especially good position to reflect that it is a rather small price, after all.

Source: The New Republic, April 22, 1978, pp. 5–6, 8. Reprinted by permission of *The New Republic*.

10.3.   The Nazis' Message Should Not Be Protected

In his famous World War I dissenting opinion in Abrams v. United States, *Justice Oliver Wendell Holmes, Jr., proclaimed that the best test of "truth" is its ability to prevail in the "marketplace of ideas." This metaphor has since underscored most liberal arguments defending freedom of speech. Political scientist Hadley Arkes of Amherst College challenged this premise in his criticism of the ACLU's defense of Nazi messages in the Skokie* case. *In his view, the Nazi message was itself indefensible and thus unworthy of First Amendment protection.*

For the leadership of the ACLU, it would be accurate to say that there is ultimately no "truth" in matters political—that all ideas about the proper form of government over men come to rest at the end on personal beliefs or opinions, which cannot finally be measured as true or false. As far at least as the right to speak is concerned, the case for a regime of law and the case for a regime of genocide must be counted, in this view, as equally deserving of a claim *to be heard* and (ultimately) approved by the public. David Hamlin, the executive director of the Illinois division of the ACLU, was moved to say, regarding the Nazis, that "the First Amendment . . . affords us the unique opportunity to hear every *imaginable* idea, and to voice opinions on any one. *It protects all ideas—popular or despised*, good or bad . . . so that each of us can make a free and intelligent choice." (Emphasis added.) In Mr. Hamlin's understanding, it is a matter of being "popular" or "despised": to be despised is to be "unpopular." It is apparently no part of his own understanding that certain things are in themselves, in principle, despicable.

Mr. Hamlin is quite plain on the point that we must be free to hear the Nazis in order to preserve our freedom to *choose* the Nazis if we wish. But of course the Constitution was never meant to be neutral in this way about the choice between despotism and free government. The Founders understood that the case for government by consent began with a self-evident truth grounded in nature; as Madison put it during the first Congress, the natural equality of human beings—their capacity for self-governing—had to be understood as an "absolute truth." And if the political order was indeed established on a necessary, self-evident truth, the perspective represented by the Nazis simply cannot be treated for a moment as plausible and legitimate. It cannot be regarded as plausible, that is, without calling into question the truth of those premises on which all constitutional rights depend. In the last analysis, then, it is a mistake to pretend that the Constitution is indifferent to the character and ends of the Nazis.

What the Constitution commends, however, may be one thing; what the Supreme Court has wrought in recent years is another. At this moment our law faces in two directions. On the one hand the Supreme Court has eroded those standards that the law has used over the years to restrain assaults carried out through speech or expression. A majority of the Court has even gone so far as to suggest that there is no principled way to mark off forms of speech that are insulting or defamatory, as against forms of speech that are neutral or inoffensive. Working on this assumption, the Court has made it very difficult to sustain any local ordinance on "provocative" and insulting speech, and, as a result of the decisions that have been taken in this vein over the last seven years, it does in fact become harder to restrain the Nazis in their march in Skokie.

But on the other hand the Court has never overturned the precedents that provided the foundation at an earlier time for the restriction of injurious speech. In fact, the Court has found it necessary in recent years to firm up its commitments to those older precedents; when it comes to the matter of confirming the power of local governments to restrain obscenity and public lewdness, the Court has been compelled to explain, in a more traditional, familiar voice, that not all forms of speech and expression can claim the protection of the Constitution.

The authority that the Court cites most importantly on these occasions is the classic case of *Chaplinsky* v. *New Hampshire*. . . .

When the ACLU came to offer its brief for the Nazis in Skokie it insisted that the concept "fighting" words applied only to personal epithets that arose in "face-to-face" encounters. For some reason it seemed to be assumed that these personal encounters were more likely to "incite an immediate breach of the peace" (more likely, say, than attacks that were made on a whole racial or religious group). At the same time, since the test in *Chaplinsky* was narrowed to assaults of the most personal nature, it was argued that the holding was not meant to cover speech with a larger political significance. In these interpretations the ACLU was essentially following the direction of the Court in recent years, as a majority of the Court has sought to narrow the holding in *Chaplinsky*.

... [But] ... *Chaplinsky* ... also encompassed words "which by their utterance inflict injury," even if they are not accompanied by overt acts that involve a physical assault.... [T]here is such a thing as psychological injury or shock, which may be quite as grave—and as much of a concern in the eyes of the law—as an assault on one's body, or a broken leg. When all of these points were taken together, the *Chaplinsky* case suggested in a rather compelling way that people had a claim to be protected from unprovoked or unjustified assaults (including verbal or psychological assaults) when they ventured into a public place.

... One need only imagine, in a hypothetical case, that a crowd gathers before the house of the first black family to move into the neighborhood. No violence is initiated; no rocks or bottles are thrown. The crowd merely stands there, perhaps chanting in a low tone, and, as the day wears on, the crowd may go long stretches in which it makes no sound at all. There is no breach of peace, nor even anything that fits the usual notion of a public disturbance. But when the people leave [home] they have to face the crowd, and the crowd simply stands there, intimidating by its very presence.

Since the crowd refrains from violence it might be said that it is engaged in a "peaceable assembly" or perhaps even a form of public protest. For despite the fact the harassment is aimed at a private family, the gathering of the crowd has a larger political significance: the aim of the crowd, quite clearly, is to have an effect on the character of the community by keeping blacks out. In pursuing this form of intimidation outside the law, the object is to encourage the members of the family from exercising rights that are theirs in the law, and perhaps also to frustrate the ends of a public policy that seeks to bring down the barriers to racial integration. The fact that the crowd refrains from speech or discussion is not enough in itself to reduce the event to an instance of "conduct" rather than "speech": it has already been established over a long train of cases that "expression" may cover symbolic acts or gestures that involve no speech or writing at all: e.g., the rendering of a flag salute, the burning of a draft card, the wearing of an armband.

If the police intervened and dispersed the crowd outside the house, they would clearly be restricting political expression; and yet it should be apparent that the police would be quite justified in intervening. But if the law can reach a case of this kind it is because it is possible to recognize the nature of the words and gestures themselves, *in the context in which they are used*, and understand that they were meant to intimidate or assault.

When it comes ... to the American Nazis and their freedom of expression, the obligations of the regime are nowhere near as one-sided as libertarians suggest. To the extent that the Nazis have any legitimate role to play at all in the political life of this Republic—a proposition I indulge only hypothetically—the most the polity is obliged to do is respect their liberty to hold meetings, conduct discussions, and make themselves part of the public discourse. But it is not obliged to let them make use of the public streets to carry the symbols of assault and genocide to the very homes of the people who would feel most acutely and properly threatened by them.

. . . For years, the ACLU has professed to believe, with Justice Holmes, that "the best test of truth is the power of the thought to get itself accepted in the competition of the market." With all proper allowances for that curious proposition, one may still ask: What unresolved issue in the marketplace of ideas may the Nazis help to settle for us? In the judgment of the ACLU, is there something in the perspective of the Nazis which has a plausible claim to truth? If we restrict the speech of the Nazis is it conceivable that we may shield ourselves from ideas that may turn out one day to be valid? Is it possible, for example, that a convincing case could yet be made for genocide if people were given a bit more time to develop the argument? Might it be that the commitment to a democratic regime itself stands on premises that may be shown one day to be doubtful?

These possibilities could not be ruled out if, in fact, all judgments of moral right and wrong rested on nothing more than "opinion." But the wrongness of genocide arises from the concept of morals itself, and therefore no amount of discussion, now or in the future, could possibly have any effect on its moral status. The wrongness of the act inheres in the willingness to put to death a whole group of people with no reference to criminal acts, with no discriminations to be made between the innocent and the guilty. Genocide will continue to be wrong as long as the notion of morals itself exists—as long as it is possible to speak of the difference between innocence and guilt, of the difference between killings that are justified and those that are unjustified.

In the meantime, however, the ACLU is helping to preserve the Nazis as an established part of the public arena, and the public lessons that are drawn from the experience are not apt to be wholesome. If the ACLU bends its efforts, after all, to support a *right* of the Nazis to march, what other lesson does it hope to teach but that the Nazis must be regarded as *legitimate*—that their claim to exist and speak stands on the same plane of legitimacy as that of any other group within the country? But if the Nazis are legitimate, they cannot be dismissed out of hand as implausible, and if the perspective they represent is regarded as plausible, then the self-evident "truth" on which the American regime is founded cannot in fact be a "truth." It must be merely an "opinion," no more or less likely to be true than any other "opinion" about the nature of a good political regime, including the "opinion" represented by the Nazis.

But the consequence that arises from this understanding was set forth long ago by Lincoln: If democracy were not founded on a natural truth—on the capacity of human beings for moral judgment—then it had to be founded merely on "opinion": it had to arise merely because it was the form of government that happened to be approved by the opinions of a majority. And if the opinions of the majority were the only authoritative source of law, there could be no ground on which one could challenge the decisions of a majority in the name of a more fundamental law. It would be within the competence of a majority, then, to forgo democratic government for the entire society or to withdraw the protections of the Constitution from any minority. The irony is that the ACLU sees itself as defending at this moment the freedom of a minority, but the principles on which it mounts that defense would cut the ground out from under constitutional government itself and, in that sense, would also imperil the freedom of all minorities.

. . . As the ACLU seeks now to resist the use of the law in restraining acts of assault and intimidation, it is also seeking to alter in a radical way the understanding of the public about the foundations on which its own freedom is established. The result of this teaching, however, is to render those foundations less firm. . . . [L]awyers and professionals who have borne the largest responsibility for the preservation of constitutional government no longer seem to understand the moral premises on which that government rests.

Source: Hadley Arkes, "Marching Through Skokie," *National Review*, May 12, 1978, pp. 588–593. © 1978 by National Review, Inc., 215 Lexington Avenue, New York, NY 10016. Reprinted by permission.

10.4.   The Skokie Ordinances Are Unconstitutional

The federal judiciary is divided geographically into twelve "circuits" of the United States, with a court of appeals within each circuit serving as the highest federal court, just below the U.S. Supreme Court. These courts decide cases in panels of three judges. In the following case, which in effect ended the Skokie litigation, the Court of Appeals for the Seventh Circuit, which sits in Chicago, ruled (2–1) on May 22, 1978, that the Skokie laws, designed to block the march, were unconstitutional.

[Judge Wilbur F. Pell, Jr., wrote the majority opinion.]

We cannot then be unmindful of the horrors associated with the Nazi regime of the Third Reich, with which to some real and apparently intentional degree [members of the National Socialist Party of America—

NSPA] associate themselves. Nor does the record allow us to ignore the certainty that [they] know full well that, in light of their views and the historical associations they would bring with them to Skokie, many people would find their demonstration extremely mentally and emotionally disturbing, or the suspicion that such a result may be relished by [the NSPA].

But our task here is to decide whether the First Amendment protects the activity in which [members of the NSPA] wish to engage, not to render moral judgment on their views or tactics. [O]ur constitutional system protects minorities unpopular at a particular time or place from governmental harassment and intimidation, [and] that distinguishes life in this country from life under the Third Reich.

These [NSPA] activities involve the "cognate rights" of free speech and free assembly. . . . [M]arching, parading, and picketing, because they involve conduct implicating significant interests in maintaining public order, are less protected than pure speech, [but] they are nonetheless subject to significant First Amendment protection. . . .

We . . . consider [the 995] ordinance . . . prohibiting the dissemination of materials which would promote hatred towards persons on the basis of their heritage. The Village would apparently apply this provision to NSPA's display of swastikas, their uniforms, and, perhaps, to the content of their placards. The ordinance cannot be sustained on the basis of some of the more obvious exceptions to the rule against content control. While some would no doubt be willing to label [such] views and symbols obscene, the constitutional rule that obscenity is unprotected applies only to material with erotic content. Furthermore although the Village introduced evidence in the district court tending to prove that some individuals, at least, might have difficulty restraining their reactions to the Nazi demonstration, the Village tells us that it does not rely on a fear of responsive violence to justify the ordinance, and does not even suggest that there will be any physical violence if the march is held. . . . The concession also eliminates any argument based on the fighting words doctrine of *Chaplinsky v. New Hampshire* (1942). . . . Again, the Village does not seriously contest this point.

[Several] arguments are advanced by the Village to justify the content restrictions of 995. First, it is said that the content criminalized by 995 is "totally lacking in social content," and that it consists of "false statements of fact" in which there is "no constitutional value." . . . We disagree that, if applied to the proposed demonstration, the ordinance can be said to be limited to "statements of fact," false or otherwise. No handbills are to be distributed; no speeches are planned. To the degree that the symbols in question can be said to assert anything specific, it must be the Nazi ideology, which cannot be treated as a mere false "fact."

We may agree with the district court that if any philosophy should be regarded as completely unacceptable to civilized society, that of plaintiffs, who, while disavowing on the witness stand any advocacy of genocide, have nevertheless deliberately identified themselves with a regime whose record of brutality and barbarism is unmatched in modern history, would be a good place to start. But there can be no legitimate start down such a road.

Under the First Amendment there is no such thing as a false idea. However pernicious an opinion may seem, we depend for its correction not on the conscience of judges and juries but on the competition of other ideas. In the words of Justice [Robert H.] Jackson, "[E]very person must be his own watchman for truth, because the forefathers did not trust any government to separate the true from the false for us." The asserted falseness of Nazi dogma, and, indeed, its general repudiation, simply do not justify its suppression.

The Village [relies on] *Beauharnais v. Illinois* (1952). There a conviction was upheld under a statute prohibiting, in language substantially (and perhaps not unintentionally) similar to that used in the ordinance here, the dissemination of materials promoting racial or religious hatred. The closely-divided [Supreme] Court stated that the criminal punishment of libel of an individual raised no constitutional problems, relying on *Chaplinsky v. New Hampshire.* . . .

In our opinion *Beauharnais* does not support ordinance 995, for two independent reasons. First, the rationale of that decision turns quite plainly on the strong tendency of the prohibited utterances to cause violence and disorder [which was not relevant here]. . . . [T]he Village, as we have indicated, does not assert [the NSPA's] possible violence, an audience's possible responsive violence, or possible violence against third parties by those incited by [the NSPA], as justifications for 995. Ordinance 995 would apparently be applied in the absence of any such threat. The rationale of *Beauharnais*, then, simply does not apply here. . . .

The Village asserts that *Beauharnais* implicitly sanctions prohibiting the use of First Amendment rights to invoke racial or religious hatred *even without reference to fears of violence*. In the light of our discussion of *Beauharnais'* premises, we do not find the case susceptible of this interpretation. Even if it were, however, we agree with the district court that decisions in the quarter-century since *Beauharnais* have abrogated the *Chaplinsky* dictum, made one of the premises of *Beauharnais*, that the punishment of libel "has never been thought to raise any Constitutional problem." *New York Times Co. v. Sullivan* (1964) [is] indisputable evidence that libel does indeed now raise serious and knotty First Amendment problems, sufficient as a matter of constitutional law to require the substantial rewriting of both criminal and civil state libel laws. . . .

The Village [also argues] that the Nazi march, involving as it does the display of uniforms and swastikas, will create a substantive evil that it has a right to prohibit: the infliction of psychic trauma on resident holocaust survivors and other Jewish residents. . . . It would be grossly insensitive to deny, as we do not, that the proposed demonstration would seriously disturb, emotionally and mentally, at least some, and probably many of the Village's residents. The problem with engrafting an exception on the First Amendment for such situations is that they are indistinguishable in principle from speech that "invite[s] dispute . . . induces a condition of unrest, creates dissatisfaction with conditions as they are, or even stirs people to anger." . . . It is perfectly clear that a state many not "make criminal the peaceful expression of unpopular views." . . .

It is said that the proposed march is not speech, or even "speech plus," but rather an invasion, intensely menacing no matter how peacefully conducted. The Village's expert psychiatric witness, in fact, testified that the effect of the march would be much the same regardless of whether uniforms and swastikas were displayed, due to the intrusion of self-proclaimed Nazis into what he characterized as predominately Jewish "turf." There is room under the First Amendment for the government to protect targeted listeners from offensive speech, but only when the speaker intrudes on the privacy of the home, or a captive audience cannot practically avoid exposure.

This case does not involve intrusion into people's homes. There *need be* no captive audience, as Village residents may, if they wish, simply avoid the Village Hall for thirty minutes on a Sunday afternoon, which no doubt would be their normal course of conduct on a day when the Village Hall was not open in the regular course of business. Absent such intrusion or captivity, there is no justifiable substantial privacy interest to save 995 from constitutional infirmity, when it attempts, by fiat, to declare the entire Village, at all times, a privacy zone that may be sanitized from the offensiveness of Nazi ideology and symbols.

We conclude that 995 may not be applied to criminalize the conduct of the proposed demonstration. . . .

Although we would have thought it unnecessary to say so, it apparently deserves emphasis in the light of the dissent's reference to this court apologizing as to the result, that our *regret* at the use [the NSPA] plan[s] to make of their rights is not in any sense an *apology* for upholding the First Amendment. The result we have reached is dictated by the fundamental proposition that if these civil rights are to remain vital for all, they must protect not only those society deems acceptable, but also those whose ideas it quite justifiably rejects and despises.

Source: *Collin v. Smith*, 578 F.2d 1197 (May 22, 1978).

10.5.   U.S. Supreme Court Denies Review

The Village of Skokie made a final appeal to the nation's highest court, which, without any explanation, refused to review the case by denying "certiorari" (a writ of review over which the Court has complete discretion). Denials of review are usually unanimous, and the denial has no legal significance except to uphold the lower court immediately below. Here, however, two justices dissented from this denial and expressed the reasons why.

[Justice Harry A. Blackmun, joined by Justice Bryon R. White, dissented:]

It is a matter of regret for me that the Court denies certiorari in this case, for this is litigation that rests upon critical, disturbing, and emotional facts, and the issues cut down to the very heart of the First Amendment.

. . . [The] facts and . . . chronology [of this case] demonstrate, I believe, the pervading sensitivity of the litigation. On the one hand, we have precious First Amendment rights vigorously asserted and an obvious concern that, if those asserted rights are not recognized, the precedent of a "hard" case might offer a justification for repression in the future. On the other hand, we are presented with evidence of a potentially explosive and dangerous situation, enflamed by unforgettable recollections of traumatic experiences in the second world conflict. Finally, Judge Sprecher of the Seventh Circuit observed that "each court dealing with these precise problems (the Illinois Supreme Court, the District Court and this Court) feels the need to apologize for its result."

Furthermore, in Beauharnais v. Illinois (1952), this Court faced up to an Illinois statute that made it a crime to exhibit in any public place a publication that portrayed "depravity, criminality, unchastity, or lack of virtue of a class of citizens, of any race, color, creed or religion," thereby exposing such citizens "to contempt, derision, or obloquy." The Court, by a divided vote, held that, as construed and applied, the statute did not violate the liberty of speech guaranteed as against the States by the Due Process Clause of the Fourteenth Amendment.

I stated in dissent when the application for stay in the present litigation was denied that I feel the Seventh Circuit's decision is in some tension with Beauharnais. That case has not been overruled or formally limited in any way.

I therefore would grant certiorari in order to resolve any possible conflict that may exist between the ruling of the Seventh Circuit here and

Beauharnais. I also feel that the present case affords the Court an opportunity to consider whether, in the context of the facts that this record
appears to present, there is no limit whatsoever to the exercise of free
speech. There indeed may be no such limit, but when citizens assert, not
casually but with deep conviction, that the proposed demonstration is
scheduled at a place and in a manner that is taunting and over-
whelmingly offensive to the citizens of that place, that assertion, uncomfortable though it may be for judges, deserves to be examined. It just
might fall into the same category as one's "right" to cry "fire" in a
crowded theater, for "the character of every act depends upon the circumstances in which it is done."

Source: Smith, President of the Village of Skokie v. Collin, 439 U.S. 916 (October 16,
1978), (dissenting opinion).

ANNOTATED RESEARCH GUIDE

Downs, Donald A., *Nazis in Skokie: Community and the First Amendment*. Notre
    Dame, IN: Notre Dame University Press, 1985. A sensitive and balanced
    analysis of the issues, the importance of community-building, and the law.
Gibson, James L., and Richard D. Bingham. *Civil Liberties and Nazis: The Skokie
    Free Speech Controversy*. New York: Praeger, 1985. Presents a case study
    with a rich analysis of the civil rights and civil liberties issues (especially
    freedom of speech) raised by this divisive episode.
Hamlin, David. *The Nazi/Skokie Conflict*. Boston: Beacon Press, 1980. A case study
    written by the executive director of the Illinois branch of the ACLU ex-
    plaining the issues and the ACLU's interest in this case.
Lukas, J. Anthony. "The A.C.L.U. against Itself." *New York Times Magazine*, July
    9, 1978, pp. 9–31. Focuses on the disarray that befell the ACLU for de-
    fending the Nazis' right to demonstrate.
Neier, Aryeh. *Defending My Enemy: American Nazis, the Skokie Case, and the Risks
    of Freedom*. New York: E.P. Dutton, 1979. Defends the ACLU's controver-
    sial legal representation of Frank Collin and the American Nazis, arguing
    that one defends the enemy's right to speak to ensure one's own right to
    speak. Neier was the national executive director of the ACLU at the time
    of the decision to represent Collin in court.
Strum, Philippa. *When the Nazis Came to Skokie: Freedom for Speech We Hate*.
    Lawrence: University Press of Kansas, 1999. An in-depth case study of the
    event (including the various rounds of litigation) that propelled to national
    prominence the debate about whether "hate speech" ought to be protected
    by the First Amendment.
Walker, Samuel. *Hate Speech: The History of an American Controversy*. Lincoln: Uni-
    versity of Nebraska Press, 1994. Puts the *Skokie* case in the context of the
    development of hate speech generally in American history.

Video Resources

Skokie. Academy Entertainment Distributors, 1990. A two-hour film, starring Danny Kaye and other luminaries and directed by Herbert Wise, tells the story of the *Skokie* case through the lenses of a Hollywood feature film.

Skokie, Rights or Wrong. Wayne, NJ: New Day Films, 1980. A twenty-seven-minute documentary videotape highlighting the events and personalities in this controversial episode.

Web Site

http://www.skokie.lib.il.us/march78/. The Skokie Public Library has established this page with links to digitized newspaper accounts of the *Skokie* case.

11

Political Correctness and Free Speech on Campus

Post-Vietnam America became a nation of increasing diversity. Social movements in the 1960s and 1970s "liberated" African Americans, women, gays, and other groups from previous conditions of second-class citizenship. Americans were far more diverse than white, male, and heterosexual. Colleges and universities promoted this diversity to foster a more propitious and comprehensive learning environment. Proponents claimed that diversity in the classrooms, in dormitories, and in extracurricular activities on campus not only stimulated and enriched the academic environment but also helped educate people more ably to make the transition to an increasingly global and heterogeneous society. Special recruitment efforts brought in diversity to colleges and universities where it had not previously existed. Academic curricula integrated "multiculturalism" through courses exposing students to alternative histories, music, cultures, and literature, beyond—and sometimes in place of—the traditional Western, white, and male counterparts that had been the canon for generations of students before.

Promoting diversity and multiculturalism meant rooting out sexism, racism, homophobia, and other forms of prejudice. Crimes motivated by hatred and bigotry toward minorities and women have a long tradition in American history, and pressure swelled from various sectors urging government to prohibit not just discrimination but also "hate crimes," such as a beating or shooting driven by racism or homophobia or some other unacceptable prejudice. Illegal conduct such as shooting or beating had always been punishable by law, but advocates of hate crime legislation demanded enhanced penalties when these crimes were predicated on animosity against certain groups—sending an official message that prejudicially motivated crimes are worse than the crimes themselves. Pressure mounted in the 1980s and 1990s amidst frequent news reports of brutal episodes of gay bashing and violence against women and racial minorities. Two such hate crimes that shocked the nation, and mobilized support for hate crime enforcement and new laws, were the attacks on Matthew Sheppard in Oklahoma, a young gay man who was savagely beaten while tied to a picket fence and left to die, and James Byrd, Jr., a black man who in Jasper, Texas, was chained to a motor vehicle and dragged miles to his death.

Advocates of tolerance argued that certain expressions should be avoided, discouraged, prohibited, and perhaps punished. "Sticks and stones may break my bones but names will never hurt me" was a childhood ditty that was never really true. Common, everyday parlance expressed prejudices no longer acceptable. "Political correctness," or PC, was a term coined by critics of this trend on college campuses, in many personnel offices of corporate America, and even in government. The efforts at achieving "neutral," or nonoffensive, speech extended to basic vocabulary. The word "freshman" denoted a male-dominated society; the same was true of "chairman" and the generic use of "he," "him," and "his" that dominated the English language. New words such as "freshers" and "chairs" were invented to promote a neutral vernacular. Some feminist groups spelled "women" as "womyn" to extirpate as much as possible the remnants of patriarchy that saturated the nation's culture. Language was political; language was power. Words and phrases were expunged to reduce prejudice and increase respect for differences. The U.S. Department of Education's Office for Civil Rights in May 1993, for example, instructed the senior staff to refer to the blind as "persons with a visual impairment" or deaf children as "young people with hearing impairments."

This movement exposed itself to ridicule, and pundits and comedians seized the occasion. Bill Maher, for example, mocked it with his highly popular TV program *Politically Incorrect*. A motion picture lampooned campus life in a film called *PCU*, released in 1994. Critics gloated on news from the nation's capital where David Howard, a white aide to Washington, D.C.'s mayor, resigned in controversy owing to his use of the word "niggardly" in a conversation during a staff meeting held on January 15, 1999. The controversial adjective meaning "stingy" or "miserly" originated in the 1500s and has nothing to do with race, but staff employees mistook it for a racial slur. Sophisticated conservative critics, like Dinesh D'Souza, saw the PC syndrome as a form of brainwashing fostered by liberal academics who had lost their influence in Washington under the twelve-year reign of Republican presidents. In his bestselling book *Illiberal Education*, D'Souza argues that America's colleges and universities implemented a regime of thought control and intolerance of dissent from conservative students and faculty, all part of a scheme to inculcate in impressionable minds the liberal agenda repeatedly rejected by American voters. In May 1991, President George Bush delivered the commencement address at the University of Michigan, in which he, too, described an "inquisition" reigning over academic life that intimidated faculty and students to adopt the values of the liberal Left—or to keep quiet.

Defenders dismiss the claims of their conservative detractors as grumbling from the privileged who fear any threat to their dominant place in the power structure. Educator David Droge replied that opponents concocted the term "politically correct" as a derisive epithet to denounce affirmative action and multicultural education because such programs broaden opportunities once reserved for an exclusive class of males. Other sympathetic observers contend that neither multicultural education nor "political correctness" dominates college curricula and that there is no concerted or programmatic mission to indoctrinate students. The hyperbole, Droge said, is the product of the media and over-generalizations drawn by political opponents who oppose extending opportunities to groups previously excluded.

Many of the episodes of repressed speech or expression on campus recounted by conservative critics and their organizations, such as Accuracy in Academia, were, in fact, actions undertaken by student groups, not faculty or administrators. In March 2001, for instance, the Brown University *Daily Herald* published David Horowitz's "Ten Reasons" not to make reparations to black Americans as compensation for slavery; many other college newspapers around the country refused to run the ad. The Brown newspaper provoked a coalition of angry student protesters who made demands on the newspaper, which were refused, and a few days later coalition members destroyed batches of the *Herald* left at distribution points on campus. However, there are many other examples of perhaps good intentions of faculty and administrators conflicting with individual freedom of students and other faculty. Professor Mary Daly at Boston College for years had prohibited men from taking her class on women's liberation, and men who complained were snubbed by Daly's admirers as disgruntled men angry about losing control of their erstwhile dominance in society. Administrators ordered Daly to admit men and dismissed her for not doing so. The University of New Hampshire suspended a communications professor, under its sexual harassment policy, because in class he equated good and focused writing with sex. The latter case highlights the fine line between freedom of speech and sexual harassment, but a federal district court concluded that the university's policy was unconstitutionally applied to the professor's academic freedom in the classroom.

There is also a class of offensive expression (racial and ethnic insults and slurs), which—while not necessarily hate crimes—became known as "hate speech" made to vilify and hurt people because of certain traits. Colleges and universities throughout the country sought ways, consistent with the right of freedom of speech, to curb the use of bigoted, racist, anti-Semitic, sexist, or homophobic remarks and epithets. The entire academic community seemed preoccupied with this issue in the late 1980s and early 1990s, as reports mounted of ugly racial and antigay epithets chalked or spray-painted on buildings and written on dorm room doors and walkways on college campuses all across the United States. Certain words—such as "faggot," "nigger," "gook," "spick," "kike," and words that taunt or insult women—convey little cognitive information and have virtually no use in spoken English except to harass or cause injury. Administrators and faculty in higher education responded by adjusting their codes of student conduct. The goal was to promote civil discourse and nurture tolerance.

Liberals confronted a dilemma and divided among themselves. For decades they had fought both to liberate women and minorities *and* to protect freedom of speech. Now they faced the challenge that the First Amendment might protect illiberal individuals who harm women and minorities through offensive, hateful speech. In trying to rid higher education of society's biases and bigotry, liberals faced the task of promoting free expression or promoting equality by suppressing offensive speech. This dilemma appeared also within the feminist movement, on this issue and pornography. Some feminists objected to pornography as an assault on women; other, more liberal feminists treated it as expression showing that women, as well as men, can enjoy sex. To the "radical" feminists, however, the multibillion-dollar pornography industry gratified men by degrading women in films, videos, and magazine and thus perpetuated the image of women as sexual objects and slaves of men. Social conservatives and religious groups supported the radical feminists, not necessarily because of the sexist messages heard by their allies but because they opposed pornography as immoral. Together these groups succeeded in enacting municipal laws giving women a right to sue producers, sellers, and distributors of pornography. The mayor of Minneapolis vetoed the city ordinance there, but another, from Indianapolis, passed but was immediately challenged in court and declared unconstitutional.

Hate speech exposed the dilemma more clearly. There was nothing new about either laws against or "hate speech" itself, which is as old as human prejudice; it can be found in some versions of the Bible; and the Supreme Court had dealt with it before. In *Beauharnais v. Illinois* (1952) a narrowly divided Court upheld a "group libel" law that punished those who publicly degraded whole classes of people because of their race, color, creed, or religion. Although that case has never been formally overruled, many commentators argue that the Court's reasoning is obsolete, undermined and eroded by later rulings, especially those developing the momentous holding in the *New York Times v. Sullivan* (1964) libel case. Nonetheless, a decade before *Beauharnais* the Court had unanimously held in a still very much-cited case, *Chaplinksy v. New Hampshire* (1942), that certain types of speech are by their nature unprotected because they contain either no socially valuable ideas or ideas outweighed by more important interests. "Fighting words" constitute one such class still considered unprotected expression—expression intentionally uttered either to provoke a fight or to inflict injury on the listener. *Chaplinsky* also acknowledged that the First Amendment does not protect hateful words designed to hurt and injure.

More than 300 institutions of higher education introduced, at one point or another by 1992, codes of student behavior to prohibit and punish certain forms of expression that stigmatize, victimize, or pejoratively characterize religious and racial minorities, women, gays and lesbians, and other particular groups. The American Civil Liberties Union, consistent with its controversial defense of the Nazis in Skokie, officially opposed these hate speech codes insofar as they prohibited or punished "speech." It agreed that colleges and universities could—and should—prohibit behavior or "conduct" constituting harassment or intimidation. More universities would have instituted these codes, but professors on campus successfully persuaded the faculty that their proposed codes could not survive in court. Under established First Amendment law the "fighting words" doctrine seemed the only principle on which these codes could safely be built, but over the years since *Chaplinsky* the judiciary has whittled down the "fighting words" exception to mean essentially *face-to-face* insults or vulgarities likely to provoke a fight or cause injury. Also, the judiciary has required government to be "content neutral" when regulating expression. Presumably, "hate speech" is unprotected only if it is face-to-face and the codes proscribing such expression are content neutral. Does a student in a classroom have a right to say that "blacks are inferior to whites" or that "homosexuality is immoral"? Critics of these codes argue that unpopular opinions, whether valid or not, are under attack not because of the context in which they are made but because of the content of the message itself.

In September 1989, a federal court in Michigan invalidated the University of Michigan's prohibition against pejorative speech (the prohibition swept across "race, ethnicity, religion, sex, sexual orientation, creed, national origin, ancestry, age, marital status, handicap or Vietnam-era veteran status").[1] The judge found the university policy so overbroad as to invade free speech rights and berated the university for failing to reconcile its attempt to combat discrimination with First Amendment principles. At the Eau Claire campus of the University of Wisconsin, a student in 1991 sent an Iranian a computer message: "Death to all Arabs. Die, Islamic scum bags." The student, who apparently was unaware that Iranians are not Arabs, was put on probation, but students from the Milwaukee campus successfully sued in a federal court in Wisconsin. A fraternity at George Mason University staged an "ugly woman" contest to raise money for charity, in which many of the fraternity brothers dressed in drag. One wore blackface and a black wig and stuffed pillows into his shirt and pants to represent large breasts and buttocks. Several students complained, and the university suspended the fraternity from social or sports activities for two years. A federal court in Virginia subsequently ruled that the university violated the free speech rights of the fraternity brothers; if a person has a right to burn the American flag, the court ruled, the university has no right to censor other messages because of their offensive content.

At Brown University a drunken student from his dorm window shouted obscenities coupled with the words "nigger" and "faggot." Although he was not aiming his tirades at any particular person, he was expelled from the university. The First Amendment reaches only "state action," that is, governmental action, and many private universities, such as Brown, might successfully claim in court that the First Amendment does not affect them. Some private universities, however, can be deemed "state actors" if they receive sufficient funds from the state or federal government, as many research institutions do. After a federal court had thrown out a speech policy from the University of Pennsylvania, the university revised its policy in 1989. A student later faced the university's judicial inquiry officer in a case widely reported as the "Water Buffalo Affair." On January 13, 1993, first-year student Eden Jacobowitz was in his dorm room writing an English paper when he was disturbed by a group of black sorority members celebrating outside below his window. He yelled out, "Please keep quiet," but twenty minutes later as the noise below increased, he shouted: "Shut up you water buffalo! If you want a party, there's a zoo a mile from here."[2] Others in the high-rise dorm annoyed by the clamor below shouted expressions such as "black asses" and "black bitches,"[3] but university police were unable to locate the source. Jacobowitz came forward as the shouter of "water buffalo" and was charged with racial harassment. The term "water buffalo" was a translation of an insult he had learned as a child and apparently had no reference to race at all. He was asked to apologize in exchange for dropping the charges, but he refused. With little to go on, the judicial inquiry officer dropped the charges.

A major blow for hate speech codes on campus occurred on February

27, 1995, when a state court invalidated the policy of Stanford University, designed by law professor Thomas Grey, one of the country's leading constitutional law experts. Stanford is a private university, but it does receive significant funding from public sources. More specifically, California law prohibited private universities from violating the First Amendment rights of students. The court ruled that Stanford's policy abridged freedom of speech—even though it tried to curtail hate speech as "fighting words."

Despite the extensive public debate on these matters, and the poor track record of campus codes in courts, the legal questions have not been clearly resolved. Some campus codes are being reconsidered, such as that at the University of Wisconsin at Madison. Shortly after the 1999 flap over the use of the word "niggardly" in the nation's capital, a student at the University of Wisconsin at Madison complained to the faculty senate about an English professor's use of that word in class. Political science professor Donald A. Downs, who attended the senate meeting in opposition to the reintroduction of the code, noted: "If that's an example of the kind of sensitivity that's out there, it shows you the danger of speech codes. We couldn't ask for a better example of why to vote against them."[4]

The Supreme Court entered the debate in the early 1990s, but its contributions infused more fog than clarity. In 1990 the city of St. Paul, Minnesota, passed the Bias-Motivated Crime Ordinance that stated:

Whoever places on public or private property a symbol, object, appellation, characterization or graffiti, including but not limited to, a burning cross or Nazi swastika, which one knows or has reasonable grounds to know arouses anger, alarm, or resentment in others on the basis of race, color, creed, religion or gender commits disorderly conduct and shall be guilty of a misdemeanor.[5]

Two years later, on June 22, 1992, the Court unanimously invalidated this law as a violation of the First Amendment, though the justices split on the reasons why.

In this case, teenagers in the predawn hours of June 21, 1990, jumped a fence onto the private yard of a black family and burned a makeshift cross, constructed from broken chair legs. Officials could have charged them with violations of several existing laws against trespass, arson, and even terrorist threats. Instead, the charge was based on the Bias-Motivated Crime Ordinance. Justice Antonin Scalia's majority opinion striking down this ordinance rested on a novel principle. Accepting the city's interpretation that its law punished only "fighting words," Scalia declared such a category of expression is not by definition "entirely invisible to the Constitution."[6] Government may not select which messages are punishable and cannot create "content-based" distinctions when invoking the fighting words doctrine to punish (or to favor) certain kinds of expression. Fighting words are unprotected, Scalia said, not because of the message being sent but because of the manner in which that message is sent. He drew an analogy to a noisy sound truck which government may regulate. "As with the sound truck . . . so also with fighting words: The government may not regulate use based on hostility—or favoritism—towards the underlying message expressed."[7] Thus, because the city ordinance did not cover *all* targets of hate speech as fighting words, it could not prohibit and punish *some* hate speech as fighting words. "The First Amendment does not permit St. Paul to impose special prohibitions on those speakers who express views on disfavored subjects."[8]

Justice Byron White, joined by three other justices, asserted that the St. Paul measure was unconstitutional because the city ordinance was both too vague (the language was unclear) and overbroad (it swept so far as to punish some protected expression, however repugnant it might be). Nevertheless, he complained about Scalia's reasoning:

> It is inconsistent to hold that the government may proscribe an entire category of speech because the content of that speech is evil . . . but that the government may not treat a subset of that category differently without violating the First Amendment; the content of the subset is by definition worthless and undeserving of constitutional protection. . . . [By] characterizing fighting words as a form of "debate" . . . the majority legitimates hate speech as a form of public discussion.[9]

Justice Harry A. Blackmun agreed that the St. Paul law was unconstitutional, and he also criticized the Court's reasoning: "I fear that the Court has been distracted from its proper mission by the temptation to decide the issue over 'politically correct speech' and 'cultural diversity,' neither of which is presented here. If this is the meaning of today's opinion, it is perhaps even more regrettable."[10]

The *R.A.V.* holding induced at least some universities and colleges to reconsider, if not abandon, their hate speech codes. The University of Delaware's faculty senate, for instance, in 1993 rescinded section 4(b) of the student code of conduct prohibiting offensive speech, after a long debate in which the dean of students expressed doubt that the provision could survive in court.

In 1993 the Democrats took control once again of the White House with the inauguration of former Arkansas governor William J. Clinton, who, during two terms as president, strongly supported affirmative action and policies against both hate speech and hate crimes. In 1994, however, the Republican Party—for the first time since 1952—captured control of both houses of Congress. Many newly elected and reelected Republican legislators attributed their stunning victory to "politically incorrect" working people across America who recoiled from oppressive political correctness. Yet by the year 2000, it was still clear that political correctness had neither been routed nor confined to college campuses, as seen in the uproar that greeted Atlanta Braves star closing pitcher John Rocker. In a sports interview the young left-hander had made unfocused but derogatory remarks about New York City, particularly its blacks and gays. The erupting clamor induced Baseball Commissioner Bud Selig to impose both a suspension and a $20,000 fine on Rocker, though the fine was ultimately reduced to $500 and the suspension was dramatically cut. The Braves a year later traded Rocker to the Cleveland Indians, but he was still "booed" by fans in New York and elsewhere. The event also reminded America that the names "Braves" and "Indians" are insensitive and politically incorrect. The *Skokie* case activated a national debate about hate speech that later swept across college campuses and that in the new millennium still remains unsettled.

NOTES

1. *Doe v. University of Michigan*, 721 F.Supp. 852, 853 (E.D. Mich. 1989).

2. As quoted in Alan C. Kors and Harvey A. Silvergate, *The Shadow University: The Betrayal of Liberty on America's Campuses* (New York: Free Press, 1998), p. 9. Professor Kors defended Eden Jacobowitz.

3. As quoted in ibid., p. 12.

4. As quoted in the *Chronicle of Higher Education* (February 12, 1999): A12.

5. *R.A.V. v. St. Paul*, 505 U.S. 377, 380 (1992).

6. Id. at 383.

7. Id. at 386.

8. Id. at 391.

9. 505 U.S. at 401, 402 (concurring opinion).

10. 505 U.S. at 415–416 (concurring opinion).

DOCUMENTS

11.1.   "PC" and the Liberal Domination on Campus

Dinesh D'Souza has been one of the leading critics of "political correctness" and speech codes at American colleges and universities. His book Illiberal Education *(1991) became a national bestseller. In this essay, he surveys higher education to evaluate the state of political correctness or what he viewed as an imperious reign of liberalism on college campuses.*

The term "political correctness" seems to have originated in the early part of the century, when it was employed by various species of Marxists to describe and enforce conformity to their preferred ideological positions. Books, films, opinions, even historical events were termed politically correct or politically incorrect depending on whether or not they advanced a particular Marxist view. There is no indication that the revolutionary ideologues and activists of that period spoke of political correctness with any trace of irony or self-mockery.

Eventually the term dropped out of the political lexicon, only to be revived in the early 1980's when it came into use by spokesmen for assorted contemporary ideologies: black consciousness and black power, feminism, homosexual rights, and to a lesser degree pacifism, environmentalism, the counterculture in general. The new *Webster's College Dictionary,* published by Random House, defines political correctness as "marked by or adhering to a typically progressive orthodoxy on issues involving especially race, gender, sexual affinity, or ecology." These days, as most people know, the home of such "typically progressive orthodoxy" is the American university.

Like the Stalinists and Trotskyites of an earlier era, contemporary campus activists maintain that "everything is political," and thus to them it seems quite proper to inquire whether classroom lectures, the use of language, and even styles of dress and demeanor reflect a politically correct stance or not. Indeed, many of today's activists are nor content with espousing politically correct views themselves, but seek to impose them by force on the new generation of students. So it is that as American society at large is moving toward greater tolerance of heterodox opinion, American universities, ostensibly dedicated to the free traffic of ideas, have been moving in the opposite direction, becoming (in the memorable phrase of Abigail Thernstrom) "islands of repression in a sea of freedom."

More than a hundred universities have instituted censorship codes which typically outlaw racially and sexually "stigmatizing" or offensive speech. Many of the codes are quite broad and elastic: at the University of Connecticut, for example, violations of the ethnic harassment policy, for which the penalty ranges from a reprimand to expulsion, include the "use of derogatory names," "inconsiderate jokes," and even "misdirected laughter" and "conspicuous exclusion from conversation." Although a federal judge struck down as unconstitutional the censorship code in place at the University of Michigan—where a student, hauled up before a disciplinary council for making negative remarks about homosexuality, was recently sentenced to write an apology and to attend sensitivity sessions to transform his unenlightened views—similar regulations are being enforced on many other campuses, and at private colleges they may be immune from First Amendment scrutiny.

The greatest obstacle to free speech on campus, however, is not the explicit censorship code but a political and social atmosphere in which politically incorrect opinions are discouraged, vilified, and ostracized. Although not a numerical majority, PC activists on campus constitute a kind of "moral majority," enjoying enormous leverage over a predominantly liberal community which is already hypersensitive to hints of racism or bigotry. In several cases, some highly publicized and others relatively unknown, professors who have dissented from PC nostrums have found themselves unemployed, or disgraced by administrative rebuke and sanctions. Many other professors and students have gotten the message: rather than risk being drawn into a vortex of accusations, sensitivity indoctrination, or censure, they simply abstain from articulating unpopular views; they censor themselves.

. . . [M]any mass publications took their first notice of political correctness *per se* only about a year ago. In "The Rising Hegemony of the Politically Correct" (New York *Times*, October 29, 1990), Richard Bernstein reported a pressure to conform to an "unofficial ideology" among students and faculty of American universities. At a conference in Berkeley, "Political Correctness and Cultural Studies," Bernstein interviewed a number of academics who did not deny that they were engaged in a project of ideological consciousness-raising, but asserted that it was justified by the need to topple "patriarchal hegemony" and the "white male power structure."

Then on December 24, 1990, *Newsweek*, itself a magazine with a "progressive" reputation, surprised everyone with a cover story on today's campus "Thought Police." The article was a parade of horror stories, each showing how professors and students who trespassed on prevailing orthodoxies were made to suffer. Still, the article implied that university leaders who permitted excesses were in pursuit of a good cause, and historical and demographic changes on campus were anyway bound to provoke tensions.

In early January of this year, *New York* magazine entered the fray with a vehement blast from John Taylor, "Are You Politically Correct?" Taylor made cruel fun of the PC lexicon, according to which, for instance, pets must be called animal companions and, in one extreme version, short people "vertically challenged." Chuckle we may, wrote Taylor, but many university officials take this very seriously; an official document at Smith College, for instance, warns students to eschew not only such evils as racism and sexism, but also heterosexism and even lookism—"the belief that appearance is an indicator of a person's value; the construction of a standard for beauty and attractiveness; oppression through stereotypes and generalizations of both those who do not fit the standard and those who do."

While the article in *New York* accurately captured the Star Chamber quality of the political environment on campus, it gave no plausible explanation of who precisely the new McCarthyites were and what they sought to accomplish. Like the *Newsweek* story, however, Taylor's article did help somewhat to delegitimize the PC authoritarians. PC was starting to look uncool.

What followed was an avalanche of critical scrutiny, both in the serious and the popular press, and on television. On February 18, the *New Republic* published a special issue, "Race on Campus," which included troubling vignettes from several prestigious campuses, an editorial attack on politically correct conformism, and a curious but important article by Irving Howe defending the traditional Western canon. . . . In April, *Time* magazine warned of a "culture of forbidden questions" and a "new intolerance" on campus. . . .

How have these spokesmen responded to criticism of the policies they have devised and implemented? So far, with only a couple of exceptions, by a deafening silence.

At first this could perhaps be attributed to the simple bewilderment of a class of people so accustomed to approbation that they had lost even the reflex habit of self-defense. But when weeks and months passed without response or rebuttal, one could only conclude that university leaders were unable to account effectively for their policies, and had decided to lie low until the storm passed—a strikingly pusillanimous posture for those usually so quick to claim a special social prerogative to engage issues of principle.

In any event, the burden of defending PC policies fell at first to political columnists, many of whom had not set foot on a campus for years, and to faculty radicals. In the case of the latter, the results were embarrassing. At the June conference of the Modern Language Association, for example, the consensus seemed to be that no defense was necessary. The problem was instead that ordinary Americans did not understand the incredible complexities of academia—"It's like trying to reduce a Henry James novel to a telegram," protested Martha Banta of UCLA's English department—or were just plain stupid, "people who don't know the difference between Plato and Nato," in the words of Berkeley sociologist Todd Gitlin, who was head of Students for a Democratic Society in the late 1960's. The only practical suggestion came from Professor Gene Ruoff of the University of Illinois, who urged that radical faculty mount a massive letter-writing and op-ed offensive to explain current academic trends to the general public. But he also conceded the risks of such a campaign; after all, many if not most Americans hold convictions diametrically opposed to those he wished to defend.

. . . [A]n argument on behalf of political correctness [was] advanced by Henry Louis Gates, Jr., chairman of Afro-American Studies at Harvard[:] as America becomes a more diverse society, the rules of academic life, heretofore shaped by white males of European origin, will have to be modified in order to reflect multiple voices and interests. Current university policies are based on the recognition that persons of color cannot be expected to homogenize themselves into "an America in cultural white lace." A new social compact needs to be negotiated and then institutionalized. . . . A similar line was taken by the feminist scholar Catharine Stimpson of Rutgers. In the first place, she maintained, the curriculum has always harbored acknowledged or covert ideological bias. And in the second place, PC activists are not politicizing the curriculum but only attempting to make higher dedication more accessible, to open closed doors, to promote inclusion. . . .

On the MacNeil-Lehrer show, Professor Stanley Fish of Duke University asserted that freedom of speech is only one of several competing values worth preserving; sometimes it must be balanced against, or subordinated to, other desiderata. Richard Rosser, president of the Association of Independent Colleges and Universities, while conceding that university codes of censorship may be regrettable, asserted that they are the only way to curb the current campus epidemic of hate speech and racial epithets.

Mainly, however, the defenders of PC have not sought to justify university policies but to shift the burden to the other side. The threat, they say, is a manufactured one, or at the very least has been greatly exaggerated by conservatives for their own nefarious political ends. "Where's this left-wing reign of terror on campus?" asks the columnist Michael Kinsley in mock-innocence. . . . The *Village Voice* and the *Nation* have also treated the PC threat as a mythic concoction of the right wing, and Brent Staples of the New York *Times* went so far as to imply that it was a "bogeyman magnified by leftover cold-war hysteria." The darkest pitch of all came from Joel Conarroe, president of the Guggenheim foundation, who suggested that the true goal of critics of PC is to legitimize racism, sexism, and homophobia "as a matter of high principle."

Unfortunately, for those who would deny the reality of PC, however, the facts continue to speak for themselves. . . . Yale president Benno Schmidt, for instance, has warned that nowhere is free speech more endangered today than on the American campus. In his annual report to the Harvard community, outgoing president Derek Bok cited the politicization of the university, primarily along race and gender lines, as one of the greatest perils to liberal education.

If there is any good news, it lies in these isolated voices from within the community of university administrators, bolstered by an un-PC faculty organization like the National Association of Scholars; but it lies even more in the public criticism that has been aired. That criticism has indeed placed PC cadres somewhat on the defensive, a little less quick to ostracize dissenters—especially when there is a chance their activities may be exposed by the media. . . . When it comes to the curriculum, although the drive to replace Western-culture requirements with "multicultural" or non-Western programs is already far advanced, it now has to contend with an intellectual opposition, sometimes from emboldened faculty liberals.

But the bad news is that the radicals are deeply entrenched in academia, and have no plans to go elsewhere. In many departments, particularly ones like ethnic and women's studies, faculty ideologues seek to perpetuate their position by hiring only like-minded people, limiting the range views in some disciplines to what Eugene Genovese terms "a diversity of radical positions." Policies such as racial preference are also thoroughly institutionalized, and have generated vested interests not only among beneficiary groups but also among enforcement bureaucracies.

In short, although the fight against political correctness has so far gone well in the open air of public opinion, the fight on the ground has barely begun.

Source: Dinesh D'Souza, " 'PC' So Far," *Commentary* 92 (October, 1991): 44–46. Reprinted from COMMENTARY, October 1991, by permission; all rights reserved.

11.2.   In Defense of "Hate Speech" Codes

A prominent liberal scholar, Professor Thomas C. Grey of the Stanford University Law School, wrote Stanford's hate speech policy that became effective in June 1990, serving as a prototype for scores of other colleges and universities around the country. He tried to steer a course between freedom and equality, and his policy was quite narrow in its coverage. Still, a California court in 1995 struck it down as an abridgment of free speech. Here, Grey explains the Stanford approach and how it accommodated two important but conflicting principles.

Let me . . . describe the proposal I originally drafted, which was recently adopted as a disciplinary rule covering discriminatory verbal harassment at Stanford. The provision is an attempt to accommodate competing values, to mediate the incommensurable conflict of civil-liberties and civil-rights approaches on this issue. I . . . believe that some such accommodating solution, as against a "principled" choice implementing one approach to the exclusion of the other, is needed.

The first section of the provision restates Stanford's policy on free expression, including an insistence that students must learn to "tolerate even expression of opinions which they find abhorrent." Counterposed is a second section restating the university's existing policy against discrimination "in the administration of its educational policies" on the basis of "sex, race, color, handicap, religion, sexual orientation, or national and ethnic origin," and adding that harassment on the basis of these characteristics can, when cumulated, constitute hostile environment discrimination under the policy. The third section notes that the free expression and anti-discrimination on policies conflict on the issue of verbal harassment; it provides that "protected free expression ends and prohibited discriminatory harassment begins" at the point where expression of opinion becomes "personal vilification" of a student on the basis of one of the characteristics stated in the anti-discrimination policy.

The operative part of the provision comes in the fourth and last section, which defines "personal vilification" as speech or other symbolic expression that (a) is intended to insult or stigmatize individuals on the basis of one of the designated characteristics; (b) is "addressed directly" to those insulted or stigmatized; and (c) makes use of "insulting or fighting words," defined . . . as words (or non-verbal symbols) that "by their very utterance inflict injury or tend to incite to an immediate breach of the peace."

Finally, the proposal adds a narrowing proviso designed to adapt the . . . insulting-or-fighting words concept to civil-rights enforcement. In the context of discriminatory harassment, punishable words (or symbols) are defined as those "commonly understood to convey direct and visceral hatred or contempt for human beings on the basis of" the characteristics specified in the anti-discrimination policy—a phrase meant to capture the sense of the common expression "racial epithets" and to extend it to other prohibited forms of discrimination.

To summarize, the rule would punish speech directed to individuals: speech meant to insult them on the basis of a protected characteristic that also makes use of one of the gutter epithets of bigotry. . . . [I]t prohibits only expression that falls roughly within the categories of fighting words or intentional infliction of emotional distress doctrines. The provision therefore only prohibits a very narrow category of expression, immunizing even the vilest hate-speech addressed generally to a campus audience as well as many serious face-to-face discriminatory verbal assaults. Many students of color and other civil-rights advocates at Stanford have opposed it, for these reasons, as too weak an anti-discrimination measure.

At the same time, narrow as it is, the proposal retains enough of the civil-rights approach to trouble most civil libertarians. It seems to violate the second central civil-liberties tenet: not only can speech be regulated only to the minimum extent necessary to prevent immediate and otherwise unremediable harm; further, any speech regulation must be *neutral*—generally neutral as to content, certainly neutral as to viewpoint. The provision's apparent violation of the neutrality constraint results directly from its being framed as civil-rights protection or anti-discrimination measure. . . .

The Stanford provision . . . suggest[s] a category of speech, objectively "insulting" in character, that attacks the very identity of its victim in such a way as to stimulate the familiar "fight or flight reaction." Among certain classes of hearers, particularly young males socialized to be physically aggressive, the typical reaction to a vile personal insult may be "fight." For others—many men; perhaps most children, most older people, most women; invalids—the typical reaction to this kind of verbal assault is some combination of extreme fear, numbness, and impotent rage: reactions calculated to produce the sort of "severe emotional distress" to which [tort law] makes reference. We should . . . identif[y] two distinct kinds of reactions (fight or flight) to the same category of intolerable speech when it speaks, respectively, of utterances that "tend to incite an immediate breach of the peace" and those that "by their very utterance inflict injury."

The Stanford provision identifies discriminatory "personal vilification" as a class of utterances of which any instance is particularly likely to produce one or the other of the kinds of injury covered by the "fighting words" and "emotional distress" analysis. These are, in Richard Delgado's phrase, "words that wound"—utterances directed to members of groups specially subject to discrimination, intended to insult or stigmatize them, and making use of the small class of commonly recognized words or symbols that have no other function but to convey hatred and contempt for these groups.

Professor Delgado offers as the test for liability under his proposal the requirement that the words directed to the victim be such as "a reason-able person would recognize as a racial insult." In a campus context, where claims of insult and ideological debate are often intertwined, this phrasing raises special, and I think avoidable, civil-liberties problems. Some ideas might be taken as racial or ethnic insults by virtue of their content alone: for example, claims that the Holocaust never happened, or that blacks are genetically inferior to whites. To avoid banning ideas as such on the basis of propositional content, on campus or elsewhere, the Stanford regulation prohibits only verbal abuse including actual racial epithets, or their equivalents for other forms of discrimination. These are the all-too-familiar words that carry with them so inseparable a message of hatred and contempt that apologies are in order for the affront involved in even quoting them: "nigger," "kike," "faggot," "cunt," and the like.

Racial and other discriminatory hatred and contempt can be effectively expressed without using these words, of course, but (partly in the interests of avoiding vagueness and its chilling effect) such cases are not included under the regulation. A white student can tell a black student, face-to-face, "you people are inferior and should not be here," but not be guilty of harassment. In addition, even gutter epithets are immunized when uttered to the campus or public at large, in order to give the widest possible leeway for speech in the public forum; the Klan or the neo-Nazis may demonstrate and display their symbols and shout their words of hatred with impunity. This very much narrows the reach of the proposal and exposes it to the charge, mentioned before, that it is mere tokenism. But at the same time, it helps meet traditional and legitimate civil-liberties concerns about public political expression, and about vagueness and its accompanying chilling effect.

The Stanford provision has also been drafted with an eye on another concern—one rooted in the civil-rights perspective, and often noted as well in civil-libertarian objections to "hate speech" or "group defamation" regulations. The concern is illustrated by one of the cases that occurred under the Michigan regulation. A black woman law student, in the course of a heated argument, called a classmate "white trash." She was charged with a violation of the harassment rule; she ultimately agreed to write a formal letter of apology to the classmate in settlement of the charge.

Under the Stanford provision, calling a white student "white trash" would not constitute harassment. In its commonly understood meaning, the term is (like "redneck") derogatory to the poor whites of the rural South by virtue of their class, not their race. If the student addressed came from that social background, and if class bias were a form of discrimination covered by the proposal (as it is not), there might be a disciplinary case. But as a white person, she is not a victim of discriminatory *racial* harassment; the term "white trash" is clearly not "commonly understood" to convey hatred or contempt for whites on the basis of their race as such—a requirement for liability under the provision. This is not to deny that the black woman student intended to express race-based hatred or contempt, or that she may have effectively conveyed a racial insult, just as a white student does who tells a black student that "you people are inferior and shouldn't be here." In neither case, though, is the regulation violated, because in neither case is there use of one of the required "commonly understood" assaultive epithets or symbols of discriminatory contempt.

The point of the "white trash" case can be generalized, and in a way that is most troubling to civil libertarian defenders of viewpoint neutrality. As best I can see, there are *no* epithets in this society at this time that are "commonly understood" to convey hatred and contempt for whites *as such*. The same can be said, I believe, of males as such, and heterosexuals as such. If this is indeed a socio-linguistic fact, it is of course one not fixed in stone; on the other hand, it is no accident. The denigrating epithets covered by the Stanford provision are able to inflict the serious and distinctive injuries characteristic of legally prohibited invidious discrimination because they strike at groups subjected to long-standing and deep-rooted prejudices widely held and disseminated throughout our culture. American children grow up with the negative stereotypes of blacks, women, and homosexuals in their bones and in their souls. This is tragically true, too, of children who are black, female, or later identify themselves as homosexual.

The denigrating epithets draw their capacity to impose the characteristic civil-rights injury to "hearts and minds" from the fact that they turn the whole socially and historically inculcated weight of these prejudices upon their victim. Each hatemonger who invokes one of these terms summons a vicious chorus in his support. It is because, given our cultural history, no such *general* prejudices strike against the dominant groups that there exist no comparable terms of universally understood hatred and contempt applicable to whites, males, and heterosexuals as such.

The Stanford provision, then, while neutral on its face, will foreseeably be asymmetric in its application. This aspect of the provision allows its interpretation to reflect a state of affairs central to civil-rights analysis— the continued existence of asymmetric social relations of group domination and subjugation in the United States. Contrary to the democratic ideal, American society (like other societies) is still characterized by a hierarchy of relatively stable ascriptive status groups. To rephrase the point from the jargon of sociology to the rhetoric of movement politics, there still exist "oppressor" and "oppressed" (or, to lower the political pitch, "privileged" and "subordinated") groups, identified as such by characteristics such as race, gender, class, and sexual preference.

Source: Thomas C. Grey, "Civil Rights versus Civil Liberties: The Case of Discriminatory Verbal Harassment," *Social Philosophy and Policy* 8, no. 2 (Spring 1991): 90–96. Reprinted with the permission of Cambridge University Press.

11.3.   Campus "Hate Speech" Codes Degrade and Weaken Students

Former U.S. assistant secretary of state, frequent contender for the Republican presidential nomination, and cable TV talk-show host, Alan L. Keyes opposes hate speech codes, claiming that they are based on moral but debatable presuppositions made by liberals. He also argues that such codes weaken, degrade, and insult students.

The debate over the regulation of speech at universities . . . is really about moral education—about how we establish, encourage, and maintain moral behavior.

The most intriguing aspect of seeing the problem in this light is that the very conduct restricted by campus speech regulation lies at the foundation of serious moral education . . . [which] involves apportioning praise and blame to guide our conduct. . . . We believe that some things are repugnant, nasty, or unacceptable, and thus we would not do them. Likewise, we believe that some things are attractive, wonderful, or acceptable, and thus we would do them. Therefore, to instill moral feelings we must be able to use the vocabulary of praise and blame, appreciation and opprobrium.

In this regard, insult is actually a very useful tool. Insults can attack immoral behavior by exposing it, by ripping off its mask and allowing us to see the corrupt for what they really are. As a result, we should not banish the vocabulary of insult from our society as long as it is effective in fighting emotionally those who engage in immoral conduct. . . .

. . . [U]niversity codes of conduct . . . represent an effort to establish and teach new moral standards to replace older moral standards. Moreover, in their dependence on coercion, the new standards may run directly counter to the older ones.

The treatment of homosexuality is a very good illustration of this phenomenon. Homosexuality was, until recently, a taboo word on campuses and elsewhere. Parents taught their children that it was ugly and dirty. They did so in order to turn their moral conviction that homosexual conduct was bad into moral actions by their children. Repugnance at homosexual behavior was seen as necessary to defend against whatever temptation it might present.

Some may claim that this method of teaching was discriminatory. Nonetheless ... this method has been commonly used to translate moral precepts into moral actions throughout human history. People point a finger at certain conduct and call it bad, ugly, shameful, dirty, or repugnant. They ridicule and revile it. Many books of the Bible, for instance, contain pages filled with invectives against the wicked.

... [But] we no longer think that invectives used in biblical times constitute fighting words. For example, if we singled out those people in this room who have engaged in any form of premarital sexual activity and called them fornicators and whoremongers, they would probably shrug off or pay no attention to the attack. Over time, then, fighting words may change along with our sense of what constitutes acceptable and unacceptable behavior.

At the same time, if we singled out people who engaged in homosexual acts and called them sodomites or other names, these would still be fighting words. Homosexual rights advocates argue that the use of such words is cause for the intervention of coercive force. In fact, what they are really arguing for is the protection of a still-controversial moral judgment about homosexuality. Because heterosexual promiscuity is generally acceptable, it requires no such formal defense. We do not establish rules to punish its opponents. Homosexuality, by contrast, has not yet achieved the same accepted status. Nonetheless, its defenders seek to create rules to stigmatize its critics. They have even invented a word to convey this stigma: homophobia.

... If homophobia is a true phobia, then it is a neurosis for which people are not responsible. If this is the case, why punish them for it? After all, the fear of immoral behavior is, in many, an uncontrollable impulse. Such people reflexively remove themselves from the presence of what they believe to be evil. They involuntarily try to oppose and destroy immorality.

... [W]hile everyone understands the general meaning of the term "sexual orientation," the fact remains that people have all kinds of odd sexual tastes. As a society, we are in basic agreement that some of these tastes, such as bestiality, are repugnant. Consequently, we should have the right to raise our children to regard certain behavior as worthy of opprobrium. Those who engage in bestiality, therefore, are rightly ridiculed and scorned in order to support the moral feelings we try to inculcate in our young. Yet, by broadly protecting "sexual orientation," are we not suppressing all forms of praise and blame directed at any sexual behavior whatsoever? Do we not thereby undermine the ability to impart any kind of moral education based on this or other standards?

This is just a general aspect of the problem, but we can only start dealing with it when we face the reality that the issue here is not one of minority rights versus free speech. Instead, the issue is one of identifying both the correct moral standards for universities to uphold and the proper methods for upholding these standards. In this regard, the question becomes whether rules against harassment on the basis of race, gender, or sexual orientation are desirable or justified.

. . . [T]he basic problem with the speech restrictions meant to protect various minorities, including blacks, is that they weaken students' ability to seek and pursue truth.

These restrictions are, at the outset, based on patronizing and paternalistic assumptions. Telling blacks that whites have the moral character to shrug off epithets, and they do not, is an insult. Saying that whites have the innate capacity to defend themselves against verbal attack, and blacks do not, compounds the insult. Finally, building this imputed genetic weakness into codes of conduct for the protection of blacks makes perhaps the most insulting, most invidious, most racist statement of all.

These codes are more than insulting; they are ultimately incapacitating. Students come to a university to learn how to engage in the pursuit of truth, in the battle of ideas. This battle is like any other; it requires effective training. . . . [I]sn't education supposed to prepare students to seek truth, to pursue it, and to persist in this endeavor despite the obstacles? Should students really be protected from these obstacles instead of preparing for them? If a black student steps out of Stanford University into his first argument with a gutter fighter over an important issue, gets called a racial epithet, and loses his mind, should he not go back to Stanford and seek a refund?

The most fundamental problem with campus speech restrictions is that in protecting certain students they ultimately make these students weaker. The restrictions institutionalize victimization by leaving the victimized unprepared to fight against it. This effect might be tolerable as long as minorities live underneath the paternalistic wing of universities such as Stanford. But it is likely to be devastating when they go into a world where no protection exists. That world is the real world, regardless of the laws we make.

Education must offer something more, particularly to those who wish to be free. Freedom is in essence the ability to defend oneself. It does not consist of seeking champions for one's defense—that is not freedom, but feudalism. Therefore, instead of looking for rulers and laws to defend us, we must be able to rule ourselves and make our own laws. This ability must be inside every individual. It should be the result of a liberal education that, true to its name, strengthens people and prepares them to be free.

Source: Alan L. Keyes, "Freedom through Moral Education," *Harvard Journal of Law and Public Policy* 14 (Winter 1991): 165–171. Reprinted courtesy of *Harvard Journal of Law and Public Policy*.

11.4.   Do "Hate Crimes" Violate the First Amendment?

Just one day after the Supreme Court had announced the confusing ruling in R.A.V. v. St. Paul, *the Wisconsin Supreme Court, in a 5–2 opinion, expressly cited* R.A.V. *to invalidate the state's penalty enhancement "hate crime" statute under which a defendant convicted of assault had received an additional two years in prison because his conduct was found to be motivated by racial animosity, in violation of the statute. The state appealed to the U.S. Supreme Court, which a year later unanimously reversed the ruling of Wisconsin's highest court, holding that* R.A.V. *had dealt with "speech," whereas the defendant's action here was "conduct."*

[Chief Justice Heffernan delivered the opinion of the Wisconsin Supreme Court.]

The sole issue before the court is the constitutionality . . . [of] the "hate crimes" statute. . . . We hold that the statute violates the First Amendment and is thus unconstitutional. . . .

The facts are not in dispute. [Todd Mitchell, nineteen at the time, on October 7, 1989, provoked a group of other blacks to beat up Gregory Reddick, a white teenager, who was passing by. The beating put him in a coma for several days and inflicted possible brain damage. The jury agreed that the beating was racially motivated.] . . .

. . . Nearly every state in the country has enacted some form of hate crime legislation. . . . The Wisconsin legislature's response was to enact [a law] which enhances the potential penalty for a criminal actor if the state proves that the actor intentionally selected the victim because of the victim's race, religion, color, disability, sexual orientation, national origin or ancestry. . . .

The hate crimes statute violates the First Amendment directly by punishing what the legislature has deemed to be offensive thought and violates the First Amendment indirectly by chilling free speech.

. . . The First Amendment protects not only speech but thought as well. . . . Even more fundamentally, the constitution protects all speech and thought, regardless of how offensive it may be. . . . As Justice Holmes put it: "If there is any principle of the Constitution that more imperatively calls for attachment than any other it is the principle of free thought—not free thought for those who agree with us but freedom for the thought we hate." . . .

Without doubt the hate crimes statute punishes bigoted thought. The state asserts that the statute punishes only the "conduct" of intentional selection of a victim. We disagree. Selection of a victim is an element of the underlying offense, part of the defendant's "intent" in committing the crime. In any assault upon an individual there is a selection of the victim. The statute punishes the "because of" aspect of the defendant's selection, the *reason* the defendant selected the victim, the *motive* behind the selection.

... Because all of the crimes under [the law] are already punishable, all that remains is an additional punishment for the defendant's motive in selecting the victim. The punishment of the defendant's bigoted motive by the hate crimes statute directly implicates and encroaches upon First Amendment rights.

... Merely because the statute refers in a literal sense to the intentional "conduct" of selecting, does not mean the court must turn a blind eye to the intent and practical effect of the law—punishment of offensive motive or thought. The conduct of "selecting" is not akin to the conduct of assaulting, burglarizing, murdering and other criminal conduct. It cannot be objectively established. Rather, an examination of the intentional "selection" of a victim necessarily requires a subjective examination of the actor's motive or reason for singling out the particular person against whom he or she commits a crime. ...

In this case, Todd Mitchell selected Gregory Reddick because Reddick is white. Mitchell is black. The circumstantial evidence relied upon to prove that Mitchell selected Reddick "because" Reddick is white included Mitchell's speech—"Do you all feel hyped up to move on some white people?"—and his recent discussion with other black youths of a racially charged scene from the movie "Mississippi Burning." This evidence was used not merely to show the intentional selection of the victim, but was used to prove Mitchell's bigoted bias. The physical assault of Reddick is the same whether he was attacked because of his skin color or because he was wearing "British Knight" tennis shoes. Mitchell's bigoted motivation for selecting Reddick, his thought which impelled him to act, is the reason that his punishment was enhanced. In Mitchell's case, that motivation was apparently a hatred of whites.

The statute commendably is designed to punish—and thereby deter—racism and other objectionable biases, but deplorably unconstitutionally infringes upon free speech. The state would justify its transgression against the constitutional right of freedom of speech and thought because its motive is a good one, but the magnitude of the proposed incursion against the constitutional rights of all of us should no more be diminished for that good motive than should a crime be enhanced by a separate penalty because of a criminal's bad motive.

The state admits that this case involves legislation that seeks to address bias related crime. The only definition of "bias" relevant to this case is "prejudice." A statute specifically designed to punish personal prejudice impermissibly infringes upon an individual's First Amendment rights, no matter how carefully or cleverly one words the statute. The hate crimes statute enhances the punishment of bigoted criminals because they are bigoted. The statute is directed solely at the subjective motivation of the actor—his or her prejudice. Punishment of one's thought, however repugnant the thought, is unconstitutional.

In *R.A.V.*, decided June 22, 1992, the United States Supreme Court held . . . that the government may not constitutionally regulate even otherwise unprotected speech on the basis of hostility towards the idea expressed by the speaker. . . . In other words, while the government may regulate all fighting words, it may not regulate only those fighting words with which it disagrees. Such a prohibition is nothing more than a governmental attempt to silence speech on the basis of its content.

While the St. Paul ordinance invalidated in *R.A.V.* is clearly distinguishable from the hate crimes statute in that it regulates fighting words rather than merely the actor's biased motive, the Court's analysis lends support to our conclusion that the Wisconsin legislature cannot criminalize bigoted thought with which it disagrees. The Court stated:

"[T]he only interest distinctively served by the content limitation is that of displaying the city council's special hostility towards the particular biases thus singled out. That is precisely what the First Amendment forbids. The politicians of St. Paul are entitled to express that hostility—but not through the means of imposing unique limitations upon speakers who (however benightedly) disagree." . . . The ideological content of the thought targeted by the hate crimes statute is identical to that targeted by the St. Paul ordinance—racial or other discriminatory animus. And, like the United States Supreme Court, we conclude that the legislature may not single out and punish that ideological content.

Thus, the hate crimes statute is facially invalid because it directly punishes a defendant's constitutionally protected thought. The hate crimes statute is also unconstitutionally overbroad. . . . For example, if A strikes B in the face he commits a criminal battery. However, should A add a word such as "nigger," "honkey," "jew," "mick," "kraut," "spic," or "queer," the crime becomes a felony, and A will be punished not for his conduct alone—a misdemeanor—but for using the spoken word. . . .

. . . As disgraceful and deplorable as these and other hate crimes are, the personal prejudices of the attackers are protected by the First Amendment. The constitution may not embrace or encourage bigoted and hateful thoughts, but it surely protects them.

Because we wholeheartedly agree with the motivation of the legislature in its desire to suppress hate crimes, it is with great regret that we hold the hate crimes statute unconstitutional—and only because we believe that the greater evil is the suppression of freedom of speech for all of us.

Source: *Wisconsin v. Mitchell*, 169 Wis 2d 153 (June 23, 1992).

11.5.   Censuring the Censors of Free Speech

In March 1993 the University of Chicago's law school held a symposium on combating speech that degrades minorities and women, bringing together an unusual alliance of feminists who see pornography as degrading to women and advocates of "hate speech" codes on college campuses. Nadine Strossen, professor of law at New York Law School and president of the American Civil Liberties Union, criticized what she saw as an assault on the First Amendment.

Will the recent alliance between two censorship movements, forged at a University of Chicago Law School conference last March, jeopardize 1st Amendment protections?

Those who champion a robust freedom of speech guarantee and who view our nation's law schools as special sanctuaries for constitutional values were doubly distressed by this organizing conference. It featured leaders of two influential movements to limit 1st Amendment protection for certain words and images, both spearheaded by law professors: the movement among some feminists to suppress certain sexually oriented expression, which they label "pornography"; and the movement to restrict racist and other forms of "hate speech" through such measures as "speech codes" on university campuses.

The Chicago Law School conference gave an unprecedented opportunity to the anti-pornography feminists and the hate speech opponents to chart a common strategy to weaken 1st Amendment rights. It attracted a large, enthusiastic group of participants, including many law students and professors.

To be sure, the University of Chicago Law School and any conference organizers it opts to host have rights to select speakers with certain viewpoints, consistent with 1st Amendment principles. What is troubling, though, is the extent to which "revisionist" approaches to the 1st Amendment have become fashionable at elite law schools such as the University of Chicago, dominating not only conferences, but also faculty appointments and promotions, law journal publications and certain law school courses.

Even more disturbingly, some of these forums purport to be neutral, but in fact virtually—or even completely—exclude censorship opponents. For example, the University of Chicago conference was entitled "Feminist Legal Perspectives on Pornography and Hate Propaganda," thus indicating that it included a range of feminist perspectives. Yet not a single speaker represented the substantial segment of feminists who oppose censoring pornography or hate speech.

Although the procensorship viewpoint appears to be disproportionately influential in law schools, several feminist organizations oppose censorship specifically on feminist grounds. They maintain that, far from promoting women's rights and interests, it would on the contrary undermine them. They say, for example, that any censorship scheme would inevitably encompass some works that are valuable to feminists and that any scheme would most likely be enforced in a way that discriminates against the least popular, least powerful groups in our society, including feminists and lesbians. They also contend that censorship perpetuates patronizing stereotypes about women and our allegedly innate sexual vulnerability.

The Chicago conference also excluded civil rights activists and members of racial minorities who oppose censoring racist speech because they believe such censorship subverts the civil rights of racial minorities. Censorship, they contend, increases attention to, and sympathy for, bigots; drives racist expression underground, thus making response more difficult; reinforces paternalistic stereotypes about members of minority groups, suggesting that they need special protection from offensive speech; and diverts resources from measures addressing discriminatory attitudes and conduct.

Beyond academia, the advocates of censoring sexual expression and hate speech also seem to be unduly dominating media discussions, and hence public perceptions, of these issues. For example, there appears to be a widespread misimpression that if you are a feminist—or even a woman—you must support censoring pornography. A *New York Times* account of the Chicago conference was symptomatic. The reporter simply asserted, without explanation, that "virtually all feminists agree that pornography is detrimental to women." But this statement is patently untrue.

The movements to censor pornography and hate speech will continue to gain power unless free speech proponents raise our voices to counter them. We must stress what history consistently has shown: Those who advocate racial, gender and other forms of equality have the most to gain from free speech, and are the first to suffer from its repression. And we must emphasize that the most effective response to any speech with which we disagree is also the response that is true to the 1st Amendment: more speech, rather than restriction.

Although free speech champions have been fighting a defensive battle in some segments of academia and the news media, so far we have prevailed in the courts. For example, federal courts recently invalidated restrictive hate speech codes at the Universities of Michigan and Wisconsin (in lawsuits brought by the American Civil Liberties Union), and in 1992 the Supreme Court struck down a St. Paul, Minn., ordinance that criminalized hate speech. In 1986, the Supreme Court affirmed lower court rulings that the 1st Amendment was violated by an Indianapolis anti-pornography ordinance that law professor Catharine MacKinnon—a leader of the feminist anti-pornography camp—had helped to draft.

But the purpose of the Chicago conference was precisely to devise new strategies to convert academic and popular momentum into court rulings cutting back on 1st Amendment protection for pornography and hate speech. We should not dismiss the possibility that new strategies could succeed.

In 1992 the Canadian Supreme Court essentially rewrote Canada's obscenity law to incorporate the theory of anti-pornography feminists. It ruled that Canada's equivalent of our 1st Amendment does not protect speech that is "degrading" or "dehumanizing" to women. Inspired by this decision, Professor MacKinnon and her supporters have vowed to pursue similar rulings in the United States. Moreover, some leading constitutional scholars have predicted that this strategy will ultimately succeed.

This prediction is supported by the fact that the current U.S. Supreme Court, consistent with previous courts, treats sexually oriented expression as less worthy of constitutional protection than expression dealing with other themes. Participants in the Chicago conference may also draw hope from other recent Supreme Court rulings, indicating that the court might not protect expression that could be deemed to constitute workplace "sexual harassment" or a "hate crime."

All free speech advocates, inside and outside academia alike, have a vital responsibility to anticipate new arguments for limiting speech and to disseminate our views about protecting it. If we do not do so, the law itself may well be caught up in, and transformed by, the speech-repressive momentum that has been on the rise in our nation's law schools. In the memorable words of then-law professor Felix Frankfurter: "In the last analysis, the law is what the lawyers are. And the law and the lawyers are what the law schools make them."

Source: Nadine Strossen, "Censoring the Censors of Free Speech," *Chicago Tribune*, September 2, 1993, p. 27. Reprinted courtesy of Nadine Strossen.

ANNOTATED RESEARCH GUIDE

Academic Questions. Summer ed. New Brunswick, NJ: Transaction Publishers, 1997. A symposium on the issue of campus free speech that included presentations by Professor Thomas C. Grey of Stanford Law School and Nadine Strossen of the American Civil Liberties Union.

Cleary, Edward J. *Beyond the Burning Cross*. New York: Random House, 1994. Takes an in-depth look at the controversial 1992 *R.A.V.* case and evaluates the impact of that holding in the field of First Amendment law. Cleary was the attorney who defended R.A.V. in the litigation.

D'Souza, Dinesh. *Illiberal Education: The Politics of Race and Sex on Campus*. New York: Free Press, 1991. Argues that while much of the rest of America was becoming increasingly tolerant, intolerance of dissent was prospering on college campuses.

Friedman, Marilyn, and Jan Narveson. *Political Correctness: For and Against*. Lanham, MD: Rowman & Littlefield, 1995. Provides a "pro" and "con" discussion of the broader issue of "political correctness," including conflicting feminist perspectives.

Greenawalt, Kent. *Fighting Words: Individuals, Communities, and Liberties of Speech*. Princeton, NJ: Princeton University Press, 1995. Comprehensively analyzes the Supreme Court's "fighting words" doctrine. Chapter 5 focuses specifically on campus speech codes in light of the "fighting words" doctrine.

Haiman, Franklyn S. *"Speech Acts" and the First Amendment*. Carbondale: Southern Illinois University Press, 1993. Attempts to differentiate between protected free speech and various forms of unprotected expressive conduct.

Kors, Alan C., and Harvey A. Silvergate. *The Shadow University: The Betrayal of Liberty on America's Campuses*. New York: Free Press, 1998. A frontal attack on suppression of free speech at America's universities and colleges.

MacKinnon, Catharine A. *Only Words*. Cambridge, MA: Harvard University Press, 1993. Makes the case that mere "words" can often be sharp instruments of hurt and injury and develops MacKinnon's reasons why pornography degrades women, a position to which other, liberal feminists are strongly opposed.

Matsuda Mari. J., et al., eds., *Words That Wound: Critical Race Theory, Assaultive Speech, and the First Amendment*. Boulder, CO: Westview Press, 1993. A collection of essays that address the many dimensions of hate speech and the extent of protection that should be provided by the First Amendment.

Shiell, Timothy C. *Campus Hate Speech on Trial*. Lawrence: University Press of Kansas, 1998. One of the best general introductions to the campus speech code controversy. It is scholarly and incisive yet highly readable for those unfamiliar with this contentious debate.

Strossen, Nadine. "Regulating Racist Speech on Campus: A Modest Proposal?" In *Speaking of Race, Speaking of Sex*, ed. H.L. Gates et al. New York: New York University Press, 1994, pp. 181–256. Strossen, a law professor and in 1994 president of the American Civil Liberties Union, suggests a way to accommodate equality with free speech.

Tuman, Joseph Sargon. " 'Sticks and Stones May Break My Bones, But Words Will Never Hurt Me': The Fighting Words Doctrine on Campus." In *Free Speech Yearbook*. Carbondale: Southern Illinois University Press, 1992, 30: 114–128. A clear and concise and illustrated overview of the constitutional doctrines as they have been applied in cases challenging campus speech codes.

Wilson, John K. *The Myth of Political Correctness: The Conservative Attack on Higher Education.* Durham, NC: Duke University Press, 1995. Makes a strong case for narrowly defined codes that target "fighting words," intimidation, and harassment. As the title indicates, the author takes issue with the claim that universities and colleges are attempting to indoctrinate students with liberal biases.

Video Resources

Campus Culture Wars. Santa Monica, CA: Direct Cinema Ltd., 1993. An eighty-two-minute film recounting five stories about political correctness and free speech on campus.

Higher Learning. Culver City, CA: Columbia TriStar Home Video, 1995. Produced as a feature film, a two-hour drama about a first-year college student who gets a crash course in cultural diversity.

Sexual Harassment: Building Awareness on Campus. Northhampton, MA: The Media Education Foundation, 1995. A brief documentary that explores the difference between free speech and sexual harassment through words as well as actions.

A World of Difference. Pacific Grove, CA: Brooks/Cole, 1994. A set of two videos that looks at how cultural differences among college students can create miscommunication and hurt.

Web Sites

http://bailiwick.lib.uiowa.edu/journalism/medialaw/hateSpeech.html. Constructed and maintained by Karla Tonella of the University of Iowa, this site is filled with links to other sources that focus on hate speech, especially on the Internet.

http://www.cise.ufl.edu/~tpearson/freedom/speech.html. Titled "Speech Codes," this site links to cases, episodes, and model—and actual—campus codes.

http://www.free-market.net/spotlight/hatespeech. Managed by J.D. Tucille, this site monitors current events and episodes pertaining to hate speech. It has numerous links to a welter of resources, including books, magazines, and commentary.

12

The Internet

In the early days of the American Republic communication depended on word of mouth, handwritten letters, a rudimentary rotary press, and a primitive postal system that relied on horses, carriages, and naval vessels. Prosecutions under the Sedition Act of 1798, for example, were brought against public speakers, newspapers, and printers of leaflets and pamphlets, all of which had limited circulation. Technological inventions and innovations during the next two centuries fundamentally broadened and reconstructed the means and character of communication and raised issues of freedom of speech in ways that even the most gifted and sagacious Founding Fathers could not have imagined. The telegraph, steam engine, telephone, celluloid film, radio, television, videotape, fiber-optic cable, computers, satellites, microchips, and wireless transmissions via pulses of laser light: These have all—one after the other—revolutionized communication in America and throughout the world. The changes forced a refashioning of an eighteenth-century yet durable constitutional principle of free speech and the more general commitment to free expression that has evolved as an indispensable feature of American political culture.

Technology affects the speed and quality of communication, the number of speakers, and the size of the audience. Hundreds of millions of people go online, use cell phones, and watch CNN all over the world. Communication that once took days, weeks, or months to penetrate the social and political systems now is instantaneous or nearly so, and the audience has become global. No more vivid or traumatic example exists than the media coverage of the second jetliner crashing and exploding into the South Tower of the World Trade Center on the morning of September 11, 2001. Frightening pictures and reports, from New York and later from the Pentagon, certified to a stunned world community that the United States was under terrorist attack.

While radio and television are still the world's reigning mass communications media, the most dynamic innovations pertaining to freedom of speech have come from the microchip and computer technology driving the Internet. No communications network has developed so rapidly, affecting so much of the world's population, and so quickly in the last twenty years, than this new medium. An international system of interconnected computers, the modern Internet developed from a 1969 military program called ARPANET, created to enable computers operated by the military, defense contractors, and research universities to communicate with each other. The number of "host" computers needed to store and transmit information on the embryonic Internet in 1981 was approximately 300. As the world approached the millennium, that number had risen to approximately 10 million.

The growth of the microchip and its phenomenal productivity rates in such a short time have catapulted the Internet as an instrument of worldwide communication that has changed business, economies, societies, political systems, and law. Since ARPANET, "information processing capacity, relative to cost, has increased one million-fold, making it possible to pack the power of a 1960s mainframe computer into a hundred gram cell phone today." To comprehend that change, imagine a $60,000 luxury car that in less than a decade on the market would cost under $500. Or if a first-class roundtrip flight from New York to Paris cost $2,500 today, "your children could count on paying 25 cents for the same trip in 2017."[1]

By mid-2001, some 60 percent of households in the United States were linked to the Internet, with people spending an average of sixteen hours per month online. Users of the Internet are expected by 2005 to top more than 215 million—*just* in the United States.[2] "Bytes" of information circulating in cyberspace are almost as pervasive as electricity. Political advocacy in American history, as we have seen, has manifested itself in many ways, and the Internet has added an unprecedented new feature. The Congressional Management Foundation in Washington estimated that the U.S. Congress in the year 2000 received 80 million e-mail messages. Some, of course, were blanket "spam" messages sent in bulk format, but there is little doubt that Americans are increasingly equipped to make their complaints and support known to members of Congress via electronic mail. And most congressional offices respond to these messages when they recognize the sender as a constituent from the home district. This new "cyber-advocacy" furthers citizen participation and democratic self-government. The Internet can furnish the means to extend "grassroots" political organizing to wider national, and even international, cooperation.

The vast scope of the Internet has required even a new vocabulary to convey and understand its dimensions. Lifted from William Gibson's "cyber" novels, the term "cyberspace" has emerged as a common word to convey, as legal scholar Laurence Tribe writes, "a place without physical walls or even physical dimensions—where ordinary telephone conversations 'happen,' where voice-mail and e-mail messages are stored and sent back and forth, and where computer-generated graphics are transmitted and transformed, all in the form of interactions, some real-time and some delayed, among countless users, and between users and the computer itself."[3] As an Arizona court explained: [T]he Internet "negates geometry [and] is profoundly anti-spatial. You cannot say where it is or describe its memorable shape and proportions or tell a stranger how to get there. But you can find things in it without knowing where they are. The [Internet] is ambient—nowhere in particular and everywhere at once."[4] The "telecosm" is a new word describing the network of zillions of bits of information traveling through lasers, satellites, the Internet, and other telecommunications technology that connect users all over the planet. The World Wide Web is clearly the best-known category of the Internet. The "Web" allows users to find and retrieve information housed in remote computers all over the world, information stored in a computer file that can be read online. Web "pages" can be elaborate, with their own addresses and "links" to other documents created by the author of the Web page or to other Web sites altogether. The "shrinkage of time and space" is one prominent consequence of this "information age." "Internet 2," a second phase of the digital revolution, can produce live digitized voice and images to facilitate instantaneous worldwide conferencing, providing a "virtual" presence anywhere in the world.

Cyberspace is so different from any other medium that law, government, and society have been challenged in ways never before contemplated. In the United States the judiciary has been expected to update constitutional principles created when no one could have foreseen the complex world of cyberspace—where "virtual realities" defy even the traditional jurisdiction of law and regulations. The consequences and astounding speed of the information revolution have forced "the law" and judges, both more comfortable with incremental and guarded adjustments, to keep pace with every change. The Internet has tested established law with an array of peculiar problems and too many free speech issues to recount in the short space allowed, but some more prominent concerns are noteworthy.

Intellectual property rights have been circumvented through "music piracy" whereby individuals download copyrighted songs from the Internet onto their own MP3 players. Software programs exist to allow users to see and copy each other's files over the Internet. User A could copy songs from user B, who has uploaded them from a CD (compact disc) through a central commercial Web site such as Napster. Users connected to Napster's central servers could connect with each other. This central accountability is how the RIAA (Recording Industry Association of America) was able fairly easily to target Napster and shut it down. Gnutella was quickly invented as a new network protocol by which Gnutella-compatible software lets users find and connect directly to each other without going through a central hosting company. No single company is thereby accountable for potential copyright infringement. Bearshare is one name brand of Gnutella.

Privacy and security have been revamped as government—and private entities—attempt to eavesdrop, for both illegitimate and legitimate reasons, such as the U.S. government's war against terrorism and the traffic in illegal drugs. The Uniting and Strengthening America by Providing Appropriate Tools Required to Intercept and Obstruct Terrorism Act was rushed through Congress and signed into law on October 25, 2001, by President George W. Bush. This "USA Patriot Act" allows the U.S. or any state attorney general, without the normal authorization needed from a judge, to install Carnivore, the controversial e-mail "wiretapping" system, to combat suspected terrorism. Advertising and selling prescription drugs on the Web present new challenges in the still uncertain terrain of "commercial speech." Unsuspecting messengers fill the Internet with e-mails infected with disruptive computer viruses designed to contaminate and wreak havoc on personal computers and comprehensive computer networks, for example, in the corporate sector.

From the amount of legislative effort expended to date, it seems that sexually explicit images have been the federal government's biggest concerns about the Internet, at least as they affect children. Graphic depictions of nudity and sexual acts inhabit an unusually vast domain of the World Wide Web, and anyone can access these sites. Some have estimated as many as 60,000 Web sites specializing in sex-oriented imaging. Courts have never interpreted the First Amendment to protect "pornography," but clear and precise definitions have always eluded the judiciary and other lawmakers. Supreme Court Justice Potter Stewart, in a 1964 case, frankly conceded that he could never define pornography but that he knew it when he saw it. Such refreshing candor would never suit a court of law, however, and the Supreme Court's official and still current definition dates to a 5–4 ruling in *Miller v. California* (1973). The *Miller* test asks whether the material in question, examined as a whole and applying contemporary community standards, appeals to the average person's prurient interests in sex by depicting or describing, in a patently offensive way, sexual conduct specifically defined by law and has no serious literary, scientific, political, or artistic value. Each part of this test must be met before a photographic, film, video, or digital display of sex or nudity can be deemed pornographic and thus unprotected by the First Amendment. It is impossible, however, to define what is "patently offensive," who is the "average person," or what is "serious" value. The Supreme Court has acknowledged that arousal of "normal" or "healthy" lust is not a reflection of "patently offensive" matter. It has also stated that the "contemporary community standards" are local in measuring "patently offensive" but that the "serious" value measure is national (or perhaps international). These definitional uncertainties convey some of the frustration that prompted Justice Stewart's honest admission (though his exasperation came a decade before the *more* precise *Miller* test).

The judiciary has imported the *Miller* test to evaluate sex in cyberspace, where local and national boundaries are virtually nonexistent. One can sit at home, "surf" the Web, and peek into sexually explicit Web sites anywhere in the world. Government, especially recently, has rarely prosecuted cyber peddlers of pornography. However, elected officials and "family values" interest groups have energetically sought ways to excise it from the Internet and in particular to isolate such expression from the reach of children. Web sites specializing in sexually explicit images usually warn viewers of the nature of these sites and even require some affirmation that they are not underage, but there has been little on the Internet to prevent minors from clicking their way into these sites, as disclaimers and declarations about age are not verifiable. Traditionally, courts have given wide latitude to governmental efforts to block pornography from underage children, but when the issue was transposed to the Internet, the judiciary seemed less willing to indulge lawmakers.

In comprehensive legislation designed to overhaul and update federal regulations of the vast telecommunications industry, Congress in 1996 passed the Telecommunications Act, a section of which was fashioned to shield minors from indecency and obscenity on the Internet as well as from predators who lure minors into underage and illegal sexual activity. Passed by impressive majorities in both Congress and the Senate, this Communications Decency Act (CDA) was very hastily tacked onto the larger bill, but it was evidently poorly crafted. Some fifty different groups, representing interests ranging from libraries to businesses, coalesced behind the American Civil Liberties Union to challenge in court the CDA's constitutionality. The law prohibited "indecent" or "obscene" online transmissions to those under eighteen and also the "patently offensive" display of sexual materials to persons under eighteen. If good faith, reasonable, effective, and appropriate steps were taken by providers to keep such materials from minors, they were not liable under the act's prohibitions. In 1997, in its first foray into this new world of communications, the Supreme Court ruled that the First Amendment applied to the Internet and that these two legislative provisions were too vague and uncertain to meet constitutional standards. The Court insisted that the government could not confine the Internet to materials fit for children. Sexual images or other materials that meet the *Miller* test could still be banned from the Internet—though proving those standards in court is an unusually difficult task.

Despite the judicial setback, persistent lawmakers on October 21, 1998, two weeks before congressional elections, passed the Child Online Protection Act (COPA) that prohibits posting on the World Wide Web any communication available and harmful to minors. This time the law defined such materials in accord with the *Miller* test, but in so doing COPA amended the *Miller* guidelines. COPA included the phrases "patently offensive with respect to minors" and "normal or perverted sexual act, or a lewd exhibition of the genitals or post-pubescent female breast," and these uncertain additions assured another battle in court. The day COPA became law, the ACLU and other groups challenged its constitutionality in federal court in Philadelphia, and less than a month later Judge Lowell A. Reed, Jr., issued a temporary restraining order to halt enforcement of the law. On June 22, 2000, a federal court of appeals agreed and declared COPA unconstitutional, and in late February 2001 the Justice Department formally petitioned the U.S. Supreme Court, which on May 21 accepted the case for review. On November 28, the justices heard arguments in the case, known as *Ashcroft v. ACLU*, and almost six months later on May 13, 2002, the Court remanded it to the appeals court for further proceedings but left the restraining order temporally in force.

Courts, lawmakers, and society have shown little patience for what is called "child pornography," where children are depicted in sexual acts. Use of children in such a business is itself criminal exploitation of minors. However, in cyberspace "virtual" children can be digitally fabricated so that "kiddie porn" can be made not only very explicit but without using real children at all. In 1996 Congress expanded existing federal legislation banning child pornography to address this wonder of cyberspace in the Child Pornography Prevention Act (CPPA). The law bans a sexual image if it merely "appears to be" explicit sexual conduct of children. "Congress found not only that pedophiles use such images to whet their own appetites and lure children into sexual activities, but also that virtual porn can 'desensitize the viewer to the pathology of sexual abuse or exploitation of children.' "[5] Having to differentiate between "actual" and "virtual" child pornography, the Federal government claims that it would be impossible to enforce any ban against child pornography. On December 17, 1999, a federal Court of Appeals in California invalidated this statute on First Amendment grounds, claiming, among other things, that the phrase "appears to be" was too vague. On January 22, 2001, the Supreme Court accepted the government's petition to review this ruling, and on October 30, 2001, both sides in the case of *Ashcroft v. The Free Speech Coalition* presented oral arguments as the justices took up this controversial dispute. On April 16, 2002, a 6–3 majority agreed that the CPPA violated the First Amendment.

In December 2000, Congress passed yet another bill, managed through the legislature by the popular Senator John McCain, called the Children's Internet Protection Act (CIPA), which cuts off federal funds to libraries and schools that do not use "filtering" software, such as Cyber Patrol, even if they employ other methods to protect children from online sexually explicit materials. CIPA employs one of the more successful instruments at the disposal of Congress—the withholding of federal subsidies. In the 1990s, Congress had created "E-rate" funds to expand Internet access in schools and libraries across the country, especially for children in families unable to afford their own home computers. Opponents see the filtering devices, which are not always very efficient, as not only blocking legitimate materials from reaching children but also confining adult users of libraries to Internet information suitable for minors. The U.S. government replied that, while imperfect, such blocking software is at least "efficient" in protecting children from harmful displays on the Internet. Despite the Supreme Court's strong inclination to allow Congress wide discretion to regulate what it subsidizes, the American Library Association and the ACLU began legal challenges in February and March 2001, convening a special three-judge federal district court in Philadelphia. The trial ended on April 5, 2002, but as of this writing the court had yet to issue its final ruling. Whatever the result, the case is almost surely to end up in the Supreme Court. When a special three-judge panel, such as this one in Philadelphia, is convened, any appeal by the losing party goes directly to the U.S. Supreme Court.

Many states have joined in the fight against online pornography, but cyberspace has created all sorts of jurisdictional problems. For example, under the *Miller* test, "patently offensive" sexual depictions are legal judgments made using local community standards. But what might be deemed patently offensive in one community may be readily available online by clicking onto a Web site loaded on the Internet somewhere else. Arizona made it a crime to transmit through the Internet materials deemed "harmful to minors," but a federal court in Tucson invalidated the law because it was overboard and vague and also because the law effectively blocked access to such materials by persons in other states where such materials were not considered so harmful.

Groups specializing in "hate speech" have invaded the Internet. Testifying before the Senate Judiciary Committee in September 1999, the Southern Poverty Law Center and the Anti-Defamation League noted anywhere from 254 to 600 hate groups on the Web.[6] Separating hate speech from unprotected "fighting words" makes it difficult for the government to regulate this expression. Also, by confining fighting words to "face-to-face" confrontations, the judiciary exempts hate speech on the Internet because online speech is never actually face-to-face. Moreover, expression often emanates from outside the jurisdiction of the United States, but is still widely received by Americans.

Or what is prohibited overseas may be protected in the United States. For example, a French court ruled that because online displays of Nazi memorabilia messages are illegal in France, Yahoo, Inc., a Delaware-based corporation, must also limit such displays in the United States. Through the Internet, these forbidden symbols and messages are accessible to computer-equipped French citizens who surf the world of cyberspace. However, in *Yahoo, Inc. v. La Ligue Contre le Racisme et L'Antisemitisme* (LICRA), decided November 7, 2001, a California court ruled that Yahoo's right to display these symbols and messages was protected in the United States by modern First Amendment law.

Government could punish online speech that *clearly incites* imminent criminal behavior, expression that the judiciary has never protected. The controversial "Nuremberg Files" anti-abortion Web site raised this issue in 1998. It featured images of the tiny legs and arms of babies, dripping blood, in the remains of aborted fetuses. It also listed doctors who performed abortions (or "baby butchers," according to the Web site). Several of these physicians were eventually murdered, and the Web page managers crossed a line through each name on the list just hours after each physician had been killed. Pro-abortion entertainers, elected officials, and family planning clinics were also identified, and viewers were encouraged to submit names and as much information as possible about other "baby butchers." The original Internet server shut down the Nuremberg Files, but its editor and backers found "mirror sites" elsewhere on the Internet. In criminal court it is very difficult to prove that the Web page incited murder. In a civil case the burden of proof is lower, and an Oregon jury awarded more than $100 million in damages to those threatened and the families of the murdered physicians. Backers of the Nuremberg Files defended it as merely a free speech exercise in collecting information about crimes (like the war crimes tried against German Nazis after World War II) for the day of reckoning when abortion again becomes illegal. In the spring of 2001, an appeals court reversed the damage judgment awarded by the jury.

There have also been cases of libel on the Internet. One major problem here is that defamatory statements ruining reputations can often appear anonymously on the Internet, by individuals who assume fake names or identifications when creating network e-mail accounts. The Supreme Court has twice ruled in the last thirty years that the First Amendment protects anonymous leaflets. Anonymity abounds on the Internet. If someone anonymously defames another, the plaintiff in court would never win or collect monetary damages if no defendant could be tracked down. The defamed could not sue the ISP (the Internet Service Provider), which would certainly be known, because Section 230 of the Communications Decency Act that survived court challenge declares that ISPs are not "publishers" and are thus not liable for the content of what they carry on the Internet.

Like all technological innovations, the Internet has profoundly affected civilization, in both negative and positive ways. It magnifies the power of groups, whether they are concerned citizens, radicals, or even terrorists. Activists can pressure social and political institutions that have Web sites with "virtual" protests or demonstrations. More radical groups skilled in computer "hacking" may discover that their opponents are more vulnerable in cyberspace than in the real physical world. The Internet has provided a soapbox for millions, and it has amplified their voices. It has allowed for the ready mobilization of people across a broad expanse, as has been evidenced in the 1990s with the use of the Internet to organize protests against the World Trade Organization meetings and political party gatherings. Anyone equipped with a computer and a modem or Ethernet connection can send e-mails or even create a personal Web page. Online he or she can reach the world audience with opinions, pictures, or messages. And that same Internet user can be reached by others. Political and legal boundaries mean little in cyberspace, making regulation of the Internet difficult and almost by default protecting "free speech." Sorting out the legality and efficacy of regulating speech on the Internet has become one of the most pressing concerns of government and society in the new century.

NOTES

1. L.R. Wilson, "The New Frontier: Cyberspace and the Telecosm," *Vital Speeches of the Day* 64 (January 1, 1998): 182.

2. These figures are taken from Stella Anne Harrison, "The Internet, Cyberadvocacy, and Citizen Communication," *Vital Speeches of the Day* 67 (August 1, 2001): 624.

3. Laurence H. Tribe, "The Constitution in Cyberspace: Law and Liberty beyond the Electronic Frontier," © 1991, online at http://www.epic.org/free_speech/tribe.html

4. *Doe v. Roe*, 955 P.2d 951, 956 (Ariz. 1998).

5. *Newsweek*, March 19, 2001, p. 51.

6. These figures are from the "News Release—Statement of Senator Orin Hatch," Chairman of the Senate Judiciary Committee, September 14, 1999.

DOCUMENTS

12.1.   The Communications Decency Act Declared Unconstitutional

---

> *Part of the Telecommunications Act of 1996, the "Communi-*
> *cations Decency Act" (CDA) was designed to protect children*
> *from "obscene" and "indecent" materials available on the Inter-*
> *net. Individuals who knowingly transmitted such material—in-*
> *cluding the Internet Service Provider (ISP)—were subject to*
> *punishments ranging up to two years in prison and a $250,000*
> *fine. The ACLU sued Attorney General Janet Reno to prevent*
> *enforcement, and a special three-judge federal district court in*
> *Philadelphia invalidated these provisions. The government ap-*
> *pealed to the Supreme Court, which addressed the Internet for*
> *the first time and agreed that the CDA was unconstitutional.*

[Justice John Paul Stevens delivered the opinion of the Court.]

At issue is the constitutionality of two statutory provisions enacted to protect minors from "indecent" and "patently offensive" communications on the Internet. Notwithstanding the legitimacy and importance of the congressional goal of protecting children from harmful materials, we agree with the three judge District Court that the statute abridges "the freedom of speech" protected by the First Amendment.... We agree with its conclusion that our cases provide no basis for qualifying the level of First Amendment scrutiny that should be applied to this medium....

... [T]he many ambiguities concerning the scope of [the CDA's] coverage render it problematic for purposes of the First Amendment. For instance, each of the two parts of the CDA uses a different linguistic form. The first uses the word "indecent," ... while the second speaks of material that "in context, depicts or describes, in terms patently offensive as measured by contemporary community standards, sexual or excretory activities or organs" ... Given the absence of a definition of either term, this difference in language will provoke uncertainty among speakers about how the two standards relate to each other and just what they mean. Could a speaker confidently assume that a serious discussion about birth control practices, homosexuality ... or the consequences of prison rape would not violate the CDA? This uncertainty undermines the likelihood that the CDA has been carefully tailored to the congressional goal of protecting minors from potentially harmful materials.

. . . [T]he CDA is a content based regulation of speech. The vagueness of such a regulation raises special First Amendment concerns because of its obvious chilling effect on free speech. . . . [Also], the CDA is a criminal statute. In addition to the opprobrium and stigma of a criminal conviction, the CDA threatens violators with penalties including up to two years in prison for each act of violation. The severity of criminal sanctions may well cause speakers to remain silent rather than communicate even arguably unlawful words, ideas, and images. . . .

The Government argues that the statute is no more vague than the [*Miller*] obscenity standard. . . . But that is not so. . . . [T]his Court . . . set forth in *Miller* the test for obscenity that controls to this day:

"(a) whether the average person, applying contemporary community standards would find that the work, taken as a whole, appeals to the prurient interest; (b) whether the work depicts or describes, in a patently offensive way, sexual conduct specifically defined by the applicable state law; and (c) whether the work, taken as a whole, lacks serious literary, artistic, political, or scientific value." . . .

Because the CDA's "patently offensive" standard (and, we assume *arguendo*, its synonymous "indecent" standard) is one part of the three prong *Miller* test, the Government reasons, it cannot be unconstitutionally vague.

The Government's assertion is incorrect as a matter of fact. The second prong of the *Miller* test—the purportedly analogous standard—contains a critical requirement that is omitted from the CDA: that the proscribed material be "specifically defined by the applicable state law." This requirement reduces the vagueness inherent in the open ended term "patently offensive" as used in the CDA. Moreover, the *Miller* definition is limited to "sexual conduct," whereas the CDA extends also to include (1) "excretory activities" as well as (2) "organs" of both a sexual and excretory nature.

. . . Just because a definition including three limitations is not vague, it does not follow that one of those limitations, standing by itself, is not vague. Each of *Miller*'s additional two prongs—(1) that, taken as a whole, the material appeal to the "prurient" interest, and (2) that it "lack serious literary, artistic, political, or scientific value"—critically limits the uncertain sweep of the obscenity definition. The second requirement is particularly important because, unlike the "patently offensive" and "prurient interest" criteria, it is not judged by contemporary community standards. . . . This "societal value" requirement, absent in the CDA, allows appellate courts to impose some limitations and regularity on the definition by setting, as a matter of law, a national floor for socially redeeming value. The Government's contention that courts will be able to give such legal limitations to the CDA's standards is belied by *Miller's* own rationale for having juries determine whether material is "patently offensive" according to community standards: that such questions are essentially ones of *fact.* . . .

. . . Given the vague contours of the coverage of the statute, it unquestionably silences some speakers whose messages would be entitled to constitutional protection. That danger provides further reason for insisting that the statute not be overly broad. The CDA's burden on protected speech cannot be justified if it could be avoided by a more carefully drafted statute.

We are persuaded that the CDA lacks the precision that the First Amendment requires when a statute regulates the content of speech. In order to deny minors access to potentially harmful speech, the CDA effectively suppresses a large amount of speech that adults have a constitutional right to receive and to address to one another. That burden on adult speech is unacceptable if less restrictive alternatives would be at least as effective in achieving the legitimate purpose that the statute was enacted to serve. . . .

It is true that we have repeatedly recognized the governmental interest in protecting children from harmful materials. . . . But that interest does not justify an unnecessarily broad suppression of speech addressed to adults. As we have explained, the Government may not "reduce the adult population to . . . only what is fit for children." . . . "Regardless of the strength of the government's interest" in protecting children, "the level of discourse reaching a mailbox simply cannot be limited to that which would be suitable for a sandbox". . . .

The District Court was correct to conclude that the CDA effectively resembles the ban on "dial a porn" invalidated [earlier by this Court]. . . . [We] rejected the argument that . . . nothing less than a total ban would be effective in preventing enterprising youngsters from gaining access to indecent communications. . . . [Our decision] made clear that the mere fact that a statutory regulation of speech was enacted for the important purpose of protecting children from exposure to sexually explicit material does not foreclose inquiry into its validity. . . . [Courts must determine] that Congress has designed its statute to accomplish its purpose "without imposing an unnecessarily great restriction on speech."

In arguing that the CDA does not so diminish adult communication, the Government relies on the incorrect factual premise that prohibiting a transmission whenever it is known that one of its recipients is a minor would not interfere with adult to adult communication. The findings of the District Court make clear that this premise is untenable. Given the size of the potential audience for most messages, in the absence of a viable age verification process, the sender must be charged with knowing that one or more minors will likely view it. Knowledge that, for instance, one or more members of a 100-person chat group will be minor—and therefore that it would be a crime to send the group an indecent message—would surely burden communication among adults.

The District Court found that at the time of trial existing technology did not include any effective method for a sender to prevent minors from obtaining access to its communications on the Internet without also denying access to adults. The Court found no effective way to determine the age of a user who is accessing material through e-mail, mail exploders, newsgroups, or chat rooms. . . . As a practical matter, the Court also found that it would be prohibitively expensive for noncommercial—as well as some commercial—speakers who have Web sites to verify that their users are adults. . . . These limitations must inevitably curtail a significant amount of adult communication on the Internet. By contrast, the District Court found that "despite its limitations, currently available *user based* software suggests that a reasonably effective method by which *parents* can prevent their children from accessing sexually explicit and other material which *parents* may believe is inappropriate for their children will soon be widely available."

The breadth of the CDA's coverage is wholly unprecedented. . . . [T]he scope of the CDA is not limited to commercial speech or commercial entities. Its open-ended prohibitions embrace all nonprofit entities and individuals posting indecent messages or displaying them on their own computers in the presence of minors. The general, undefined terms "indecent" and "patently offensive" cover large amounts of nonpornographic material with serious educational or other value. Moreover, the "community standards" criterion as applied to the Internet means that any communication available to a nation-wide audience will be judged by the standards of the community most likely to be offended by the message. The regulated subject . . . may also extend to discussions about prison rape or safe sexual practices, artistic images that include nude subjects, and arguably the card catalogue of the Carnegie Library.

. . . Under the CDA, a parent allowing her 17-year-old to use the family computer to obtain information on the Internet that she, in her parental judgment, deems appropriate could face a lengthy prison term. . . . Similarly, a parent who sent his 17-year-old college freshman information on birth control via e-mail could be incarcerated even though neither he, his child, nor anyone in their home community, found the material "indecent" or "patently offensive," if the college town's community thought otherwise.

The breadth of this content based restriction of speech imposes an

especially heavy burden on the Government to explain why a less restrictive provision would not be as effective as the CDA. It has not done
so. . . . [W]e are persuaded that the CDA is not narrowly tailored if that
requirement has any meaning at all.
      . . . [T]he Government advances three additional arguments for sus-
taining the Act's affirmative prohibitions: (1) that the CDA is constitutional because it leaves open ample "alternative channels" of
communication; (2) that the plain meaning of the Act's "knowledge" and
"specific person" requirement significantly restricts its permissible applications; and (3) that the Act's prohibitions are "almost always" limited
to material lacking redeeming social value.
      The Government first contends that, even though the CDA effectively
censors discourse on many of the Internet's modalities—such as chat
groups, newsgroups, and mail exploders—it is nonetheless constitutional
because it provides a "reasonable opportunity" for speakers to engage
in the restricted speech on the World Wide Web. . . . The Government's
position is equivalent to arguing that a statute could ban leaflets on certain subjects as long as individuals are free to publish books. In invalidating a number of laws that banned leafletting on the streets *regardless
of* their content—we explained [in an earlier case] that "one is not to
have the exercise of his liberty of expression in appropriate places
abridged on the plea that it may be exercised in some other place." . . .
      The Government also asserts that the "knowledge" requirement . . .
saves the CDA from overbreadth. Because both sections prohibit the dissemination of indecent messages only to persons known to be under 18,
the Government argues, it does not require transmitters to "refrain from
communicating indecent material to adults; they need only refrain from
disseminating such materials to persons they know to be under 18." . . .
This argument ignores the fact that most Internet fora—including chat
rooms, newsgroups, mail exploders, and the Web—are open to all com-
ers. The Government's assertion that the knowledge requirement somehow protects the communications of adults is therefore untenable. Even
the strongest reading of the "specific person" requirement . . . cannot
save the statute. It would confer broad powers of censorship, in the form
of a "heckler's veto," upon any opponent of indecent speech who might
simply log on and inform the would-be discoursers that his 17-year-old
child—a "specific person . . . under 18 years of age," . . . —would be present.
      Finally, we find no textual support for the Government's submission
that material having scientific, educational, or other redeeming social
value will necessarily fall outside the CDA's "patently offensive" and
"indecent" prohibitions. . . .
      [The Court then rejected several other defenses offered by the govern-
ment to save the CDA, one of which was requiring a credit card verification to assure that the recipients were over eighteen.] . . . [T]he

Government failed to adduce any evidence that these verification techniques actually preclude minors from posing as adults. Given that the risk of criminal sanctions "hovers over each content provider, like the proverbial sword of Damocles," the District Court correctly refused to rely on unproven future technology to save the statute. The Government thus failed to prove that the proffered defense would significantly reduce the heavy burden on adult speech produced by the prohibition on offensive displays.

We agree with the District Court's conclusion that the CDA places an unacceptably heavy burden on protected speech, and that the defenses do not constitute the sort of "narrow tailoring" that will save an otherwise patently invalid unconstitutional provision. In [a previous case] we remarked that the speech restriction at issue there amounted to " 'burn[ing] the house to roast the pig.' " The CDA, casting a far darker shadow over free speech, threatens to torch a large segment of the Internet community. . . .

In this Court, though not in the District Court, the Government asserts that—in addition to its interest in protecting children—its "[e]qually significant" interest in fostering the growth of the Internet provides an independent basis for upholding the constitutionality of the CDA. . . . The Government apparently assumes that the unregulated availability of "indecent" and "patently offensive" material on the Internet is driving countless citizens away from the medium because of the risk of exposing themselves or their children to harmful material.

We find this argument singularly unpersuasive. The dramatic expansion of this new marketplace of ideas contradicts the factual basis of this contention. The record demonstrates that the growth of the Internet has been and continues to be phenomenal. As a matter of constitutional tradition, in the absence of evidence to the contrary, we presume that governmental regulation of the content of speech is more likely to interfere with the free exchange of ideas than to encourage it. The interest in encouraging freedom of expression in a democratic society outweighs any theoretical but unproven benefit of censorship.

For the foregoing reasons, the judgment of the district court is affirmed.

Source: Reno v. ACLU, 521 U.S. 844 (June 26, 1997).

12.2.   Quiet in the Library! Children Viewing Porn

After the Supreme Court invalidated the challenged provisions of the Communications Decency Act (CDA), Congress reacted by drafting new legislation such as the Child Online Protection

Act (1998) and the Children's Internet Protection Act (2000). In this essay written soon after the Court struck down the CDA, Neil Munro, a policy reporter for Washington Technology, *describes some of the circumstances that might have induced the determined Congress to act as it did.*

The American Library Association has an answer for parents who are concerned about pornography on library computers: Buzz off. What's more, the association recommends that libraries furnish private booths in which patrons, including children, may view Internet porn undisturbed. A growing number of protesters-parents, social conservatives, and some librarians themselves are fighting back.

Their protests stem from the decision of the Supreme Court . . . to void half of the 1996 Communications Decency Act—the half that sought to outlaw the display of online smut to minors. Although the library association, the American Civil Liberties Union, and other groups claim credit for the court's decision, none of them dared challenge the law's other half—the one that bars the display to minors of "obscene" material, the type of porn that fails to meet the legal test of literary, artistic, political, or scientific value. Outside certain business and free-speech enclaves, this law is popular: One poll found that 80 percent of Americans believe government should curb Internet pornography.

This sentiment is shared by most librarians, who have traditionally refused to buy pornographic or otherwise obscene books. Over the last few years, however, more than 40 percent of the nation's libraries have each paid at least $3,000 to buy a computerized portal into the Internet—and so have stocked their electronic shelves with an array of cyberspace porn, complete with color, sound, and full-motion-video action.

The most interesting portion of the Internet is the World Wide Web, which consists of endlessly interlinked series of "Web sites," each containing a storehouse of images and information. To find your way through these millions of pages, you can use any of dozens of electronic indexes, called "search engines." Thus, if you type in "puppy," you will be led to hundreds of Web sites, dedicated to pictures of well-groomed canines, advertisements for pet products, a rock band named Skinny Puppy, a fishing-tackle outfit called Mud Puppy—and a group of deviants at "alt.sex.bestiality," where "Happiness is a warm puppy."

In this way does the Internet provide libraries with instant access to a world of useful information but also convert computer-equipped libraries—including those in schools—into government-funded peep shows. Says Mitzi Brown of the National Law Center for Children and Families in Fairfax, Va., "It is illegal to allow minors into an adult bookstore. Why are we allowing them into the porn sections of the Internet?" Her group advocates restrictions on the Internet links of library computers, contending that the Supreme Court's decision has left online "non-obscene pornography" with even fewer restrictions than porn videos and magazines or *The Simpsons* on television (which is rated TV-PG for bad language).

For parents, politicians, and decency-minded librarians, one obvious solution is a type of software that severs libraries' Internet links to offensive Web pages. Naturally, the first generation of this software has had problems, largely because it is difficult to find every pornographic needle in the fast-growing Internet haystack. For example, one product barred access to Web pages containing the words "sex" and "couple," thus blocking a Web page created by the good citizens of Middlesex, England, as well as the White House Web page, which featured the first couple.

This sort of defect has provided ammunition to the library association and allied groups, which call the smut-filtering software "censorware" and argue that developers secretly build into it right-wing political ideology, preventing access to pages that support abortion, homosexuality, or drug use. That objection is being answered by improved technology and trial-and-error experiments. Librarians in Austin, Texas, for instance, have worked with a software developer to narrow the filters to block only obscenity and "gross depictions," while librarians in Boston use very broad filters in the children's corners. The local government in Loudoun County, Va., has voted to install filters in all its computers, while other libraries reject any filter at all, simply keeping their computers near check-out desks, where middle-aged ladies tend to shame the underaged away from porn.

This jumble of experiments may look like a democratic compromise-in-progress, but the American Library Association will have none of it. Its lobbyists adamantly oppose any and all use of filtering technology and have distributed tip-sheets and legal briefs in support of their cause. According to Judith Krug, director of the association's Office for Intellectual Freedom, any use of smut-filtering software in government-funded libraries is an unconstitutional violation of free-speech rights. In her opinion, no filtering software could be constitutionally valid because no developer can devise a filter that excludes all obscenity while keeping the door open to all less-than-obscene pornography. "Porn is erotica, and that is constitutionally protected speech, and if you don't want your children to access that information, you had better be with your children when they use a computer," she says. And those little booths? They are needed, she maintains, to protect users' privacy. Of parents concerned about Internet porn, Krug is dismissive: "Their number is so small that it is almost laughable." Only one child "out of a trillion billion" might use library computers to seek out porn, she believes.

Krug's touching faith in the virtue of American youth aside, the association's laissez-faire fundamentalism clashes with several facts. First, it is a federal crime to display obscene materials to children. Second, industry is selling cyberspace maps that prod users toward favored Web sites, many of which will soon receive quality ratings. These maps and ratings are prepared by search-engine companies, which make their money by nudging users to corporate Web pages that buy advertising slots or pay for prominent positions in the electronic index. Thus, the association's hands-off approach would, in essence, invite online advertisers to take over the librarians' task of indexing and grading the content of libraries.

Third, the association is entirely willing to push kids to certain sites— liberal ones. It has developed a guide to 700 politically correct sites, including those for Young Feminists in NOW, the Sierra Club, multiculturalism, Latin American issues, American Indians, and origami "Cranes for Peace." (There is even one for Louis Farrakhan's Nation of Islam.) Krug says that selecting World Wide Web content is "exactly what librarians are doing, but not in the way [those on the right] want us to do it." . . .

On the smut-filtering issue, the association works hand-in-glove with the American Civil Liberties Union (ACLU). "I don't think [any kind of screening] technology can do the job of a jury and judge" in determining what material meets the legal test of obscenity, says Ann Beeson, an ACLU staff attorney. As for the little booths, she says, "I think that's a good idea." Beeson is threatening to sue libraries that use filters—which is hardly surprising. The ACLU argues that parents should have no right to limit their children's use of library computers, and it backed a California lawsuit that sought to legalize computerized simulations of adult-child sex.

At its base, the argument advanced by the library association and its friends is that the Web should—and will—treat all information equally, undermining traditional morality and promoting "diversity," sexual autonomy, and moral relativism. So far, it seems that they are correct— much to the benefit of corporations, which are delighted to supplant the judgment of librarians with the sell-anything-now ethos of an online marketplace carefully segmented by age, race, wealth, education, and sexual urges.

So, what should conservatives do in response? They could adopt a libertarian stance: shut down the libraries and let citizens do their own Web searches at home, with or without filters. Or they could try to take the libraries back from the American Library Association; perhaps local politicians could fire recalcitrant librarians, which would free up cash for computer-equipped charter schools whose librarians treat parents' concerns with respect. The Republican Congress could pass a law that helps parents sue librarians who fail to take reasonable measures to abide by the Communications Decency Act. Congress could even go a step further and prod the Justice Department to jail careless librarians when the computers under their charge are used to break the law.

There is room for optimism: Several legislators, including Republican senator Dan Coats of Indiana, have drafted bills designed to curb commercial online pornography. Some of the larger Internet companies are eager to buy respectability in suburbia—and protection from porn-related lawsuits brought by outraged parents—by exiling their lucrative online-porn business to backwater reservations in cyberspace, from which filters can bar children. Industry's increased support for filters allows [advocates] to trumpet those filters as "seat-belts for the information superhighway" without worrying about a hostile reaction from Silicon Valley—a reaction that would surely ensue if the Justice Department actually prosecuted online-obscenity cases.

In this debate over technology and morality, conservatives will need a ready-for-TV answer whenever they are slammed as [opponents of] free speech. . . . Judith Krug says of conservatives, "I don't want their view of the world to affect what my kids have access to." Maybe conservatives can simply echo her.

Source: Neil Munro, "Quiet in the Library! Children Viewing Porn," *Weekly Standard* 3, December 22, 1997, pp. 27–29. Reprinted with permission of *Weekly Standard*.

12.3.   Free Speech Entangled in the Internet

Governmental restrictions on speech have always been the principal target of free speech proponents, but as freelance writer, and former Washington editor of the American Prospect, *Joshua Marshall argues, curbs on the free flow of information on the Internet come not from government alone but also from the private sector. In this intriguing essay, Marshall explains how and calls for a reassessment of the role and meaning of freedom of expression in our society.*

When the Supreme Court overturned the Communications Decency Act (CDA) in the summer of 1997, its decision seemed to put to rest much of the controversy over Internet free speech. But there are now a host of more limited efforts afoot to prune back the range of Internet content and limit access to various kinds of online material. Such technical innovations as "content filtering" and "censor-ware" make it possible for individuals, employers, Internet service providers, and others to block out selected portions of the online world. . . . [T]hese new forms of control pose more subtle and incremental threats—and should force us to confront whether keeping the government out of the censorship business will be sufficient to assure freedom online. . . .

. . . While Congress was hashing out what would become the Communications Decency Act, a group of Internet policy planners began to formulate a system that would allow individual users to decide what could and could not appear on their computer screens. Rather than banning information at the "sending" end, Internet users would be able to block offensive material at the "receiving" end. Everybody could then carve out his or her own zone of comfort on the Internet, with just the right mix of Puritanism and prurience. It was an ingenious solution—a kinder, gentler version of the CDA. It would assuage the fears of parents, conciliate free speech advocates, and short-circuit the political argument for a broad regime of Internet censorship.

The PICS project [the Platform for Internet Content Selection] was co-ordinated and directed through the World Wide Web Consortium, an independent body that has taken a leading role in formalizing standards and protocols for the Web, with support from many of the biggest Internet industry companies. . . . They designed PICS not as a set of ratings or categories but as a format for devising a variety of different ratings systems, each reflecting different cultural and political perspectives. To understand the distinction, consider the difference between a word processing format like Microsoft Word and the infinite variety of documents that one could author in that format. PICS is not a rating system; it is a format that can be used to create many different rating systems.

PICS envisions at least two basic models in which rating systems might operate. The first—and conceptually more straightforward—is self-rating. Publishers of Web sites rate their own material, alerting viewers to coarse language, nudity, or violence. Publishers would choose whether to rate their sites and, if so, what ratings system to use. PICS would also allow third-party rating. Different organizations or companies could set up "rating bureaus" that would rate sites according to their own political, cultural, or moral standards. Thus the Christian Coalition might set up its own rating bureau, as could the National Organization for Women. Individual users could then decide whether to filter material using the voluntary self-ratings or subscribe to a rating bureau that suited their personal sensibilities.

Given the obvious similarities, many have compared PICS to an Internet version of the much-touted V-chip. But the V-chip analogy is only partly correct, and the differences are telling. The weight of the argument for the content filtering approach is that individuals decide what they will and will not see. But PICS-based content filtering is actually much more flexible and scalable than this standard description implies. There are many links in the information food chain separating your personal computer from the source of information. And what you see on the Internet can potentially be filtered at any of those intermediate points. You can block material at your computer, but so can libraries, your employer, your Internet service provider, your university, or even—depending on where you live—your nation–state. With the V-chip you control what comes on your television set. But with PICS the choice may not be yours.

There are already a host of new software products on the market that allow this sort of "upstream" content filtering. They are being introduced widely in the workplace and, to a lesser degree, in schools and libraries. This so-called Internet access management software . . . can monitor what *individual* users view on the Web and how long they view it. It can even compile percentages and ratios of how much viewing is work related, how much is superfluous, and how much is simply inappropriate. These less savory uses of the technology won't necessarily be used. But the opportunities for abuse are obvious and they reach far beyond issues of free speech into elemental questions of personal privacy.

The other problem with PICS is more subtle and insidious. You often do not know just what you are not seeing. Because of a perverse but seemingly inevitable logic, companies that provide content filtering or site blocking services must keep their lists hidden away as trade secrets. The logic is clear enough. The companies expend great resources rating and compiling lists of prohibited sites; to make those lists public would divest them of all their value. But whatever the rationale, this practice leads to numerous tangled situations. Public libraries that have installed site blocking software are in the position of allowing private companies to determine what can and cannot be viewed in the library. Even the librarians don't know what is blocked and what is not.

The possible integration of search engine technology and PICS-based rating holds out the prospect of a Web where much of the material that would not appear on prime-time television just slips quietly out of view. Even more unsettling, many Internet search engine companies—with a good deal of prodding from the White House—have announced plans to begin refusing to list sites that will not, or cannot, rate themselves. Again, the implications are far-reaching. With the increasing size and scope of material on the Web, most people use search engines as their gateway to finding information online. Not being listed is akin to having the phone company tell you that you are welcome to have as many phone numbers as you like but no listings in the phone book. This is one of the ways in which "voluntary" self-rating can quickly become a good deal less than voluntary. There are also bills pending before Congress that would either mandate self-rating or threaten sanctions for "mis-rating" Internet content. This is the sort of creeping, indirect censorship that makes PICS so troubling.

. . . [C]ontent filtering makes censorship quiet, unobtrusive, and thus all the more difficult to detect or counter. It is difficult to quantify just what is different about the new information technology. But the essence of it is an increasing ability to regulate the channels over which we communicate with one another and find out new information.

To all these criticisms the creators of PICS say simply that they and their technology are neutral. But this sort of "Hey, I just make the guns" attitude is hardly sufficient. To their credit, they also point to the more positive uses of content filtering. And here they have a point. In its current form the Internet is a tangled jumble of the useful, the useless, and the moronic. PICS could help users cut through the clutter. Topic searches could become more efficient. In one oft-cited example, content filtering could allow Internet searches for information about a particular medical condition that would produce only material from accredited medical organizations. Of course, the question then becomes, who accredits? There are standards of authority and discrimination we will gladly accept about information for treating breast cancer that we would never accept if the topic is, say, art or political speech. And in any case none of these potentially positive uses negates, or really even speaks to, the reality of possible abuses.

This new debate over content filtering has sliced apart the once potent coalition of interests that banded together to defeat the Communications Decency Act. One of the striking features of the anti-CDA fight was how it lined up technologists, civil libertarians, and major corporations on the same side. What became clear in the aftermath, however, was that companies like Microsoft, Netscape, and IBM were not so much interested in free speech, as such, as they were in preventing government regulation—two very distinct concepts that we now tend too often to conflate.

In fact, the seamless and adaptable censoring that makes civil libertarians shudder is precisely what makes it so attractive to business. Businesses do not want to refight culture wars in every locale where they want to expand Internet commerce. If parents from the Bible Belt are afraid that their children will find gay rights literature on the Web, they won't let them online to buy Nintendo game cartridges either. The same logic is even more persuasive when commerce crosses international borders. International Internet commerce is widely seen as one of the most lucrative prospects for the Internet industry, and much of that trade would take place with countries that either do not share American standards of cultural permissiveness or that routinely censor political material. Content filtering will let American companies sell goods to China over the Internet without having to worry that pro-Tibetan independence Web sites will sour the Chinese on the Internet altogether. Content filtering allows us to carve the Internet up into countless gated communities of the mind.

. . . [T]he technologies and principles that we formulate now will ripple into a future when the Internet—and its successor technologies—will be more and more tightly stitched into the fabric of everyday communication. In a world of books and print, the "Government shall make no law" formulation may be adequate. But in a world of digitized information, private power to censor may be just as deleterious as public power, and in many respects may be more so.

... In a political climate such as ours, which is generally hostile to government power, a subtle and perverse shift can take place in our understanding of the First Amendment and the importance of free speech. ... We seem to be moving toward a public philosophy in which we would shudder at the thought of government censoring a particular book or idea but would be more than happy if major publishing companies colluded together to prevent the same book's publication.

Our political and cultural landscape is replete with examples. We see it in support for the V-chip, government's strong-arming of TV networks to adopt "voluntary" ratings, and in the increasingly fashionable tendency for political figures to shame entertainment companies into censoring themselves. The sort of public shaming of which Bill Bennett has made a career has a very good name in our society, and too few speak up against it. The move to rate television programming may well be benign or, at worst, innocuous in itself. But it points to a broader trend for government to privatize or outsource its powers of censorship. This sort of industry self-regulation is said to be voluntary. But more and more often it is "voluntary" in the sense that Senator John McCain must have had in mind when he threatened to have the Federal Communications Commission consider revoking the broadcasting licenses of NBC affiliates if the network did not agree to adopt the new "voluntary" TV rating system.

... [B]asic structural forces in the computer and software industries make it likely that we will have one or two dominant operating systems rather than five or six. The Web browser market has followed a similar trend toward consolidation. ... Effectively rating even a minute portion of the Web would be an immense undertaking. The resources required to rate the Web and constantly update those ratings could be recouped only by signing up legions of subscribers. Far more likely than the "let a hundred flowers bloom" scenario is one in which there would be a few large companies providing content filtering and site blocking services. And these would be exactly the kind of companies that would become the targets of crusading "family values" politicians trying to add new candidates to the list of material to be blocked.

The novelty of this new information technology calls on us to think and act anew. We cannot now foresee what changes in technology are coming or what unexpected implications they will have. What is clear, however, is that there is no easy translation of real-world standards of intellectual freedom into the online world. Our current conceptions of First Amendment rights are simply unequal to the task. It is easy enough to say that the First Amendment should apply to cyberspace, but crude applications of our current doctrines to the online world involve us in unexpected and dramatic expansions and contractions of intellectual freedoms and free speech. In the architecture of the new information economy, private power will have a much greater and more nimble ability to regulate and constrict the flow of information than state power will. Taking account of this will mean updating both the jurisprudence and the public philosophy of free speech rights. . . .

Partly this will mean focusing more on the goals of First Amendment freedoms and less on the specific and narrow mechanics of preventing government regulation of speech. It may even mean considering some informational equivalent of antitrust legislation—a body of law that would intervene, not to regulate the content, but to ensure that no private entity or single corporation gained too great a degree of control over the free flow of information. What it certainly does mean is that we must abandon that drift in public policy that allows government to outsource its power to censor under the guise of encouraging industry self-regulation. Government may not be fully able to alter some of the pernicious directions in which information technology is evolving—and it may be good that it cannot. But government can at least avoid policies that reinforce the negative tendencies. "Voluntary" industry self-regulation should really be voluntary and we should inculcate within ourselves—and particularly our policymakers—a critical awareness of the implications of new technologies. Whatever the merits of creating PICS and the infrastructure of content filtering, now that it exists we must be vigilant against potential abuses. We should make critical distinctions between the narrow but legitimate goals of content regulation—like providing mechanisms for parents to exercise control over what their children see—and the illegitimate uses to which these technologies can easily be applied.

There are many ways in which we can subtly adjust the law of intellectual property, civil liability, and criminal law to tip the balance between more or less restrictive regimes of free speech, privacy, and individual expression. . . . Sensible public policy can be devised to safeguard the values of an open society in the information age. But too often we are letting technology lead public policy around by the nose.

. . . Though we strain mightily to avoid government censorship, there is little public commitment in our society today to a culture of free expression on its own merits. Public calls from Bill Bennett to shame media companies into "doing the right thing" are widely acclaimed. Political leaders too often take a wink-and-a-nod approach when private bodies take on the censoring role that government itself cannot. But the myopic focus on government as the singular or most significant threat to free speech rests on a basic misreading of our history. In America, the really pointed threats to free speech and free expression do not come from government. They never have. They have always come from willful majorities intent on bullying dissenters into silence. The new information technology and content filtering make that even more feasible than it has been in the past. And that is the problem.

Source: Joshua Micah Marshall, "Will Free Speech Get Tangled in the Net?" *American Prospect* (January–February, 1998): 46–50. Reprinted with permission from *The American Prospect*, Volume 9, Number 36: January 1–February 1, 1998. The American Prospect, 5 Broad Street, Boston, MA 02109. All rights reserved.

12.4. Should "Virtual" Child Pornography Be Protected Speech?

Congress passed the Child Pornography Prevention Act (1996) to prohibit on the Internet sexually explicit images of actual underage minors (under eighteen years old) but also "virtual," fabricated images that "appear to be" underage minors. A federal appeals court in California invalidated this law as unconstitutionally vague in December 1999, and the Supreme Court took up the U.S. government's appeal during its October 2001 term. Jane Eisner, a columnist for the Philadelphia Inquirer, *explores the issues raised by this law.*

Once upon a time, the central objection to child pornography was that it unquestionably harmed real children—the children who, before reaching the legal age of consent, were forced to do things in front of a camera that most of us would find utterly disgusting.

That standard was set by the U.S. Supreme Court in 1982; that was, technologically speaking, a long, long time ago. And the world is changing fast.

Which is why the venerable justices of the court last week found themselves weighing the harm of "virtual" pornography—computergenerated images of children engaging in sexually explicit conduct that looks awfully like the real thing.

Congress voted in 1996 to ban the creation and distribution of virtual child porn in legislation that has been challenged in courts ever since. No matter what the high court eventually decides about the Child Pornography Protection [sic] Act, the larger issues it raises will find no neat, storybook resolution.

That's because the line between what is real and what is virtual is

blurring before our very eyes, and we haven't even gotten past the open-
ing credits. *Final Fantasy: The Spirits Within*, last summer's cinematic attempt to replace live actors with computer-generated look-alikes, will
surely be only the initial foray into that brave new world on film.

The ability to create lifelike computerized images may advance society's health and well-being in ways we can only now imagine. But just
as certainly, it will be used to harm and manipulate those who most
deserve society's protection. Virtual child porn may be the first, crude
warning sign of a troubling trend.

Which is why I think we could be heading toward a colossal constitutional dilemma: Does freedom of speech forever enshrine freedom of
image?

It's a question the Founding Fathers never could have anticipated, because the ubiquity of image is a modern phenomenon with an impact
we're only beginning to appreciate, particularly on children. Research
already has shown that exposure to media violence—in films, TV or
video games—can negatively influence a child's behavior.

"You can feel as threatened by fiction as you can by reality," notes
Joanne Cantor, author of Mommy, I'm Scared.

But the fiction has to feel authentic. If the depiction of a naked child
performing sexual acts in a virtual porno film looks as made-up as Mary
Martin did flying through the air in the original Peter Pan, it may be no
more harmful than a risqué cartoon.

"As long as people hold in mind that this is not real, the effects will
not be as pronounced as with real porn," says Jennings Bryant, director
of the Institute for Communication Research at the University of Alabama. "But will younger people make those kinds of discriminations?
Will they come to accept reality as an altered image without the distinctions of the past?"

Those who favor the 1996 child protection act say it is a law for the
21st century, a preemptive attempt to protect children against what will
likely be a growing threat.

They have a point.

If virtual reality looks real, then the pernicious effects of child porn on
children will be real, too. Anecdotal research shows that illicit films with
live actors are used to "groom" the next victim—by persuading the child
that the sex acts are fun and legitimate. Virtual child porn is just another
indoctrination tool.

"We have a new way to create, but the consequences are the same,"
says Susan Kreston, deputy director of the National Center for Prosecution of Child Abuse.

If the law is upheld, it will mark the first time Congress has banned
the distribution of an image, and the consequences of that are worrying,
too—especially since the language of the act is sweeping and the proven

harmful effects are only indirect. Do we then ban beer commercials because they could induce someone to drive while drunk?

The justices are faced with a delicate balancing act, weighing the harm
to free speech against the potential harm virtual pornography represents
to children, who have traditionally received special protection under the
law.

I suspect that the American aversion to curtailing speech will prevail,
and it probably should. But I'd bet my ambivalence is shared by a great
many Americans. It's compounded by the sense that the line between
reality and virtual reality will only grow fainter, and the need to control
the images placed before our children will be ever more urgent.

Source: Jane Eisner, "Virtual Child Pornography an Issue before the Supreme
Court," *Philadelphia Inquirer*, November 4, 2001, p. D2. © November 4, 2001, The
Philadelphia Inquirer, reprinted with permission.

12.5. Patriotism and Internet Privacy

*By lopsided margins (98–1 in the Senate, and 356–66 in the
House of Representatives) and with nearly unprecedented
speed, Congress passed, and on October 26, 2001, President
George W. Bush signed into law, what is popularly known as
the USA Patriot Act—designed to fight terrorism. One provision
allows government to "wiretap" the Internet to intercept messages that might be used to communicate information among
possible terrorists. Sonia Arrison is director of the Center for
Freedom and Technology at the San Francisco-based Pacific Research Institute, and argues that the law has the ironic potential
to invade rights that define America.*

The Uniting and Strengthening America By Providing Appropriate Tools
Required To Intercept and Obstruct Terrorism (USA Patriot) Act was
rushed through Congress with remarkable speed.

This quick movement, combined with a fear that the administration
calls the "new normalcy," allowed for legislation that would have been
difficult to pass pre-Sept. 11 or even months from now. While it is important to defend the country against terrorist acts, it can and should be
done without whittling away America's liberties. For instance, the act
unnecessarily impinges upon Fourth Amendment protections because it
significantly changes how search warrants are executed. Previously, before the government could enter a house and search through an individual's property and documents, a warrant had to be obtained and notice

had to be given to the person being searched (except in very limited circumstances where a person's electronic communications were being searched).

Notice is important to ensure that the individual being searched can assert his or her Fourth Amendment rights. For example, making sure that the police are only searching the areas allowed by the warrant.

The new law changes this so that police can delay giving notice when conducting searches in any criminal case. That means the police can search your home or office when you're not there and tell you about it after the fact.

This ability to search secretly gives government broader powers, justified as a means to protect America against its enemies. Unfortunately, law enforcement has a history of snooping on "enemies" that are a far cry from terrorists, such as Martin Luther King, Jr. and John Lennon.

The law also expands Internet surveillance by making Carnivore, the controversial e-mail wiretapping system, official even though there is a real danger that it over-collects information. And while a judge must monitor Carnivore use after the fact, now the system can be installed by order of a U.S. or state attorney general without going to a judge.

Financial privacy is at risk, too. Without a doubt, there is a need to freeze the assets of known terrorists and that's already been done. But the USA Patriot Act goes too far, forcing financial institutions to monitor daily financial transactions of all customers more closely and requiring that information be shared with other federal agencies, such as the Central Intelligence Agency.

The re-integration of the CIA with the FBI in this way is unsettling. The functions of the two agencies—foreign and domestic intelligence— were separated in the 1970s after evidence of surreptitious spying in the United States and the collection of data overseas by means that would be illegal under U.S. law.

The terrorist crisis is pulling America back to circumstances that did not work well in the past and do not bode well for the future.

The law also takes steps toward making legitimate political dissent a terrorist act—a problem for a country that values free speech and political association. It does this by creating a new crime called "domestic terrorism." It is unclear why this new category is necessary as the Sept. 11 attacks violated the three definitions already on the books: international terrorism, terrorism transcending national borders, and federal terrorism.

Under the new law, someone is guilty of domestic terrorism if he engages in acts of political protest that are dangerous to human life. The American Civil Liberties Union asserts that this means the World Trade Organization protesters "have engaged in activities that could subject them to prosecution as terrorists."

Obviously, acts such as damage to persons or property should be prosecuted, but that already can be done without these new provisions.

To equate protest acts with terrorist acts goes too far and threatens legitimate political association—especially since the law also makes it a crime to allow a terrorist to stay in one's home. There's also a new crime called "cyberterrorism," which classifies computer hacking as a terrorist act—a rather extreme move.

While much of this act is unsettling, at least parts of it were given sunset clauses. Perhaps when the sunset clauses expire in four years, Congress will come back to its senses and reaffirm America's fundamental liberties.

Source: Sonia Arrison, "New Anti-Terrorism Law Goes Too Far," *San Diego Union-Tribune*, October 31, 2001, p. B9. This article was written by Sonia Arrison of the Pacific Research Institute for Public Policy. It was originally published by Knight Ridder News Service.

12.6.   Supreme Court Invalidates Provisions of the Child Pornography Prevention Act

---

In the Child Pornography Prevention Act (CPPA) passed in 1996, Congress outlawed, on the Internet and elsewhere, the display of images of minors engaged in explicit sexual acts, with punishments as long as thirty years in prison. Section 2256(8) B of this law prohibited even computerized or "virtual" images of children, who are not real people, and images of young adults who appear to be underage. A federal court of appeals struck down two key provisions of the CPPA, and U.S. Attorney General John Ashcroft appealed to the Supreme Court, which (6–3) agreed with the court of appeals. The following excerpt is from the majority opinion which found section 2256(8)B overbroad and therefore in violation of the First Amendment.

Justice [Anthony] Kennedy delivered the opinion of the Court.

. . . The CPPA extends the federal prohibition against child pornography to sexually explicit images that appear to depict minors but were produced without using any real children. [It] prohibits, in specific circumstances, possessing or distributing these images, which may be created by using adults who look like minors or by using computer imaging. The new technology, according to Congress, makes it possible to create realistic images of children who do not exist. . . .

By prohibiting child pornography that does not depict an actual child,

the statute goes beyond *New York v. Ferber* . . . (1982), which distinguished child pornography from other sexually explicit speech because
of the State's interest in protecting the children exploited by the production process. . . . As a general rule, pornography can be banned only if
obscene, but under *Ferber*, pornography showing minors can be proscribed whether or not the images are obscene under the definition set
forth in *Miller v. California*. . . . *Ferber* recognized that the *Miller* standard
. . . does not reflect the State's particular and more compelling interest in
prosecuting those who promote the sexual exploitation of children.

. . . The principal question to be resolved, then, is whether the CPPA
is constitutional where it proscribes a significant universe of speech that
is neither obscene under *Miller* nor child pornography under *Ferber*.

I

Before 1996, Congress defined child pornography as the type of depictions at issue in *Ferber*, images made using actual minors. . . . The
CPPA retains that prohibition . . . and adds three other prohibited categories of speech, of which the first . . . and the third . . . are at issue in
this case. [Section 2256 (8) B] prohibits any visual depiction, including
any photograph, film, video, picture, or computer or computer-generated
image or picture that is, or appears to be, of a minor engaging in sexually
explicit conduct. The prohibition on any visual depiction does not depend at all on how the image is produced. . . .

These images do not involve, let alone harm, any children in the production process; but Congress decided the materials threaten children in
other, less direct, ways. Pedophiles might use the materials to encourage
children to participate in sexual activity. A child who is reluctant to
engage in sexual activity with an adult, or to pose for sexually explicit
photographs, can sometimes be convinced by viewing depictions of other
children having fun participating in such activity. . . . Furthermore, pedophiles might whet their own sexual appetites with the pornographic
images, thereby increasing the creation and distribution of child pornography and the sexual abuse and exploitation of actual children. . . . [The
rationale is that] harm flows from the content of the images, not from
the means of their production. In addition, Congress identified another
problem created by computer-generated images: Their existence can
make it harder to prosecute pornographers who do use real minors. . . .
As imaging technology improves, Congress found, it becomes more difficult to prove that a particular picture was produced using actual children. To ensure that defendants possessing child pornography using real
minors cannot evade prosecution, Congress extended the ban to virtual
child pornography. . . .

II

* * *

As we have noted, the CPPA is much more than a supplement to the existing federal prohibition on obscenity. Under *Miller v. California* (1973), the Government must prove that the work, taken as a whole, appeals to the prurient interest, is patently offensive in light of community standards, and lacks serious literary, artistic, political, or scientific value. . . . The CPPA, however, extends to images that appear to depict a minor engaging in sexually explicit activity without regard to the *Miller* requirements. . . . Any depiction of sexually explicit activity, no matter how it is presented, is proscribed. The CPPA applies to a picture in a psychology manual, as well as a movie depicting the horrors of sexual abuse. . . .

The CPPA prohibits speech despite its serious literary, artistic, political, or scientific value. The statue proscribes the visual depiction of an idea, that of teenagers engaging in sexual activity, that is a fact of modern society and has been a theme in art and literature throughout the ages. Under the CPPA, images are prohibited so long as the persons appear to be under 18 years of age. . . . This is higher than the legal age for marriage in many States, as well as the age at which persons may consent to sexual relations. . . . It is, of course, undeniable that some youths engage in sexual activity before the legal age, either on their own inclination or because they are victims of sexual abuse.

Both themes, teenage sexual activity and the sexual abuse of children, have inspired countless literary works. William Shakespeare created the most famous pair of teenage lovers, one of whom is just 13 years of age . . . [and this drama] has inspired no less than 40 motion pictures, some of which suggest that the teenagers consummated their relationship. . . .

Contemporary movies pursue similar themes. [The popular film] *Traffic* . . . portrays a teenager, identified as a 16-year-old, who becomes addicted to drugs. The viewer sees the degradation of her addiction, which in the end leads her to a filthy room to trade sex for drugs. The year before, *American Beauty* won the Academy Award for Best Picture. . . . In the course of the movie, a teenage girl engages in sexual relations with her teenage boyfriend, and another yields herself to the gratification of a middle-aged man. The film also contains a scene where, although the movie audience understands the act is not taking place, one character believes he is watching a teenage boy performing a sexual act on an older man.

. . . Whether or not the films we mention violate the CPPA, they explore themes within the wide sweep of the statute's prohibitions. If these films, or hundreds of others of lesser note that explore those subjects, contain a single graphic depiction of sexual activity within the statutory definition, the possessor of the film would be subject to severe punishment without inquiry into the work's redeeming value. This is inconsistent with an essential First Amendment rule: The artistic merit of a work does not depend on the presence of a single explicit scene. . . . Under *Miller*, the First Amendment requires that redeeming value be judged by considering the work as a whole. . . . For this reason, and the others we have noted, the CPPA cannot be read to prohibit obscenity, because it lacks the required link between its prohibitions and the affront to community standards prohibited by the definition of obscenity.

The Government seeks to address this deficiency by arguing that speech prohibited by the CPPA is virtually indistinguishable from child pornography, which may be banned without regard to whether it depicts works of value. . . . Where the images are themselves the product of child sexual abuse, *Ferber* recognized that the State had an interest in stamping it out without regard to any judgment about its content. . . . The production of the work, not its content, was the target of the statute. The fact that a work contained serious literary, artistic, or other value did not excuse the harm it caused to its child participants. It was simply unrealistic to equate a community's toleration for sexually oriented materials with the permissible scope of legislation aimed at protecting children from sexual exploitation. . . . *Ferber* upheld a prohibition on the distribution and sale of child pornography, as well as its production, because these acts were intrinsically related to the sexual abuse of children. . . .

In contrast to the speech in *Ferber*, speech that itself is the record of sexual abuse, the CPPA prohibits speech that records no crime and creates no victims by its production. Virtual child pornography is not intrinsically related to the sexual abuse of children, as were the materials in *Ferber*. While the Government asserts that the images can lead to actual instances of child abuse . . . the casual link is contingent and indirect. The harm does not necessarily follow from the speech, but depends upon some unquantified potential for subsequent criminal acts.

The Government says these indirect harms are sufficient because, as *Ferber* acknowledged, child pornography rarely can be valuable speech. . . . [But] *Ferber's* judgment about child pornography was based upon how it was made, not on what it communicated. The case reaffirmed that where the speech is neither obscene nor the product of sexual abuse, it does not fall outside the protection of the First Amendment.

. . . *Ferber* did not hold that child pornography is by definition without value. On the contrary, the Court recognized some works in this category might have significant value . . . but relied on virtual images, the very images prohibited by the CPPA, as an alternative and permissible means of expression: "[I]f it were necessary for literary or artistic value, a person over the statutory age who perhaps looked younger could be utilized. Simulation outside of the prohibition of the statute could provide another alternative." *Ferber*, then, not only referred to the distinction between actual and virtual child pornography, it relied on it as a reason supporting its holding. *Ferber* provides no support for a statute that eliminates the distinction and makes the alternative mode criminal as well.

III

The CPPA, for reasons we have explored, is inconsistent with *Miller* and finds no support in *Ferber*. The Government seeks to justify its prohibitions in other ways. It argues that the CPPA is necessary because pedophiles may use virtual child pornography to seduce children. There are many things innocent in themselves, however, such as cartoons, video games, and candy, that might be used for immoral purposes, yet we would not expect those to be prohibited because they can be misused. The Government, of course, may punish adults who provide unsuitable materials to children, . . . and it may enforce criminal penalties for unlawful solicitation. The precedents establish, however, that speech within the rights of adults to hear may not be silenced completely in an attempt to shield children from it. . . .

Here, the Government wants to keep speech from children not to protect them from its content but to protect them from those who would commit other crimes. The principle, however, remains the same: The Government cannot ban speech fit for adults simply because it may fall into the hands of children. The evil in question depends upon the actor's unlawful conduct, conduct defined as criminal quite apart from any link to the speech in question. This establishes that the speech ban is not narrowly drawn. The objective is to prohibit illegal conduct, but this restriction goes well beyond that interest by restricting the speech available to law-abiding adults.

The Government submits further that virtual child pornography whets the appetites of pedophiles and encourages them to engage in illegal conduct. This rationale cannot sustain the provision in question. The mere tendency of speech to encourage unlawful acts is not a sufficient reason for banning it. The government cannot constitutionally premise legislation on the desirability of controlling a person's private thoughts. . . . First Amendment freedoms are most in danger when the government seeks to control thought or to justify its laws for that impermissible end. The right to think is the beginning of freedom, and speech must be protected from the government because speech is the beginning of thought. . . . The government may not prohibit speech because it increases the chance an unlawful act will be committed at some indefinite future time. . . . The Government has shown no more than a remote connection between speech that might encourage thoughts or impulses and any resulting child abuse. Without a significantly stronger, more direct connection, the Government may not prohibit speech on the ground that it may encourage pedophiles to engage in illegal conduct.

The Government next argues that its objective of eliminating the market for pornography produced using real children necessitates a prohibition on virtual images as well. Virtual images, the Government contends, are indistinguishable from real ones; they are part of the same market and are often exchanged. In this way, it is said, virtual images promote the trafficking in works produced through the exploitation of real children. The hypothesis is somewhat implausible. If virtual images were identical to illegal child pornography, the illegal images would be driven from the market by the indistinguishable substitutes. Few pornographers would risk prosecution by abusing real children if fictional, computerized images would suffice. . . .

Finally, the Government says that the possibility of producing images by using computer imaging makes it very difficult for it to prosecute those who produce pornography by using real children. Experts, we are told, may have difficulty in saying whether the pictures were made by using real children or by using computer imaging. The necessary solution, the argument runs, is to prohibit both kinds of images. The argument, in essence, is that protected speech may be banned as a means to ban unprotected speech. This analysis turns the First Amendment upside down.

The Government may not suppress lawful speech as the means to suppress unlawful speech. Protected speech does not become unprotected merely because it resembles the latter. The Constitution requires the reverse. . . .

Source: *Ashcroft v. Free Speech Coalition*, 122 S. Ct. 1389 (April 16, 2002).

ANNOTATED RESEARCH GUIDE

Eisenstein, Zillah R. *Global Obscenities: Patriarchy, Capitalism, and the Lure of Cyberfantasy*. New York: New York University Press, 1998. A study of the Internet, its strengths and dangers, from the twin perspectives of Marxist and feminist theory.
Friedman, Samuel J. *Children and the World Wide Web: Tool or Trap?* Lanham, MD: University Press of America, 2000. Analyzes the Internet and children and the social aspects of censorship.
Godwin, Mike. *Cyber Rights: Defending Free Speech in the Digital Age*. New York: Times Books/Random House, 1998. Designed for the nonprofessional audience, this survey by an attorney for the Electronic Frontier Foundation, a group sometimes called the ACLU of cyberspace, covers a variety of free expression problems, with many illustrations that have surfaced with regard to the Internet.

Hawke, Constance. *Computer and Internet Use on Campus: A Legal Guide to Issues of Intellectual Property, Free Speech and Privacy.* San Francisco: Jossey-Bass, 2000. A fairly brief but useful volume that introduces the fledgling law, including its application to free speech issues, in this new medium of communication.

Jordan, Tim. *Cyberpower: The Culture and Politics of Cyberspace and the Internet.* New York: Routledge, 1999. An account of how cyberspace and the Internet have augmented the political power of individuals and groups to mobilize and change public policy.

Lane, Frederick S, III. *Obscene Profits: The Entrepeneurs of Pornography in the Cyber Age.* New York: Routledge, 2000. A comprehensive examination of sexual representations on the Internet.

Lipschultz, Jeremy Harris. *Free Expression in the Age of the Internet.* Boulder, CO: Westview Press, 2000. Explores the terrain of free speech issues pertaining to the Internet from the perspective of communications theory.

Margolis, Michael, and David Resnick. *Politics as Usual: The Cyberspace "Revolution."* Thousand Oaks, CA: Sage Publications, 2000. Examines the impact of cyberspace and the Internet on modern politics.

O'Donnell, James J. *Avatars of the Word: From Papyrus to Cyberspace.* Cambridge, MA: Harvard University Press, 1998. A comprehensive history of technology's influence on the development of communications.

Video Resources

Censorship and Content Control on the Internet. New York: Insight Media, 1996. An eighty-minute video that examines ethical as well as legal justifications, and technological solutions, for controlling online access to controversial material.

The Constitution in Cyberspace: Law and Liberty beyond the Electronic Frontier. Topanga, CA : Sweet Pea Productions, 1996. A sixty-eight-minute video that examines some important constitutional issues raised by the Internet.

Hate and the Internet: Web Sites and the Issue of Free Speech. ABC News, 1992. A twenty-two-minute video of Ted Koppel of *Nightline* interviewing First Amendment attorney Floyd Abrams and Don Black, the founder of the Web site *Storm Front,* which advocates white nationalism.

Hate.com: Extremists on the Internet. HBO, 2000. A forty-two-minute film that examines how messages of hate and violence have been spread via the Internet.

Web Sites

http://jurist.law.pitt.edu/sg_cyb.htm. The official page of *Jurist: The Legal Education Network,* this site follows legal developments in the new, relatively uncharted waters of cyberspace law.

http://www.epic.org/. A page maintained by the Electronic Privacy Information Center, that covers a vast assortment of issues pertaining to the Internet. It has a link to an excellent site devoted to free speech issues.

http://www.findlaw.com/01topics/10cyberspace/index.html. A professional center maintained by Find Law, with links to all sorts of legal developments in this field.

http://www.techlawjournal.com. Full of links to court cases and current events, this Web page will inform students interested in nearly every legal issue affecting the Internet.

Selected Bibliography

Abraham, Henry J., and Barbara A. Perry. *Freedom and the Court: Civil Rights and Liberties in the United States.* 7th ed. New York: Oxford University Press, 1998.

Academic Questions. Summer ed. New Brunswick, NJ: Transaction Publishers, 1997.

Barson, Michael. *Better Red Than Dead: A Nostalgic Look at the Golden Years of Russia Phobia, Red-baiting, and Other Commie Madness.* New York: Hyperion, 1992.

Belknap, Michal R. *Cold War Political Justice: The Smith Act, the Communist Party, and American Civil Liberties.* Westport, CT: Greenwood Press, 1977.

Bennett, D.R.M. *Anthony Comstock: His Career of Cruelty and Crimes.* New York: DaCapo Press, 1971.

Besiel, Nicola. *Imperiled Innocents: Anthony Comstock and Family Reproduction in Victorian America.* Princeton, NJ: Princeton University Press, 1998.

Bloom, Jack M. *Class, Race, and the Civil Rights Movement.* Bloomington: Indiana University Press, 1987.

Branch, Taylor. *Parting the Waters: America in the King Years, 1954–1963.* New York: Simon & Schuster, 1988.

———. *Pillar of Fire: America in the King Years, 1963–1965.* New York: Simon & Schuster, 1998.

Broun, Heywood, and Margaret Leech. *Anthony Comstock: Roundsman of the Lord.* New York: A.C. Boni, 1927.

Campbell, Clarice T. *Civil Rights Chronicle.* Jackson: University Press of Mississippi, 1997.

Carmichael, Stokely, and Charles V. Hamilton. *Black Power: The Politics of Liberation in America.* New York: Random House, 1967.

Carson, Clayborne, et al., eds. *The Eyes on the Prize Civil Rights Reader*. New York: Penguin Books, 1991.

Chafee, Zechariah, Jr. *Free Speech in the United States*. Cambridge, MA: Harvard University Press, 1948.

———. *Freedom of Speech*. 1920. Birmingham, AL: Legal Classics Library, 1990.

Chapin, Bradley. *Early America*. Rev. ed. Englewood, NJ: J.S. Ozer, 1984.

Cleary, Edward J. *Beyond the Burning Cross*. New York: Random House, 1994.

Corker, Charles, ed. *Digest of the Public Record of Communism in the United States*. New York: Fund for the Republic, 1955.

Curtis, Michael Kent. *Free Speech, The People's Darling Privilege: Struggle for Freedom of Expression in American History*. Durham, NC: Duke University Press, 2000.

———. "Lincoln, Vallandigham, and Anti-War Speech in the Civil War." In *First Amendment Law Handbook*, ed. James L. Swanson. St. Paul, MN: West Group, 1999, pp. 461–566.

De Benedetti, Charles. *An American Ordeal: The Antiwar Movement of the Vietnam Era*. Syracuse, NY: Syracuse University Press, 1990.

Dickerson, Donna Lee. *The Course of Tolerance: Freedom of the Press in Nineteenth-Century America*. Westport, CT: Greenwood Press, 1990.

Dillon, Merton Lynn. *Slavery Attacked: Southern Slaves and Their Allies, 1619–1865*. Baton Rouge: Louisiana State University Press, 1990.

Domino, John C. *Civil Rights & Civil Liberties: Toward the 21st Century*. New York: HarperCollins, 1994.

Downs, Donald A. *Nazis in Skokie: Community and the First Amendment*. Notre Dame, IN: Notre Dame University Press, 1985.

D'Souza, Dinesh. *Illiberal Education: The Politics of Race and Sex on Campus*. New York: Free Press, 1991.

Eaton, Clement. *Freedom of Thought in the Old South*. Durham, NC: Duke University Press, 1940.

Farber, David. *The Age of Great Dreams: America in the 1960s*. New York: Hill and Wang, 1994.

Fariello, Griffin. *Red Scare: Memories of the American Inquisition—An Oral History*. New York: W.W. Norton, 1995.

Foner, Eric. *The Story of American Freedom*. New York: W.W. Norton, 1998.

Forer, Lois G. *A Chilling Effect: The Mounting Threat of Libel and Invasion of Privacy Actions to the First Amendment*. New York: W.W. Norton, 1987.

Foster, Stuart J. *Red Alert!: Educators Confront the "Red Scare" in American Public Schools, 1947–1954*. New York: Peter Lang, 2000.

Friedman, Marilyn, and Jan Narveson. *Political Correctness: For and Against*. Lanham, MD: Rowman & Littlefield, 1995.

Gibson, James L., and Richard D. Bingham. *Civil Liberties and Nazis: The Skokie Free Speech Controversy*. New York: Praeger, 1985.

Godwin, Mike. *Cyber Rights: Defending Free Speech in the Digital Age*. New York: Times Books/Random House, 1998.

Grant, Alfred. *The American Civil War and the British Press*. Jefferson, NC: McFarland, 2000.

Greenawalt, Kent. *Fighting Words: Individuals, Communities, and Liberties of Speech*. Princeton, NJ: Princeton University Press, 1995.

Haiman, Franklyn S. *"Speech Acts" and the First Amendment*. Carbondale: Southern Illinois University Press, 1993.

Hamlin, David. *The Nazi/Skokie Conflict*. Boston: Beacon Press, 1980.

Harper, Robert S. *Lincoln and the Press*. New York: McGraw-Hill, 1951.

Harris, Brayton. *Blue & Gray in Black & White: Newspapers in the Civil War*. Washington, DC: Batsford Brassey, Inc., 1999.

Heineman, Kenneth J. *Campus Wars: The Peace Movement at American State Universities in the Vietnam Era*. New York: New York University Press, 1993.

Hopkins, Mary Alden. "Birth Control and Public Morals: An Interview with Anthony Comstock." *Harper's Weekly*, May 22, 1915, pp. 489–490.

Hyman, Harold M. *A More Perfect Union: The Impact of the Civil War and Reconstruction on the Constitution*. New York: Alfred A. Knopf, 1973.

Hyman, Harold M., and William M. Wiecek. *Equal Justice under Law: Constitutional Development, 1835–1875*. New York: Harper & Row, 1982.

Hynd, Alan. "Comstock: Crusader Against Sin." *The American Mercury*. (August 1949): 184–191.

Kalven, Harry, Jr. *The Negro and the First Amendment*. Chicago: University of Chicago Press, 1965.

———. *A Worthy Tradition: Freedom of Speech in America*. New York: Harper & Row, 1988.

Kennedy, Sheila Suess, ed. *Free Speech in America: A Documentary History*. Westport, CT: Greenwood Press, 1999.

Kors, Alan C., and Harvey A. Silvergate. *The Shadow University: The Betrayal of Liberty on America's Campuses*. New York: Free Press, 1998.

Kutler, Stanley I. *The American Inquisition: Justice and Injustice in the Cold War*. New York: Hill and Wang, 1982.

———. *Judicial Power and Reconstruction Politics*. Chicago: University of Chicago Press, 1968.

Lane, Frederick S., III. *Obscene Profits: The Entrepeneurs of Pornography in the Cyber Age*. New York: Routledge, 2000.

Levy, Leonard. *The Legacy of Suppression: Freedom of Speech and Press in Early American History Students*. Cambridge, MA: Harvard University Press, 1960.

Levy, Peter B. *The Civil Rights Movement*. Westport, CT: Greenwood Press, 1998.

Lewis, Anthony. *Portrait of America: The Second American Revolution*. New York: Random House, 1964.

Lipschultz, Jeremy Harris. *Free Expression in the Age of the Internet*. Boulder, CO: Westview Press, 2000.

Lukas, J. Anthony. "The A.C.L.U. against Itself," *New York Times Magazine*, July 9, 1978, pp. 9–31.

MacKinnon, Catharine A. *Only Words*. Cambridge, MA: Harvard University Press, 1993.

Martin, James P. "When Repression Is Democratic and Constitutional: The Federalist Theory of Representation and the Sedition Act of 1798." In *First Amendment Law Handbook*, ed. James L. Swanson. St. Paul, MN: West Group, 1999, pp. 567–637.

Matsuda, Mari J., et al., eds. *Words That Wound: Critical Race Theory, Assaultive Speech, and the First Amendment*. Boulder, CO: Westview Press, 1993.

McCullough, David. *John Adams*. New York: Simon & Schuster, 2001.

Miller, John Chester. *Crisis in Freedom: The Alien and Sedition Acts*. Boston: Little, Brown, 1951.

Miller, William Lee. *Arguing about Slavery: The Great Battle in the United States Congress*. New York: Alfred A. Knopf, 1996.

Murphy, Paul L. *The Meaning of Freedom of Speech: First Amendment Freedoms from Wilson to FDR*. Westport, CT: Greenwood Press, 1972.

———. *World War I and the Origins of Civil Liberties in the United States*. New York: W.W. Norton, 1979.

Navasky, Victor S. *Naming Names*. New York: Viking Press, 1980.

Neely, Mark E., Jr. *The Fate of Liberty: Abraham Lincoln and Civil Liberties*. New York: Oxford University Press, 1991.

———. *Southern Rights: Political Prisoners and the Myth of Confederate Constitutionalism*. Charlottesville: University Press of Virginia, 1999.

Neier, Aryeh. *Defending My Enemy: American Nazis, the Skokie Case, and the Risks of Freedom*. New York: E.P. Dutton, 1979.

Nye, Russell B. *Fettered Freedom: Civil Liberties and the Slavery Controversy 1830–1860*. East Lansing: Michigan State University Press, 1963.

O'Reilly, Kenneth. *Hoover and the Un-Americans: The FBI, HUAC, and the Red Menace*. Philadelphia: Temple University Press, 1983.

Powers, Richard Gid. *Not Without Honor: The History of American Anticommunism*. New York: Free Press, 1995.

Powers, Thomas. *Vietnam: The War at Home—Vietnam and the American People, 1964–1968*. Boston, MA: G.K. Hall, 1984.

Rabban, David M. "An Ahistorical Historian." *Stanford Law Review* 37 (February 1986): 795–856.

———. *Free Speech in Its Forgotten Years*. New York: Cambridge University Press, 1997.

Reynolds, Donald E. *Editors Make War: Southern Newspapers in the Secession Crisis*. Nashville, TN: Vanderbilt University Press, 1970.

Robbins, Mary Susannah, ed. *Against the Vietnam War: Writings by Activists*. Syracuse, NY: Syracuse University Press, 1999.

Rollins, Peter C., and John E. O'Connor, eds. *Hollywood's World War I: Motion Picture Images*. Bowling Green, OH: Bowling Green State University Popular Press, 1997.

Rose, Lisle A. *The Cold War Comes to Main Street: America in 1950*. Lawrence: University Press of Kansas, 1999.

Rudenstine, David. *The Day the Presses Stopped: A History of the Pentagon Papers*. Berkeley: University of California Press, 1996.

Sachsman, David B., S. Kittrell Rushing, and Debra Reddin van Tuyll, eds. *The Civil War and the Press*. New Brunswick, NJ: Transaction Press, 2000.

Shiell, Timothy C. *Campus Hate Speech on Trial*. Lawrence: University Press of Kansas, 1998.

Simon, Paul. *Freedom's Champion: Elijah Lovejoy*. Carbondale: Southern Illinois University Press, 1994.

Small, Melvin. *Covering Dissent: The Media and the Anti-Vietnam War Movement*. New Brunswick, NJ: Rutgers University Press, 1994.

Small, Melvin, and William D. Hooper, eds. *Give Peace a Chance: Exploring the Vietnam Antiwar Movement*. Syracuse, NY: Syracuse University Press, 1992.

Smith, James Morton. *Freedom's Fetters: The Alien and Sedition Laws and American Civil Liberties*. Ithaca, NY: Cornell University Press, 1956.

———, ed. *The Republic of Letters: The Correspondence between Jefferson and Madison*. Vol. 2. New York: W.W. Norton, 1995, chap. 23–27.

Smith, Jeffrey A. *War and Press Freedom*. New York: Oxford University Press, 1999.

Steinberg, Peter L. *The Great "Red Menace": United States Prosecution of American Communists, 1947–1952*. Westport, CT: Greenwood Press, 1984.

Stewart, James Brewer, ed. *The Constitution, the Law, and Freedom of Expression 1787–1987*. Carbondale: Southern Illinois University Press, 1987.

Strossen, Nadine. "Regulating Racist Speech on Campus: A Modest Proposal?" In *Speaking of Race, Speaking of Sex: Hate Speech, Civil Rights, Civil Liberties*, ed. H.L. Gates et al. New York: New York University Press, 1994, pp. 181–256.

Strum, Philippa. *When the Nazis Came to Skokie: Freedom for Speech We Hate*. Lawrence: University Press of Kansas, 1999.

Tuman, Joseph Sargon. " 'Sticks and Stones May Break My Bones, But Words Will Never Hurt Me': The Fighting Words Doctrine on Campus." In *Free Speech Yearbook*. Carbondale: Southern Illinois University Press, 1992, 30: 114–128.

Walker, Samuel. *Hate Speech: The History of an American Controversy*. Lincoln: University of Nebraska Press, 1994.

———. *In Defense of American Liberties: A History of the ACLU*. 2nd ed. Carbondale: Southern Illinois University Press, 1999.

Wilson, John K. *The Myth of Political Correctness: The Conservative Attack on Higher Education*. Durham, NC: Duke University Press, 1995.

Wise, David. *The Politics of Lying: Government Deception, Secrecy, and Power*. New York: Random House, 1973.

Zaroulis, Nancy, and Gerald Sullivan. *Who Spoke Up?: American Protest against the War in Vietnam, 1963–1975*. Garden City, NY: Doubleday, 1984.

Zinn, Howard. *SNCC: The New Abolitionists*. Boston, MA: Beacon Press, 1964.

Index

Abolitionist movement, 43–51; anti-slavery societies in, 44; documents of, 52–66; intellectual climate for, 4, 43–44; mail campaigns of, 45, 47–48; mob violence against, 5, 49–50; opposition to, 43, 44; and the press, 44–45, 47–48, 49

Abrams, Jacob, 125

Academic freedom, wartime suppression of, 127

Adams, John, 2, 19–20, 22, 23, 26, 47

Adams, John Quincy, 47

African Americans: and Black power movement, 182–83; and reparations, 247; and urban race riots, 183. *See also* Civil rights movement; Slavery

Alien Acts of 1798, 2, 45; Alien Enemies Act, 20, 122; Alien Registration Act, 150–51, 153; citizenship and, 20; Naturalization Act, 20–21; outrage against, 21; and Virginia Resolution, 2, 21, 27, 29–31

Allen, Raymond B., 160

American Anti-Slavery Society, 44, 45

American Civil Liberties Union (ACLU), 269, 271, 302; defense of pornography, 279, 280, 281, 282, 292; establishment of, 130; and hate speech codes on campus, 249; and Skokie case, 223, 226, 230, 232, 234–38

American Library Association, and Internet filters, 281, 290–91

American Nazi Party, 223

American Protective League (APL), 127

American Student of Art, The, 101, 112–13

Amherst College, 49

Antiwar movement, 201–9; and campus teach-ins and sit-ins, 203; and draft protests, 202, 204, 206, 210–13; and government intelligence gathering, 205–6; and 1960s protest activities, 201–2; and public schoolchildren's rights to protest, 213–16; and self-immolation, 204. *See also* New Left movement

Ashcroft v. The Free Speech Coalition, 280–81, 303–8

Atomic Energy Act, 148
Aurora (newspaper), 21

Bachel, Benjamin Franklin, 21
Banta, Martha, 257
Barenblatt v. United States, 154, 248–49
Beauharnais v. Illinois, 227, 240, 242–43, 248–49
Beecher, Henry Ward, 96
Beeson, Ann, 282
Bennett, De Robigne M., 98–99
Bernstein, Richard, 255
Bill of Rights, 7
Birney, James, 44, 47, 49
Birth control literature, censorship of, 8, 9, 97, 99, 100, 102–4
Birth of a Nation (film), 123
Black reparations, 247
Black, Hugo L., 151, 154, 155, 169, 181–92, 193, 207, 208, 214
Blackmun, Harry A., 252
Blackstone, William, 23–24, 34
Blasphemy, and free speech, 95, 99
Blockade (film), 159
Bok, Derek, 258
Bollinger, Lee C., 228–29
Boston Anti-Slavery Society, 44
Brandeis, Louis D., 126, 129, 138, 151
Brandenburg v. Ohio, 223–24
Brennan, William J., Jr., 190–93
Brotherhood of Man, The (film), 159
Brown University: *Daily Herald*, 247; speech policy of, 250
Brown, Mitzi, 290
Brown v. Board of Education, 176, 177
Bryant, William Cullen, 44, 64–66
Buchanan, James, 46
Buckley, James M., 98, 100, 108–10
Buckley, William, 223–24
Bundy, McGeorge, 203
Burleson, Albert, 126
Burnside, Ambrose, 7, 76–77
Burr, Aaron, 24
Bush, George, 247
Bush, George W., 278

Calhoun, John C., 5, 46, 47–48, 55–58
Carnivore wiretapping system, 278, 302
Censorship: of abolitionist movement, 45–51; of birth control literature, 97, 99, 100, 102–4; during Civil War, 73–77; Post Office Department and, 4–5, 47–48, 53–54; of the press, 77, 78–79, 123–24; and World War I Army Index, 123. *See also* Comstock Act
Central Intelligence Agency (CIA): establishment of, 148; and USA Patriot Act, 302
Chaplinsky v. New Hampshire, 224, 225, 228, 235–36, 239, 249
Chapman, Mary Weston, 44
Chicago *Times*, 76–77
Child Online Protection Act (COPA), 280, 289
Child Pornography Prevention Act, 299–301; Supreme Court invalidation of, 303–8
Children's Internet Protection Act (CIPA), 281
Cincinnati *Volksblatt*, 133
Citizens' Commission to Investigate the FBI (CCIFBI), 206
Citizenship, and Alien Acts, 20
Civil Rights Act of 1965, 179
Civil rights movement, 175–96, 201–2; boycotts of, 177, 178; documents of, 185–96; and "equal protection under the law," 175; and freedom of expression and association, 175, 176, 178, 179–80; and freedom rides of 1961, 178; and Freedom Summer of 1964, 179; and NAACP litigation, 175–76, 180; nonviolence and civil disobedience in, 176–79, 180–81; and school desegregation, 177, 179–80; and Selma-to-Montgomery march, 179; sit-in campaign, 177–78, 181; and Supreme Court's support and reversals, 179–82; and voter registration drives, 178–79; and voting rights, 175, 176

Civil War military campaign, 59–72; Bull Run/Manassas battles in, 73–74; constitutionality of, 69, 78, 83–87; and Copperhead movement, 72, 77; documents of, 80–92; and draft opposition, 91–92; freedom of expression issues in, 5–6, 74, 87–88, 90–92; martial law in, 71; military censorship in, 73–77; and mob violence, 70, 74; newspaper coverage of, 71–74; and political polarization, 72

Claflin, Tennessee, 96, 97

Clark, Tom, 153

Clay, Henry, 46

Clinton, William J., 252

Cohen, Carl, 228

Cohen v. California, 207–8

Cold War era: anticommunist crusade of, 149–55; containment policy of, 199; free speech infringements of, 148–55; regime of repression in, 147–48. *See also* Vietnam War

Coleman, Henry S., 204

Collin, Frank, 225, 226, 227, 230

Columbia University, antiwar protests at, 204

Columbia, South Carolina, civil rights march in, 180, 187–89

Commentaries on the Laws of England (Blackstone), 23–24

Commercial speech: constitutional protection of, 224; and the Internet, 278

Committee on Public Information (CPI), 123, 131

Communications Decency Act, 279; applied to the Internet, 280; and Internet Service Providers, 283, 284; language of, 279, 284; Supreme Court's invalidation of, 284–89

Communist Control Act of 1954, 153

Communist Party members: and Alien Registration Act, 150–51, 153; arrests and deportation of, 128–29; and Cold War paranoia, 147–55; and House Committee on Un-American Activities, 148–50, 154, 155; and McCarthy crusade, 152–53; and Palmer raids, 128, 129, 142–44; and "Red Scare," 128–29, 142–44; registration requirements, 151

Comstock, Anthony, 7–8, 96–98, 109, 117–18

Comstock Act, 8–9, 95–118; and censorship of art and literature, 101–2, 110–11; background of, 95–97; and contraception, 9, 99, 100, 102–8; and *Hicklin* rule, 99; and proliferation of obscenity, 96–97

Congress: anti-Communist legislation of, 151, 153, 154; and Civil War censorship, 74; and Comstock Act, 97, 105–8; and crimes of treason, 122; e-mail messages to, 276; erotic and birth control literature suppressed by, 8, 97; Gag rules of, 4–5, 46–47; Internet legislation of, 280–81, 284–89, 290–93, 296, 299–301; and scientific data flow, 148; and selective service laws, 206; and World War I legislation, 122. *See also* House Committee on Un-American Activities

Congress of Racial Equality (CORE), 178

Conscription. *See* Draft, the

Constitution: Bill of Rights, 7; Civil War amendments, 7; interpretation and enforcement of, 2; Lincoln administration and, 5–6. *See also* First Amendment

Copperhead movement, 6, 72

Corning, Erastus, 83

Craddock, Ida, 102

Creel, George, 123, 131

Cronkite, Walter, 176

Daly, Mary, 247

Davidson, William C., 206

Debs, Eugene, 124

Decker, Bernard, 226

Declaration of Independence, slavery and, 52

Defense Department, and Pentagon Papers, 208

Democracy: and cyber-advocacy, 276–77; and loyal political opposition, 23, 25; and moral judgment, 238

Democratic newspapers, and Lincoln's war policies, 6–7, 71, 72

Democratic Party, 6, 7, 72, 252

Denmark Vesey conspiracy, 4, 45

Dennis v. United States, 151, 153, 155

Diversity and multiculturalism: in academia, 245–46; and social movements of 1960s and 1970s, 245. *See also* Political correctness movement

Dix, John A., 76

Douglas, William O., 150, 193

Douglass, Frederick, 44

Draft, the, 122; Civil War, 91–92; and constitutional rights, 125; and Vietnam War protests, 202, 204, 206; and voting rights, 209

Draft card destruction, Supreme Court's rulings on, 206–7, 210–13

Dred Scott v. Sandford ruling, 64, 70, 71

Droge, David, 247

D'Souza, Dinesh, 246–47, 254–58

Easton, Clement, 49

Educational institutions: feminist curricula in, 247; and high school students' right to protest, 207, 213–16; Internet filtering software in, 281; multicultural curricula in, 245, 247, 258; and school desegregation, 177, 179–80; sexual harassment in, 247–48; southern Civil War era, 48–49, 61–64

Eisenhower, Dwight: desegregation and, 177; summit with Khrushchev, 151–52

Eisner, Jane, 299

Espionage Act of 1917: and acts of treason, 124; arbitrary enforcement of, 125, 126–27; convictions, 147; enactment of, 124; and wartime seditious expression, 138

Evening Post, 44

Faubus, Orval, 177

Federal Bureau of Investigation (FBI), 128, 153; burglary of, 206; Counter Intelligence Programs (COINTELPRO), 205, 206; directory of untrustworthy groups, 148; and Hoover's "fifth column" Communists, 148; noncriminal intelligence gathering of, 205–6; and USA Patriot Act, 302

Federal employee loyalty-screening program, 148

Federal lawmaking power, and First Amendment, 22–23

Federalist Party, 2, 3, 19–20; and the Alien Acts, 20–21, 22; 1800 election and, 24

Feminist movement: and feminist curricula, 247; and hate speech censorship, 269–71; and pornography, 248, 269–71

Ferber case, 304, 306, 307

Fifteenth Amendment, and voting rights, 175, 179

Fifth Amendment, and Communist sympathizers, 150, 153

Film industry: House Committee on Un-American Activities' investigation of, 149–50, 157–60, 167–69; teenage sexual activity depicted in, 305; wartime censorship of, 123

First Amendment, 1; absolutist interpretation of, 22, 169–72; and Alien and Sedition laws, 21–22; and anonymous leaflets, 282; and draft card destruction, 206–7, 204–13; and government secrecy, 208; and Internet issues, 277–82, 283, 285, 298–99; and libel, 182, 189–93; and peaceful assembly, 187–89; and pornography, 278–79; and protests on government property, 193–96; and right to petition, 46; and seditious libel, 3, 125; states' applicability, 45, 129; and symbolic speech, 213–16; and Vietnam War protests, 206–8, 204–13

Fish, Stanley, 257

Flanders, Ralph E., 153

Foote, Edward Bliss, 102

Fortas, Abe, 207

Founding Fathers: and concept of loyal political opposition, 23; and First Amendment rights, 1; and offices of president and vice president, 20

Fourteenth Amendment, equal protection clause of, 7, 175, 178

Fourth Amendment, and USA Patriot Act, 301–3

France, diplomatic crisis with, 19–20, 22

Franco, Francisco, 149

Frankfurter, Felix, 271

Free Speech League, 9, 103, 114

Freedom of assembly: and civil rights movement, 175, 176, 178, 179; and disclosure of membership lists, 179–80, 185–86; and peaceful marches, 187–89; and protests on public/government property, 193–96

Freedom of speech and expression, 45; abolition and, 4–5; and "bad tendency" test, 129; in British legal system, 23–24, 34–37; and civil rights movement, 175, 176, 178, 179; Civil War suppression of, 69–79, 90–92; and "clear and present danger" test, 125–26; and criticism of slavery, 48–51, 64–66; and "fighting words" concept, 224, 225, 227, 235, 249, 251–52; and hate speech codes, 249; historical overview of, 1–17; and obscenity and blasphemy, 95, 224; and party politics, 1–2; and political correctness movement, 247–53; and pornography, 278–81, 282, 292; and privacy in group affiliation, 185–86; as prohibition against prior restraint, 23; in public schools, 213–16; and right to dissent, 3, 135–37, 206–8, 210–13; and "slippery slope" arguments, 227; and wartime censorship, 121–30. See also First Amendment

Freedom of the press: and antislavery newspapers, 44–45, 47–48, 49; and Lincoln's war policies, 6–7, 72–77,

78–79; and McCarthy witch hunts, 152

Frémont, John C., 5, 51

Fuchs, Klaus, 147

Fuller, E. N., 76

Garrison, William Lloyd, 44, 45, 49, 52–53

Gates, Henry Louis, Jr., 257

Gayle v. Browder, 177

Genius of Universal Emancipation newspaper, 44, 52

Genovese, Eugene D., 203, 204–5

George Mason University, speech policy of, 250

German Americans, and World War I, 121–22, 132–34

Gibson, William, 277

Gitlin, Todd, 203–4, 257

Gitlow v. New York, 129

Goldman, Emma, 103, 128

Goldwater, Barry, 200

Government secrecy, and First Amendment principles, 208

Great Britain: and Jay Treaty with United States, 19; legal definition of "freedom of speech" in, 23–24, 34–37

Greeley, Horace, 83

Gregory, Thomas W., 122

Grey, Thomas C., 258–63

Group libel law, and Skokie case, 225, 226, 227–28, 248–49

Group membership disclosure, 151, 179–80, 185–86

Habeas corpus, presidential suspension of, 71

Hamilton, Alexander, 24, 130

Hamlin, David, 234

Harlan, John Marshall, 153, 154, 185, 207, 208; and Pentagon Papers case, 216–18

Harmon, Moses, 101

Hate crime(s): legislation, 245–46; and "fighting words" doctrine, 249, 251–52, 268; and First Amendment, 266–69

Hate speech: and campus codes of
conduct, 248, 249–52, 255; federal
court rulings on, 249–50; and group
libel law, 248–49; on the Internet,
281–82; and racial/ethnic insults,
224–25; and white epithets, 261–62
Heywood, Ezra, 100–101
Holmes, Oliver Wendell, 79, 125–26,
138–40, 151
Homophobia, and hate crimes, 245–
46
Hoover, J. Edgar, 128, 148; and antiwar protesters, 205, 206
Horowitz, David, 247
House Committee on Un-American
Activities (HUAC), 154; constitutional authority of, 148–49; and
Hollywood entertainment industry,
149–50, 157–60, 167–69; and labor
unions, 150; and social/professional
ostracism, 150
House of Representatives: and 1800
election, 24; Gag Rules adopted by,
46–47
Humphrey, Hubert, 183

Illiberal Education (D'Souza), 246–47
Immigrants, national distrust of, 122
Independent Progressive Party, 135
Intellectual property rights, Internet
tests of, 277–78
Intelligence gathering: and antiwar
protesters, 205–6; on Internet, 278,
301–3
Internal Security Act of 1950, 151, 153,
155; Truman's veto of, 165–67
International Workers of the World
(IWW), 124
Internet, 275–83; and anti-abortionists,
282; content filtering devices, 281,
291–92, 293–95; development and
expansion, 275–77; and First
Amendment rights, 277–82, 283,
285, 298–99; and government eaves-
dropping, 278, 301–3; hate speech
on, 281–82; and incitement to murder, 282; and libel, 282–83; and music piracy, 277–78; PICS project

(Platform for Internet Content Selection), 294–99; privacy/security
concerns, 278, 301–3; rating systems, 294; sexually explicit images
on, 278–81; and virtual protests, 283;
and World Wide Web, 277, 290,
292
Internet pornography: child and "virtual child," 280–81, 299–301, 306–7;
children's access to, 279–80, 281;
Ferber case and, 304, 306, 307; and
First Amendment protections, 278–
79; legislation, 279, 280–81, 284–89;
in libraries and schools, 289–93; and
Miller test, 280, 304, 305, 307
Internet Service Provider (ISP), and
Communications Decency Act, 283,
284
Interstate commerce regulation, and
obscenity laws, 95
Irish ethnic groups, and World War I,
121–22

Jackson, Andrew, 4, 47, 53–54
Jackson State killings, 205
Jacobowitz, Eden, 250
Jay Treaty, 19
Jefferson, Thomas, 2, 3, 19–20, 21–22,
24, 25; Kentucky Resolution of, 37–
39
Jessup, Morris K., 96
Johnson, Lyndon B., 176; and Civil
Rights Act passage, 179; and stu-
dent teach-ins, 203; Vietnam policy
of, 199, 200, 203
Joint Anti-Fascist Refugee Committee
(JAFRC), 149
Journal of Commerce, 6, 73, 76
Justice Department: Central Intelli-
gence Division of, 128; and Com-
munist Party, 128–29, 142–44, 150;
and espionage cases, 126–27; and
seditious conduct, 122; and student
antiwar protests, 205

Kattenburg, Paul M., 201
Kazan, Elia, 167–69
Kendall, Amos, 47

Kennedy, Anthony, 303
Kennedy, John F., 179; and civil
    rights, 178; inaugural address of,
    199
Kennedy, Robert F., assassination of,
    183
Kent State killings, 205
Keyes, Alan L., 263–65
Khrushchev, Nikita, 151
King, Martin Luther, Jr., 176, 177, 178,
    190; assassination of, 183; "I Have a
    Dream" speech of, 179
Kinsley, Michael, 257
Krug, Judith, 291–92
Ku Klux Klan (KKK), 179

Labor unions, and anti-Communist
    crusades, 150
LaFollete, Robert M., 135–37
Lawson, John Howard, 158, 159
Leaves of Grass (Whitman), 101
Lee, Robert E., 76
Legacy 1 Suppression, The (Levy), 23–
    24
Levy, Leonard, 23–24
Libel: and "actual malice" test, 182;
    and First Amendment, 181–82, 189–
    93; group, 225, 226, 227–28; Internet
    and, 282–83; Sullivan case and, 181–
    82; Supreme Court protection for,
    224
Liberal left: and New Left movement,
    202–4; and political correctness
    movement, 247, 248; and suppres-
    sion of offensive speech, 248
Liberator (newspaper), 44, 45, 52–53
Libraries, and children's access to
    pornography, 281, 289–93
Lincoln, Abraham: Albany Commit-
    tee's censure of, 83, 87–89; and Bal-
    timore riots, 70–71; and due process
    of law, 69; executive fiat rule of, 5–
    6, 70; Fort Sumter crisis response
    of, 70; and suppression of the press,
    6, 69, 71–73, 74; and suspension of
    writ of habeas corpus, 71; war poli-
    cies defense of, 83–87; and wartime
    censorship, 6–7, 74–77

Little Rock (Arkansas) Central High
    School, desegregation of, 177
Lovejoy, Elijah, 5, 50, 59–61
Lowell, James Russell, 44
Lucifer: The Light-Bearer (journal), 101
Lundy, Benjamin, 44
Lyon, Matthew, 22, 39–40

MacKinnon, Catharine, 271
Madison, James, 21–22, 190, 192
Maher, Bill, 246
Mail. See Post Office censorship
Malcom X, 182–83
Man and Superman (Shaw), 102
Mao Zedong, 152
Marshall, Joshua, 293
Marx, Karl, 153
Mass media: and communist witch
    hunts, 149–50, 157–60, 167–69; in-
    vestigative journalism of, 200; pres-
    entation of Vietnam War in, 201;
    and wartime censorship, 123–24,
    126. See also Press, the
Mayer, Louis B., 160
McCain, John, 281, 297
McCarthy, Joseph R., 152–53; formal
    censure of, 153
McClellan, George B., 75
McNamara, Robert S., 200
McNutt, Paul, 158
Meredith, James, 178
Merriam, C. L., 97
Miller v. California, 278–79; and Inter-
    net pornography, 280, 304, 305,
    307
Milligan case, 7, 77
Mills, C. Wright, 202
Milwaukee Germania, 134
Mississippi Freedom Democratic
    Party, 179
Montgomery Bus Boycott, 177, 178
Mother Earth (magazine), 103
Munro, Neil, 290
Murrow, Edward R., 152

NAACP v. Alabama, 179–80
NAACP v. Button, 180
Napster, 278

Nat Turner slave revolt, 4, 44–45
Nation, The, 203
Nation of Islam, 182–83
National Anti-Slavery Standard, 44
National Association for the Advance-
    ment of Colored People (NAACP):
    civil rights litigation of, 175–76, 180;
    and membership lists battle, 179–80,
    185–86. *See also* Civil rights move-
    ment
National Defense Association, 101
National Law Center for Children
    and Families, 290–92
National Liberal League, 101
Nationalist Socialist Party of America,
    225, 230
Nationalist Socialist Party v. Skokie, 225.
    See also Skokie case
Nazi march on Skokie, Illinois. *See*
    Skokie case
Nazi symbols, online display of, 282
New England Anti-Slavery Society,
    44
New Left movement: "Ban the Bomb"
    rally of, 202; and Berkeley Free
    Speech Movement, 203; FBI pursuit
    of, 204; Port Huron statement of,
    202. *See also* Antiwar movement
New Republic, 256
New York *Herald,* 71, 73
New York magazine, 256
New York *Daily News,* 73
New York Times, 110–11, 117–18, 203,
    216, 255, 256, 257
New York Times v. Sullivan, 181–82,
    249
New York *Tribune,* 83, 142
New York *World,* 6, 76–77
Newark, New Jersey *Evening Journal,*
    76, 91–92
Newsweek magazine, 203, 255–56
Ngo Diem, 199
Nicholas, John, 34
Nixon, Richard M., 183; and *Pentagon
    Papers* case, 208, 216–18; and Viet-
    nam War protests, 204–5; and Wa-
    tergate scandal, 200, 209
North Star journal, 44

O'Brien, David Paul, 210–13
Obscenity: Comstock Law and, 8–9;
    and English common law, 98–99;
    regulation and defining of, 95; and
    sexual expression in American soci-
    ety, 95–96. *See also* Internet pornog-
    raphy; Pornography
Observer newspaper, 50
Olds, Frank Perry, 132–34

Palmer, A. Mitchell: raids and depor-
    tations of, 128; self-defense docu-
    ment of, 142–44
Parks, Rosa, 176–77
PCU (film), 246
Pentagon Papers case, 208; Justice Har-
    lan's dissent in, 216–18
Philanthropist newspaper, 44, 47
PICS project (Platform for Internet
    Content Selection), 294–99
Pinckney, William, 46
Political advocacy, and the Internet,
    276–77, 283
Political correctness movement, 245–
    53; and campus episodes of re-
    pressed speech, 247–50; and codes
    of student conduct, 248, 249–52, 255;
    criticism and ridicule of, 246–47,
    254–58, 263–65; defense of, 247, 255–
    63; and free speech issues, 247–53;
    and hate speech, 248–51, 255; and
    liberal left values, 247, 248; press
    coverage of, 255–56; as student ac-
    tivism, 247; and Supreme Court rul-
    ings, 248–49, 251–52
Political parties, 19, 20; Civil War pol-
    icies and, 72; development of, 23
Political speech: First Amendment
    protection of, 224; and "heckler's
    veto", 227; and wartime censorship,
    124–26
Politically Incorrect (TV program), 246
Pornography: censorship of, 269–71;
    feminist opposition to, 248, 269–71;
    and *Miller* test, 278–79, 281, 285; Su-
    preme Court's official definition of,
    278–79. *See also* Internet child
    pornography; Internet pornography

Port Huron Statement of the Students for a Democratic Society, 202

Post Office censorship: and abolitionist literature, 4–5, 47–48, 53–54; and birth control information, 8, 103; and left-wing press, 126; and obscene materials, 95, 97; and President Jackson's Postal Bill, 55; and suppression of newspapers, 73; during World War I, 126

Press, the: and Bull Run/Manassas defeats, 73–74; Civil War positions in, 71–72; editorial wars and advocacy journalism of, 72; and freedom of speech, 6–7, 44–45, 47–48, 49, 72–77, 78–79, 152; German, and World War I, 132–34; and military control of telegraph lines, 123–24; Northern, official suppression of, 77, 78–79; postal suppression of, 73, 126; Southern, destruction and suppression of, 77–78; Treason Act and, 75; and Union military machine, 75–77; and wartime censorship, 74. *See also* Mass media

Prize cases, 70

Public transport desegregation, 178

Quakers, and abolition movement, 43, 44, 45

Racial minorities, and hate crimes/hate speech, 245–46, 270

Racial segregation: in public schools/transportation, 177; Supreme Court rulings on, 176–78, 179–82, 183. *See also* Civil Rights Movement

Radical libertarianism, and Comstock Law, 99, 100–101

Radio industry: and House Committee on Un-American Activities, 149; wartime censorship of, 124

R.A.V. v. St. Paul, 266–69

Reconstruction Acts, 7

Regina v. Hicklin, 98; and Hicklin test, 8–9

Republican newspapers, Civil War positions of, 71

Republican Party, 5, 51, 152, 183, 253; Civil War and, 6; Jeffersonian, 20, 21–22, 26; Radical, 71

Right to associate. *See* Freedom of assembly

Right to dissent: and criticism of government, 3; during wartime, 121–30, 135–37. *See also* Freedom of speech and expression

Right to petition, and congressional Gag Rules, 46

Rivers, L. Mendel, 206

Rocker, John, 253

Rosenberg, Julius and Ethel, 147

Rosser, Richard, 257

Rudd, Mark, 204

Rule of law, and Civil War military edicts, 69

Sanford, Edward T., 129

Sanger, Margaret H., 9, 103–4

Sanger, William, 103–4

Scalia, Antonin, 251

Schenck v. United States, 125, 126

Schmidt, Benno, 258

Schroeder, Theodore, 103, 114–17

Sedition Act of 1918, 2, 3, 20–25, 26–27, 45, 122, 137–38, 275; constitutionality of, 21–22; convictions and punishments under, 124, 125–27, 138–42; and diplomatic crisis with France, 19, 20, 22; and First Amendment rights, 21–23, 24, 25; and Kentucky and Virginia Resolutions, 2, 21, 27, 29–31, 37–39; outrage against, 21; and seditious libel, 21, 24, 25, 26–27; and Supreme Court's dissent opinions, 138–40; and wartime dissent, 138

Seditious libel: British law on, 3; Espionage Act and, 138; First Amendment and, 125; state laws against, 129

Selective service laws, and draft card destruction, 206. *See also* Draft, the

Self-incrimination, Fifth Amendment prohibition against, 150, 153

Senate anti-Communist committees, 151, 152

Senate Internal Security Subcommittee, and student antiwar protests, 205

Seward, William H., 71, 74–75

Shaw, George Bernard, 8, 101–2

Sheppard, Matthew, 246

Skokie case, 223–29; and "clear and present danger" argument, 232–33; federal court ruling on, 226, 230, 238–41; and "fighting words" concept, 224, 225, 227, 235; as First Amendment issue, 223–27, 230–31; and genocide and concept of morals, 237; and indefensibility of Nazi message, 234–35; as obscenity case, 232; press reactions to, 226–27; and state Supreme court, 226, 230; and Supreme Court rulings, 225, 226, 242–43; and Village ordinances, 225–26, 233, 238–41

Slavery: and Congressional Gag rules, 4–5, 46–47; and *Dred Scott* ruling, 70, 71; early opposition to, 3, 43; and religion, 58–59; and slave revolts, 44–45. *See also* Abolition movement

Smith, Margaret Chase, 152, 163–64

Smith Act. *See* Alien Registration Act

Smith College, speech codes of, 256

Socialist newspapers, denial of mailing privileges to, 126

Socialist Party, 124, 125

Southern Christian Leadership Conference (SCLC), 176

Southern educational institutions: and antislavery speech, 48–49; banning of blacks from, 49; central university proposal, 61–64; desegregation of, 177, 179–80

Soviet Union, as nuclear threat to U.S., 147, 155. *See also* Cold War era

Spirit of '76 (film), 123

Spock, Benjamin, 218–20

St. Paul, Minnesota, Bias-Motivated Crime Ordinance, 251–52

Stanford University, speech policy of, 250, 258–63

Stanton, Edwin M., 74

Staples, Brent, 257

State(s): and federal constitutional constraints, 129; law, and federal law, 2–3, 27–29, 55; libel laws, 182; regulation of obscene expression, 95; rights, and Bill of Rights provisions, 7; and Sedition Act, 29–31; standards of free speech, 3; and World War I civil liberty restrictions, 127

States, southern: banning of antislavery speech in, 45, 48–49; education and proslavery ideas in, 48–49, 61–64; "Slave" and "Black" codes in, 48

Stevens, John Paul, 187, 278, 279

Stimpson, Catharine, 257

Stockman, Alice, 102

Stone, I. F., 149, 157

Strossen, Nadine, 269–71

Student Non-violent Coordinating Committee (SNCC), 177–79

Student political movement of 1950s, 202. *See also* Antiwar movement; New Left movement

Sullivan, L. B., libel case of, 181–82, 189–93

Supreme Court: and absolutist view of First Amendment, 169–72; and advocacy of overthrowing the government, 153; and antiwar activism, 206–8, 210–13; appellate jurisdiction of, 154–55; and balancing of conflicting interests, 169–70; and Child Pornography Prevention Act, 303–8; and "clear and present danger" test, 125–26, 129, 151; and civil rights movement, 179–82; commercial speech doctrine of, 224; and Communist witch hunts and prosecutions, 150–51, 153–55; and declaration of war, 70; and disclosure of group affiliation, 185–86; generous speech-protective stance of, 224; and group libel law, 227–28; and hate speech, 248–49, 251–52; and Internet regulation, 280, 284–89; and libel, 181–82, 189–93, 224; Nixon appointees to, 183; and peaceful marching, 187–89; pornography defined by (*Miller* test), 278–79, 285;

pornography rulings of, 271, 299–301; and protesters' free speech claims, 183; and public transportation desegregation, 178; and school desegregation, 177; Sedition Act dissent opinions, 138–40; Skokie case rulings of, 225–26, 242–43; slavery ruling of, 64, 70, 71; and "symbolic" speech cases, 176–81, 207–8; and World War I censorship, 123, 124–25

Sweezy, Paul, 153–54

Symbolic speech: and First Amendment protections, 297–8, 213–16; and Supreme Court civil rights decisions, 176–81, 207–8

Taney, Roger B., 71

Taylor, John, 256

Telecommunications Act, and Internet pornography, 279

Telegraph, and military censorship, 73, 75, 123–24

Television, and communist witch hunts, 149

Thirteenth Amendment, slavery prohibition in, 125

Thomas, J. Parnell, 158

"Threats against the President Act," 122

Time magazine, 256

Tinker v. Des Moines School District, 207, 213–16

Tom Jones (Fielding), 110

Trading with the Enemy Act, 126

Traffic (film), 305

Treason, and Wilson administration policies, 122

Treason Act, 75

Truman, Harry S., 151; criticism of, 152; loyalty-screening program of, 148; veto of Internal Security Bill, 165–67

United States ex rel. Milwaukee Social Democrat Publishing Co. v. Burleson, 126

United States v. O'Brien, 207

Uniting and Strengthening America by Providing Appropriate Tools Required to Intercept and Obstruct Terrorism Act. *See* USA Patriot Act

University of California at Berkeley, Free Speech Movement, 203

University of Chicago Law School, conference on pornography and hate speech, 269–71

University of Delaware, speech policy of, 252

University of Michigan: campus teach-ins, 203; speech policy of, 249–50, 255

University of Mississippi, desegregation of, 178

University of Pennsylvania, speech policy of, 250

University of Wisconsin, speech policy of, 250, 251

USA Patriot Act, 278; and invasion of privacy, 301–3

Vallandigham, Clement L., 6–7, 77, 83, 85–87, 88, 89

Vice presidential office, and early electoral process, 20

Vietnam Moratorium Day, 204

Vietnam War, 199–209; documents of, 210–20; and domestic upheaval, 201–2; escalation of, 200, 201; and First Amendment issues, 206–8; graphic depictions of, 201; public disillusion with, 200–201; Tonkin Gulf Resolution, 199–200; and Watergate scandal, 208. *See also* Antiwar movement

Voting rights: and civil rights movement, 175, 176, 178–79; and the draft, 209

Voting Rights Act of 1965, 179

Wallace, George C., 183

War correspondents, and censorship rules, 124

War in the Air (Wells), 123

Warner, Jack, 159–60

Warren, Earl, 154, 210

Wartime censorship: of mail materials, 126; of mass media, 123–24, 126; of political speech, 124–26
Washington Post, 216
Washington, George, 2
Watergate scandal, and public trust, 200, 208
Watkins v. United States, 154, 169
Wells, H. G., 123
White, Byron, 252
Whitman, Walt, 101
Wilson, Woodrow: and civil rights restrictions, 122–24; criticized by Theodore Roosevelt, 140–42; Espionage Act enforcement of, 124; Executive Order regarding Federal Employees, 122; patriotic reelection campaign of, 122; war powers of, 128
Wisconsin Supreme Court, hate crimes ruling of, 266–69
Woman Rebel, The (magazine), 103
Women: in abolition movement, 44; in birth control and free speech movement, 102–4; and "freedom amendments," 7; violence against, and hate crimes legislation, 246

Women's International League of Peace, 202
Woodhull, Victoria, 96–97
Word, The (journal), 100
World, The (newspaper), 6, 90–91
World War I, 121–30; and academic freedom, 127; Americans' opposition to, 121; anti-German and anti-radical campaign, 123; and arrests for violating wartime prohibitions, 127–28; and internal security system, 122–23; and mob violence, 127; and postwar sabotage, 128; and repression of freedom of expression, 121–30; and right to dissent, 130, 135–37; and state and local government restrictions of civil liberties, 127; and Soviet Union invasion, 125
World War II, and U.S.-Soviet alliance, 147

Yahoo, Inc. v. La Ligue Contre le Racisme et L'Antisemitisme, 282
Yiddish *Daily Forward*, 126

Zenger, John Peter, 24